William John Fitzpatrick

Secret Service under Pitt

Elibron Classics
www.elibron.com

Elibron Classics series.

ISBN 1-4021-6875-6 (paperback)
ISBN 1-4021-1942-9 (hardcover)

This Elibron Classics Replica Edition is an unabridged facsimile of the edition published in 1892 by Longmans, Green, and Co., London and New York.

SECRET SERVICE UNDER PITT

SECRET SERVICE UNDER PITT

BY

W. J. FITZPATRICK, F.S.A.

AUTHOR OF 'LIFE, TIMES, AND CORRESPONDENCE OF BISHOP DOYLE'
'LIFE OF LORD CLONCURRY'
'CORRESPONDENCE AND MEMOIRS OF DANIEL O'CONNELL'
'IRELAND BEFORE THE UNION' ETC.

SECOND EDITION, ENLARGED

LONDON
LONGMANS, GREEN, AND CO.
AND NEW YORK: 15 EAST 16th STREET
1892

PRINTED BY
SPOTTISWOODE AND CO., NEW-STREET SQUARE
LONDON

PREFACE

THESE notes—begun long ago and continued at slow intervals—were put aside during the onerous task of editing for Mr. Murray the O'Connell Correspondence. The recent publication of Mr. Lecky's final volumes, awakening by their grasp a fixed interest in pre-Union times, and confirming much that by circumstantial evidence I had sought to establish, affords a reason, perhaps, that my later researches ought not to be wholly lost. Mr. Lecky's kindness in frequently quoting me[1] merits grateful acknowledgment, not less than his recognition of some things that I brought to light as explanatory of points to which the State Papers afford no clue. This and other circumstances encourage me in offering more.

My sole purpose at the outset was to expose a well-cloaked case of long-continued betrayal by one of whom Mr. Froude confesses that all efforts to identify him had failed;[2] but afterwards it seemed desirable to disclose to the reader a wider knowledge of an exciting time. In various instances a veil will be found lifted, or a visor unlocked, revealing features which may prove a surprise. Nor is the story without a moral. The organisers of illegal societies will see that, in spite of the apparent secrecy and ingenuity of their system, informers sit with them at the same council-board and dinner-table, ready at any moment to sell their blood; and that the wider the ramifications of conspiracy, the greater becomes the certainty of detection.

I felt that it was better to lay before the reader my facts

[1] Vide *England in the Eighteenth Century*, vii. 211; viii. 42-44, 45, 191, 240, etc.

[2] See Froude's *English in Ireland*, vol. iii. sec. vi.

and proofs, solid and unvarnished, than to dissolve them in a flowing narrative, more pleasing to the eye, though less satisfactory as evidence. Had it been possible for my researches to have taken a chronological rather than a biographic shape, the result might have proved easier reading. Yet if there is truth in the axiom that men who write with ease are read with difficulty, and *vice versâ*, these chapters ought to find readers. Every page had its hard work. Tantalising delays blocked at times the search for some missing—but finally discovered—link. Indeed, volumes of popular reading, written *currente calamo*, might have been thrown off for a tithe of the trouble.

'If the power to do hard work is not talent,' writes Garfield, 'it is the best possible substitute for it. Things don't turn up in this world until somebody turns them up.' Readers who, thanks to Froude and Lecky, have been interested by glimpses of men in startling attitudes, would naturally like to learn the curious sequel of their subsequent history. This I have done my best to furnish. The present volume is offered as a companion to the two great works just alluded to. But it will also prove useful to readers of the Wellington, Castlereagh, Cornwallis, and Colchester Correspondence. These books abound in passages which, without explanation, are unintelligible. The matter now presented forms but a small part of the notes I have made with the same end.

A word as regards some of the later sources of my information. The Pelham MSS. were not accessible when Mr. Froude wrote. Thomas Pelham, second Earl of Chichester, was Irish Secretary from 1795 to 1798, but his correspondence until 1826 deals largely with Ireland, and I have read as much of it as would load a float. Another mine was found in the papers, ranging from 1795 to 1805, which filled two iron-clamped chests in Dublin Castle, guarded with the Government seal and bearing the words 'Secret and Confidential: Not to be Opened.' These chests were for a long time familiar objects exteriorly, and when it was at last permitted to disturb the rust of lock and hinge, peculiar interest attended the exploration. Among the contents were 136 letters from Francis Higgins, substantially supporting all that I had ventured to say twenty years before in the book which claimed to portray his career. But neither the Pelham Papers in London nor the archives at Dublin Castle reveal the great secret to which Mr. Froude points.

That so many documents have been preserved is fortunate. Mr. Ross, in his preface to the Cornwallis Correspondence, laments that 'the Duke of Portland, Lord Chancellor Clare, Mr. Wickham, Mr. King, Sir H. Taylor, Sir E. Littlehales, Mr. Marsden, and indeed almost all the persons officially concerned, appear to have destroyed the whole of their papers.'[1] He adds: 'The destruction of so many valuable documents respecting important transactions cannot but be regarded as a serious loss to the history of these times.'

I have freely used the Registry of Deeds Office, Dublin—a department peculiar to Ireland. Originating in penal times, its object was to trace any property acquired by Papists—such being liable to 'discovery and forfeiture.' This office served as a valuable curb in the hands of the oppressor, and ought to prove a not less useful aid to historic inquirers; but, hitherto, it has been unconsulted for such purposes. Few unless legal men can pursue the complicated references, and —unlike the Record Office—fees attend almost every stage of the inquiry. Here things stranger than fiction nestle; while the genealogist will find it an inexhaustible store.

I have to thank the Right Hon. the O'Conor Don, D.L.; Sir William H. Cope, Bart.; Mrs. John Philpot Curran; Daniel O'Connell, Esq., D.L.; D. Coffey, Esq.; Jeremiah Leyne,

[1] To these names may be added that of Lord Clonmell (see Grattan's *Life*, ii. 145). A fatality seemed to attend other valuable collections. The late Lord Londonderry, referring to a voluminous correspondence with his brother, Castlereagh, writes: 'Many years since, I placed this collection in the hands of the Rev. S. Turner, who was at that time nominated and going out as Bishop of Calcutta. This excellent divine had been tutor to my son Castlereagh; and, feeling a deep interest in the family, he had undertaken to arrange these papers. . . . The vessel, however, that sailed to India with Mr. Turner's baggage, papers, etc., was unfortunately wrecked.'—*Memoirs, &c., of Viscount Castlereagh*, London, 1848, i. 143.

Esq.; the late Lord Donoughmore, and the late Mr. Justice Hayes for the communication of manuscripts from the archives of their respective houses. The Rev. Samuel Haughton, F.T.C.D., kindly copied for me some memoranda made in 1798 by the Rev. John Barrett, Vice-Provost T.C.D., regarding students of alleged rebel leanings. So far back as 1880 Sir Charles Russell, when M.P. for Dundalk; Mr. Denis Caulfield Brady, Newry, Mr. James Matthews, and Rev. J. O'Laverty, P.P. Holywood, obligingly made inquiries respecting the object of my suspicion—Samuel Turner.[1] Mr. Lecky transcribed for me a curious paper concerning Aherne, the rebel envoy in France, and has been otherwise kind. My indebtedness to Sir Bernard Burke, Keeper of the Records, Dublin Castle, dates from the year 1855.

The late Brother Luke Cullen, a Carmelite monk, left at his death a vast quantity of papers throwing light on the period of the Rebellion. No writer but myself has ever had the use of these papers, and I beg to thank the Superior of the Order to which Mr. Cullen belonged for having, some years ago, placed them in my hands.

There is a figure in this book of whom I wish to say a final word. Mr. Froude brands the Rev. Arthur O'Leary with having been a spy (p. 230, *post*). After a very protracted inquiry, throughout which I carefully weighed all available evidence, I am of opinion that the charge against this priest has not been proven. An examination of the circumstances that surrounded his career also proved useful in turning up some of those things which my critic in the 'Saturday Review' described as 'curiosities of history.'

49 Fitzwilliam Square, Dublin:
September, 1892.

[1] On this point see p. 383, *post*.

CONTENTS

CHAPTER		PAGE
I.	A MYSTERIOUS VISITOR	1
II.	ARRESTS MULTIPLY	8
III.	FATHER O'COIGLY HANGED	15
IV.	THE BETRAYER'S INTERVIEW WITH TALLEYRAND	24
V.	LORD CLONCURRY SHADOWED	35
VI.	THE MASK TORN OFF AT LAST	44
VII.	DR. MACNEVIN'S MEMORIAL INTERCEPTED	52
VIII.	GENERAL NAPPER TANDY	70
IX.	ARREST OF JÄGERHORN IN LONDON—THE PLOT THICKENS—TURNER SHOT THROUGH THE HEAD	91
X.	EFFORTS TO EXCITE MUTINY IN THE ENGLISH FLEET	105
XI.	THE BETRAYER OF LORD EDWARD FITZGERALD	116
XII.	WILLIAM TODD JONES—EMMET'S REBELLION	156
XIII.	THOMAS COLLINS—PHILLIPS, THE SACERDOTAL SPY	163
XIV.	LEONARD MCNALLY	174
XV.	FATHER ARTHUR O'LEARY	211
XVI.	ARTHUR O'LEARY IN LONDON	227

CHAPTER PAGE

XVII. THE REGENCY—STRUGGLE BETWEEN WHIG AND TORY CAMPS—O'LEARY AND THE PRINCE OF WALES . . 253

XVIII. BISHOP HUSSEY 280

XIX. PRESBYTERIAN MINISTERS DEEP IN TREASON—PLOT AND COUNTER-PLOT 290

XX. THOMAS REYNOLDS: SPY, AND BRITISH CONSUL . . 301

XXI. ARMSTRONG AND THE SHEARESES—GENERAL LAWLESS 308

APPENDIX (BEING NOTICES OF CURIOUS INCIDENTS) . . 335

INDEX 401

Corrigenda.

Page 88 (note) for "the Hague" read Hamburg.

SECRET SERVICE UNDER PITT

CHAPTER I

A MYSTERIOUS VISITOR

It is now some years since Mr. Froude invested with new interest the Romance of Rebellion. Perhaps the most curious of the episodes disclosed by him is that where, after describing the plans and organisation of the United Irishmen, he proceeds to notice a sensational case of betrayal.[1]

An instance has now to be related [he writes] remarkable for the ingenious perfidy with which it was attended, for the mystery which still attaches to the principal performer, and for his connection with the fortunes and fate of Lord Edward Fitzgerald.

Lord Edward's movements had for some time been observed with anxiety, as much from general uneasiness as from regret that a brother of the Duke of Leinster should be connecting himself with conspiracy and treason. His proceedings in Paris in 1792 had cost him his commission in the army. In the Irish Parliament he had been undistinguished by talent, but conspicuous for the violence of his language. His meeting with Hoche on the Swiss frontier was a secret known only to a very few persons ; Hoche himself had not revealed it even to Tone ; but Lord Edward was known to be intimate with McNevin. He had been watched in London, and had been traced to the lodgings of a suspected agent of the French Directory ; and among other papers which had been forwarded by spies to the Government, there was one in French, containing an allusion to some female friend of Lady Edward, through whom a correspondence was maintained between Ireland and Paris. Lady Edward's house at Hamburg was notoriously the resort of Irish

[1] *The English in Ireland* (Nov. 1797), iii. 278.

refugees. Lord Edward himself was frequently there, and the Government suspected, though they were unable to prove, that he was seriously committed with the United Irishmen. One night, early in October, 1797,[1] a person came to the house of Lord Downshire in London, and desired to see him immediately. Lord Downshire went into the hall and found a man muffled in a cloak, with a hat slouched over his face, who requested a private interview. The Duke (*sic*) took him into his Library, and when he threw off his disguise recognised in his visitor the son of a gentleman of good fortune in the North of Ireland, with whom he was slightly acquainted. Lord Downshire's 'friend' (the title under which he was always subsequently described) had been a member of the Ulster Revolutionary Committee. From his acquaintance with the details of what had taken place it may be inferred that he had accompanied the Northern delegacy to Dublin and had been present at the discussion of the propriety of an immediate insurrection. The cowardice or the prudence of the Dublin faction had disgusted him. He considered now that the conspiracy was likely to fail, or that, if it succeeded, it would take a form which he disapproved; and he had come over to sell his services and his information to Pitt. In telling his story to Lord Downshire he painted his own conduct in colours least discreditable to himself. Like many of his friends, he had at first, he said, wished only for a reform in parliament and a change in the constitution. He had since taken many desperate steps and connected himself with desperate men. He had discovered that the object of the Papists was the ruin and destruction of the country, and the establishment of a tyranny worse than that which was complained of by the reformers; that proscriptions, seizures of property, murders, and assassinations were the certain consequences to be apprehended from their machinations; that he had determined to separate himself from the conspiracy.[2] He was in England to make every discovery in his power, and if Lord Downshire had not been in London he had meant to address himself to Portland or Pitt. He stipulated only, as usual, that he should never be called on to appear in a court of justice to prosecute any one who might be taken up in consequence of his discoveries.

Lord Downshire agreed to his conditions; but, as it was then

[1] It was October 8, 1797.

[2] But it will appear that he continued to the end to play the part of a flaming patriot.

late, he desired him to return and complete his story in the morning. He said that his life was in danger even in London. He could not venture a second time to Lord Downshire, or run the risk of being observed by his servants. Downshire appointed the empty residence of a friend in the neighbourhood. Thither he went the next day in a hackney coach. The door was left unlocked, and he entered unseen by anyone. Lord Downshire then took down from his lips a list of the principal members of the Executive Committee by whom the whole movement was at that time directed. He next related at considerable length the proceedings of the United Irishmen during the two past years, the division of opinion, the narrow chance by which a rising had been escaped in Dublin in the spring, and his own subsequent adventures. He had fled with others from Belfast in the general dispersion of the leaders. Lady Edward Fitzgerald had given him shelter at Hamburg, and had sent him on to Paris with a letter to her brother-in-law, General Valence.[1] By General Valence he had been introduced to Hoche and De la Croix. He had seen Talleyrand, and had talked at length with him on the condition of Ireland. He had been naturally intimate with the other Irish refugees. Napper Tandy[2] was strolling about the streets in uniform and calling himself a major. Hamilton Rowan[3] had been pressed to return, but preferred safety in America, and professed himself *sick of politics*. After this, 'the person'—as Lord Downshire called his visitor, keeping even the Cabinet in ignorance of his name—came to the immediate object of his visit to England.

He had discovered that all important negotiations between the Revolutionary Committee in Dublin and their Paris agents passed

[1] Cyrus Marie Valence, Count de Timbrune, born 1757, died 1822. His exploits as a general officer are largely commemorated in the memoirs of his friend, Dumouriez. After having been severely wounded, he resided for some time in London; but was expelled by order of Pitt on June 6, 1793. He then took up his residence in a retired outlet of Hamburg, which our spy soon penetrated; and he at last wormed himself into the confidence of Valence. The General afterwards resumed active military service, and fought with distinction in Spain and Russia.—Vide *Discours du Comte de Ségur à l'occasion des Obsèques de M. Valence*; *Souvenirs de Madame Genlis, &c.*; Alison's *Hist. Europe*, 1789–1815, x. 189.

[2] The strange career of Tandy—who was made a general by Bonaparte—is traced in chapter viii. *infra*.

[3] Some notice of Hamilton Rowan's adventurous courses will be found in chapter xiii. *infra*.

through Lady Edward's hands. The Paris letters were transmitted first to her at Hamburg. By her they were forwarded to Lady Lucy Fitzgerald [1] in London. From London Lady Lucy was able to send them on unsuspected. Being himself implicitly trusted, both by Lady Edward and by Lady Lucy, he believed he could give the Government information which would enable them to detect and examine these letters in their transit through the post.

Pitt was out of town. He returned, however, in a few days. Downshire immediately saw him, and Pitt consented that 'the person's' services should be accepted. There was some little delay. 'The person' took alarm, disappeared, and they supposed that they had lost him. Three weeks later, however, he wrote to Downshire from Hamburg, saying that he had returned to his old quarters, for fear he might be falling into a trap. It was fortunate, he added, that he had done so, for a letter was on the point of going over from Barclay Teeling [2] to Arthur O'Connor,[3] and he gave Downshire directions which would enable him to intercept, read, and send it on.

Such an evidence of 'the person's' power and will to be useful made Pitt extremely anxious to secure his permanent help. An arrangement was concluded. He continued at Hamburg as Lady Edward's guest and most trusted friend, saw everyone who came to her house, kept watch over her letter-bag, was admitted to close and secret conversations upon the prospect of French interference in Ireland with Reinhard, the Minister of the Directory there, and he regularly kept Lord Downshire informed of everything which would enable Pitt to watch the conspiracy. One of his letters, dated November 19, 1797, is preserved:—

'A. Lowry writes from Paris, August 11, in great despondency on account of Hoche's death, and says that all hopes of invading Ireland were given over.

[1] Lady Lucy Fitzgerald, sister of Lord Edward, married in 1802 Admiral Sir Thos. Foley, K.C.B., died 1851.

[2] Bartholomew Teeling was his correct name. In 1798 he was hanged in Dublin.

[3] Arthur O'Connor, nephew and heir of Lord Longueville, sat in Parliament for Philipstown, and spoke so ably on Indian affairs that Pitt is said to have offered him office. In November 1796 he joined the United Irishmen, and from that date his life is one of much activity and vicissitude. Excitement and worry failed to shorten it. He became a general in the French service, and died, aged eighty-eight, April 25, 1852.

'I then saw Reinhard, the French Minister, who begged me to stay here, as the only mode in which I could serve my country and the Republic. I instantly acquiesced, and told him I had arranged matters with Lord Edward Fitzgerald in London for that purpose. I showed him Lowry's [1] letter. He said that things were changed. Buonaparte would not listen to the idea of peace, and had some plan which I do not know. I told him the spirit of republicanism was losing ground in Ireland, for the Catholics and Protestants could not be brought to unite. I mentioned then what Fitzgerald told me in London, viz., that after I left Ireland they had thoughts of bringing matters to a crisis without the French. Arthur O'Connor was to have had a command in the North, he himself in Leinster, Robert Simms [2] at Belfast; that the Catholics got jealous of this, and Richard McCormick,[3] of Dublin, went among the societies of United Men and denounced the three as traitors to the cause, and dangerous on account of their ambition. All letters to or from Lady Lucy Fitzgerald ought to be inspected.

'She, Mrs. Matthieson, of this place, and Pamela [4] carry on a correspondence. Lewins, Teeling, Tennant, Lowry, Orr, and Colonel Tandy are at Paris. Tone expects to stay the winter there, which does not look like invasion. Oliver Bond is treasurer. He pays Lewins and McNevin in London. Now for myself. In order to carry into effect the scheme which you and

[1] Alexander Lowry was the treasurer for Down. Tone describes Lowry and Tennant as 'a couple of fine lads, whom I like extremely.'—*Life*, ii. 433. Aug. 1797. Their youth and ingenuousness would make them easy prey.

[2] Robert Simms had been appointed to the chief command of the United Irishmen of Antrim; but he is said to have wanted nerve. James Hope, in a narrative he gave Dr. Madden, said that Hughes, the Belfast informer, once proposed to him to get rid of Simms by assassination. Hope pulled a pistol from his breast and told Hughes that if ever he repeated that proposal he would shoot him.

[3] Richard McCormick, originally secretary of the Catholic Committee, and afterwards an active 'United Irishman,' and styled by Tone, in his *Diary* 'Magog.'

[4] The wife of Lord Edward Fitzgerald. Moore's *Life of Lord Edward Fitzgerald* says that she was the daughter of Mde. de Genlis by Philippe Egalité, Duke of Orleans; but a letter appears in Moore's *Memoirs* from King Louis Philippe denying it, and Mde. de Genlis calls her a child by adoption. Pamela was a person of surpassing beauty; her portrait arrests attention in the gallery of Versailles. R. B. Sheridan proposed for her, but she rejected him in favour of Lord Edward. Died 1831; her remains were followed to Père la Chaise by Talleyrand.

Mr. Pitt had planned, it was requisite for me to see my countrymen. I called on Maitland,[1] where I found A. J. Stuart,[2] of Acton, both of them heartily *sick of politics.* Edward Fitzgerald had been inquiring of them for me. I went to Harley Street, where Fitz told me of the conduct of the Catholics to him and his friends. He said he would prevail on O'Connor, or some such, to go to Paris. If not, he would go himself in order to have Lewins removed. Mrs. Matthieson[3] has just heard from Lady Lucy that O'Connor is to come. I supped last night with Valence, who mentioned his having introduced Lord Edward and O'Connor to the Minister here in the summer, before the French attempted to invade Ireland. They both went to Switzerland, whence O'Connor passed into France, had an interview with Hoche, and everything was planned.[4]

'I feared lest Government might not choose to ratify our contract, and, being in their power, would give me my choice either to come forward as an evidence or suffer martyrdom myself. Having no taste for an exit of this sort, I set out and arrived here safe, and now beg you'll let me know if anything was wrong in my statements, or if I have given offence. If you approve my present mode of life, and encourage me so to do, with all deference I think Mr. Pitt may let me have a cool five hundred,[5] which shall last me for six months to come. To get the information here has cost me three times the sum, and to keep up the acquaintance and connections I have here, so as to get information, I cannot live on less.'[6]

[1] The allusion may be to Captain Maitland—afterwards General Sir Thomas Maitland, Governor of Ceylon, a son of Lord Lauderdale. He was in Parliament from 1774 to 1779, and from 1790 to 1796, when he sat for the last time in the House—a circumstance which may, perhaps, explain the remark that he was sick of politics. Died 1824. In 1800 he was Colonel Maitland, and in the confidence of Lord Cornwallis.

[2] Who Stuart was, see p. 36 *infra*; also Lord Cloncurry's *Memoirs*, p. 63.

[3] Madame de Genlis states in her memoirs that her niece, Henriette de Sercey, married M. Matthiessen, a rich banker of Hamburg. The General Count Valence married a daughter of Madame de Genlis, and resided near Hamburg on a farm where the latter wrote several of her works.

[4] The expedition of Hoche to Bantry Bay in December, 1796.

[5] 'I just made a couple of betts with him, and took up a *cool* hundred.'—*The Provoked Husband*, by Vanbrugh and Cibber, ii. i. 311, ed. 1730. See also Smollett's *Don Quixote*, bk. iii. c. viii.

[6] Froude, iii. 277 *et seq.*

The betrayer, before his interview with Downshire closed, supplied him with a list of the Executive Committee of United Irishmen. This list, duly given by Mr. Froude, includes—

Jackson and his son; Oliver Bond; John Chambers; James Dickson; Casey, a red-faced Dublin priest; Thomas Addis Emmet; Dr. McNevin, a physician who had great weight with the papists;[1] Braughall, John Keogh and R. McCormick, who belonged to the committee, though they did not attend; Samuel Turner; Lord Edward Fitzgerald; Arthur O'Connor; Alexander Stewart; two Orrs, one an attorney and a dangerous person, the other of Derry, described as a clever, sensible, strong-minded man; B. Teeling; Tenants, of Belfast; Agnew, of Larne; Lawless, Lord Cloncurry's son; Hamill, of Dominick Street[2]; Inishry,[3] a priest, a canting, designing man, who swore in Lord Edward Fitzgerald and Lawless.[4]

Lord Downshire, who negotiated in this affair, had weight with Pitt. The husband of an English peeress, and the son of Lord North's Secretary of State, he was a familiar figure at Court. He had sat for two English constituencies; while in the Irish Parliament as senator, borough proprietor, governor of his county, and one of the Privy Council, he wielded potent sway. His later history and fall belong to chapter ix.

[1] Alexander Knox, in his *History of Down*, errs in saying (p. 26) that 'Dr. McNevin was an influential member of the Established Church.'

[2] All these men, unless Hamill and Inishry, are to be found in books which treat of 1798. The first is noticed in the *Dublin Penny Journal*, March 1, 1834 (p. 274). In 1797 Mr. Hamill was indicted for defenderism and acquitted, 'and the witnesses for the Crown were so flagrantly perjured that the judge, I have heard, ordered a prosecution' (Speech of Henry Grattan in Parliament, May 13, 1805—*Hansard*, ii. 925).

[3] As regards 'Inishry,' no such cognomen is to be found in the pedigrees of MacFirbis or O'Clery, or any name to which it might be traced. The name that the spy gave was probably Hennessy—which Downshire, in writing from dictation, may have mistaken for 'Inishry.'

[4] Long before the publication of Mr. Froude's book, Arthur O'Connor, in a letter to Dr. Madden, states that 'Lord Edward took no oath on joining the United Irishmen.'—Vide their *Lives and Times*, ii. 393.

CHAPTER II

ARRESTS MULTIPLY

It was not easy to separate the threads of the tangled skein which Mr. Froude found hidden away in the dust of the past. But, lest the process of unravelling should tax the reader's patience, I have transferred to an Appendix some points of circumstantial evidence which led me, at first, to suspect, and finally to feel convinced, that 'the person' was no other than Samuel Turner, Esq., LL.D., barrister-at-law, of Turner's Glen, Newry—one of the shrewdest heads of the Northern executive of United Irishmen.[1] Pitt made a good stroke by encouraging his overtures, but, like an expert angler, ample line was given ere securing fast the precious prey.

One can trace, through the public journals of the time, that the betrayer's disclosures to Downshire were followed by a decided activity on the part of the Irish Government. The more important of the marked men were suffered to continue at large, but the names having been noted Lord Camden was able, at the threatened outburst of the rebellion, to seize them at once. Meanwhile an influential London paper, the 'Courier' of November 24, 1797, gave a glimpse of the system that then prevailed by announcing the departure from Dublin for England of Dr. Atkinson, High Constable of Belfast, charged, it is said, with full powers from Government to arrest such persons as have left Ireland, and against whom there are charges of a treasonable or seditious nature.

[1] In chapter vii. my contention will be found established on conclusive testimony, which had failed to present itself until years had been given to a slow process of logical deduction. *Vide* also Appendix, pp. 335–40 *infra*.

The former gentleman is well known, and will be long remembered by the inhabitants of Belfast, for the active part he took in assisting *a Northern Marquis*,[1] and the young apostate of the County Down, to arrest seven of their fellow-citizens on September 16, 1796; since which period these unfortunate men have been closely confined without being allowed to see their friends, and now remain without hope of trial or liberation.

'The young apostate of Down'—thus indicated for English readers ninety years ago—was Lord Castlereagh, afterwards Minister for Foreign Affairs, and well twitted by Byron for his Toryism; but who, in 1790, had been elected, after a struggle of two months' duration and an outlay of 60,000*l.*, Whig Member for Down. Like Pitt, he began as a reformer; like Disraeli, he avowed himself a Radical; and presided at a banquet where toasts were drunk such as 'Our Sovereign Lord the People.' Ere long his policy changed, and his memory is described as having the faint sickening smell of hot blood about it.

Mr. Froude's work has been several years before the world; it has passed through various editions. Thousands of readers have been interested by his picture of the muffled figure gliding at dark to breathe in Downshire's ear most startling disclosures, but no attempt to solve the mystery enshrouding it has until now been made.[2]

The name of Samuel Turner obtains no place on the list of Secret Service moneys[3] expended by the Irish Government in 1798—thus bearing out the statement of Mr. Froude that the name of the mysterious 'person' was not revealed in the most secret correspondence between the Home Office and Dublin Castle. At the termination of the troubles, however, when the need of secrecy became less urgent, and it was

1 'The Northern Marquis' was, of course, Lord Downshire.

2 'A Lanthorn through some Dark Passages, with a Key to Secret Chambers,' was the title originally chosen for the present book, but I finally laid it aside as being too much in the style of old Parson Fry's 'Pair of Bellows to Blow away the Dust.'

3 How this book got out of the Castle and was sold for waste paper by a man named Fagan is a curious story in itself. The volume is now preserved in the Royal Irish Academy.

desirable to bestow pensions on 'persons who had rendered important service during the rebellion,' the name of Samuel Turner is found in the Cornwallis Papers as entitled to 300*l*. a year. But a foot-note from the indefatigable editor—Mr. Ross—who spared no labour to acquire minute information, confesses that it has been found impossible to procure any particulars of Turner.

For years I have investigated the relations of the informers with the Government, and Samuel Turner is the only large recipient of 'blood-money' whose services remain to be accounted for. Turner's name never appeared in any printed pension list. Mr. Ross found the name at Dublin Castle, with some others, in a 'confidential memorandum,' written for the perusal of the Lord Lieutenant, whose fiat became necessary. The money was 'given by a warrant dated December 20, 1800,' but the names were kept secret—the payments being confidentially made by the Under-Secretary.

At this distance of time it is not easy to trace a life of which Mr. Ross, thirty years earlier, failed to catch the haziest glimpse; but I hope to make the case clear, and Turner's history readable.

Previous to 1798 he is found posing in the double *rôle* of martyr and hero—winning alternately the sympathy and admiration of the people. Mr. Patrick O'Byrne, formerly of Newry, and long connected with an eminent publishing firm in Dublin, has replied to a letter of inquiry by supplying some anecdotes in Turner's life. It is a remarkable proof of the completeness with which Turner's perfidy was cloaked that Mr. O'Byrne never heard his honesty questioned.[1]

In 1836 there was a tradition current in Newry of a gentleman named Turner, who in the previous generation had resided in a large red brick house situated in the centre of a fine walled-in park called Turner's Glen, on the western side of Newry, in the County Armagh. Mr. Turner had been in 1796 a member of the great confederacy of United Irishmen, one of the leaders who, for self and fellows, 'pledged

[1] A prisoner named Turner, Christian name not given, indicted for high treason, is announced as discharged in December 1795, owing to the flight of a Crown witness.—*Irish State Trials* (Dublin: Exshaw, 1796); Lib. R. I. A.

his life, his fortune, and his honour' to put an end to British supremacy in Ireland.[1] About the date mentioned the notorious Luttrell, Lord Carhampton, who was commander of the forces in Ireland at the time, and was then making a tour of inspection of the army, had to pass through Newry. The chief hotel in Newry at that time adjoined the post-office. The gentry and merchants of Newry generally went to the post-office shortly after the arrival of the mails to get their letters, and while waiting for the mail to be assorted promenaded in front of the hotel, or rested in the coffee-room. Mr. Turner wore the colours he affected—a large green necktie. Lord Carhampton, while his horses were being changed, was looking out of the coffee-room windows of the hotel, and his eye lighted on the rebel 'stock:' here was a fine opportunity to cow a rebel and assert his own courage—a quality for which he was not noted. Accordingly he swaggered up to Mr. Turner and, confronting him, asked 'Whose man are you, who dares to wear that rebellious emblem?' Mr. Turner sternly replied, 'I am my own man. Whose man are you, who dares to speak so insolently to an Irish gentleman?' 'I am one who will make you wear a hempen necktie, instead of your flaunting French silk, if you do not instantly remove it!' retorted Lord Carhampton. 'I wear this colour,' replied Mr. Turner courageously, 'because I like it. As it is obnoxious to you, come and take it off.' Carhampton, finding that his bluster did not frighten the North Erin rebel, turned to leave; but Turner, by a rapid movement, got between him and the door, and, presenting his card to the general, demanded his address. Carhampton told him he would learn it sooner than he should like. Turner thereupon said, 'I *must* know your name; until now I have never had the misfortune to be engaged in a quarrel with aught but gentlemen, who knew how to make themselves responsible for their acts. You cannot insult me with impunity, whatever your name may be. I will yet find it out, and post you in every court as a coward.' The Commander of the Forces withdrew from Newry, having come off second best in the quarrel he had provoked. Mr. Turner, for reasons connected with the cause in which he had embarked, was obliged to lie *perdu* soon after, and so Carhampton escaped the 'posting' threatened by the Northern fire-eater.[2]

[1] Their object at first was quite constitutional. See p. 89 *infra*.

[2] Letter of Mr. Patrick O'Byrne to W. J. F., Dublin, September 6, 1880. Since the first edition of this book appeared I have received a communication from Mr. O'Byrne, saying that my discovery of Turner's treachery has come upon him like a thunderclap.

The general accuracy of Mr. O'Byrne's impressions is shown by the 'Life and Confessions of Newell the Informer,' printed for the author at London in 1798.[1] Newell travelled with the staff of Lord Carhampton, and in April, 1797, witnessed the scene just described.

Newell's pamphlet, which created much noise at the time and had a large circulation, did not tend to weaken popular confidence in Turner. It appeared soon after the time that he had begun to play false; but Newell, with all his cunning, had no suspicion of Turner.

The late Mr. J. Mathews, of Dundalk, collected curious details regarding the rebel organisation of Ulster in 1797. With these details the name of Samuel Turner is interwoven, but, although the object of Mathews was to expose the treachery of some false brothers, he assigns to Turner the rank of a patriot and a hero. How the authorities, by a *coup*, made a number of arrests, is described; and how Turner, after some exciting adventures, got safely to France.[2]

The spy on this occasion was Mr. Conlan, a medical practitioner in Dundalk. A sworn information, signed by Conlan, is preserved among the Sirr MSS. in Trinity College, Dublin. It is dated 1798, when Turner himself was betraying his own colleagues to Pitt! Conlan states that one evening, after Turner had left his house at Newry to attend a meeting of United Irishmen at Dundalk, the officer in command at the barracks of Newry got orders to march on Dundalk and arrest the leaders. An officer's servant apprised Corcoran, who was an adherent of Turner's. Corcoran mounted a horse and galloped to Dundalk, where he arrived in time to warn Turner. Conlan recollected Turner and Teeling travelling through Ulster and holding meetings for organisation at Dundalk, Newry, Ballinahinch (the site of the subsequent battle), Ronaldstown, Glanary, and in Dublin at

[1] *Vide* pp. 21–2. Newell's pamphlet will be found in the Haliday Collection, vol. 743, Royal Irish Academy.

[2] *Vide* Mr. Matthew's narrative in *The Sham Squire*, sixth edition, pp. 355–363.

Kearn's, Kildare Street,[1] where the principal meetings were held.[2]

I find in the Pelham MSS. the examination of Dr. John Macara, one of the Northern State prisoners of 1797. It supplies details of the plan of attack which had been foiled by the arrests. 'Newry was to be attacked by Samuel Turner, of Newry aforesaid, with the men from Newry and Mourn.'[3]

It was not Conlan alone who reported Turner's movements to the Crown. Francis Higgins, the ablest secret agent of Under-Secretary Cooke, announces that Turner had sent 'letters from Portsmouth for the purpose of upholding and misleading the mutinous seamen into avowed rebellion;'[4] and some weeks later he states that 'Turner had returned from Hamburg with an answer to the Secret Committee of United Irishmen.'[5]

We know on the authority of James Hope, who wrote down his 'Recollections' of this time at the request of a friend, that Turner, having fled from Ireland, filled the office of resident agent at Hamburg of the United Irishmen. The Irish envoys and refugees, finding themselves in a place hardly less strange

[1] This place of rendezvous was, doubtless, chosen because of its proximity to Leinster House, where Lord Edward mainly lived.

[2] Major Sirr's Papers (MS.), Trinity College, Dublin. Conlan's information makes no mention of a remarkable man, the Rev. William Steel Dickson, D.D., a Presbyterian pastor of Down, and described by the historians of his Church as ready to take the field. Dr. Dickson, in his *Narrative*, admits (p. 193) that he had been 'frequently in the company of Lowry, Turner, and Teeling.' Turner was a Presbyterian and possibly wished to spare a pastor of his Church.

[3] The Pelham MSS. Examination dated September 6, 1797. Pelham, afterwards Lord Chichester, was Chief Secretary for Ireland at that time, and his papers are a useful help in throwing light upon it. Quite an armful are occupied by a correspondence with Generals Lake and Nugent regarding Dr. Macara; he offered to inform if let out on bail. Lake hoped that he would prove a valuable informer; and, as he was far from rich, could not afford to reject pecuniary reward; but, although Macara at first seemed to consent, his replies were finally found to be evasive.

[4] Higgins to Cooke, MS. letter, Dublin Castle, June 7, 1797.

[5] *Ibid.*, August 29, 1797. Five weeks later Turner makes his disclosure to Downshire.

than Tierra del Fuego, ignorant of its language, its rules and its ways, sought on arrival the accredited agent of their brotherhood, hailed him with joy, and regarded the spot on which he dwelt as a bit of Irish soil sacred to the Shamrock. The hardship which some of the refugeës went through was trying enough. James Hope, writing in 1846, says that Palmer, one of Lord Edward's bodyguard in Dublin, travelled, 'mostly barefooted, from Paris to Hamburg, where he put himself into communication with Samuel Turner.' The object of Palmer's mission was to expose one Bureaud, then employed as a spy by Holland. 'Palmer,' writes Hope, 'gave Turner a gold watch to keep for him.' He enlisted in a Dutch regiment, and was found drowned in the Scheldt. When Turner,' adds Hope, 'was applied to for the watch by Palmer's sister, he replied that he forgot what became of it.'

Hamburg in troubled times was a place of great importance for the maintenance of intercourse between England and France. Here, as Mr Froude states, 'Lord Downshire's friend' had vast facilities for getting at the inmost secrets of the United Irishmen. Hope's casual statement serves to show how it was that this 'person' could have had access to Lady Edward Fitzgerald's confidence, and that of her political friends at Hamburg.

CHAPTER III

FATHER O'COIGLY HANGED

Mr. Froude, after a perusal of the letters of Downshire's friend, and other documents, states that a priest named O'Coigly or Quigley 'had visited Paris in 1797, returned to Dublin, and had been with Lord Edward Fitzgerald at Leinster House; that he was now going back to Paris, and Arthur O'Connor determined to go in his company.'[1] Their mission, though ostensibly for presenting an address from the London corresponding society of United Irishmen to the French Government, was really for the double purpose of urging upon it the prompt despatch of an invading fleet to Ireland, and of deposing the Irish envoy, Lewins, who, instead of Turner, had begun to be suspected. Mr. Lawless, afterwards Lord Cloncurry, invited O'Coigly to dinner in London; and it was on this occasion that O'Connor met the priest for the first time. O'Coigly, under the name of Captain Jones, with Allen[2] seemingly as his servant, and Leary, left London for Margate, on their mission of mystery. O'Connor travelled by another route to Margate, took the name of Colonel Morris, and was accompanied by Binns. On the following day, at the King's Head Inn, Margate, all the party were arrested by two Bow Street officers. O'Coigly and O'Connor had dined at Lawless's lodgings more than once; and here, though not necessarily with his knowledge, the travelling arrangements seem to have been made. Whether Turner was a guest does not appear; but he was certainly in London at this time, and as one of the Executive

[1] *The English in Ireland*, iii. 312.

[2] Allen, a draper's assistant in Dublin, afterwards a colonel in the service of France.

Committee is likely to have been invited. Presently it will be shown that from this quarter came all the information which enabled Pitt to seize O'Connor and O'Coigly at Margate *en route* to France, although, to elude observation, they had journeyed by different roads. The prisoners, meanwhile, were removed to London, examined before the Privy Council, and then transmitted to Maidstone Jail to await their trial. The source of the information which caused these historic arrests on February 27, 1798, has hitherto remained a mystery. Father O'Coigly, while in jail, wrote some letters, in which he failed to avow his share in the conspiracy, but admitted to have made a previous visit to Cuxhaven. This was part of the city of Hamburg. Turner, in addition to being the official agent of the United Irishmen at Hamburg, was an old Dundalk acquaintance of O'Coigly's, and no doubt was promptly hailed by the country priest.

Turner and O'Coigly are mentioned in Hughes's information. They belonged to the same district organisation. After describing Teeling, Turner and Lowry working in concert in 1797, Hughes adds that priest Quigly or O'Coigly introduced him at that time to Baily and Binns.[1] The paper revealed by Mr. Froude, now shown to be Turner's, and other letters from the same hand in the 'Castlereagh Papers,' show that the writer always felt a strong dislike to work with the 'Papists,' especially priests. 'Casey, the red-faced, designing Dublin priest,' was one of the leading men he met in Dublin, and whose 'prudence or cowardice' disgusted him. Immediately after O'Coigly's return to London we find the authorities on his track. The priest himself refers to an abortive attempt to arrest him by night at Piccadilly.[2] Mr. Froude, dealing with this case, does not seem to have suspected that the arrival in London of Downshire's friend, at the time of the arrests at Margate, was other than accidental. Yet clearly it was business of no ordinary moment which brought him back to London

[1] *Report of the Secret Committee*, p. 31. (Dublin, 1798.)

[2] *Life of the Reverend James Coigly*, p. 28. (London, 1798.) Haliday Collection, R.I.A., vol. 743.

at this time. It will be remembered that, panic-stricken and fearing death from the assassin's knife, he had returned to Hamburg in October 1797, ere an answer came from Pitt to the proposition of betrayal conveyed by Lord Downshire.

It happened that at this particular time [writes Mr. Froude] that Downshire's friend was in London, and Pelham (the Irish Secretary) knew it. If the 'friend' could be brought over, and could be induced to give evidence, a case could then be established against all the United Irish leaders. They could be prosecuted with certainty of conviction, and the secrets of the plot could be revealed so fully that the reality of it could no longer be doubted.

Most earnestly Camden [1] begged Portland [2] to impress on the 'friend' the necessity of compliance. 'Patriotism might induce him to overcome his natural prejudice.' If patriotism was insufficient, there was no reward which he ought not to receive.[3] Portland's answer was not encouraging: 'The friend,' he said, 'shall be detained. As to his coming over to you, I have reason to believe that there is not any consideration on earth which would tempt him to undertake it. He is convinced that he would go to utter destruction. Better he should stay here and open a correspondence with some of the principal conspirators, by which means you may be apprised of their intentions. If I could be satisfied, or if you would give it as your positive opinion that this person's testimony or presence would crush the conspiracy, or bring any principal traitor to justice, I should not, and Lord Downshire would not, hesitate to use any influence to prevail on his friend to run any risk for such an object. But if he should fail and escape with his life, he could render no further service. Weigh well, therefore, the consequence of such a sacrifice.'[4]

After describing the arrest at Margate of Father O'Coigly, O'Connor, and Binns, Mr. Froude writes:—

O'Connor wrote a hurried note to Lord Edward, telling him not to be alarmed, nothing having been taken upon them which compromised any individual.[5] The messenger to whom the note was

[1] The Lord Lieutenant of Ireland. [2] The Home Secretary.

[3] Camden to Portland, March 1, 1798. *English in Ireland*, iii. 310.

[4] Portland to Camden, March 7, 1798.

[5] In O'Connor's valise were found 900*l.*, a military uniform, and some papers relating to Lord Edward Fitzgerald.—W. J. F.

entrusted was unfortunate or treacherous, for it fell into the hands of the Government. *Had O'Connor known the connection between the Government and Lord Downshire's friend, he would have felt less confident.* There was evidence, if it could only be produced, which would send both Lord Edward and himself to the scaffold.

It may be observed here—*en parenthèse*—that Downshire must have felt conflicting emotions when called upon to communicate information which might bring Lord Edward to the block. His father had married the sister of James, Duke of Leinster; Lord Edward was, therefore, the first cousin of Lord Downshire.

One of the most truthful chapters of the laudatory life of Reynolds, the informer,[1] is that aiming to show that he could not have been the spy who caused the arrests at Margate. But the biographer is unable to offer any suggestion as to who that agent was—so carefully veiled from Reynolds, one of their own confidential prompters, was the part played by Turner in that episode.

The information which led to the arrest of O'Connor, O'Coigly, and his companion cannot have come from Ireland, because in the 'Book of Secret Service Monies expended in the Detection of Treasonable Conspiracies'[2] no entry appears connected with the above incident, unless 'Dutton's Expenses going to England to attend Quigly's Trial,' and where he had merely to swear to the priest's handwriting. For his courage in doing this—having once seen him sign a lottery ticket at Dundalk—50*l.* is paid to 'Dutton on June 12, 1798.' The names of Newell and Murdoch certainly appear in the 'Secret Service Money' book about that time; but it is clear from Newell's narrative—doubtless a genuine confession—that neither he nor Murdoch had any hand in tracing the movements of O'Coigly and O'Connor.

Lord Castlereagh was now acting for Pelham as Chief Secretary for Ireland. On July 25, 1798, a secret letter—

[1] *Life of Thomas Reynolds*, by his Son. (London, 1830.)

[2] 'Per affidavit of Mr. Cooke,' Under Secretary, Dublin Castle (p. 9 *ante*).

printed in the 'Castlereagh Papers'—is addressed to him from the Home Office:—

I am directed by the Duke of Portland to inform your Lordship that I have received intelligence from *a person very much in the confidence of [Reinhard] the French Minister at Hamburg*,[1] that several French officers and soldiers have lately arrived at that place, where they have purchased sailor's dresses, clothed themselves in them, and gone on to Denmark and Sweden, from whence it is intended that they should embark for the North of Ireland.[2] I know not what credit is to be given to this information, which must be received with caution, as it does not appear to have reached his Majesty's Minister at Hamburg.

It comes, however, from a person[3] whose reports while he was in this country[4] were known to his Excellency as singularly accurate and faithful—*the same who gave such an accurate account of the proceedings of O'Connor and Coigly* whilst they were in this country, and on whose authority those persons were apprehended.[5]

Some of the letters of 'Lord Downshire's friend,' not being forthcoming in the official archives, Mr. Froude assumed that they had been destroyed; but, however masked, they are recognisable in the 'Castlereagh Correspondence.' Several anonymous papers, furnishing information of the movements of the United Irishmen about Hamburg and elsewhere, crop up in that book, having been enclosed from Whitehall for the guidance of Dublin Castle. One of these letters makes special reference to information already sent to Lord Downshire.[6]

[1] For proofs of the intimacy between Reinhard and Turner at Hamburg, see *Castlereagh Papers*, i. 277 *et seq.*; and my chapter on McNevin, *infra.*

[2] In August, 1798, Humbert and 900 Frenchmen arrived in Killala Bay.

[3] 'The person' is the name by which Downshire's friend, the betrayer, is usually styled in the letters from the Home Office to Dublin Castle. The words, 'while he was in this country,' show that he had left England, as Downshire's friend admittedly did, in panic.

[4] '*I.e.* in October 1797, when he called upon Downshire; and again in March 1798, when Portland offered him large sums if he would openly prosecute.

[5] Mr. Lecky describes this arrest, and rather suggests that it may have been due to Higgins in Dublin (*vide* viii. 55). The above evidence points surely to the Hamburg spy.

[6] See *Castlereagh Papers*, i. 231–6.

Another long letter of the same batch will be found the first placed in the second volume of Castlereagh, though an examination of it shows that it belongs to the middle of the previous volume. Detailed reference is made to Father O'Coigly's mission and movements, both in France and in London. One is struck by the accuracy of its information regarding the Ulster United Irishmen, of whom Turner was one. Of MacMahon, who travelled to Paris with O'Coigly, we learn that, '*tired of politics*, especially those of France, he is to write to Citoyen Jean Thomas,[1] *à la poste restante à Hamburg*, whom he looks on as a good patriot.'[2] It will be remembered that a similar phrase occurs in the letter of Downshire's friend, printed by Froude, *i.e.* Rowan had 'professed himself sick of politics.' Again, 'I found Maitland and Stewart, of Acton, both heartily sick of politics.'

How to hang O'Coigly was now the difficulty. The Government knew—from somebody who had worked with him—that he was deep in the treason; but nothing could persuade the informer to prosecute him openly.

On April 11, 1798, Wickham writes from Whitehall:—

> It is most exceedingly to be lamented that no person can be sent over from Ireland to prove Coigly's handwriting. Proof of that kind would be so extremely material, that I have no doubt that the law officers would think it right to put off the trial if they could have any hope of any person being found, in a short time, who could speak distinctly to his handwriting.[3]

The secret adviser who, as Portland said, 'should be detained,' worked his brain until at length a man, hailing from a place suspiciously familiar to Turner, is sent for to swear to the point. Samuel Turner, formerly of Newry, had intimate knowledge of every man in the place. One Frederick Dutton, described as 'of Newry,' was now subpœnaed by the Crown to swear to O'Coigly's handwriting in a letter addressed to Lord Edward Fitzgerald. 'He claimed to have seen Coigly write his name for the purpose of getting a watch raffled which

[1] Of course one of Turner's many aliases. See p. 97, *infra*.

[2] *Castlereagh Correspondence*, ii. 1 7.   [3] *Ibid.* i. 178.

belonged to a poor man under sentence of death.' Dutton had been a dismissed servant and had kept a public-house at Newry without a licence.[1]

It will be seen on turning to p. 30 that 'Downshire's friend' got back to London on Tuesday, May 15, 1798. What secret help he gave to the law officers can only be inferred, for they promised that he should never be asked to come forward publicly. Though O'Connor, O'Coigly, and Binns[2] were arrested in February, their trials did not take place till late in May 1798. The Duke of Norfolk, Lords Moira, Suffolk, Oxford, John Russell, and Thanet, Fox, Sheridan, Whitbread, Erskine, Grattan, all testified to O'Connor's character. All the prisoners were acquitted, except the priest, notwithstanding that Lord Cloncurry paid a counsel to defend him. He was hanged on Penenden Heath, June 7, 1798. Judge Buller had leant heavily on O'Coigly in his charge.

O'Coigly [writes Lord Holland] was condemned on false and contradictory evidence. I do not mean to aver, as Lord Chancellor Thurlow assured me he did to Judge Buller, who tried him, that '*if ever a poor man was murdered it was O'Coigly*,' but simply to allude to a circumstance which, in the case of a common felon, would probably have saved his life. The Bow Street officer who swore to finding the fatal paper in his pocket-book, and remarked in court the folding of the paper as fitting that pocket-book, had sworn before the Privy Council that the same paper *was found loose in O'Coigly's great-coat, and, I think, had added that he himself had put it into the pocket-book.* An attorney of the name of Foulkes[3] gave me this information, and I went with it to Mr. Wickham, who assured me that the circumstance should be carefully and anxiously investigated before the execution. But the

[1] Dutton, on his examination, said that he had sworn in Ireland against one 'Lowry.' This is the man whom Turner, in his letters, constantly points to. Dutton admitted that he had previously sworn secrecy to the Society of United Irishmen, but the oath had been sworn only on a spelling-book.

[2] Trial of Arthur O'Connor and James Quigley at Maidstone. Howell's *State Trials*, vols. xxvi. and xxvii.

[3] Foulkes was the attorney whom Lawless engaged to defend O'Coigly. Lord Cloncurry, in his *Memoirs*, writes very inaccurately of the facts. He says that the arrests took place at Whitstable, instead of Margate, and that O'Coigly was hanged on May 7, whereas he should have written June. See p. 67.

order had gone down, and while we were conversing the sentence was probably executed.[1]

Lord Holland adds that when the Judge was descanting on the mildness and clemency of the Administration, O'Coigly quietly took a pinch of snuff and said 'Ahem!'

When no evidence was produced in court which could legally ensure a verdict against O'Coigly, it seems reasonable to assume from the tone of the law officers and the Judge that they possessed some secret knowledge of his guilt, for in point of fact, though O'Coigly declared his innocence, he was deeply pledged to the conspiracy.

'O'Connor was leaving the court in triumph,' writes Mr. Froude, 'but the Government knew their man too well to let him go so easily. He was at once re-arrested on another charge, and was restored to his old quarters in Dublin Castle.'[2] From whom the fatal whisper came does not appear, but the sequel seems to leave no doubt that to Turner it was due. MacMahon and other prominent rebels were Presbyterian clergymen of Ulster. It was an object now with those who desired the collapse of the conspiracy to detach the Presbyterian party from the 'Papists.' Binns was a staunch Presbyterian rebel, a colleague of O'Coigly. In a letter dated Philadelphia, 1843, Binns, addressing Dr. Madden, states that great efforts were used to try and persuade O'Coigly to implicate him, 'offering Mr. Coigly his life if he would criminate me agreeable to the instructions of the Government, which proposal he indignantly refused to accede to. Though heavily ironed, he pushed the gentlemen out of his cell, when he there lay under sentence of death.'

We have seen that when severely tried he resorted to snuff. He had other small consolations. Even in his irons he talked irony. One of several letters of protest addressed by the priest to Portland, shortly before his death, tells him that he is 'one of his Grace's envoys to the other world, charged with tidings of his mild and merciful administration.'

[1] *Memoirs of the Whig Party.* By Lord Holland, afterwards a Cabinet Minister.
[2] Froude's *English in Ireland*, iii. 301.

As O'Coigly's memory has been all but beatified as a martyr's, it is due to the interests of historic truth to add—especially after the remarks of Lord Holland—the following from a letter written by Arthur O'Connor in 1842 :—

Though there was not legal evidence to prove that the paper found in Coigly's coat-pocket was Coigly's, yet, the fact is, it was his, and was found in his riding-coat ; for when the five prisoners were brought to Bow Street, a report was spread that the papers taken on the prisoners were lost ; for the first time Coigly said it was fortunate the papers were lost, for that there was one in his pocket that would hang them all. He never made a secret to his fellow-prisoners that he got that paper from a London society. In my memoirs I will clear up this point.

O'Connor's promised work, however, never appeared.

As regards Dutton, the witness who swore to O'Coigly's handwriting, his subsequent career was cast on a spot also frequented by Turner.[1] He is found at Cuxhaven, not very far from Hamburg, and, until 1840, holding office in its postal and diplomatic departments, and the husband of a lady well connected.[2] Cuxhaven, as gazetteers record, was from 1795 a place of the utmost importance for the maintenance of intercourse between England and the Continent.

[1] See p. 31, *infra*.

[2] In the Pelham MSS. is a letter signed Frederick Dutton, regarding his Vice-Consulate, and dated Dec. 19, 1825.

CHAPTER IV

THE BETRAYER'S INTERVIEW WITH TALLEYRAND

The letters of secret information in the well-known 'Castlereagh Correspondence' being mostly without date are inserted regardless of chronological sequence, and are often, from dearth of explanation, wholly unintelligible. One of these secret reports follows a letter of Portland's[1]—to be found later on—regarding the intercepted memorial which Dr. McNevin had addressed to the French Government. The particular references to Lord Downshire, to Hamburg, to Fitzgerald, and to the North of Ireland, of which Turner was a native—not to speak of his 'tone of injured innocence,' 'the dread of those from whom I come as to the ascendency of the Papists'—all point to him as the writer.

His tone as usual is hostile to Lewins, a Roman Catholic envoy of great honesty, whose reputation he is ever seeking to injure; and the intrigue, it may be added, very nearly succeeded in getting Lewins superseded. Mr. Froude, it will be remembered, when describing his unmasked informer writes:

> Lady Edward Fitzgerald had sent him on to Paris with a letter to her brother-in-law, General Valence. By Valence he had been introduced to Hoche and De la Croix. He had seen Talleyrand and had *talked* at length with him on the condition of Ireland.

It was in February, 1798, that Mr. Froude's spy reappeared in London.[2] He had interviews at the Home Office, where he received some instructions, which are not stated.

[1] See *Castlereagh Papers*, i. 251. See also chapter vii. of the present volume.

[2] Froude, iii. 301.

Camden urged Portland to beg of him to give evidence publicly, and to offer reward to any amount. But all to no effect. At last it was decided, as the next best thing to do, 'that he should open a correspondence with the principal conspirators, by which means you may be apprised of their intentions.' This is exactly what he is now found doing. On April 17 he goes to Paris, no doubt sent by the Home Office, to ascertain what arrangement had been made by O'Coigly and O'Connor as regards the long-sought French expedition to Ireland.

De la Croix will be chiefly remembered as the Minister for Foreign Affairs with whom Tone had to do. But he had been personally offensive to Lord Malmesbury, the English Minister, and M. Talleyrand was appointed to succeed La Croix on July 15, 1797.[1]

The following letter is to be found in the 'Castlereagh Papers' (i. 231–6), and derives additional importance from its close connection with Talleyrand:—

SECRET INTELLIGENCE.

April 17th [1798], arrived in Paris.

On the 19th waited on the Minister for Foreign Affairs; it being Décadi, he was gone to the country. Left my name, and called next day, at eleven; instantly admitted; *talked* over the purport of my visit, which I had brought in writing, as follows:—

'Citizen Minister,—Since I had the honor of seeing you in September last, I understand attempts have been made to injure my character here by some persons equally despicable as malicious (I mean Lewines and his associates), from whom, though United Irishmen, I pride myself in differing, both in sentiment and conduct; nor should I condescend to answer their infamous charges.[2]

'I, however, take great pleasure in acquainting you with what I have been about, viz., trying to bring over to the side of the United Irish what is called the Independent Interest, *alias* the Country Gentlemen, all of whom have commands either in the Yeomanry or

[1] See *M. de Talleyrand*, par M. de Villemarest, ch. viii.; *Hist. du Directoire*, par M. de Barante, liv. iv.

[2] Of infidelity to the rebel cause.

Militia,[1] and to whom the safety of the interior will be entrusted, whilst the regular troops march against the enemy. These gentlemen have always been much against the Government, but feared, in a revolution, the loss of their property, especially such as held their estates by grants of Oliver Cromwell. For some time past a union has been formed among this body for the purpose of forcing England into whatever measures they choose as soon as an invasion takes place; all of my most particular friends are of this association, and they have infused into the minds of the rest the idea that English faith is not to be relied on. In consequence, they are all now completely up to the formation of a Republic and a separation from Britain, provided the French Directory will give, under their seal, the terms and conditions Ireland has a right to expect and demands. I took upon me to say France never meant to treat Ireland has a conquered country; that, certainly, they would expect a contribution towards defraying the great expense incurred in supporting the cause of liberty; but what the sum would be, I could not take upon me to mention. They insist upon having that specified, and any other conditions for this purpose.

'Citizen Minister, I now apply to you; to none other have I hinted my business, and the most profound secrecy will be requisite in order to completely deceive the English Government. I shall mention to you the channel of correspondence, &c., with the ciphers I'll make use of, if it is requisite to write, but which I sha'n't do without your permission, and giving you the letter to enclose to Hamburg.[2]

'I have the honour to remain,' &c.

---

[1] Mr. Froude, speaking of 'the second arrest of two of the leading committees of Belfast,' says (iii. 237) that 'Lake seized papers which revealed the correspondence with France, the extent of the revolutionary armament, and the measures taken for the seduction of the army and militia. The papers were sent to Dublin and were laid before a secret committee.' See also correspondence *in re* McNevin's Memorial, ch. vii. *infra.*

[2] The spy sought to deceive the French Government in this report. The Cromwellian Settlers never thought of joining the United Irishmen. One of Turner's objects seems to have been to get a written undertaking from Talleyrand that the estates of these Settlers should be left intact, and money sent to promote an alleged treasonable conspiracy of Cromwellian Settlers against England, but which, in point of fact, did not exist. The Ulster Presbyterians were, no doubt, rebels; but these men were the descendants, not of the Cromwellian adventurers, but of King James's Planters.

Thus far the letter of Turner to Talleyrand—for Turner it assuredly is. It does not follow that the Minister believed all he was told. The quondam Bishop of Autun could read a soul. He was a diplomat, however, and showed to his visitor that cautious courtesy which he had learned when a hierarch. He who said that speech is given to conceal thoughts,[1] was not the man to be at once swayed by words. The despatch now before us had been addressed to the Home Office, and must be one of the papers Mr. Froude thought destroyed. The copy of his letter to Talleyrand having been submitted to Portland, the spy thus resumes:—

The Minister then said it was a matter extremely interesting, that other things were on the *tapis* at present, but desired I would call again on the second uneven day from that, and he'd[2] enter into particulars. I did so, and gave him the following letter. He said he had laid my first before the Directory; that their opinions coincided with his, but that they could not give anything under their hands or seal, nor he either; that I had perfectly expressed their intentions. I told him this was perfectly satisfactory to me, but I feared it would not be so to them. 'Surely,' says he, 'they have a confidence in you, and you shall have it from the Directory, if you choose.' I said I hoped that would be sufficiently satisfactory to my friends, and begged to know when I could see him again—the 1st of the next decade, as they were still very busy.

Copy of the Letter to Talleyrand.

'Citizen Minister,—Wishing to give the Government every satisfaction on the point of my mission, I now have the honour of laying before you every particular. I am extremely glad to find it appears to you interesting, which induces me to hope as little delay will be given as possible. I think it incumbent on me to state to you that the spirit of the North is completely broken,[3] and

[1] This phrase is assigned to Talleyrand by Harel in the *Nain Jaune*; but the thought had been previously expressed by Bishop Jeremy Taylor.

[2] The contractions 'he'd' and 'sha'n't' are entirely consistent with Turner's 'you'll' in the letter to Downshire, transcribed by me from the Pelham MSS. See p. 50, *infra*; also Turner's acknowledged letter to Cooke, p. 97.

[3] Captain Taylor, writing to Wickham (Dublin Castle, August 21, 1798) says, 'the Rebellion is more deeply rooted in the North than anywhere else.'—*Cornwallis*, ii. 390.

I fear shortly the rest of Ireland will be in the same predicament.[1] A vast number of the persons concerned in persecuting the United Irish are those from whom I come; for at present they dread, and with good reason, the ascendency of this body. As soon as you set these gentlemen's minds at ease in regard to their property, the business of revolution will get leave to go on, and the British Government will find themselves clogged in their system of terror, without knowing why. The enclosed paper contains the mode in which I am to act, &c., &c. I have the honour, &c.'

Turner then adds:—[2]

Enclosure, containing the ciphers I sent to the Marquess of Downshire, and the following postscript:—

'The intention of the ciphers was, if I thought it requisite to write from Paris, to say who I had had communication with and as a channel of conveying any intelligence you might allow me to send during my stay. The letter to be addressed to Charles Ranken,[3] Esq., at Mr. Elliot's, Pimlico, London, to be put in the common post-office at Hamburg, and sealed with a particular seal I have for the purpose. As soon as I receive the proper paper or document, in order to save time, I am to get, if possible, into England; if that can't be done with safety, I'm to go to either Bremen or Hamburg, write thence to Ranken, who comes over before him. I attest the business on oath, and he goes instantly for Ireland. Ranken,[4] having been a banker at Belfast, a man of good property,

[1] This alternate blowing of hot and cold worked its end. A long letter from the Home Office furnishing secret items to Dublin Castle goes on to say (*Castlereagh*, ii. 361): 'Lewins had often complained that the conduct of the French Government had been hitherto so indecisive with respect to Ireland that all their projects had naturally failed.' However, it was admitted by Talleyrand that 'Ireland was the only vulnerable part of the British Empire.'

[2] The Cabinet, Mr. Froude says, was kept in utter ignorance of his name, and in the most secret despatches of the Home Office he is known only as 'Lord Downshire's friend.' These precautions will remind us of the cipher of the Louvais despatches, which has hitherto baffled all efforts to identify the Man in the Iron Mask.

[3] The narrative of Edward J. Newell—the spy who turned against his employers—states (London, 1798, p. 59) that he was asked to give information 'against Charles Rankin and others for high treason.'

[4] Our spy often refers to Rankin and others of Belfast: 'He [the betrayer] had fled with others from Belfast at the general dispersion of the leaders,' writes Mr. Froude, iii. 280.

and looked on by Government as a friend, can pass and repass as if to settle accounts at Hamburg.

'I beg leave once more to inform you that delay will be looked on, I fear, as non-compliance; and, if there's any particular point on which you wish for accurate information, I think I can undertake to obtain it.'

The spy's letter then proceeds :—

He (Talleyrand) seemed to disapprove of my venturing to Ireland or England; asked me if I knew anything of Fitzgerald.[1]

Waited on him the first of the following decade; he said nothing was resolved on. I asked if the Irish were to wait for their coming or not. He said by all means to wait, and not to risk or expose themselves. 'May I assure them you'll come in the course of three months?' 'No, we cannot fix a time; it may be more, or not so long. I shall depend on you to obtain for me as accurate a statement, with as much information as you can collect.' I desired to know on what particular point, otherwise I should be at a loss; he said he could not mention any particular. I then promised as much as I could collect in general, with a particular and accurate one of Ireland. I then asked if I might venture to assert that the French Government would be content with being paid the expense of their former expedition, and of that which will be sent; that they will leave the Irish to choose a constitution for themselves as soon as English influence is destroyed; guaranteeing to every individual their property, without respect to old Catholic claims and to their political conduct prior to the time of actual invasion. 'You may venture to assure them that the property of no individual will be seized upon, but the reverse. On the other points we cannot give an answer.'—'When shall I see the Directory?'—'On the ninth of this decade I shall speak to the President, and you may bring to me one of your acquaintance that is known to him, who will introduce you;' or that I might go alone, as my name was sufficiently known to him. Between that and the 9th I spoke to Abbé Grégoire[2] to accompany me; but he

[1] Whatever he knew of Lord Edward Fitzgerald is told in the first letter. See pp. 5, 6, *ante*.

[2] This was Henri Grégoire, the celebrated Bishop of Blois—a most influential member of the National Convention, and afterwards of the Council of Five Hundred. The *aplomb* of our spy in hailing such men as friends will be appreciated. Grégoire was a cautious man, who voted against the divorce of

declined it, as did Stone;[1] upon which I wrote, on the 8th, to the Minister, to say that these two had refused, and that they thought he himself ought to do it, or give me a note of introduction to the President; but that, if it was disagreeable, I would not press the matter further, as I looked on his word as that of the Directory, and that I would call next day at the Directory, when, if I could get an audience, so much the better; if not, I thought it imprudent to wait longer.

Next day I called at the Directory and sent in my name. I there met Duckett,[2] who told me it would be impossible to see any of them that day; for a letter, which he had just brought them, which came from Leonard Bourdon,[3] would give them, he believed, work enough, as he understood it contained some very interesting matter. I was to have seen some of them that day likewise; an answer came to us both that they were too much occupied. I then went to the Minister, and sent in my name, as did, at the same time, Colonel La Harpe and the Swiss Deputies. We were all sent off, as he was very busy. I left a note with his Secretary, saying I would set out next day, which I did, the 20 Floreal, alias Wednesday, the 9th May; arrived at Cuxhaven the Wednesday following; sailed the next day, landed at Lowestoff on Tuesday morning, got to town [London] that night, accompanied by one Jeffrey,[4] who passes himself off for a Scotchman, was coming to Yarmouth as an American, was in Paris last September, speaks French as a Frenchman, looks extremely like one, and lodges at the New Hummums, Covent Garden.

It is quite clear that the above letter was written by the same nameless spy who poses in Froude's book as 'Lord

Napoleon and Joséphine, and opposed the Emperor's marriage with Marie-Thérèse. During the 'Reign of Terror,' when urged to follow the Archbishop of Paris and abjure his priestly duties, he refused. B. 1750, d. 1831.

[1] Stone, see p. 33 *infra*.

[2] Duckett, an Irish rebel agent, falsely suspected by Tone of being a spy, will figure in chapter x.

[3] See p. 110 *infra*.

[4] Possibly John Jeffrey, brother of Francis. He was a Scotchman, and usually resided in America (*Life of Jeffrey*, by Lord Cockburn, i. 50). How completely a Republican spirit possessed him is shown by his brother's letters to him in 1797, beginning 'My dear Citizen' (ii. 30 *et seq.*). The subsequent Lord Jeffrey was also a democrat, and his movements may have been shadowed, as those of Coleridge notoriously were.

Downshire's friend.' '*One* of his letters, dated November 19, 1797, is preserved,' writes Mr. Froude; but, no doubt, a few others are preserved too, and may be found in the correspondence of Lord Castlereagh. How they escaped destruction is a marvel. Wickham, on January 11, 1799, writes, regarding 'United Irishmen' at Hamburg: 'The enclosed very curious papers the Duke of Portland desires may be laid before the Lord Lieutenant, *and afterwards destroyed*.'

So careful was the spy of his reputation that he vouchsafes not a signature. Internal evidence, however, shows that he was the man who made his disclosure to Downshire, and was by him put in correspondence with Portland.

From the letter just quoted it appears that, after his efforts to pick news from Talleyrand and fish in Irish channels at Paris, he returned, *viâ* Cuxhaven, to London, where he arrived on Tuesday night, May 15, 1798. This date is worthy of note. The spy feared to show himself in London and felt that his life was unsafe. What brings him back to London on May 15, 1798? His favourite post was Cuxhaven or Hamburg. O'Coigly, Binns, and Leary, though arrested in February *en route* to France, were not put on their trial until Monday, May 21, 1798. This case is reported at extraordinary length in Howell's 'State Trials' and would fill a volume. Scott, afterwards Lord Eldon, prosecuted. The mass of secret information which the Crown contrived to acquire strikes very forcibly. Letters written in cipher by O'Coigly to Lord Edward Fitzgerald and others are translated and expounded by Scott. All the parties concerned in the conspiracy had false names. Mrs. Mathiessen[1] is called 'Marks;' 'a man going to William's,' means 'going to France,' etc. It was largely on evidence of this sort that O'Coigly was convicted and hanged.[2]

The betrayer tells Talleyrand that 'the spirit of the North was completely broken.' In point of fact, however, it was in the North that the real martial spirit of the United Irishmen

[1] See Froude, iii. 283, or *ante*.

[2] Compare letter from 'Castlereagh to Wickham,' p. 44 *ante*.

blazed, and there the best battles were afterwards fought under the leadership of Orr and Monroe. Turner was anxious to make the French turn their thoughts of invasion to other points on the Irish coast, and he so far succeeded that in August, 1798, Humbert's expedition, with less than 1,000 men, landed at Killala, among the starved and unarmed peasantry of Connaught. He calculated on meeting enthusiastic support; but, as Mr. Lecky says, it soon became apparent how fatally he had been deceived. After winning one battle, and losing another, Humbert surrendered to Cornwallis.

'May I assure them that you'll come in three months?' Talleyrand is asked. The object of this and other questions, which, to a casual reader, seem hardly consistent with Turner's treachery to his friends, is now pretty plain. Great doubt prevailed as to whether an invasion of Ireland was really to be attempted. The First Consul blew hot and cold upon it. If the spy, as an envoy of the United Irishmen, could only extort from Talleyrand an explicit reply in writing avowing the intention to invade, and telling the exact time on which the descent on Ireland was to be made, England would thus be well prepared, and her fleet able to destroy the French armament as she had already destroyed that of De Winter. Why Bonaparte, at first so anxious for invasion, should have changed his mind, is explained, in the recently published Memoirs of Gouverneur Morris, as due to the conflicting reports of Irish envoys. At St. Helena he told Las Cases that his mistake in '98 was to have gone to Egypt and not to Ireland.[1]

Mr. Froude states that the betrayer had discovered one of the objects of the Papists to be the seizure of property, and had determined to separate himself from the conspiracy. Attention is requested to that part of the foregoing letter[2] where the writer refers to the Cromwellian holders of estates in Ireland, and asks that every individual be guaranteed his

[1] *Mémoires de Sainte-Hélène.*

[2] The precise and careful wording is that of a lawyer, which Turner was.

property without respect to old Catholic claims and to their political conduct prior to the time of actual invasion. Samuel Turner represented some of the Cromwellian Settlers, and 'his most particular friends,' as he calls them, were amongst those who held grants of land in succession to the old Papist proprietary. The descendants of these men viewed invasion with alarm, lest their lands should go, just as the property of the Papists had already gone.[1]

Talleyrand's caution in talking with Turner contrasts with the freedom with which he opened his mind on the same subject to his *confrères*. A very important book was published in 1890 at Paris by M. Pallain, 'Talleyrand sous le Directoire.' It depicts his diplomatic life, and gives the pith of his despatches. From Turner and Duckett he probably derived some impressions regarding Great Britain and Ireland. He augurs well from the Irish rebellion, which has been 'cemented,' adds Talleyrand, 'by the blood of celebrated victims.' Its first victim was the Rev. William Jackson, in 1794. Talleyrand urges the invasion of Ireland and the establishment of an Irish Republic 'for the instruction or chastisement of England.' 'Nelson's fleet,' he says, 'is manned almost exclusively by Irishmen,' and that their patriotism 'will teach them to see in the English their oppressors and enemies.' Talleyrand's sketch of 'Irish Landed Proprietors' is full and curious.

Another man who, besides Talleyrand and Grégoire, dealt cautiously with Turner was Stone, as Turner in his secret letter to the Home Office admits. Stone had been tried in England for high treason and sent into exile.[2] At Hamburg

[1] Mr. J. P. Prendergast, in his *Cromwellian Settlement of Ireland*, prints, from original MSS., a 'list of adventurers for land in Ireland' (p. 417). Among them we find: 'Samuel Turner of London, merchant taylor, £200.' 'Richard Turner, senior and junior, taylors, £200.' These persons are also found subscribing the same sum, he adds, as 'adventurers, for the sea-service' (p. 417). The hereditary feelings and predilections of a Cromwellian Settler can be traced in the letter to Talleyrand.

[2] I find in the contents of the long-sealed chest at Dublin Castle, 'The Examination of Samuel Rogers, of Cornhill, Banker,' regarding his relations with Stone, dated May 10, 1794. With it is preserved an autograph statement by

and at Paris he belonged to the set mentioned by Mr. Froude's cloaked spy [1] as including Lady Edward Fitzgerald (Pamela), Lady Lucy Fitzgerald, Mrs. Matthiessen, and General Count Valence. Madame de Genlis in her 'Memoirs' mentions Stone conjointly with her daughter Madame de Valence and her 'niece' Pamela.[2]

Richard Brinsley Sheridan, technically called his examination, embracing ten folios, dated May 9, 1794, and explaining his intercourse with Stone.

[1] *Vide* p. 5, *ante*.

[2] *Memoirs of Madame de Genlis*, iv. 130–36.

CHAPTER V

LORD CLONCURRY SHADOWED

Discoveries and arrests now multiplied, despite the care with which Reinhard and Lady Edward persuaded themselves that all negotiations had been fenced.

Lord Cloncurry in his Memoirs writes of his 'dear friend Lord Edward Fitzgerald,' and readers of that book will remember the touching narrative given of the writer's arrest and long confinement in the Tower. This peer seeks to show that he himself was innocent of treason, but Mr. Froude states, after studying the letters of Lord Downshire's friend, that 'Lord Cloncurry was a sworn member of the Revolutionary Committee.'[1] The betrayer's first interview with Downshire took place on October 8, 1797. In that interview he ranked among the marked men, Lawless, afterwards Lord Cloncurry. During the next month we find his movements narrowly watched. One of Mr. Froude's sensational surprises is a statement in reference to this subsequent British Peer and Privy Councillor. Pelham, Chief Secretary for Ireland, writing to the Home Office on November 7, 1797, refers to the fact—if fact it is—that

'Mr. Lawless, Lord Cloncurry's eldest son, is going to England this night, charged with an answer to a message lately received from France. I have sent Captain D'Auvergne in the packet with Mr. Lawless, with directions to find where he means to go in London, and to give you immediate information.'[2]

[1] Froude, iii. 287.

[2] This announcement had its origin in one of the secret letters of McNally (MSS. Dublin Castle). Lawless was to sail for London 'to-morrow night,' he wrote, 'and ought to be watched every hour'; but nothing is said of the answer to

A story never loses in its carriage; and Portland was perturbed by the news. The Hamburg spy, who was the first to mention Lawless's name, was now consulted.

Two secret letters from the Home Office, dated June 8, 1798, and printed in Lord Castlereagh's 'Correspondence,' speak of a communication received from '*a person* in Hamburg,' and how

'His Majesty's confidential servants have found it necessary to take into custody and detain several natives of Ireland, now resident here, of whose intimate connection and correspondence with the leaders and inciters of the present rebellion in Ireland there was no room whatever to doubt. . . . Communicate this information to the Lord Lieutenant, that the Honourable Mr. L——, Mr. S., of Acton,[1] and Messrs. T., A., and C.,[2] of the Temple, have been apprehended here, and Messrs. McG—— and D—— at Liverpool;[3] and that warrants for apprehending the following have been granted: Dr. O'K——, C——[4] of Abbey Street, Dublin, and Mr. H——.[5]

Lord Cloncurry states that the Duke of Leinster, Curran, and Grattan, who happened to be visiting him, were also

France, of which Pelham declares he was the bearer. McNally lived in Dublin, was a United Irishman, and confidential lawyer of the body, but had been bought over. The strange story of his life is told in a succeeding chapter. This man was now asked to find out all he could about Lawless.

[1] Lord Castlereagh, in a letter addressed to Colonel Lord William Bentinck, dated, Dublin Castle, June 24, 1798, and given to me by Mr. Huband Smith, states that, according to the information received, 'Mr. Stewart had accepted the post of Adjutant-General for Armagh in the rebel army. Bentinck, writing to General Nugent three days later, says that Stewart, when his prisoner, 'confessed to me privately that he was a United Irishman.' This tends to show how generally accurate was the information communicated through Downshire.

[2] Trenor, Agar, and Curran. Trenor was the secretary of Lawless. Cloncurry's Memoirs state (p. 68) that the hardships to which Trenor was exposed brought on illness and caused his death.

[3] It appears from a letter of Wickham's (*Castlereagh*, i. 313) that the two men arrested at Liverpool were McGuckin and Dowdall.

[4] The *Dublin Directory* for 1798 records the name of 'John Chambers, 5, Abbey Street.' Here again the handiwork of Downshire's 'friend' is traceable. The private list of the executive, which he gave him, includes Chambers,s name. Mr. Chambers, grandson of the above, tells me that when the warrani was issued, a judge of unpopular antecedents hid the rebel in his house.

[5] The imprisonment of Hamilton, the nephew of Russell, is noticed in the letter from Hamburg. *Castlereagh Papers*, ii. 5.

taken into custody; but this statement is not wholly borne out by contemporary accounts.

Wickham's second letter of June 8, 1798, recurs to the arrests and speaks of 'most secret, though accurate, intelligence received from Hamburg,' adding:—

There are some papers found in Mr. Lawless's possession that tend directly to show his connection with some of the most desperate of the Republican party here, as well as with those who are in habitual communication with the French agents at *Hamburgh*, and his Grace is in daily expectation of some material evidence *from that place*, tending more directly to implicate that gentleman in a treasonable correspondence with the enemy.[1]

'Braughall' was another name which will be found in the list written out by Downshire from his visitor's dictation. Lord Cloncurry, in his Memoirs, describes Braughall as 'his business agent and confidential friend;' while Tone constantly refers to him in cordial terms. The newspapers of the day record his arrest and how 'papers of a very seditious nature were found in his house.'[2] Among them was a letter from Lawless urging him to contribute to the defence of unfortunate O'Coigly, and mentioning that 'Little Henry' had munificently subscribed. This passage, Lord Cloncurry states, was interpreted at Dublin Castle as referring to Henry Grattan, though the writer meant Mr. Henry of Straffan, brother-in-law to Lord Edward Fitzgerald, and as

[1] Wickham to Castlereagh, Whitehall, June 8, 1798.

[2] McNally's secret letters, scores of which I have read in MS., make frequent mention of Braughall as a man with whom he was intimate; and it is likely that the news of Lawless's intended journey to England came from Braughall innocently. McNally, while incriminating others, uniformly seeks to exculpate Braughall, whose counsel he was (MS. letter of May 25, 1798). On June 13, 1798, he expresses his opinion that 'Braughall is an enemy to force'; and a characteristic hint drops: 'If Braughall could be made a friend—and I do believe he is not disinclined to be one, for I know he always reprobates tumult—his influence is great, and his exertions would go far to restore peace.' Braughall had been secretary to the Catholic Committee, and is repeatedly mentioned by Tone in his Journal. A fine portrait of Braughall, in oils, may be seen in the board-room of the Royal Dublin Society, of which he was secretary. After his arrest, this picture was relegated to a cellar of the institution; but, thanks to Lord J. Butler, it has been recently unearthed and restored. He died in 1803.

the result of this mistake Grattan was placed under arrest, but speedily liberated.

A memoir of O'Coigly is furnished by Dr. Madden in the first edition of his 'United Irishmen,' and embodies information derived from Cloncurry. Referring to the Hon. Mr. Lawless, when in London, he says: 'Every Irishman who frequented his house was vigilantly watched by *agents of a higher department than the police.*' Pelham says that he sent Captain D'Auvergne on board the packet with Lawless, charged to find out where he went to in London; and it would seem that during the tedious journey of those days, Lawless suspected D'Auvergne's mission. 'The agent of a higher department than the police' would also apply to Turner, who was in London at this time. Who was the detective who had his berth next to young Lawless on board the boat, sat and chatted with him in the coach to London, and afterwards dogged his steps? Letters furnishing secret information, and signed 'Captain D'Auvergne, Prince of Bouillon,' may be found in the 'Castlereagh Papers.'[1] This personage represented an old and illustrious French family. The Prince, finding his patrimony sequestered during the Revolution, looked out for a livelihood, and seems to have been not fastidious as to the sort. Cloncurry states that when bidding good night at the house of a friend, he would say, 'I haven't the conscience to keep my poor spy shivering longer in the cold.' After 1798, D'Auvergne's usual post was Jersey, whence his letters in the 'Castlereagh Papers' are dated, and furnish the fruit of espionage, including all warlike preparations made by the French at Brest.[2]

[1] *Castlereagh*, i. 250, 373, 382; ii. 104, 162, &c.

[2] He obtained the rank of Post-Captain, R.N., in 1784; and at the time that he was with Lord Camden at Dublin Castle he commanded the 'Bravo' gunboat. In 1805 he was gazetted 'Rear-Admiral of the Blue.' His name crops up now and then in the Wellington Correspondence. Thus, on November 15, 1814, when the Bourbons had been restored, this gentleman, now signing himself 'D'Auvergne, Duke of Bouillon, &c.' writes from 'Bagatelle, Jersey,' thanking his Grace for the condescending interest he had shown in recovering for him the small sovereignty of Bouillon. *Vide* also a piquant memoir of His Serene Highness Philip d'Auvergne, Prince de Bouillon, in *Public Characters*

Mr. Froude quotes a letter from Portland, part of which is to the same effect as that already given, and announcing the discovery of important papers 'in Mr. Lawless's [Cloncurry's] possession that tend directly to show his connection with some of the most desperate of the Republican party in England, as well as with those who are in habitual communication with the French agents at Hamburg; and yet,' he continued, 'under present circumstances, and with evidence of the nature of that of which the Government here is in possession, strong and decisive as it is, none of those persons can be brought to trial without exposing secrets of the last importance to the State, the revealing of which may implicate the safety of the two kingdoms.'[1] But although the leading men could not be brought to trial, it was fit to hold them fast, that thus the teeth of the conspiracy might be drawn. One important man—Stewart of Acton—was certainly let out on bail; but he was a cousin of Lord Castlereagh's.

These rough notes ought not to close without some notice of a reply to Portland's criminatory remarks, which the late Lord Cloncurry has placed on record. When the 'Castlereagh Papers' appeared he was an octogenarian and enjoying, it is to be hoped, an unimpaired memory; but it is an open secret that tho book known as 'Lord Cloncurry's Personal Memoirs' was fully prepared for publication, and its style strengthened throughout, by a practised writer connected with the Tory press of Dublin, and who believed that Cloncurry had been wrongly judged in 1798.

As to the papers alleged by Mr. Wickham to have been found in my possession, [Lord Cloncurry is supposed to write] and tending directly to show my connection with some of the most desperate of the Republican party in London and Hamburgh, I now solemnly

for 1800–1, pp. 545, 561. His father, though of ancient lineage, embarked in commercial pursuits; and it is added that at Jersey 'a multitude of spies were kept in constant pay.' A love of epistolary intrigue seems to have been hereditary with Captain d'Auvergne, Prince of Bouillon. History records that Cardinal d'Auvergne Bouillon, during the War of the Succession, held a culpable correspondence with the enemy, *i.e.* Marlborough, Orrery, and Galloway.

[1] Portland to Camden, June 8.—S. P. O.

declare that I believe the statement to be *a pure fiction*, and that no papers were found, as I am most certain that, with my knowledge, no papers existed which could have had any such tendency, more directly or indirectly than, perhaps, a visiting ticket of Arthur O'Connor's, or a note from O'Coigly in acceptance of my invitation to dinner.[1]

On the other hand, it is stated in a letter to the Home Office, dated July 24, 1799, that rebel despatches had been regularly addressed to Mr. Lawless in the Temple, 'whose fate,' it is added, 'is much lamented at Paris.'[2] Lord Cloncurry himself admits that in the autumn of 1797 he was elected—but without his desire or knowledge—a member of the Executive Directory of the United Irishmen, 'when, for the first and only time, I attended a meeting held at Jackson's in Church Street.'[3] This date furnished fresh proof of the promptitude and accuracy of Turner's information to Downshire (supplied also in the autumn of 1797)—information which revealed the adhesion of Lawless, afterwards Lord Cloncurry, to the Executive Directory. Jackson's name is also to be found in the list as dictated by Turner. Of course Lawless must have been already a United Irishman, or he could not be eligible for election to a seat in the Directory. Binns, who was arrested with O'Connor and O'Coigly at Margate, says: 'Coigly was no stranger to Lawless; he made him a United Irishman in his father's house, in Merrion Street, Dublin.'[4] Cloncurry's Memoirs state merely that O'Coigly, who was the finest-looking man he had ever seen, presented to him a letter of introduction, descriptive of Orange persecution, which it was alleged he had suffered.

Lawless and O'Coigly had opinions in common; and both

[1] *Personal Recollections of Lord Cloncurry.*

[2] *Castlereagh Papers*, ii. 361.

[3] *Personal Recollections of Lord Cloncurry*, p. 38.

[4] Purchased by the father of Lord Cloncurry from Lord Mornington (Cloncurry's *Recollections*, p. 8). In this house the Duke of Wellington was most certainly born in 1769, though his Grace was himself ignorant of the fact, as his Census return, in 1850, shows. It is now the headquarters of the Land Commission.

were much together in London. The former never forgave O'Connor for having—as he said—unfairly sacrificed O'Coigly during the trials at Maidstone.[1] In collecting evidence to hang the priest, renewed attention fell upon Lawless. His first imprisonment lasted for six weeks. On April 14, 1799, on the eve of his marriage with Miss Ryall, who at last died of a 'broken heart,' he was again arrested on Portland's warrant and committed to the Tower, where he remained two years. Lord Cloncurry states that his father, in dread of confiscation following his son, left away from him 65,000*l.* However, the Irish rebel lived to become a British peer, a Privy Councillor, and the adviser of successive Viceroys. Dr. Madden, who received much help from Cloncurry when compiling his 'Lives of the United Irishmen,' states that Robert Emmet dined with this peer in Paris, previous to leaving France on his ill-fated enterprise; and Madden, in his second edition (ii. 137), says he knows not how to reconcile the account of the interview, as supplied in 'Cloncurry's Personal Memoirs,' with a verbal account of the same given by his lordship to himself.

The list noted by Downshire from the dictation of his visitor, though complete as regards the Rebel Executive of 1797, far from embraced all the names which more careful thought must have brought to the recollection of the informer. It had now become second nature to him to discharge, almost daily, letters of fatal aim, jeopardising the lives and reputations of men who implicitly trusted him. He also, as it appears, 'opened a correspondence' with leading United Irishmen. It is not sought to be conveyed that all the information came from Turner; but the following remarks of Mr. Froude, although they repeat a few names already mentioned, are important, as connecting 'Lord Downshire's friend' with the harvest of captures in midsummer 1798:—

Every day was bringing to the private knowledge of the Cabinet how widely the mischief had spread, *as the correspondence which continued with Lord Downshire's friend added to the list of accom-*

[1] Statement of Lord Cloncurry to Mr. O'Neill Daunt.

plices. Lord Cloncurry's son was no sooner arrested, than Stewart of Acton, a young Agar, a young Tennent, young Curran, McGuckin, Dowdall, and twenty others,[1] whose names never came before the public, were found to be as deeply compromised as he.[2]

The question was even mooted as to whether he and others should not be excepted by name from the Bill of Indemnity, or even specially attainted by a Bill of Pains and Penalties, in consideration of the impossibility of convicting them by the ordinary course of the law.[3]

Turner's knowledge and duties as a United Irishman having been mainly confined to Ulster, it seemed strange that one of the Northern Committee could be so intimate with O'Connor and Lord Edward. Even in the betrayer's first interview with Downshire he reveals much intimate acquaintance with both. All this can be readily understood now. In November, 1796, O'Connor took a house near Belfast, preparatory to offering himself for the representation of Antrim. Dr. Madden states that Lord Edward and O'Connor lived together for some months, and during their stay maintained friendly intercourse with the Northern leaders.[4] Soon after we find the command in Ulster assigned to O'Connor. 'Arthur O'Connor,' resumes Mr. Froude, describing the events of December, 1797, 'after spending a few months in the Castle,'[5] had been released on bail, Thomas Addis Emmet and Lord Edward Fitzgerald being his securities. "*The person*" *who had come to Lord Downshire* had revealed the secret of the visit to Switzerland; but without betraying his authority Camden could not again order O'Connor's arrest.'[6] After an interval, however, and

[1] Stewart of Acton, Tennent, McGuckin, Hamilton, and many of the twenty others, were all, like Turner, belonging to the Ulster branch of the organisation.

[2] Froude, iii. 418; see also p. 20, *ante*.

[3] *Castlereagh Papers*, i. 163.

[4] *Lives and Times of the United Irishmen*, ii. 13.

[5] Birmingham Tower, Dublin Castle.

[6] *The English in Ireland*, iii. 288. The above passage serves to show that the important arrests made by the Lord-Lieutenant in Ireland were largely due to 'the person' who whispered in Downshire's ear.

at a critical moment, O'Connor was apprehended anew, and he remained a State prisoner until 1802.

At an early stage of this chase I met with the seeming difficulty that the name of Samuel Turner appears in the list of leading rebels which '*the person*' gave to Lord Downshire.[1] In undertaking to give a complete list of the Executive Committee, he could not well omit his own name. No doubt to invest it with increased importance, he puts it next after those of Lord Edward and Arthur O'Connor (the nephew of Lord Longueville), and before Stewart of Acton and the future Lord Cloncurry. The act is consistent with the usual swagger of the man, and shows the ingenuity by which he hoped to baffle all subsequent evidence of his treachery.

Lord Camden writes: 'The intelligence with which we are furnished would, if certain persons could be brought forward, be sufficient to bring the conspiracy to light, defeat its ill consequences, and make a salutary impression on the minds of the people.'[2] 'Unfortunately,' comments Mr. Froude, '"certain persons" declined to be brought forward. Pelham, when in London, made *large offers to Lord Downshire's friend* but without effect.'

[1] See this list, p. 7, *ante*.
[2] Camden to Portland, December 2, 1797.

CHAPTER VI

THE MASK TORN OFF AT LAST

Mr. Froude, quoting from the betrayer's letter to Downshire, writes:—'I went to Harley Street, where Fitz[1] told me of the conduct of the Catholics to him and his friends. He said he would prevail on O'Connor, or some such,[2] to go to Paris; if not, he would go himself, in order to have Lewins removed.'

Lord Edward came to this decision obviously on the representations made by his false friend regarding Lewins. The false friend will be found impugning Lewins on every opportunity. Turner and Lewins, it may be repeated, clashed as rival envoys; Lewins, a Catholic, represented the Leinster Directory, while Turner claimed to represent the Northern. Turner worked his pen and tongue to such purpose that he at last succeeded in convincing Lord Edward of Lewins's treachery. Binns, in his narrative, states that 'O'Coigly had been commissioned by the Executive to supersede Lewins in Paris, *whom some suspected of betraying the interests of Ireland.*'[3]

The letter from Hamburg (first revealed by Mr. Froude) continues:—

Mrs. Matthieson[4] has just heard from Lady Lucy that O'Connor is come. I supped last night with Valence, who mentioned his

[1] Edward J. Lewins was an attorney, and with the astuteness of that craft he had early suspected Turner, as appears from the letter to 'Citizen Minister Talleyrand' (p. 24, *ante*).

[2] The 'some such' proved to be Father O'Coigly, arrested *en route*, and hanged in 1798.

[3] Lewins, Mr. Lecky shows, proved thoroughly faithful to his party.

[4] Henriette de Sercy, the niece of Madame de Genlis, and the companion of Pamela in childhood, who married Mr. Matthiessen, the banker of Hamburg.

having introduced Lord Edward[1] and O'Connor to the Minister here[2] in the summer before the French attempted to invade Ireland.[3] They both went to Switzerland, whence O'Connor passed into France, had an interview with Hoche, and everything was planned.

I feared lest Government might not choose to ratify our contract, and, being in their power, would give me my choice either to come forward as an evidence or suffer martyrdom myself. Having no taste for an exit of this sort, I set out and arrived here safe, and now beg you will let me know if anything was wrong in my statements, or if I have given offence. . . .

One of the many unexplained letters in the Castlereagh Correspondence finds its keynote here. In August, 1798, Wickham, of the Home Office, writes as follows to Castlereagh, who then held O'Connor a prisoner in Dublin.[4] Wickham's object, though shrouded in mystery, was no doubt to check the accuracy of 'Lord Downshire's friend,' and to weigh the marketable value of his services:—

It would be a great satisfaction to me, personally, were O'Connor to be questioned on the object of his journey to Switzerland with Lord Edward Fitzgerald in 1796, and whether they, or either of them, were in France at that time, and what French agents they saw besides M. Barthélemy. I was absent with the Austrian army at the time of their arrival, so that I lost the opportunity of observing their motions.[5] If either of them went into France, which I am persuaded they did, I should be curious, for very particular reasons, to know whether they went in by way of Basle, and whether their passports were given in their own names. Should

[1] Lord Edward Fitzgerald.

[2] Reinhard.

[3] At Bantry Bay in 1796. By many, Tone was regarded somewhat as a clever adventurer; but when the French authorities saw a nobleman—brother of the Duke of Leinster—as well as O'Connor, nephew and heir of Viscount Longueville, acting in a way which meant business, their hesitancy ceased.

[4] After the arrest and death of Lord Edward Fitzgerald, and the collapse of the rebellion, the State prisoners consented to give some general information which would not compromise men by name.

[5] Wickham's correspondence illustrative of his secret mission to Switzerland, when he debauched the French minister, Barthélemy, with 'saint-seducing gold,' was published by Bentley in 1870.

there be no impropriety in questioning O'Connor on these points, as I have said before, it would be a great satisfaction to me that it should be done.[1]

Fifty pages may be turned ere the answer to this letter comes. It is headed '*Secret*,' and bears date 'Dublin Castle, August 17, 1798.' All my circumstantial evidence, aiming to show that Turner is the man whom Mr. Froude could not identify, is crowned by this letter. Castlereagh thus replies to Wickham:—

'Secret. 'Dublin Castle: August 17, 1798.

'I have endeavoured to obey your commands in examining Mr. O'Connor as to the object of his journey to Switzerland with Lord Edward Fitzgerald. At first he declined answering to this point, considering himself as only bound to state the facts which came to his knowledge after he became a United Irishman, of which body he was not then a member. Upon being pressed, without mentioning names, he stated it thus:—In the summer of 1796, as set forth in the Memoir, an agent was sent to France to arrange with the Directory the plan of invasion. This person went to Hamburg; from thence, accompanied by his friend, to Switzerland; neither went to Paris, but the person employed *had an interview* near the French frontier with a person high in the confidence of the Directory; upon a communication with whom everything was settled.[2] The reason neither proceeded to Paris was lest the English Government, in whose pay most of the officers in Paris were supposed [3] to be, should suspect the design, and arrest the persons on their return.

'This perfectly agrees with Richardson's information, which states that Lord Edward and O'Connor met Hoche, and arranged the invasion. '*R—— states that O'Connor went into France*; if he did, it was only a short distance merely to meet Hoche, and, from what O'Connor said, Lord E. seemed to be the principal.'

[1] *Castlereagh Papers*, i. 259-60.

[2] 'Everything was planned,' are the words in the betrayer's letter to Lord Downshire.

[3] In this suspicion, Lord Edward and O'Connor were not far astray. *The Confidential Letters of the Right Hon. William Wickham* reveal that Pichegru and other French generals were paid by Pitt to allow themselves to be beaten in battle.

The above paragraph is one of much importance. Richardson I have discovered to be another alias of the hydra-headed Turner. Distinct proof of this will be found presently. Castlereagh continues:—

'Should I succeed in drawing from him any further information on this point, I shall have great pleasure in transmitting it. He further stated that, when taken in Kent,[1] although he had not authorised any person to hire a vessel direct for France, but rather looked to reach a Dutch port, yet his real object was to pass through Switzerland into France, and fairly confessed that, had he reached Paris, he should not have been idle, as, though not charged with any special commission, he did believe the Directory would have considered him as an accredited agent.'[2]

Ordinary students of history are not free to search the papers of the Home Office, London after the date 1760; and the present writer ventured to ask Mr. Lecky whether he had met the name of Turner in his inquiries. The object of Mr. Lecky's history is distinct from mine, and his researches have taken a different direction; but he could not fail to observe, he said, that the Government correspondence threw not much light on questions of espionage, 'for names of informers,' he adds, 'are nearly always concealed.' However, on referring to his notes, it appeared that '*Richardson*' was the pseudonym of Samuel Turner. While thanking my correspondent, I thought it well to remind him that in the 'Castlereagh Papers'[3] 'Furnes' is stated to be the alias for this man. And I added, in order to guard against mistake, that one Thomas Richardson, a Liberal magistrate for Tyrone, was confined, in 1797, with Neilson and Teeling. The historian's reply is very satisfactory:[4] 'Samuel Turner wrote his letters to the British

[1] At Margate with Father O'Coigly.

[2] *Castlereagh Papers*, i. 309–10.

[3] General index to the *Correspondence of Lord Castlereagh*. 'Furness' is the name under which Reinhard, the French minister, refers to him when writing to his Government.

[4] Letter of W. E. H. Lecky, Esq., to W. J. F., Athenæum Club, London, July 5, 1888. Richardson, the popular author of 'Pamela,' was then a specially familiar name, and one which would readily occur to a well-read man who divulged the secrets of a real Pamela. The plot in the stories of Samuel Richardson is

Government under the name of Richardson. This,' adds Mr. Lecky, 'is not a matter of inference, but of distinct proof.'

Once only 'Richardson' is mentioned in 'Castlereagh.' It was the false name by which the Home Office, when obliged to communicate with Dublin Castle, masked Samuel Turner, LL.D., of the Irish Bar. Lord Castlereagh's letter to the Home Office confirms the intimate knowledge possessed by Turner of the doings of O'Connor and Lord Edward Fitzgerald. O'Connor was now—August, 1798—in an Irish dungeon; and Lord Castlereagh having, as he says, pressed him to answer certain questions, adds: '*This perfectly agrees with Richardson's information, which states that Lord Edward and O'Connor met Hoche and arranged the invasion.*'

Besides his horror of martyrdom by the knife, Turner had a lively dread of the martyrdom of exposure and social ostracism. Jackson's trial in 1794 had the effect of deterring approvers. Curran's skill in torturing such persons was marvellous; and Mr. Froude declares that he stretched Cockayne as painfully as ever the rackmaster of the Tower stretched a Jesuit. 'He made him confess that he had been employed by Pitt, and showed that, if Jackson was a traitor to the State, Cockayne was a far blacker traitor to the friend who trusted him.'[1]

'Richardson' is now shown to be the same man as he who gave his information to Downshire; and that 'Richardson' was an assumed name for Samuel Turner.[2] Thus the question

developed by letters, a branch of composition in which Samuel Turner was *au fait*. There seems a strange irony in this spy describing, under the *nom de plume* of Richardson, a new 'History of Pamela' and her struggles. Dr. Madden says that, after the death of her husband, Pamela returned in painfully straitened circumstances to Hamburg, the only place to which she could with prudence go. Madden little dreamt that the fugitive's retreat was the serpent's lair.

[1] The Rev. William Jackson, an Anglican clergyman, came to Dublin on a treasonable mission, accompanied, as his friend and legal adviser, by Cockayne, a London attorney. The latter was deputed by Pitt to entrap the National leaders. Cockayne prosecuted Jackson to conviction. In Ireland, unlike England, one witness then sufficed to convict for high treason.

[2] In a letter dated June 8, 1798, Wickham speaks of the source from which 'R' procured 'all the information that he has communicated to us'—meaning

of identity is established without appealing to further evidence. But inasmuch as my efforts to track Turner open up facts long forgotten, and others new to the historian, some readers may not object to follow.

As regards Lord Edward's meeting with Hoche, more than once referred to in Turner's letter to Lord Downshire and in the correspondence of the Home Office, M. Guillon, a recent investigator,[1] could find no trace of it in the French official archives. Special efforts were made at the time to veil this historic interview. No wonder, therefore, that Mr. Froude, in introducing the information furnished by Downshire's mysterious visitor, points specially to the secret meeting with Hoche, and how Hoche himself had not revealed it even to Tone.[2]

Wickham was but carrying out Portland's behest in signifying to Castlereagh that O'Connor, then a prisoner, should be questioned on points of which the Home Office had acquired private knowledge. On August 23, 1798, the same polite pumping of O'Connor is urged—a task fraught with no great labour to a man of Castlereagh's tact and powers of persuasion. 'A *private* communication,' Wickham writes, 'of the names of the persons with whom Mr. O'Connor corresponded abroad, would answer *the particular purpose* required by the Duke of Portland.' The 'particular' object is not explained. It was probably that the spy might, as previously suggested, cultivate epistolary relations with the men whom O'Connor [3] would admit to have been his correspondents.[4]

what concerned Lady Edward Fitzgerald, Valence, Mrs. Matthiessen, Reinhar and other ingenuous friends at Hamburg, who told Turner all they knew Dr. Madden and others mistook this 'R' for the incorruptible Reinhard, as M. Mignet styles him. See folio 102, *infra*.

[1] *France et Irlande* (Paris, 1888).

[2] See p. 1, *ante*.

[3] *Vide* Appendix for some revelations of fratricidal betrayal by O'Connor's brother.

[4] One letter only, from Richardson (Turner) to Lord Downshire, I have found in the Pelham MSS.; it bears date 'Hamburg, December 1, 1797':—

'My Lord,—I cannot contrive any mode of seeing Mr. Fraser without running a very considerable risque of a discovery. For this reason I now intrude to

Teeling, one of the Northern leaders, who had been closely associated with Turner, gives a curious glimpse of the easy intercourse which Castlereagh would maintain with his captives. Sometimes he made the arrests himself in the first instance, and afterwards could charm his prisoners by drawing silken bonds around them. Teeling was accompanied by his father on horseback, when 'we met,' he writes, 'Lord Castlereagh, who accosted us with his usual courtesy. We had proceeded up the street of Lisburn together, when, having reached the house of his uncle, the Marquis of Hertford, we were about to take leave of his lordship. "I regret," said he, addressing my father, "that your son cannot accompany you," conducting me at the same moment through the outer gate, which, to my inexpressible astonishment, was instantly closed, and I found myself surrounded by a military guard.' Teeling, later on, describes a visit paid by Castlereagh to him when a prisoner:—

Fatigued, and apparently much dispirited, Lord Castlereagh entered the room. He possessed the most fascinating manner and engaging address, with a personal appearance peculiarly attractive, and certainly not in character with the office he had that day assumed. For though national pride was extinct in his soul, the graces of nature were not effaced from the form, nor the polished

request you'll be so kind as to favour me with a few lines. I wrote to you on November 17, by post. Since that I have sent you two letters by Captain Gunter, of the Nautilus: the first contains seven and a half pages of letter paper; the second, a single letter with such information as I could collect, which I hope will be material. Gunter promised to put them in the Yarmouth office himself.

'It will be requisite for your lordship to lay aside every emblem of *noblesse*, and adopt the style of an Irish *sans-culotte*, for fear of accidents. If I appear worthy the further notice of your lordship, no pains on my part shall be spared to merit the honour of being ranked among your lordship's most sincere,

'J. RICHARDSON.

'December 1, 1797, Hamburg (under cover to the master of the post-office, Yarmouth).'—Pelham MSS. At p. 30 Turner also points to Yarmouth.

Placed far apart from Richardson's letter is found the despatch of Cooke, wherein it had been enclosed. 'The letters by the "Nautilus" have not been received,' he writes, 'and we know not how to direct to him.' The Pelham MSS. are pyramids in bulk, but no other letter from Richardson, alias Turner, is entombed within them.

manners of the gentleman forgotten in the uncourteous garb of the officer of police. He regretted that in his absence I had been subjected to the painful restraint of an additional guard. It was not his desire that they should have been placed within my room. A slight repast had been prepared for him, of which he pressed me to partake. The wine was generous, his lordship was polite, and the prisoner of State seemed for a moment forgotten in the kinder feelings of the earlier friend. [Lord Castlereagh then informed Teeling that they had that day arrested Neilson and Russell.] 'Russell!'[1] said I. 'Then the soul of honour is captive! Is Russell a prisoner?' Lord Castlereagh was silent. He filled his glass—he passed me the wine. Our conversation had become embarrassing. . . .[2]

[1] Neilson, Russell, Teeling, and Turner belonged to the Ulster branch of the organisation. Russell, who had been a captain in the 64th Regiment, and a J. P. for co. Tyrone, remained a prisoner untill 1802, and, on connecting himself with Emmet's scheme, was beheaded October 30, 1803. Samuel Neilson, son of a Presbyterian minister, died, after many exciting vicissitudes, on August 29 in the same year.

[2] *Personal Narrative*, by Charles Hamilton Teeling. His daughter became the first wife of Lord O'Hagan.

CHAPTER VII

DR. MACNEVIN'S MEMORIAL INTERCEPTED

ALTHOUGH the spy did not confide to Lord Downshire until October 1797 his name and secrets, there is reason to believe that he had furnished information previously. To enhance his importance he probably said nothing of this. As Mr. Froude observes, he painted his own conduct in the colours he thought best. This man had long played fast and loose. So early as May 1797 Turner was viewed with suspicion. The Castlereagh Papers contain a bundle of intercepted letters addressed by Reinhard, the French Minister at Hamburg, to De la Croix, head of the Foreign Office, Paris, of whom Tone often speaks with affection.[1] These letters, as already stated, mention Turner under the name of Furnes, which we learn from the Castlereagh Papers was an *alias* of Turner.[2] He is praised for his zeal and patriotism ; but in one letter Reinhard is found struggling with a painful misgiving. The suspicion is so dark that he does not like to write even the name of Furnes, but makes dots to tally with the letters composing it, and no name was better known to De la Croix. At last Reinhard tries to banish the thought as an unworthy suspicion ; and a subsequent letter of his reinstates Turner in full prestige.

The letter which expresses suspicion bears date May 31, but is confusingly assigned, in the Castlereagh Papers, to the year 1798. Its reference to Hoche, however, shows that it was written during the previous year—his death having occurred on September 15, 1797.

[1] *Castlereagh*, i. 282 292.

[2] *Ibid.*, General Index, iv. 504.

You must have heard [writes Reinhard to De la Croix] of the apprehension of two committees of United Irishmen at Belfast, and the publication of the papers seized, made by the secret committee of the Parliament of Ireland.[1] Among these papers is a letter from the provincial committee, informing those of Belfast that the executive committee having conducted itself in an improper manner, the provincial committee thought fit to dissolve it, retaining however, two-thirds of the former members. This letter has been printed in London in the *True Briton*, a ministerial paper. It is very remarkable that . . . . . . should never have mentioned that circumstance to me. Supposing, which is very probable, that this reorganisation of the executive took place before the departure of . . . . . . [from Ireland], it is natural enough to suppose that . . . . . . should find himself among the *excluded members*. The opinion that I have formed of him . . . . . . [adds Reinhard in words worthy of a true diplomat] is, that he is a man of haughty and violent character, without, on that account, stooping to dissimulation and deceit; so, in order to revenge himself on his countrymen, he may have betrayed his cause to Mr. Pitt. [Reinhard goes on to say that] it was letters of Lord Edward Fitzgerald which certified that this man who called upon me was the person sent to me by Lady Fitzgerald on his arrival.[2]

It seems needless to point out that this must be the 'person' whom Mr. Froude describes as being introduced by Lady Edward Fitzgerald, and having the ear of Reinhard at Hamburg; and there is hardly less doubt that the man thus noticed was the same who, having got into debt with his

[1] Further on will be seen Portland's caution to Castlereagh as to the means to be taken by the Secret Committee of the Irish Parliament in order to divert suspicion from their spy.

[2] The letter, of which this is an extract, appears in the *Castlereagh Papers* (i. 275–6). It was the interest of the spy that this letter should not be seen at the Foreign Office, Paris. It could do him no harm in the eyes of Pitt. A second intercepted letter from Reinhard states that consistently with his duties he sent Samuel Turner [of Hamburg] to General Hoche (see *Castlereagh*, i. 285). Tone mentions in his diary that Hoche one day 'seemed struck when I mentioned Hamburg, and asked me again was I going hither. "Well then," said he, "perhaps we may find something for you to do there. There is a person there whom perhaps you may see."' Tone muses, 'Who is my lover that I am to see at Hamburg, in God's name?' (*Diary*, ii. 341.) His diary is relinquished, however, just as he gets there, and his death in an Irish prison occurred soon after.

friends, addressed himself to Pelham as early as 1796. His secret letter to Pelham will be seen presently. Meanwhile the same sensitive pride and the same revengeful spirit when that pride was once wounded is also traceable in the details revealed to Lord Downshire next year. Judging from the slippery and impulsive character of the man, I cannot doubt that previous to his mission to London in October 1797, for the purpose of making a final bargain with Pitt, he had coquetted with Dublin Castle.

Lewins and Turner were rival envoys—Lewins represented the Leinster Directory; Turner claimed to speak for Ulster. Of Lewins, who stands above all suspicion, Reinhard writes to De la Croix in 1797:—'I think L . . . . . incapable of treachery, but capable of imprudence. I should not answer thus concerning *the other*. What seems further to concur in the support of my hypothesis is, that Mr. L. before his departure made it a point of great importance to ascertain whether there was any other envoy from Ireland, who addressed himself to me, and that he begged me not to give my confidence to any other than to him alone. I refrained from giving these tidings to General Hoche, not only because my means of corresponding with him are uncertain, but because all the letters from Frankfort announce his departure for Paris.'

It may not have struck Mr. Froude, as it certainly strikes me, that the man he describes[1] as visiting Lord Downshire, and at the last moment offering to betray, was the same person whom the historian, one hundred pages previously, notices as an informer, 'in the closest confidence of the *Northern Leaders*, but whose name is still a mystery.'

It will be seen that Pelham's correspondent of 1796 had fallen into debt and difficulties. This at first seems not consistent with the statement of Mr. Froude that Downshire's visitor was the son of a gentleman of good fortune in the North. But it is easy to see that the son himself had got into pecuniary straits. He tells Downshire of the expenses he is under, and asks Pitt for a 'cool 500*l.*'[2] to begin with.

[1] *English in Ireland*, iii. 278.

[2] *Ibid.* iii. 284.

In addition to a judgment debt of 1,500*l.* which Jacob Turner in his will forgives his son Samuel,[1] I find, on examining the records of the three Law Courts, that another judgment debt of 800*l.* was marked against Samuel Turner on January 26, 1793.[2]

Speaking of informers, Mr. Froude writes under date 1796:—

One of these especially, whose name is still a mystery, was in the closest confidence of the Belfast leaders. He had been among the most enthusiastic of the original members of Tone's society, but he had fallen into debt to others of the confederates and had been expelled. In revenge he sold himself to the Government, satisfied his creditors with money which he received from Pelham, and was at once taken back into confidence. Among others, be became an intimate associate of William Orr, a Belfast tradesman, afterwards executed for treason, who at this time was a member of the Head Northern Committee.

Orr told him that everything was ready. Dublin, Cork, Limerick, were waiting only for orders to rise, and when the word was given the movement was to be universal and simultaneous. They had 200,000 men already officered in regiments; they had pikes and muskets for 150,000, and more were on the way.

The militia were almost to a man United Irishmen, and in fact, according to Orr, they would have risen in the autumn but for some differences among themselves. For himself, the informer thought that nothing would be attempted till the arrival of the French.

The Belfast men, Neilson, Orr, the two Simms, the party who had taken the oath with Wolfe Tone on Cave Hill,[3] he described as wealthy, wily, avaricious, tenacious of their property, distrustful of one another, and if afraid of nothing else, desperately afraid of the Orangemen, who were five times stronger than people in general believed.[4] They had authentic news that Hoche might be expected in the fall of the year, and then undoubtedly an effort would be made. If Hoche came, they were perfectly confident that Ireland

[1] Irish Record Office. [2] Judgment Registry, Four Courts, Dublin, No. 302.

[3] Tone's *Life* (i. 128) describes how, before leaving for America in 1795, he swore to his friends who surrounded him on Cave Hill never to desist from his efforts until Ireland was free.

[4] This is quite Turner's style.

would be a republic before Christmas. The instant that the signal was given the whole Orange party were to be assassinated. . . .

The Informer concludes with these words:—

Be assured that what I have told you is true. The original agitators have been kept concealed even from the knowledge of the common people. The medium of dissemination has been the priests, and they have concealed from their congregations, on whom they have so effectively wrought, the names of those who have set them on, merely saying that there were men of influence, fortune, and power ready to come forward. The motive of the original agitators—and I mean by them the members of the Catholic Committee that sat in Dublin, and many of the Convention that were not on the Committee—was to carry the Catholic Bill through Parliament by the influence of terrorism.[1]

So much for the informer who sought the ear of the Irish Secretary in 1796. His close connection with the Northern leaders, his air of mystery, his hatred of the priests and the Catholic Committee, even his style and tone, the reference to Hoche, the prediction that the Protestants would suffer if the rebels won—all point to him as the same person who made overtures to Pitt, through Downshire, in October 1797. The alleged disaffection of the militia and the danger which menaced the estates of the aristocracy again crop up in Turner's letter to Talleyrand.[2] In both cases the same stipulation is made that he should not be called upon to give evidence publicly—the same nervous temperament is revealed. Downshire's visitor expressed mortal terror lest his life should pay the forfeit of his startling whisper. The same fear—and I believe I may add, presentiment—pervades the letter to Pelham in 1796. 'Don't name it,' he writes; 'if it get out they will know whence it came, and my life will be the certain forfeit.'[3] The 'secret' which the informer of '96 told Pelham

[1] Froude, iii. 176. The original objects of the Society of United Irishmen were parliamentary reform and Roman Catholic emancipation.

[2] *Ante*, p. 25.

[3] The Rev. Arthur McCartney, vicar of Belfast, stated that he had never heard of a Committee of Assassination existing in Belfast with the cognizance or sanction of the leaders of the United Irishmen.

was what Mr. Froude describes as 'a curious story.' 'To show you that they tell me their secrets,' writes the informer to Pelham, 'here is the account told me of the death of Mr. McMurdoch of *Lurgan*.'[1] From searches made in the Registry of Deeds Office, it appears that Samuel Turner was closely connected with Lurgan, and in a way which gave double facilities for acquiring its secrets.[2]

The reader might glance once more at Mr. Froude's account of the visit to Lord Downshire on that dark October night in 1797. The betrayer's disguise and stealthy nervous gait as though some avenging power were on his track, are things worth noting. Why was he in such dread of assassination before he unfolded his story to Downshire? Surely he must have been conscious of having earned, for a long time before, the penalty of 'Ormond steel.'[3] This, according to Dr. Conlan's sworn testimony, was a specially familiar dogma with Teeling and Turner when organising treason in Ulster. The visit to Downshire was clearly prompted by greed. This peer had got the name of having secret service money at his disposal. 'Bank notes were offered to me,' observes James Hope, the working weaver of Belfast, 'if I would implicate Will Tennant, Robert Simms and others, and it was admitted that the money came from Lord Downshire.' This was probably among the efforts which were made to induce minor conspirators to give evidence publicly against their leaders, of whose treason the Crown had private knowledge through Turner.[4] McDougall's 'Sketches of Irish Political Characters,'

[1] Froude's *English in Ireland*, iii. 175.

[2] The following memorandum, though of no political import, is useful as an authentic record of facts:—

'1791, February 13. Samuel Turner and Jacob Turner his father, both of Turner's Hill, co. Armagh, Esquires, to John McVeagh of Lurgan. Conveyance of premises in Lurgan.

'1794, October 8. Samuel Turner of Newry, and Jane Turner, late of Lurgan, now of Newry, to Thompson and others. Premises in Lurgan

The Teelings, with whom Turner claims to be intimate, came from Lurgan. See Webb's *Irish Biography*.

[3] See Conlan's sworn information, Appendix.

[4] James Hope to the late Mr. Hugh McCall, of Lisburn. See Webb's *Irish Biography* for an appreciative notice of Hope.

published in 1799, says of Lord Downshire (p. 20): 'His political conduct agrees very well with his motto, *Ne tentes, aut perfice*; he supports administration with all his might.' Downshire's visitor knew, therefore, that this peer, if he liked, could make good terms with Pitt. Much of the melodramatic character of the scene appears to have been designed to move Downshire. 'He saw Mr. Pitt,' says Froude, 'who consented that "the person's" services should be accepted.'

The Cabinet, we are told, was kept in ignorance of his name. But Pelham, the Irish Secretary previous to Castlereagh, seems to have known something of him already, for, as we learn, 'Pelham, when in London, made large offers to Lord Downshire's friend.' [1] That information had been given by the latter prior to the dark interview of October 1797, I cannot doubt.[2] Mr. Froude, describing Lord Edward's visit to Hoche on the Swiss frontier,[3] writes: 'Hoche himself had not revealed it even to Tone, but Lord Edward was known to be intimate with Macnevin. He had been watched in London, and traced to the lodgings of *a suspected agent of the French Directory*.' Downshire's visitor, it will be remembered, had interviews with Lord Edward in London.

When the betrayer threw back his disguise, Downshire, we are told, recognised him at once. This, I suspect, was not

[1] Froude's *English in Ireland*, iii. 290.

[2] There were informers from the first, but not to the extent suggested; nor can it be fairly said that they were men 'deepest in the secret.' 'This and similar information,' writes Mr. Froude, 'came in to them (the Government) from a hundred quarters' (p. 177). 'They had an army of informers' (p. 174). The historian here writes of the year '96, and rather overrates the extent of the treachery. Dr. Macnevin, writing in 1807, says that the secrets of the United Irishmen were kept with wonderful fidelity. Their society existed from 1791; it was not until 1798, when ropes were round their necks, that Reynolds and McGuckin proved false; and the same remark applies to most of the others.

[3] As regards Pelham's correspondent in 1796, and Downshire's in 1797, does Mr. Froude mistake, for two distinct betrayers, the one Informer? His striking scenes, his dramatic situations, his fine painting and accessories, remind me of a stage where the movements of a few men convey the idea of an advancing 'army.' That 'Downshire's friend' had been previously known as an informer is proved by a letter from the Viceroy Camden to Portland, dated December 9, 1797.

the first time that a communication reached Downshire from the same source. Dr. Madden quotes from the 'Northern Star' of September 16, 1796, a sensational account of the arrest at Belfast of Russell, Neilson, Sampson, and many others, and how the whole garrison, with its artillery, took part in the stirring scene, and it appears that Downshire helped to direct the proceedings. That day Neilson and Russell surrendered to his lordship, and Tone in his 'Diary' deplores the arrest as the heaviest blow which could fall on their cause.[1]

The name of the French agent in London is not mentioned by Mr. Froude. It is M. Jägerhorn, described by Reinhard, the French Minister at Hamburg, as 'that estimable Swede;' and concerning whom there is a mass of matter, often purposely misleading, in the Castlereagh Correspondence. Macnevin's memorial to the French Directory was betrayed to England in the summer of 1797. M. Jägerhorn was sent by France to treat with the Irish Directory. His mission, however, transpired, and means were taken to prevent him going farther than London, whereupon Lord Edward Fitzgerald was deputed to cross to England, and there confer with Jägerhorn.

Turner's *fracas* with tho terrorist commander-in-chief, Carhampton, was supposed to have caused his retirement to Hamburg. But that scene, with its dialogue, may have been purely theatrical.[2]

In June 1797 Turner attends several meetings of the Ulster delegates in Dublin.[3] There it was that the 'prudence or the cowardice' of the Papist leaders in Dublin, as he says, disgusted him.[4] Why should the notorious Turner be allowed to go on to Dublin, and Jägerhorn be refused?

Samuel Turner saw a good deal of Lord Edward and Jägerhorn in London. We find traces of this knowledge in

[1] *Lives and Times of the United Irishmen*, iv. 22.

[2] *Ante*, p. 11.

[3] Appendix No. 1 to Report of the Secret Committee of the House of Commons, 1798.

[4] See *ante*, p. 2; Froude, iii. 279.

Mr. Froude's notes of 'the person's' interview with Downshire —how he called Lord Edward 'Fitz' and had confidential talk with him in Harley Street. The spy tells Downshire soon after that Reinhard begged him to stay at Hamburg, 'as the only mode in which I could serve my country and the republic. I instantly acquiesced, and told him I had arranged matters with Lord Edward in London for that purpose.'

Turner played his cards so well, and personated an ardent patriot so completely, that the suspicions of his fidelity which Reinhard [1] expressed on May 31 are found removed soon after. Dr. Macnevin, of Dublin, a chief in the Executive Directory, was now coming to Paris to ask French aid. Reinhard reports progress to De la Croix:—

Hamburg: 25 Messidor [July 12].

While Mr. Lewins has suffered me to lose all traces of his journey, and Mr. Furnes [2] is gone to write [3] to him, M. Jägerhorn has returned from London, and a new Irish deputation has called upon me. All the efforts of M. Jägerhorn having failed against the obstinacy with which the Duke of Portland refused him a passport for proceeding to Dublin, he determined to call Lord Fitzgerald to London. The latter came upon pretext of accommodating his sister. The authenticity of the mission of Mr. Lewins was verified; important details respecting the state of Ireland were given; it was ascertained that there was no derangement in the plan, and in the resources of the united patriots. It is unnecessary for me to give you a circumstantial account of the information brought by Mr. F., since he enters fully into that which Mr. Macnevin has just given. The latter came surrounded by all the motives for confidence, and he did not leave Dublin till the 27th of June: his intelligence is of the latest date, and from the very source. The reports of Mr. Macnevin, who goes here by the name of Williams, and who would wish to appear always under that name, as Mr. Lewins under that of Thompson, appear to me to throw great light upon all that the Government can have an interest to know. Mr. Macnevin has been secretary

[1] The French minister at Hamburg.

[2] The noble editor of the *Castlereagh Papers* says that this name is an alias for Samuel Turner.

[3] In writing to leading rebels Turner was attempting the *ruse* suggested by Portland (see p. 17 *ante*). He was the secret enemy of Lewins (p. 44 *ante*).

of the executive committee, and all that he says proves him to be a man thoroughly acquainted with the ensemble of facts and combinations. In annexing to this despatch the Memorial[1] which he delivered to me, I shall add what I have reason to think of importance in his conference.

My first care was to clear up what the papers seized at Belfast said concerning a change made by the provincial committee in the organisation of the executive committee. It results from the answers of Mr. Macnevin, conjointly with those of *Mr. Furnes, that it was of dilatoriness and indecision that several members of the committee were accused*; that the northern province, feeling its oppression and its strength, was impatient to break forth,[2] while the committee strove to defer any explosion till the arrival of the French, and declined giving a full explanation of its relations with France; that, nevertheless, after the change of the committee, meetings were held in Dublin and in the North, at which it was resolved to wait; that the clandestine visitation of several depôts of arms, where the powder was found damp and the muskets rusty, contributed a good deal to that resolution; and that the desire for the assistance of the French had in consequence become more general than ever. It was, however, decided that a rising should take place when the prisoners were set at liberty. Macnevin and Lord Fitzgerald are of the moderate party. Furnes is for a speedy explosion; and it is some imprudences into which his ardent character has hurried him, that have obliged him to leave the country[3]; whereas, the conduct of Mr. Macnevin has been so circumspect,[4] that there is nothing to oppose his return.

Reinhard's despatch is continued at very great length, and those who care to read it should consult the 'Castlereagh Papers' (i. 282-6). He thus ends: 'I have just received a memorial in which M. Jägerhorn gives me an account of his journey. I will send it to you by the next courier. That

[1] Mr. Froude errs in stating (iii. 260) that Macnevin himself carried the Memorial to Paris.

[2] All this is exactly what Downshire's visitor told him (see chap. i.).

[3] His challenge to the commander-in-chief, Lord Carhampton, was among the 'imprudences.'

[4] Instead of the words 'circumspect' and 'moderate,' 'prudence' an 'cowardice' are applied to Macnevin's party by Turner (*vide* chap. i.).

estimable Swede has again manifested great devotedness to the cause of liberty.'

By some marvellous sleight-of-hand Jägerhorn's secret report found its way to Whitehall, instead of to Paris, and may be read in the memoirs of Lord Castlereagh.[1] Two years later, the Swede will again be found tracked from Hamburg to London, and arrested on Portland's warrant.

Mr. Froude's allusion to the facilities of command exercised by 'the person' over Lady Fitzgerald's letter-bag, the hints he gave Downshire how secret letters from Hamburg were sealed and addressed, and how they might be intercepted, read, and then passed on,[2] are only those gleams of light that shine dimly in dark places, but enough, with present knowledge, to discern a good deal.

It will be remembered that Downshire's visitor, in his list of men marked out for doom, gave prominence to Dr. Macnevin, 'a Physician who had great weight with the Papists.' 'He (the betrayer) had discovered,' writes Froude, 'that the object of the Papists was the ruin and destruction of the country, and the establishment of a tyranny worse than that which was complained of.'

The famous memorial of Dr. Macnevin, embracing a full report on the state of Ireland, and appealing to France for help, was written at this time.[3] On arrival at Hamburg he entrusted it to Reinhard, the French minister there, by whom—as we learn from the 'Cornwallis Papers'—it was translated and forwarded to Paris. Mr. Froude thinks its betrayal to the English Cabinet a very remarkable circumstance, and the more strange because 'no suspicion has been suggested of Macnevin's treachery.' A hidden hand

[1] *Castlereagh Papers*, i. 286–8

[2] Among the letters headed 'Secret Information from Hamburg,' in the *Castlereagh Papers*, is one making allusion to the writer's previous communications with Downshire, whom he mentions by name, and stating that certain letters to Charles Rankin, of Belfast, were 'to be sealed with a particular seal I have for the purpose.'—*Ibid.* i. 234.

[3] Mr. Lecky says, what previous writers do not, that Macnevin wrote the memorial *at* Hamburg.

contrived to pass on to Pitt this document destined to become historic.[1]

Wickham, writing to Castlereagh on August 15, 1798, states that the rebel executive committee directed Dr. Macnevin to proceed to Paris by the way of Hamburg; that the principal objects of his journey were to give additional weight and credit to the mission of Lewins, and to confirm the information that had already been transmitted.[2] Again the reader may be reminded that Lewins and Turner were rival envoys. Each is found constantly trying to circumvent the other. Turner, therefore, had a special object in foiling and intercepting Macnevin's memorial.

Reinhard, in the betrayed despatch of July 12, 1797, tells De la Croix, at Paris, that every confidence might be reposed in Lewins. Lewins' usual post was at Paris, just as Turner's was at Hamburg, but both passed to and fro. Of Lewins, Reinhard takes care to say that Macnevin

> not only attested that he possesses, and deserves, the utmost confidence, but that he is designated a minister at Paris in case of success. Mr. Macnevin wished much that his memorial should be communicated to him.[3]

If it was Turner's interest to intercept Reinhard's letter establishing confidence in Lewins, it was still more his interest to keep back from Lewins a document which, while vindicating his name, would protect it from further attack; and this the 'Memorial' of Macnevin was designed to do.

Camden had now ceased to be Viceroy and was succeeded by Cornwallis.[4] The latter co-operates with the Home Secretary in screening from publicity the name of their informer. The report of the Secret Committee was now in progress. Cornwallis, writing to Portland, says:—

[1] Other intercepted letters addressed to the French Minister of War will appear later on. These unanswered appeals were well calculated to damp the ardour of the Irish refugees; but they tried to keep the machine of conspiracy moving—despite the subtle insertion of so many hidden obstacles tending to clog and destroy it.

[2] *Castlereagh Papers*, i. 271.

[3] *Ibid.* i. 284.

[4] How this appointment came about, see Appendix.

The same reason may not operate against the production of Dr. Macnevin's memoir, which might be supposed to have fallen into our hands by various other means, and which, from its being produced, without connection with the other papers, might not create any alarm in the quarter where it is so necessary that the most implicit confidence in our prudence and secrecy should be preserved.

Your Grace will of course be aware that no account will be given, even to the Secret Committee, of the means by which these papers came into the hands of Government.[1]

Portland duly acknowledged Lord Cornwallis's despatch,

in which you represent the advantages which might result from laying before the Committees of Secrecy of the two Houses of Parliament in Ireland the whole, or at least a part, of the very secret and authentic documents relating to the conspiracy in that kingdom, which I had the King's permission from time to time to transmit to the late Lord-Lieutenant [Lord Camden]. I lost no time in acquainting his Majesty's confidential servants with your Excellency's sentiments upon this very important and delicate question ; and I am now to inform you that, after its having repeatedly undergone the most serious investigation and discussion, the result of our unanimous opinion is, that the communication of the whole of those papers cannot on any account, or in any situation of the country, be suffered to be made to a parliamentary committee, under whatever qualification or conditions it may be appointed, consistently with that secrecy which in certain cases the honour and safety of the State require to be observed.

We agree, however, for the reasons you have stated, that the same objection does not exist to the production of the greater part of Dr. Macnevin's memoir, and I have therefore had an extract made of such parts of it as it appears to us may be laid before the public without inconvenience. . . .

To prevent as much as possible any occasion being given which can tend to a discovery of the channels by which this intelligence has been obtained, I most earnestly recommend to your Excellency to do your utmost in procuring that the facts which are stated from it may not stand in the report of the committees in the exact order in which they are given here, but that they may be mixed with other information which has been derived from other sources.[2]

[1] *Castlereagh Correspondence*, i. 228.

[2] *Ibid.* i. 251.

The precautions taken to screen the betrayer were certainly very complete. Castlereagh tells Wickham (July 30, 1798) :—

His Excellency authorised me to read the correspondence and memorial once over to the committee of the Commons, with a strict injunction that no person should note a single fact; and I can truly state that the individuals on that committee are altogether in the dark as to the manner in which that intelligence was obtained, and, from the mode in which it was gone through, can only have a very general impression of its contents. The same precaution was used in the Lords; and, I trust, although the Duke of Portland's despatch to his Excellency does not altogether sanction what has been done, yet that his Grace and the Ministers, who have so wisely enjoined the greatest precaution to be observed in the use to be made of that most interesting and important correspondence, will be of opinion that the guarded manner in which the Lord-Lieutenant made the communication to the committees, not authorising the smallest extracts to be made, or any of the facts to be relied on in their report, without being fully authorised by his Excellency, will preclude any danger to the State from this valuable channel of intelligence being in any degree brought into suspicion.[1]

In June 1798 Lord Edward was dead. The Sheares's had been executed. Macnevin, O'Connor, T. Addis Emmet, and Sampson lay in prison in Dublin. Blood flowed on every side. The city was like a shambles. The State prisoners, on the understanding that executions should cease, and that they might be allowed to leave Ireland, consented to reveal, but without implicating individuals, the scheme of the United Irishmen. A prolonged secret inquisition by the Secret Committee took place. As soon as their evidence appeared, Macnevin and his fellow-prisoners complained, by a public advertisement, that the Crown officials who drew up the report of the Secret Committee had garbled the facts and distorted their evidence. Into all this it is not necessary now to go, but it may be observed that, while everything inconvenient was left out, an innuendo was made that the betrayal of Dr. Macnevin's memoir may have been due to Reinhard, the French Minister.

[1] *Castlereagh Correspondence*, i. 246–7.

This—apart from M. Mignet's testimony to the incorruptibility of Reinhard—serves to exculpate him, and narrows the spot on which suspicion now rests. Reinhard, in his letter to De la Croix, thinks it strange that Turner had never spoken to him about certain revelations made by 'the Secret Committee of the Parliament of Ireland;'[1] but the reason now seems intelligible enough.

Macnevin published his 'Pieces of Irish History'[2] at New York in 1807, and notices the betrayal of the memorial which he had addressed to the French Government. Up to that time, and until his death in 1840, he does not seem to suspect Turner. Had any such doubt occurred to him, he would have been the first to avow it. At p. 146 of his book Macnevin inveighs against a 'profligate informer,' 'a ruffian of the name of Reynolds;' but Reynolds' treachery was confined to the arrests at Bond's in Dublin, and did not take place until March 1798. Ten pages further on Macnevin speaks of the 'unparalleled fidelity of the United Irish Body.' Dr. Macnevin was struck by the knowledge the Government had acquired of the 'negotiations of the United Irishmen with foreign States,' and, he adds, 'at this time one of the deputies [*i.e.* himself] had personal evidence of its extent and accuracy. That knowledge was obtained from some person in the pay of England and in the confidence of France.' And Dr. Macnevin then proceeds to point to REINHARD by name!

This is just what the officials of the Home Office wished for all along. Wickham, referring to the publication of Macnevin's memorial by the Secret Committee of the House of Lords, writes: 'It may fairly be presumed that the copy has been obtained at [the Foreign Office] Paris, or from R.'s [Reinhard's] secretary at Hamburg. *This conjecture will be at least as probable as the real one.*'[3]

One circumstance struck Macnevin as 'confirmation strong' of his dark suspicion. Reinhard, as he tells us,

[1] *Castlereagh Correspondence*, i. 275–6.

[2] Allibone erroneously assigns (p. 558) the authorship of this book to Thomas Addis Emmet.

[3] *Castlereagh Papers*, i. 237.

made difficulties about giving him a passport to Paris. A most important despatch from Reinhard to De la Croix thus concludes :—

What I must particularly urge, Citizen Minister, in regard to this business, is, at least, that you will have the goodness to direct me as to Mr. Macnevin. I will not give another passport without your order.[1]

This letter—possibly written at Lady Edward Fitzgerald's house at Hamburg, and put into her post-bag—was treacherously betrayed to Pitt. When De la Croix remained ominously silent in response to the above appeal, is it surprising that Reinhard should have made difficulties and delays in giving Macnevin a passport ?[2]

Macnevin's groundless distrust of Reinhard naturally influenced the views of a most painstaking investigator. Dr. Madden, who, when he at last saw, in the 'Castlereagh Papers,' Reinhard's letters to De la Croix, regarded the circumstance as damning proof of his treachery.[3] Subsequently Mignet, the great French historian and keeper of the ministerial archives at Paris, who had ample official means of knowing the character and acts of both Reinhard and De la Croix, assured Madden in writing that both men were incorruptible. This may be taken as conclusive, for, unlike Turner, there is not a line in any English State Paper tending to compromise Reinhard or De la Croix.[4]

For the act of betrayal we must therefore look to Samuel Turner, agent at Hamburg of the United Irish Brotherhood ; the man who had access to the most secret papers in Lady Fitzgerald's house, and who, we learn, 'was admitted to close

[1] *Castlereagh Papers*, i. 281–6.

[2] Reinhard seems to have complained to the French Directory that his letters to De la Croix were not answered. The last intercepted letters are dated July 1797 ; and on the 15th of the same month Talleyrand was appointed to succeed De la Croix, who had been unjustly suspected. De la Croix survived until 1805, when he died at Bordeaux, stung by the desertion of some old friends.

[3] *Lives and Times of the United Irishmen*, ii. 290.

[4] Arthur O'Connor, at all times distrustful, seems to have suspected the upright Macnevin. They were never quite cordial afterwards, and in 1804, when both served in the Irish Legion, a duel very nearly took place between them.

and secret conversations upon the prospect of French interference in Ireland with Reinhard.' This, in fact, was the grand proof submitted by Downshire's visitor to show that he could spy to advantage, and which suffices in itself to demonstrate that Reinhard was himself no spy.

Dr. Madden's suspicion of Reinhard[1] was doubtless strengthened by a passage which for a long time puzzled myself, and occurs in Wickham's letter to Castlereagh of June 8, 1798. Wickham speaks of 'information confirmed by a person at Hamburg, who must necessarily have derived his intelligence from a very different source, and who could not but be ignorant of that from which R. had procured all that he has communicated to us.' The name thus masked is not Reinhard, but Richardson—an alias for Turner, as I proved at p. 48.

One thing greatly complicated this puzzle as regards 'R.' Wickham, in a subsequent letter, dated July 25, 1798, speaks of 'R.'—meaning not Richardson, but Reinhard, as the context shows.[2] But these blanks are due to the noble editor of the 'Castlereagh Papers,' the late Lord Londonderry; and in cloaking the name Richardson—though it inadvertently peeps out in one place, like 'Capel' instead of 'Catesby' in 'Lothair'—he doubtless thought that it was a real name.

Too long has it been assumed that with France lay the guilt of this betrayal. In 1828 Judge Robert Johnson published, under the signature of 'Fermoy,' a 'Commentary on Tone's Life.' W. C. MacDermott, in his 'Refutation' of this book, writes (p. 78): 'What are we to think of the hollow-hearted French Directory who betrayed their credulous dupes? Yes, that France, with which the patriotic Fermoy is so charmed withal . . . gave up the private communications of those men, at the moment she was pretending to repose in them her confidence, and to yield them assistance.'[3]

[1] The letters in which the Keeper of the French archives exculpated Reinhard and convinced Madden of his error have been kindly shown to me by Dr. Thomas More Madden, F.R.C.S.E., son and representative of the historian of the *United Irishmen*.

[2] See *Castlereagh Papers*, i. 237.

[3] Dublin: Clarke, 1829; Moore Library, R.I.A., vol. 989.

On February 18, 1798, Lord Moira addressed the House of Lords in favour of Catholic Emancipation, which, he declared, must be granted, as well as Parliamentary Reform. 'The greatest evil to be feared from it sinks to nothing compared to the mischief which is raging at present. The expression of a conciliatory desire on your part would suspend immediately the agitation of the public mind.'

Mr. Froude says that the members of Council knew more than Lord Moira—'if he really believed his words;' and he adds that they must have found it hard 'to sit patient under his flatulent declamation.' How much Turner's tattle had excited the Cabinet, and aroused lasting prejudice against a statesman not less able than estimable, appears from the historian's words: 'At that moment the Council were weighing intelligence from the friend at Hamburg, so serious that they had all but resolved on an immediate arrest of the entire Revolutionary Committee.'

Reinhard tells De la Croix, on July 12, 1797, that while 'Lord Edward Fitzgerald and Macnevin [1] were of the moderate party, Turner was for a speedy explosion.' [2] Turner was co-operating in a very base policy, one which unscrupulous statesmen are said to have planned. During the examination of Macnevin before the Secret Committee, Lord Castlereagh confessed that 'means were taken to make the United Irish system explode.' The policy of exciting a premature explosion before Ireland had been organised peeps forth in the Report of the Secret Committee of the Irish Parliament: 'The rebellion [we are told] would not have broken out so soon as it did, had it not been for the well-timed measures adopted by Government.'

Turner's policy changed according as the policy of his employers changed. In March 1798 the rebel Directory at Dublin were seized as they sat in council at Oliver Bond's. Soon after, three out of thirty-two counties rose; and to crush that partial revolt cost England twenty-two millions of pounds and twenty thousand men.

[1] After 1798 Macnevin migrated to America, where he filled some important medical posts, and published numerous books. He survived until July 1841.

[2] *Castlereagh*, i. 283.

CHAPTER VIII

GENERAL NAPPER TANDY

An old and very influential French newspaper, 'Le Journal des Débats,' published, on February 29, 1884, an article descriptive of the pleasure with which its writer had heard sung a touching but simple Irish lyric, 'La Cocarde Verte,' commemorative of the career of General Napper Tandy. It had been sung, he said, at Paris, by an English girl, who threw into its simple lines a power most entrancing. The melody and the words continued to haunt him at all hours,[1] and, some months later, we learn, found him in London, seeking information, but in vain, regarding Napper Tandy and the song. During a subsequent tour to the 'Giant's Causeway,' his inquiries were not much more successful. 'J'avouai que nos histoires de France ne nous parlent pas de Napper Tandy, et je quittai Portrush sans être absolument satisfait.'

When French history is silent as regards Tandy, and remote inquirers appear so much interested about him, the present chapter may not have been written in vain.

The arrest by British agencies of Tandy and others within the neutral territory of Hamburg and contrary to the law of nations was boldly denied for some time.[2] A similar tone

[1] The words of the French writer will be found at p. 78, *infra*.

[2] The *London Courier* of September 14, 1799, displays the following translation of a letter addressed to a Paris journal: 'Citizens,—*The Redacteur* has said, and many other Journalists have repeated it, that Napper Tandy had been given up by the Senate of Hamburg. I declare to you, Citizens, that not a word is said of this in any letters received in any of the Banking houses in Paris, nor in those which I myself have received. I hasten to give you this information, because the Public ought never to be *deceived*.

(Signed) 'Daniel C. Meyer,
'Consul General from Hamburgh.'

was taken by official authority as regards the subsequent surrender of Tandy to England; but how true was the story, and with what striking circumstances fraught, will presently appear.

Soon after the departure of Humbert's expedition for Ireland, Tandy, now a general in the French service, accompanied by a large staff, including Corbet and Blackwell, sailed from Dunkirk in the French ship 'Anacreon,' having on board a store of ordnance, arms, ammunition, saddles, and accoutrements. He effected a landing on the coast of Donegal, but, learning that Humbert, after having beaten Lake at Castlebar, had met with reverses and surrendered to Cornwallis, he abandoned the enterprise and re-embarked. It is told in the 'Castlereagh Papers' that the 'Anacreon,' when attacked by an English cruiser, gave battle near the Orkneys, and that 'Tandy had put two twelve-pound shot in his pockets, previous to leaping overboard in the event of striking to the English ship.'[1]

An interesting memoir of Colonel Blackwell, who died in 1809, appears in Walter Cox's 'Irish Magazine' for that year. William Murphy, an old '98 man, and afterwards the well-known millionaire, said that Cox played fast and loose, betraying his own party and the Government alternately. Cox begins by saying that 'few occurrences excited a stronger or more universal sensation than the treacherous arrest at Hamburg, in 1798, of Blackwell, Morres, Tandy and Corbet.' Cox describes Blackwell's perilous descent with Tandy on the Irish coast, and states that, when passing through Hamburg going back to France, the secret of his arrival and that of his comrades 'was betrayed to the British envoy, Crawford, by two pensioned spies of England, *Turner* and Duckett.'[2]

Cox was a shrewd man; but when suspicion is once raised

[1] *Castlereagh Papers*, i. 405. The letter, of which this is a bit, was written by a spy who contrived to accompany Tandy as a sort of aide-de-camp, and was on board the 'Anacreon' during the voyage. Wickham divulges merely his initial, 'O,' but the reader will find his name and career successfully traced in the Appendix.

[2] Cox's *Irish Magazine*, January 1809, pp. 32–4.

it is apt to extend beyond due limits. He was right as regards Turner; he wronged Duckett. His impression of at least the first was probably derived from Blackwell himself, for Cox acknowledges that some of the facts 'the writer of this sketch received from the mouth of Colonel Blackwell.'

General Corbet privately printed at Paris, in 1807, strictures on the conduct of the Senate of Hamburg for having handed him over to the British minister. Appended to this *brochure* is a letter written by Tandy some days before his death, giving an account of his arrest. 'The original,' writes Corbet, 'is in my possession.'

I arrived in Hamburg on the evening of the 22nd of November, 1798 [writes Tandy], and the next day I went with M. Corbet to visit the French minister and the Consul General Lagan to obtain passports to Paris. I passed the day with the consul general and prepared for my departure, which was to have taken place the following day. I was invited to sup the same evening by Messrs. T—— and D——, in a house where Blackwell, Corbet, and Morres supped also; we remained there till midnight, and at four o'clock went to our hotel. Towards morning I was awakened by armed men rushing into my chamber.

Cox jumped at the conclusion that the names thus cautiously initialled by Corbet, are Turner and Duckett.[1] A coming chapter will vindicate Duckett; and I am bound to conclude that this man, if he really joined the supper party, had been duped by the plausibility of Turner. Turner and Duckett have been previously shown as on friendly terms.[2]

The accuracy of the information by which Crawford, the British minister at Hamburg, was able to effect his *coup* excited general surprise. According to the 'Castlereagh Papers' tidings reached him that Tandy and others were lodged at an

[1] It will be shown, later on, that an Irish spy named 'Durnin' resided at Hamburg.

[2] See letter to Talleyrand, *ante*, p. 27. Some persons supposed that because Duckett lived at Hamburg like Turner, he used that great gangway to France for espionage. In the *Castlereagh Papers* (ii. 6) Duckett is described as 'Secretary to Léonard Bourdon.' Bourdon is noticed in the *Nouvelle Biog. Générale*, was 'l'agent du Directoire à Hambourg, d'où il fit partir les émigrés.'

inn in Hamburg called the 'American Arms,' and on November 24, 1798, soon after five o'clock A.M., this minister, accompanied by a guard, entered the house. Early as it was, Napper Tandy was found writing. The officer demanded his passport. Thereupon Tandy, with composure, said he would produce it, and going to his trunk he took out a pistol, which presenting, he said: 'This is my passport.' The officer grappled with him, and the guard rushing in secured Tandy. 'He and his associates were put in irons, and confined by order of Sir James Crawford.'[1]

And now for a short digression ere finishing the story of Tandy's woes.

People were puzzled to know how the complicated intrigue which achieved his capture—contrary to the law of nations—could have been woven in a few hours. There can be little doubt that Turner—whom Cox broadly charges with the betrayal, by furnishing information to Crawford—had ample notice of their coming.[2] Besides Turner's personal acquaintance with Tandy, official ties of brotherhood had arisen between them, and nothing was more natural than the invitation to sup.

A letter headed 'Secret Information from Hamburg,' and bearing date August 16, 1798, has found its way into Lord Castlereagh's correspondence.[3] The writer, clearly Turner, is found back at Hamburg after one of his periodic visits to Paris, where, with his usual *audace*, he claimed to be an

[1] Sir James Crawford, British minister at Hamburg from 1798 to 1803. Crawford afterwards filled a similar post at Copenhagen, where Reynolds, the Kildare informer, is also found acting as British consul. Reynolds's betrayals were long subsequent to those of Turner, and of a wholly different sort. His evidence was given in court publicly. The editor of the *Cornwallis Papers* states that Crawford died on July 9, 1839; but Mr. Ross confounds him with an utterly different man. The *Black Book*, published in 1820, records (p. 31) a pension of 1000*l*. 'continued to the family of Sir James Crawford, late minister at Copenhagen, dead.' The 'most exhaustive' works of biographical reference omit Sir James Crawford, a remarkable man, and one who played an important part in European history; and a letter of mine in *Notes and Queries*, asking for facts about him, failed to elicit a reply.

[2] *Infra*, p. 79.

[3] *Castlereagh Papers*, i. 306–9.

accredited envoy of the United Irishmen, and sought to discredit the mission of Lewins.

Before Tandy had left Paris for Dunkirk, where the 'Anacreon' was being equipped for Ireland, he had some unpleasant differences with Lewins and Wolfe Tone.[1] This afforded prospect of a golden harvest for our spy. Tone had long avoided Turner; Lewins repudiated his pretensions. Our spy now 'sided' with Tandy's party, and intrigued to such purpose that he seems to have got himself appointed *locum tenens* of the general. In this affair Muir and Madgett, with honest motives, bore a part. Muir, a distinguished Scotch advocate, had attached himself to the republican interest, and was tried for sedition.[2] Madgett—an old Irish refugee—held a post in the Foreign Office in Paris, and will be remembered by readers of Tone's Diary as in constant communication with him. It is needless to quote in full the anonymous letter of our spy. It will be found in the 'Castlereagh Papers,' vol. i. pp. 306–9. The men noticed in it, McMahon and O'Coigly, McCann and Lowry, had been old allies of Turner's; and 'Casey, brother to the priest,' Tone, Tandy, Lewins, Teeling, Orr of Derry, McCormack, all figure in the original information conveyed to Lord Downshire.

The letter begins by saying that 'Tandy, having quarrelled

[1] Why Tone's *Diary*, as published, does not once name Turner, may be due to the uncertainty as to whether Turner was alive in 1826, and perhaps Tone's son, from motives of prudence, cut out some allusions to him. Tone died in a Dublin prison on November 19, 1798, three days before the arrest of Tandy. Tone and Turner were closely associated in their studies, distinctions, and political pursuits. Turner entered Trinity College, Dublin, on July 2, 1780; Tone entered on February 19, 1780. Turner was called to the Bar in 1788; Tone in 1789.

[2] Muir's trial took place on August 30, 1793. He was transported to New South Wales, from which he escaped by American agency. After a series of great sufferings he arrived at Paris in February 1798, but died on September 27 that year from the effect of the hardships he had endured. The papers of the Home Office show that in 1793 Muir came to Dublin to confer with the United Irishmen, and on January 11 in that year was elected one of the brotherhood. *Vide* also *Life of Thomas Muir, Advocate*, by P. Mackenzie (Simpkin, 1831).

with Lewins and Tone, called a meeting of United Irishmen, at which a division took place; the numbers pretty equal.' Tandy's rupture with Lewins was quite enough to make Turner take Tandy's side. Dating from Hamburg, and believing that the real 'minister of the interior' was a good cook, he writes :—

A General Creevy, who goes with the great expedition [to Ireland], called on me one day at Paris and stayed dinner. Muir and Madgett were of the party. It was for the purpose of inquiring into Tone's character, which we gave him. Madgett and Muir swore me into the Secret Committee for managing the affairs of Ireland and Scotland in Tandy's place: there are only we three of the committee.

He then proceeds to describe his visit to the Hague, and the information he acquired there. It may be asked if any evidence exists that Samuel Turner left his usual quarters at Hamburg and was in Paris at this time, and afterwards at the Hague. On p. 409 of the same volume of Castlereagh, Turner is described by name as in Paris on business connected with the United Irishmen, and that from thence he repaired to the Hague. Here he was consulted, as he stated, by General Joubert on various points, including the 'safest places for debarkation.' The West coast, he tells Wickham, 'seemed to be the most eligible, from Derry to Galway.' In the letter to Talleyrand[1] the West coast is also suggested as the best point to invade.[2] The spy, after alluding to the 'contrivances of Lewins,' who 'strives to prevent any person doing anything with the (French) Government but himself,' reports Duckett as a most active

[1] *Ante*, pp. 25–9.

[2] A man whom he found in consultation with Joubert, planning the invasion of Ireland with a map of it before them, he describes in this and subsequent letters as O'Herne. Students of the *Castlereagh Papers* have been unable to identify this man; but it is clear that the O'Herne who figures in them was no other than Ahearne, so often mentioned by Tone in his *Diary*. The letter to Wickham mentions General Daendels as a co-conspirator with O'Herne. In Tone's *Diary* we read (p. 460): 'Received a letter from General Daendels, desiring me to send on Aherne to him, without loss of time, to be employed on a secret mission.'

rebel. He makes this statement in a paper meant for the private perusal of Portland[1] and Wickham. Thus it would appear that Blackwell and Cox wronged Duckett in accusing him of informing against Tandy. To Duckett, a man hitherto maligned, it is necessary in justice to return.

Lord Edward had died in Newgate June 4, 1798. The departure of his widow from Dublin and return to Hamburg are announced in the 'Evening Post' of August 16, ensuing. Our spy, as the 'friend' of the dead Geraldine, welcoming Pamela back and tendering sympathy and consolation, would be a good subject for a picture. Mr. Froude tells us that the great power wielded by this seeming exile of Erin lay in his intimacy with Lady Edward Fitzgerald at Hamburg. Morres had been sojourning here previous to Tandy's arrival, and, like Turner, received hospitality at her hands. 'Lord Downshire's friend,' who we are told had access to her house and post-bag, could not fail to know Morres well. It will be remembered that Dr. Madden blows hot and cold on Reinhard, the French minister at Hamburg, and suggests that he may have betrayed to Pitt his correspondence with De la Croix; but Reinhard had now been succeeded by a new man; and if further exculpation[2] of Reinhard were needed after the testimony of Mignet, it is found in the fact that the correspondence of his successor was also tampered with. The letter of 'Lord Downshire's friend,' in which he proposes to become a spy, mentions, as a striking proof of his power, that he had full access to the *bureau* of the French resident at Hamburg: M. Maragan now filled this post. A letter addressed by him to Talleyrand may be found in the 'Castlereagh Papers.'

[1] The writer mentions his election in Tandy's place as proof of his unsleeping vigilance and increased power to betray. Portland, instead of seeing that the man thus ready to take a false oath would not scruple to say anything, was so struck by the importance of the letter that he sent a copy of it to Dublin for the guidance of Lord Castlereagh. Here was a man, as Curran once said of an approver, 'willing to steep the Evangelists in blood.' Turner, in a previous letter (*ante*, p. 28), glibly writes: 'I attest the business on oath.'

[2] *Vide ante*, p. 68 *et seq.*

Most Secret. Hambourg, 29 Brumaire.

M. Harvey Montmorency Morres,[1] of Kivesallen, in Ireland, has called upon me, on the part of the interesting Lady Edward Fitzgerald: he has been outlawed, and fears that he is not safe at Hamburg. He was an intimate friend of the late Lord E. Fitzgerald's; he has, therefore, acquired a right to the kindness of the widow, and it is on this ground alone that she has allowed herself to express it. Mr. Morres was the leader of the numerous corps of United Irishmen: he is utterly ruined in consequence of his attachment to the cause of liberty. He wishes to go to France, where he has important matters to communicate. He is expecting from day to day an officer, who has commanded some expedition, and he hopes to make the journey with him.[2]

This was Tandy, as a succeeding letter explains. Tandy and Morres were seized at the same moment, and doubtless on the same whisper. Hamburg encouraged an impression that Russia prompted this arrest; but, unless on the hypothesis that Pitt had the Senate of Hamburg in his pay, it is hard to understand how orders were sent to effect arrests there, just as if it were on British territory. Mr. Secretary Elliot was a member of the family which some months previously received the peerage of Minto in acknowledgment of diplomatic service. This official, writing to Lord Castlereagh, says: 'I learn from Mr. Hammond, Canning's colleague [in the Foreign Office], that Napper Tandy is suspected to be at Hamburg, and instructions have been sent to our resident there to apprehend him.'[3] Thus Crawford must have heard in advance of Tandy's coming, and taken his steps accordingly. Of course he at once acquainted the head of his department; and hence the remark of Mr. Elliot.[4] Some historians convey that

[1] Harvey Morres, of the ennobled family of Frankfort (b. 1767), had been in the Austrian service previous to joining the Irish rebellion; married, in 1802, the widow of Dr. Esmonde who was hanged in '98. He subsequently gained the rank of a French colonel, and died in 1839.

[2] *Castlereagh Papers*, ii. 96.

[3] *Ibid.* i. 405.

[4] Tandy had borne a part in every Irish national movement from November 1783, when the Volunteer Convention met. He was a most determined man

Tandy, after his ill-fated expedition to Ireland, returned direct from Donegal to Hamburg, *en route* for France. The words of the editor of the 'Cornwallis Papers' are that 'he returned *immediately to France*.' But these accounts are most misleading. Tandy did not get back to France until after his liberation in 1802, and instead of the few days which might be supposed to intervene between the departure from Donegal and arrival at Hamburg, it was nearer to two months. Dreading renewed trouble with the English cruisers, Tandy gave orders to steer for Norway. All landed at Bergen, and after suffering many vicissitudes sought to reach France by land. The cold became so intense that, as Corbet notes, people were found frozen to death at the gate of Hamburg. Weary and footsore, Tandy arrived here at twilight on November 22, 1798. Hungry for Irish news, he readily embraced Turner's invitation to sup.[1]

This meeting between Tandy and the man whom 'wearing of the Green'[2] had forced to fly his native land may have been in the thoughts of the rebel bard when writing the rude ballad which, a century later, so excited the querist in the 'Journal des Débats:—'[3]

and a firm believer in artillery, a brigade of which he commanded in Dublin, with the words 'Free Trade or ——' inscribed on the breeches of the guns. The procession of Volunteer delegates from the Royal Exchange to the Rotunda was announced by the discharge of twenty-one cannon.

[1] It is doubtful whether the supper formed part of the plan for the arrest. All arrangements with that design had been already organised. *In vino veritas*; and the effect of the supper was, of course, an increased knowledge and command of the conspiracy, with proportionate profit to the spy. For such suppers he had a special *gusto*. 'I supped last night with Valence, who mentioned having introduced Lord Edward, &c., &c.' See letter to Lord Downshire, p. 4 *ante*.

[2] See Carhampton's command to Turner, when at Newry, to remove his green neckcloth, p. 11, *ante*. Reinhard, writing to De la Croix, says that these 'imprudences' compelled Turner to leave Ireland.

[3] These are his words: 'Pauvre de forme et bien simple de style, mais d'une puissance d'autant plus entraînante, surtout sous le charme d'une voix qui jetait toute l'intensité de la passion Anglaise dans les accens de douleur et de colère, toujours un peu vagues et flottans, de la fantaisie celtique. L'air et les paroles ne me sortaient point de l'oreille ; et, comme toute impression d'ensemble se concentre toujours sur un détail unique, il y avait surtout une strophe étrange qui me hantait.'

I met with Napper Tandy, and he took me by the hand,
And he said 'How's poor old Ireland, and how does she stand?
'Tis the most distressful country, for it's plainly to be seen
They are hanging men and women for the wearing of the Green.'

It was no isolated secret that Turner had acquired and disclosed. General Corbet, speaking of Morres, Tandy and Blackwall, gives an interesting account of their subsequent imprisonment at Hamburg, and how successive plans to effect their escape became marvellously foiled. 'I lost myself in vain conjectures,' he writes. 'It was not until a long time after that I learned the infamous treason of which I was the victim. I was very far from suspecting the author.' And then, in a foot-note, he indicates him with great caution, dreading the penalty of an action for libel.

> A man [he writes] residing at Hamburg, who had all my confidence, and that of my three companions in misfortune, was at this precise time sold to England, and was one of Crawford's numerous agents. He was informed of all our projects, and communicated them to this minister. This man is now [1807] actually in London,[1] and pensioned by the Government.[2]

It is strange that Corbet was able to anticipate by half a century the revelation made in the 'Cornwallis Papers,' that a secret pension had been given to Turner for information in Ninety-eight. But his privately printed tract may indeed be styled a sealed book.

Some hours after the arrest Maragan, the French resident, wrote to the Senate at Hamburg claiming Tandy and his colleagues as French citizens, and threatening to leave the place unless they were released. Crawford opposed the demand in terms equally strong, and, needless to say, carried

[1] The London *Post-Office Directory*, eighty years ago and later, gave the names of those only who were engaged in trade. But Holden's *Triennial Directory* for 1808 includes the name 'Samuel Turner, Esq. 21, Upper Wimpole Street.' The name disappears from the Dublin Directory about the same time.

[2] *The Conduct of the Senate at Hamburg revealed*, by William Corbet (Paris, 1807). The number of copies privately printed was small; the pamphlet is very scarce, and obtains no place in the Haliday Collection, R.I.A.

his point. The French *chargé d'affaires,* observing Tandy's critical state of health, offered a large sum to the officer of the guard to permit his escape, but the superior influence of Crawford overrode all obstacles.

The letter of Tandy, from which an extract has already been made, states that after his arrest one hundred louis d'or were taken from him and never returned. His sufferings in prison he describes as so severe that life became a burden, and more than once he prayed to be led out on the ramparts and shot.

John Philpot Curran gives us some idea of what these sufferings were :—

He was confined in a dungeon little larger than a grave; he was loaded with irons; he was chained by an iron that communicated from his arm to his leg, and that so short as to grind into his flesh. Food was cut into shapeless lumps, and flung to him by his keepers as he lay on the ground, as if he had been a beast; he had no bed to lie on, not even straw to coil himself up in if he could have slept.

The details given by Corbet of their detention are hardly less painful. At last he and Morres were removed to a new prison.

What had happened to me [he writes] would have naturally discouraged and prevented me from making any new attempts; nevertheless, I managed to correspond with my two companions in misfortune; and we all three stood so well with our guards, the greater number of whom we had gained, that we resolved to arm ourselves and place ourselves at their head, to deliver Tandy, who was in another prison, and after to repair to the house of the French ambassador. Our measures were so well taken that we hoped this time at least to recover our liberty in spite of the impediments which fortune might put in our way. But *the same traitor* who had formerly deranged my plan discovered all to the English minister, Crawford, who immediately gave orders that our guards should be changed, and even that those of the different posts of Hamburg should be doubled, which continued even to our departure. Such was the result of the last struggle we made to obtain our liberty at Hamburg.

These incidents occurred at a time when wagers had been laid that the days of French power were numbered. England Austria and Russia prepared to form an alliance. Suvarov, repulsing the French arms in Italy, had entered on French territory; the Archduke Charles advanced on the Rhine, and the Duke of York was in full march on Amsterdam. Hamburg felt that the time had come when England might be truckled to, and France slighted. At midnight on September 29, 1799, after ten months' detention, Tandy and his companions were torn from the sanctuary they had sought and put on board an English frigate which had cast anchor at Cuxhaven.

Their departure was marked by a curious incident, which General Corbet thus notices in describing his arrest and extradition:—

> In open sea, and half a league before us, an English frigate laden with gold, and on the way to Hamburg, was suddenly wrecked and only one sailor saved. What was the use of this? Was it to purchase additional mercenaries against France? Was it the price of that treachery of which the Hamburghers were just guilty? Happy would the Continent be if all the gold leaving England for such purposes had been buried in the sea! [1]

Corbet, describing his arrest in the first instance, says that he asked the soldiers by what authority they acted. 'They appeared not to be ignorant that we were French officers; they answered that they should fulfil the orders of the minister of England.' [2]

For a time France sought to stifle its wrath; but at last it was resolved that the conduct of Hamburg should be denounced to all States, allied and neutral; that all French consular officers quit the offending territory; and that every agent of Hamburg residing in France should leave in twenty-four hours. The Senate of Hamburg now became penitential, and wrote to say so. 'Your letter, gentlemen,' replied

[1] Corbet's *Narrative*. (Paris, 1807.) General Corbet did not live to see the day when the recovery of such treasure was regarded as feasible. In 1889 appeared the prospectus of the Aboukir Bay Company for recovering the treasure sunk in the 'L'Orient,' destroyed by Nelson at the Nile.

[2] *Ibid.*

Napoleon, 'does not justify you. You have violated the laws of hospitality, a thing which never happened among the most savage hordes of the desert.'

A deputation from the Senate arrived at the Tuileries to make public apology to Napoleon. He again testified his indignation, and when the envoys pleaded national weakness he said: 'Well, and had you not the resource of weak states: was it not in your power to let them escape?' In reply it was urged that such negligence would have irritated rather than appeased the Powers. Napoleon laid a fine of four millions and a half on Hamburg. This sum, it is naïvely remarked by Bourrienne, his secretary, mollified him considerably, and helped to pay Josephine's debts.

An interesting account of the arrival in England of Tandy and his companions appears in the 'Courier,' a leading London paper, of October 31, 1799.[1] A military *cortège* accompanied them from Sittingbourne to Rochester, and thence over Blackfriars Bridge, up Ludgate Hill, to Newgate.

> Had Buonaparte and his staff been sent here by Sir Sydney Smith, they could not have excited more curiosity [records the 'Courier']. A vast concourse of people was gathered at the landing place, who attended the prisoners and their escort to the garrison gates, where a new concourse was assembled, and so from stage to stage to the end of the journey, everybody, old and young, male and female, was anxious to get a peep at this wonderful man, now become, from the happy perseverance of Ministers, a new bone of contention among the powers of Europe.
>
> Napper Tandy is a large big-boned muscular man, but much broken and emaciated. His hair is quite white from age, cut close behind into his neck, and he appears much enervated. This is indeed very natural, if it be considered that he is near seventy years of age, and has just suffered a long and rigorous confinement, his mind the constant prey of the most painful suspense. He wore a large friar's hat, a long silk black grey coat, and military boots, which had a very *outré* effect.
>
> Blackwell and Morres seem to be about five and thirty. They

[1] File in possession of the writer. The British Museum, so rich in other respects, does not embrace the *Courier* for 1798–9.

are two tall handsome-looking men, wore military dresses, and have a very soldierlike appearance. The former is a man of a very enterprising genius, about the middle size, apparently not more than four or five and twenty, and has much the look of a foreigner.

Morres had not accompanied Tandy in his expedition to Ireland; and it may be asked on what grounds he was placed in irons, and made to share with the ill-starred general all the rigours of a tedious imprisonment. While Morres indignantly protested against this cruelty, he little thought that a document, seriously compromising him, and penned by his own hand, had been given up to the Crown officials. This was a memorial which, on his arrival at Hamburg as an Irish refugee, he had written, in Lady Edward's house most probably, and addressed to the French Minister at Paris. It was intercepted as usual, and may now be consulted in the 'Castlereagh Papers.' Colonel Hervey Montmorency Morres tells Bruix how he had been intrusted by Lord Edward with the direction of the intended attack upon Dublin, and especially as regarded the magazine and batteries in the Phœnix Park; how after the death of Lord Edward he escaped from Dublin, and remained concealed until the arrival of Humbert at Killala, when he assembled the men of West Meath to aid the invading force; but upon the surrender of Humbert he disbanded his followers, and, being pursued by the King's troops, made his way to England, and thence to Hamburg on October 7, 1798. In conclusion he implored the protection of France for himself and his family.[1]

After Tandy and Morres had been removed to Ireland, they were placed at the bar of the King's Bench, when the Attorney General prayed that sentence of death should be passed upon them. Historians curtly tell that the prosecution broke down on a point of law; but this explanation does not quite satisfy. The prisoners pleaded that they were arrested abroad by the King's command, and were thereby prevented from surrendering themselves for trial before the day limited by the Act of Attainder for doing so. The case was argued for

[1] *Castlereagh Correspondence*, ii. 94–6.

days. Tandy's legal position was shown to be this: 'Why did you not surrender and become amenable to justice? Because I was in chains. Why did you not come over to Ireland? Because I was a prisoner in Hamburg. Why did you not do something tantamount to a surrender? Because I was unpractised in the language of the strangers, who could not be my protectors, inasmuch as they were also my fellow-sufferers.' Counsel argued that when the Crown seized Tandy at Hamburg it thereby made him amenable, and so satisfied the law. Lord Kilwarden, a most humane judge, ruled that Tandy should be discharged.[1] But their triumph was short-lived. Tandy was transferred to Lifford, Donegal, previous to being tried in the district where two years before he had made a hostile descent from France. In Lifford gaol Tandy lay for seven months, during which time great efforts were made to ensure the conviction of so formidable a character; and April 7, 1801, was at last fixed for his trial. Several applications to postpone it were refused by the court, and divers law arguments and objections overruled.

The compact with Turner that he should never be asked to brave public odium by appearing as an approver, was of course respected; but it would seem that he was now brought over to Ireland for the purpose of assisting the law officers in their difficult and delicate task. That the quondam spy at Hamburg was in Ireland at this very time, though soon after he is back again in Hamburg, can be shown. The Registry of Deeds Office, Dublin, records that on February 25, 1801, Samuel Turner, vaguely described as 'of the United Kingdom of Great Britain,' executed to George Lysaght a conveyance of lands in Clare. In society he was well trusted, unless by a few who kept their thoughts to themselves; and at this same time also he became the trustee of the marriage settlement of John Wolcot[2] and Dorothy Mary Lyons. One can hardly realise this man, whose more fitting post would be a funeral

[1] Howell's *State Trials*, xxvii. 1194–1243.

[2] John Wolcot is a rare name. All have heard of John Wolcot, well known as 'Peter Pindar,' the merciless assailant of George the Third.

feast, presiding at a bridal breakfast and wishing joy and long life to his friends. His trip to Ireland 'killed two birds with one stone,' for the Book of Secret Service Money expenditure reveals that on July 8, 1801, 71*l.* 13*s.* 3*d.* is paid 'per *Mr. Turner* to Chapman in Cork for one year and eleven weeks, at one guinea.' Chapman I suspect to have been a minor agent employed by Turner to ferret out evidence against Morres and the Corbets (both Cork men), and in connection with the prosecution of Tandy.[1] The 'one year and eleven weeks' would cover the time that Tandy and his companions, after their removal from Hamburg, lay in an Irish gaol awaiting their trial.

Tandy, finding the evidence against him overwhelming, admitted the truth of the indictment, and was sentenced to die on the 4th of the ensuing May. In this course he was doubtless influenced by his son, with whom, as will be seen, McNally, the debauched legal adviser of the rebels, could do what he liked.[2] Meanwhile Napoleon, on his return from Egypt, claimed Tandy as a French general, and held an English prisoner of equal rank a hostage for his safety. It was now not so clear that Pitt had a legal claim to the life of a man who wore the uniform of a French officer, and had come into his hands under circumstances the most peculiar.

As regards Blackwell, the fellow-prisoner of Tandy, Portland, writing to Cornwallis, speaks of having been importuned by Mrs. Blackwell's family, whom he describes as 'of considerable influence in Somersetshire,' and imagines that 'there is no intention of inflicting any punishment on Mr. Blackwell.'[3] Soon after we find Blackwell[4] discharged, but, unlike Morres, he proudly refused to give bail. Morres after

[1] The intercepted memorial from Morres to the French Government, preserved in the *Castlereagh Papers* (ii. 96), urges: 'In case of future attempts on Ireland on the part of France, the province of Munster, which abounds in good havens, and whose men are the best republicans in Ireland, is the point to be looked to.' The capture of Cork is proposed, i. 295.

[2] See Appendix, 'James Tandy.'

[3] *Cornwallis Papers*, iii. 284.

[4] See memoir of Blackwell in Cox's *Irish Magazine of Neglected Biography* for 1811, p. 32.

an imprisonment of more than three years regained his liberty on December 10, 1801. Tandy, less fortunate, was removed to Wicklow gaol, and his son asserts that while there the French minister in London signified that Buonaparte had sent directions to his brother Joseph not to sign the treaty of peace 'at Amiens' till Tandy was restored. M. Otto had in fact, as Bourrienne states,[1] previously negotiated with Lord Hawkesbury for his release. Mr. Froude says that 'Tandy was spared as too contemptible to be worth punishing.'[2] This hardly conveys a true idea of the facts. A pardon was at last made out for him on condition of banishment to Botany Bay. To this proviso his son demurred; but, as Mr. Marsden, the Under Secretary at Dublin Castle, assured him, 'all that was required was merely the name of *transportation*, in order to strike terror into others; and that he would pledge his honour, if he acquiesced, that his father should be landed wherever he pleased, that it might appear to the world as if he made his escape at sea.'[3]

Tandy arrived at Bordeaux on March 14, 1802. Bonaparte's treaty with England was signed on the 27th of the same month. Military honours hailed Tandy. Bordeaux was illuminated, and he was promoted to the rank of a general of division. But in the midst of this jubilee the old rebel read with horror a speech of Pelham's in Parliament stating that 'Tandy owed his life to the useful information and discoveries he had given to the British Government.' He addressed a letter to Pelham, now a peer, branding the statement as mean, audacious, and false. 'This may appear uncouth language to a courtly ear,' he added; 'but it is the voice of truth. I never had any connection or correspondence with your Government, and if I had, they knew my character too well to attempt to tamper with me. Had you contented yourself with saying, "there were particular circumstances in my case," you would have adhered to the truth,

[1] *Life of Napoleon.*
[2] *English in Ireland*, iii. 488.
[3] *Appeal to the Public*, by James Tandy (Dublin, 1807), p. 108, 2nd ed. Haliday Pamphlets, vol. 915, R.I.A.

for you know the whole, though you have let out only a part!' Tandy thus concluded: 'I am, my Lord, with the same sentiments which I have uniformly cherished and supported, a friend to universal benevolence, and an enemy to those only who raise their fortunes on their country's ruin!'

Pelham probably confounded Napper Tandy with James Tandy, from whom information had been given to his confidant, McNally, and by 'Mac' conveyed to Dublin Castle. Napper told his son all, not thinking it would transpire. His feelings had been roused by the imputation, and in a letter to the 'Argus' he gave them fuller vent. 'Had discoveries been proposed to me, I should have rejected, with scorn and indignation, a baseness which my soul abhorred . . . I had made up my mind for death in a cause which no mode of execution could stamp disgrace upon. It would have been death in the cause of freedom and of my country—a cause which would have converted the scaffold into an altar, the sufferer into a victim!'

Mr. Elliot, who, I think, afterwards succeeded his brother as Lord St. Germans, echoed in Parliament the taunt cast by Pelham, and spoke of 'Tandy's ignorance and insignificant birth.'[1] Tandy, addressing Elliot, said:—

The illiberal attack which you have made upon me in your speech of the 24th of November last, in the British House of Commons, is the cause of my troubling you with this. My '*ignorance and insignificance*,' which you have painted in such glowing colours, ought, with a man of sense, to have been my protection; but you have proved yourself as deficient in this, as in point of good manners, which is the true criterion of a gentleman.

You cannot, sir, but know (for you pretend to be a man of in-

[1] This is probably the same Mr. Elliot (see *ante*, p. 77) who states that instructions had been sent to have Tandy arrested on the neutral ground of Hamburg. Elliot, who applied the term 'insignificant' to Tandy, must have read the informer's letter (since published in the *Castlereagh Papers*, pp. 405–9), where Tandy is described, among other contemptuous epithets, as 'insignificant'! Elliot is styled in the *Castlereagh Papers*, 'Military Secretary to Lord Cornwallis, the Viceroy.' 'Cornwallis Elliot' is a favourite name in the St. Germans family. Tandy addresses his assailant merely as 'Mr. Elliot.' The Elliots formed a powerful diplomatic *coterie*.

formation) that I hold a high rank in the army of this great and generous nation, which places me upon a footing with the proudest peer of your island. You know, also, that the honour of a soldier is dearer to him than life; yet, with these facts before you, you have dared to traduce my character, and have attempted to affix a stigma to my name which nothing can now wipe out but the blood of one of us. *A French officer must not be insulted with impunity*, and you, as well as the country which gave me birth, and that which has adopted me, shall find that I will preserve the honour of my station. I, therefore, demand of you to name some town on the Continent where you will be found, accompanied by your friend and your pistols—giving me sufficient time to leave this, and arrive at the place appointed.

NAPPER TANDY, General of Division.

Bourdeaux, December 12, 1802.

Eight weeks elapsed. Elliot failed to reply, and Tandy, in accordance with the fashion of the day, proclaimed him 'a calumniator, a liar, and a poltroon!' This fierce climax was preceded by a more temperate tone.

The question in debate [he said, when Elliot asailed him] was for laying a tax on Great Britain, in which I, as a French citizen, could not possibly be implicated, and, therefore, it is evident that I was wantonly dragged in for the sole purpose of calumny and abuse. Such conduct was unmanly, as no brave man would attack a defenceless person, much less an absent one.

Ignorant of the source to which his betrayal was due, it did not occur to Tandy that the speeches of Elliot and others may have aimed at diverting suspicion from their real informant. Tandy, in reply, advanced merely the suspicion that the charge of being an informer was fulminated to excite the jealousy and disgust of his adopted country France, which, unlike America, had opened her arms to afford him protection.[1]

The wearing worry of Tandy's later life had sapped his

[1] Elliot, writing to Lord Castlereagh, says: 'The Americans absolutely refuse to admit the Irish traitors into their territories' (*Castlereagh Papers*, i. 405, 411, 413, 415, 421). This is the letter which refers to the contemplated arrest of Tandy at the Hague, and in it he further says: 'I have begged Pelham to come to London immediately.' Succeeding letters describe Elliot and Pelham closeted together at various places.

strength, and left him sensitively open to hostile shafts, which his conduct provoked. His vanity was commensurate with his patriotism, and in his stoutest day was easily wounded. He gradually sank, and died at Bordeaux in 1803. 'His private character,' writes Barrington, 'furnished no ground to doubt the integrity of his public one.' He died, as he had lived, a staunch Protestant.[1]

Much has been written of the wonderful escape from Kilmainham Gaol of Corbet, afterwards a general in the French service, and one of the prisoners captured with Tandy at Hamburg, and thence removed to Dublin. Miss Edgeworth was so much struck by this romantic escape, that she made it the leading incident of her best novel. But, considering the subtle international difficulties that had arisen, and with the suggestion of Under-Secretary Marsden before us, it is a question how far Corbet's escape may not have been connived at by Castlereagh.

The sermon which Napoleon preached to the Hamburg deputies on their infringement of the law of nations was in the mouths of his admirers for years after; but it lost in impressiveness by his own violation of the neutral territory of Baden, when, on the night of March 17, 1804, he sent a strong guard

[1] The Society of United Irishmen had no treasonable design when first formed, as the following letter admitting the O'Conor Don would almost in itself convey.

Tandy writes to Charles O'Connor from Dublin, December 8, 1791:—

'Sir,—I have to acknowledge the favour of your very polite letter, and to assure you that I had particular pleasure in seconding the motion for the admission of Mr. O'Conor into the Society of United Irishmen—and that no exertion of mine shall be wanting to compleat the emancipation of my country, give her a free and general representation, and render to every man what I conceive to be his just and undoubted rights, security for his liberty and property, and a participation in the blessings of that land where Nature has placed him.'

(O'Conor Don MSS.) The Irish Parliament at that time was mainly composed of mere nominees of the Crown and traffickers in borough-mongering. Parliamentary Reform and the complete Emancipation of Catholics and Dissenters were the two objects sought; and it was only when both demands had been refused that the organisation drifted into deeper plans. Some recollections of Tandy's expedition to Ireland in 1798 will be found in the Appendix.

to seize and carry off to France the Duc d'Enghien. After a hasty trial by court-martial, and on unproven charges of conspiracy, he was cruelly put to death in the Castle of Vincennes. In the heated discussions to which this outrage gave rise, Buonaparte more than once quoted the case of Tandy, and feebly sought to find in the past conduct of Hamburg a precedent and justification.

Thomas Addis Emmet accused him of coldness and indecision as regards the long threatened invasion of Ireland, because, instead of steering for Erin in 1798, he changed his plan and went to Egypt. The arrest of Tandy in Hamburg rekindled Napoleon's hostile feeling, and shortly after the death of that general he resolved to carry out comprehensively his oft-mooted design.

The 'Correspondence of Napoleon' [1] contains a letter to Berthier, dated September 27, 1804. He says that an expedition to Ireland had been decided upon; that 18,000 men for that purpose were ready at Brest; that a simultaneous landing was to be attempted in Kent; while in Ireland the French army would march straight on Dublin. Meanwhile 200,000 men were encamped at Boulogne; but hostile plans collapsed with the smash of the French fleet at Trafalgar. A few weeks later the so-called 'Army of England' traversed the banks of the blue Danube instead of the Thames. General Mack capitulated at Ulm; Francis of Austria fled, and Napoleon's legions entered Vienna.

[1] Bingham's *Correspondence of Napoleon*, ii. 96. (Chapman and Hall, 1884.)

CHAPTER IX

ARREST OF JÄGERHORN IN LONDON—THE PLOT THICKENS—TURNER SHOT THROUGH THE HEAD

In 1799, Turner's stealthy steps can be traced once more in London. It will be remembered that Lord Edward Fitzgerald had met, by appointment near Whitechapel, M. Jägerhorn, a secret envoy of France, and gave him, in full detail, information regarding every point on which that agent had been charged to inquire. Jägerhorn was 'the estimable Swede' named by Reinhard, the French minister at Hamburg, when writing the intercepted letter. This document, dated July 12, the editor of the 'Castlereagh Papers' assigns to the year 1798;[1] but as Lord Edward was dead at that time,[2] it must belong to the previous year. Other secret missives were sent to Dublin at the same time by the Home Office, in order to guide the course of the Irish Government. These papers, filling forty pages of the book,[3] were the result of a successful stroke of espionage at Hamburg.

M. Jägerhorn is of course the person alluded to by Mr. Froude when describing the nocturnal visit to Lord Downshire. 'He [Lord Edward] had been watched in London, and had been traced to the lodgings of a suspected agent of the French Directory, and among other papers which had been forwarded by spies to the Government, there was one in French containing an allusion to some female friend of Lady Edward, through whom a correspondence was maintained between Ireland and Paris.'

[1] *Castlereagh Correspondence*, i. 282.
[2] Lord Edward Fitzgerald died on June 4, 1798.
[3] *Castlereagh Correspondence*, i. 270–309.

Hamburg was Turner's usual residence, and Jägerhorn had an estate near that place.[1]

Although the case of M. Jägerhorn is opened in the first volume of the 'Castlereagh Papers,' and misplaced among the incidents of another year, we do not find until far in the second the letters addressed to him in 1797 by General Valence and Lord Edward. In 1799 Jägerhorn had sought to renew his perilous enterprise. The same keen scent which traced Lord Edward, in 1797, to the lodgings of the confidential envoy in London, was once more on his track. Wickham, writing from the Home Office on March 28, 1799, has news for Castlereagh in Dublin: 'I have the satisfaction to inform your lordship that we have secured M. Jägerhorn, who was coming over here on a mission similar to that which he undertook some two years since, when he met Lord Edward Fitzgerald in London.'

A full report is given of Jägerhorn's examination, in which he is asked: 'Were you not charged to deliver to Lord Edward Fitzgerald a letter from somebody?' and he replied, 'Madame Matthiessen.' This was the lady, nearly connected with Lady Edward, and alluded to by Mr. Froude as a name found in secret papers. He is further questioned about Lord Edward, Lady Lucy, General Valence, and a number of other persons whose names had cropped up in the interview between Turner and Downshire; but, though the queries were searching, and Jägerhorn now seemed completely in Pitt's power, nothing material was wrung from him. England and Russia were at this time allied, and Jägerhorn, pretending that he had a pension of 2,000 roubles as a spy of Russia, rather dumbfoundered his examiners, and he at last regained his liberty. All this is to be found, with full details, in the 'Correspondence of Lord Castlereagh.'

The paltry sum which Turner received for his services now comes to be considered. This man, who had every facility of access to Lady Edward's house at Hamburg and its rebel *entourage*, held the key of a position so incalculably im-

[1] *Castlereagh Correspondence*, ii. 265.

portant that he seems never to have discerned its marketable value. Thousands would doubtless just as readily have been paid to him as 'the cool 500*l.*' that he modestly asked. 'To get the information had cost him,' he said, 'three times that sum, and to keep up the acquaintances and connections he had at Hamburg he could not live on less.'[1]

'Fresh evidence of the person's power to be useful,' writes Froude, 'made Pitt extremely anxious to secure his permanent help.' The Cornwallis papers record, but without any attempt to identify him, that the pension Samuel Turner received—dating from 1800—was but 300*l.* a year. Wellington when Irish Secretary addressed to Portland a letter in which a present payment of 5,000*l.*, and 'not more than 20,000*l.* within the year,' appears guaranteed to one nameless informer.[2]

Another case may be cited. A document placed in my hands by Sir W. Cope, Bart., records that his grandfather was told by Under-Secretary Cooke to stop at no sum, not even 100,000*l.*, in urging Reynolds to turn approver. Reynolds, not realising the importance of his evidence, consented to take 5,000*l.* and 1,000*l.* a year, with the post of British consul. The tergiversation of Reynolds did not take place until 1798, long after Turner had sold the pass.

The services of 'Downshire's friend' were more timely and, perhaps, more valuable. He told what he knew in 1797: the names he gave of the Executive Committee (p. 7, *ante*) proved more important than might appear at first sight. Reynolds, it is true, gave the hint that a Committee would

[1] 'There really seems some ground for believing that his motive was something else than greed, though what it was is uncertain. It might be love of power—the power of making important revelations to great ministers, the power of holding men's lives and properties in the hollow of his hands. If there is such a thing as an instinct for crooked and dirty ways, a love of treachery for its own sake, a hankering for gratuitous villainy, that instinct was in Samuel Turner.'—George F. Shaw, Esq., LL.D., Senior F.T.C.D., in the *Mail*, March 23, 1892. *Vide* p. 53 *ante*, where Reinhard, in noticing Turner's violent temper, says that 'in order to revenge himself on his countrymen he may have betrayed their cause to Pitt.'

[2] Letter of Sir A. Wellesley to the Duke of Portland, dated 'Holyhead, June 19, 1808.' *Wellington Correspondence* (*Ireland*), pp. 454–5.

be found sitting at Bond's on March 12, 1798, but he does not seem to have disclosed names; his son says that the names were inserted in the warrant purely 'on speculation.'[1]

As regards the more distinct whisper of Turner, the betrayal of the Belfast Directory, at the very hour that Tone was leaving Brest with a French fleet, proved in itself a paralysing blow, and one worth its weight in gold. But the arm that dealt it struck from behind unseen. However, as most of the information that Downshire's friend gave concerned the Northern organisation, he may, perhaps, be credited with this exploit. The loss of Ulster was the loss of the right arm of the rebellion. Turner made his disclosures on October 8, 1797. Besides the list of the Executive Directory, there can be no doubt that in the information which followed he named, with others, John Hughes, the date and place of whose arrest tally with the presumption that to Turner it was due. The 'History of Belfast' records:—'October 20, 1797—John Hughes, bookseller, having been apprehended *in Newry*[2] on a charge of high treason, was brought in here escorted by light dragoons.'[3] Mr. Froude says that 'Downshire's friend' kept him informed of everything.[4]

How well Turner knew Hughes is proved by the sworn testimony of the latter,[5] in which he describes a breakfast in June 1797, with Samuel Turner, Teeling, Macnevin, etc., when the fitness of the country for an immediate rising was debated. Hughes had been a great patriot previously, but now to save himself became a mercenary informer, and even sought to criminate Grattan, who thereupon was dismissed from the Privy Council, though, as Stanhope[6] admits, without just cause. In 1802 John Hughes retired to the United States and became a slave-owner.

[1] *Life of Reynolds*, by his Son, ii. 153.

[2] Newry had been Turner's home. [3] *History of Belfast*, p. 478.

[4] Immediately after the rebellion Downshire received 52,500*l*., nominally as compensation for borough seats. The magnitude of the sum has excited historic surprise; but in making this payment other services were, no doubt, weighed, including the timely information of which Turner made him the channel.

[5] Before the Secret Committee of the House of Lords, 1798.

[6] See *Life of Pitt*, *ante*, p. 36.

Wickham's letter of June 8, 1798, enumerated, for the information of Lord Castlereagh, a number of men whose arrests in England seem consequent on the information furnished by Downshire's visitor. These names include McGuckin, the attorney, who had been concerned for O'Coigly at Maidstone. The subsequent career of this once determined rebel, but who soon after his arrest in 1798 became a spy for the Crown, enhances the importance of Turner's information at a great crisis. The first recorded payment to McGuckin of secret service money is March 5, 1799. His son migrated to France, and was created a baron by Louis Philippe.

The peril of assassination which shadowed every step made by Turner was not adequately weighed by Pitt when estimating the value of his services. The risk he ran was not confined to Ireland. The life of an English spy abroad was deemed equally unsafe, and there is much reason to fear that more than one met with short shrift. Even an oily diplomat, if his subtlety touched French interests, could not regard his life as safe. The disappearance of Benjamin Bathurst, a kinsman of Earl Bathurst, has never been explained. Bathurst was sent on a secret mission to Vienna, at the time that England before opening the Peninsular campaign sought to persuade Austria to declare, by way of a distraction, war against France. Austria soon after crossed the French frontier, and Bathurst received hints of threatened personal doom. Hoping to avoid assassination, he took a northerly route in returning to England, and on reaching Perleberg in Brandenburg, he visited, in his agitation, the commandant of cuirassiers, requesting that sentries might mount guard at the inn where he stopped. These were supplied, and Bathurst spent the day in writing and destroying letters. Shortly before his carriage came to the door in the dark of a November evening, he told some troopers who escorted him that they might withdraw. While all the household was on the alert to see him off, 'he walked beyond the circle of the lantern glare, and was lost to sight at the heads of the horses.' This occurred on November 25, 1809, and Bathurst was never seen or heard of more, notwithstanding that, as we are reminded by Baring Gould, England offered 2,000*l.* reward, and Prussia 100 Friedrichs d'or, for the discovery even of his remains.

To trace the spy with whom these chapters mainly deal seemed, at the outset, almost as hopeless as to find Bathurst's bones. Of all the Government informers not one has been more ingeniously guarded from discovery. Wellington, with all his astuteness, supposed that the fact of a man's name appearing in the Banishment Act was conclusive evidence against him of having been a rebel,[1] and therefore disqualified from claiming any favour from the Crown. But had he known the secret history of Turner's case, it would have opened his eyes. A Fugitive Bill was passed in July 1798, enumerating the rebel leaders who had fled from justice. In this bill we find Samuel Turner named. During the following year Parliament was asked to lend itself to the fraud of branding as a traitor the same Samuel Turner, by passing against him an Act of Attainder. From 1797 he lived abroad, posing as an 'exile of Erin.'[2]

The sealed chest in Dublin Castle which was opened a few years ago contained the only letter I ever saw signed with Turner's name. It related to his pension, and it was neces-

[1] Vide *Irish Correspondence*, p. 386.

[2] The original of 'The Exile of Erin' was said to be an obscure democrat named McCann; but it is perhaps as likely to have been that finished actor, Turner himself. So prominent and conversable a man must have been well known to Thomas Campbell, then a strong Radical, and who, as he tells us, wrote the 'Exile,' at Altona, near Hamburg, in 1801; and it suggests conflicting emotions to speculate as to how far the figure of Turner, in his slouched hat, gazing wistfully from the beach, in search of prey, may have influenced the beautiful idea of the poet:—

'There came to the beach a poor exile of Erin,
The dew on his raiment was heavy and chill;
For his country he sighed, when at twilight repairing
To wander alone by the wind-beaten hill.
But the day-star attracted his eye's sad devotion,
For it rose o'er his own native isle of the ocean;
Where once, in the fire of his youthful devotion,
He sang the bold anthem of Erin-go-Bragh.'

sary to lay the mask aside for once. We have already seen him styled Furnes, Richardson, and especially 'Lord Downshire's friend.'[1] A new name is now adopted to puzzle posterity. He directs that 500*l.* be lodged to the account of 'J. Destinger,' and this sum he was to draw through a third party. Turner's letter is addressed, not to Dublin Castle, but to Cooke in London, that gentleman having been succeeded, as Under-Secretary for Ireland, by Mr. Marsden.

Rt. Honble Mr. Secretary Cooke.[2]

Hamburg: May 18, 1802.

Sir,—In consequence of letters I've had the honour of receiving from Lord Castlereagh and Sir James Craufurd, I take the liberty of intruding relative to a pension of 300*l.* per annum the Government has thought proper to bestow on me for information on Irish affairs.

His lordship states that you have been so kind as to offer to pay the pension to any person I would name as agent—or in any way I was to propose. At present there is no person in Ireland I'd like to trust, and till some mode is adopted, I should be extremely obliged if you'd take the trouble of lodging in any bank in London the sum of 500*l.* (British) on account of J. Destinger—the name I shall draw it under—through Sir Geo. Rumbold.[3]

Now that the war is over, and it is *supposed* all persons in my line are discharged, I make it a point to spend much more money than heretofore in order to do away any idea of my being employed and income diminished, and it is for that reason I request your attention, and beg the honour of a line through Sir George to say where the draft is to be sent.

Hoping one day or other to merit your good opinion, I remain, most respectfully, &c. &c.

S. Turner.

Turner spent money freely, and often when he could ill afford it. He had a social status to maintain: he was the son of a county magistrate; had distinguished himself in college;

[1] Also 'Jean Thomas,' *ante*, p. 20. Compare also Wellington's *Irish Correspondence*, p. 357, regarding a letter received in 1808 'from —— *alias* ——.'

[2] This letter was forwarded by Cooke to Marsden for his guidance.

[3] Sir George Rumbold was Consul-General at Hamburg. Died 1807.

belonged to an honourable profession. He was the trustee of marriage settlements. He was 'Lord Downshire's friend!' If he continued to wear his mask well, why might he not aspire to attain, in America at least, the high official rank of his late colleague and fellow-prisoner, Thomas Addis Emmet, whom she at last honoured by a public funeral and a monument raised by national subscription?

The 'Dublin Directory' for 1804 describes Samuel Turner's address as 58 St. Stephen's Green, in that city. The volume must have been compiled during the previous year, and it may be that the Irish Government, in 1803, removed him to Dublin, with the object of picking the brains of those who had been concerned in Emmet's rebellion of that year. Until the very night of its outburst, in July 1803, the existence of a slumbering volcano had not been suspected. After the vain attempts to convict and hang Tandy, Turner had returned to his old quarters.[1]

The Irish Government were wholly unprepared for Emmet's revolt. No wonder that Wickham, with the experience he had acquired, confessed amazement that the secret should have been kept so well.

The Secretary of State cried out with astonishment to think that such a preparation for revolution could be carried on in the very bosom of the seat of Government, without discovery, for so long a time, when any of the party could have made their fortunes by a disclosure of the plot; and remarked, at the same time, in presence of Mr. Stafford and the two Mr. Parrots, John and

[1] A small box of papers, labelled 'Curious and Selected,' is preserved in the Record Tower, Dublin Castle. Two unsigned letters supplying private information in 1803 have puzzled their official custodians. St. John Mason—a cousin of the ill-fated Robert Emmet—is the man mainly sought to be incriminated. The letters are endorsed 'R.' and I observed, in holding up one against the light, that the capitals 'S. T. 1801,' appear as the watermark. 'R' is the cypher by which Castlereagh points to 'Richardson,' *alias* Turner, in his letter to Wickham (p. 46, *ante*). The case of St. John Mason and his prolonged imprisonment without trial was brought before Parliament in 1812. The Duke of Richmond—then Viceroy—wrote a despatch and made allusion to the above letters. 'Who the writer may have been I know not,' observes his Grace, 'but he appears to have been some secret informer of the Government.' This despatch was ordered by the House of Commons to be printed June 2, 1812.

William, that it was because they were mostly all mechanics, or working people, that the thing was kept so profound; and said that if the higher orders of society had been connected, they would divulge the plot for the sake of gain.[1]

Turner was at once set in motion: but how? We find him put into the same gaol with a swarm of State prisoners, many of whom had been active in 1798. All daily met for exercise in the yard of Kilmainham Gaol, and had every opportunity for converse. Here Robert Emmet himself had been confined until the very day of his execution.

The execution was followed by that of several of his confederates. Let us look back. Martial law is proclaimed; a dead calm prevails. Turner is now traced stealthily making his way to the Secretary of State's Office, Dublin Castle. Anxious to avoid committing himself in writing, especially with a true signature, he seeks the safer medium of oral communication. Mr. Marsden cannot be seen; he is engaged just then in conference with the chief law officer of the Crown. Turner scribbles the following and sends it in; no signature is attached, but the paper and enclosure are endorsed, by Marsden, 'Mr. Samuel Turner':—

Understanding the Attorney-General is just with you, I take the liberty of sending in a letter of Mr. Ball, but wish to speak on other matters.

Sergeant Ball's letter to Turner is dated

Temple St., October 3, 1803.

I have looked into the Act of Parliament and considered in what manner you should proceed in order to do away the effect of the attainder thereby passed against you. Nothing short of an Act of Parliament, reversing the former as far as it affects you, will be sufficient to enable you to sue for your property in our courts of justice. I think you mentioned that some other plan had been suggested as sufficient. If you will let me know what it is, I will give it the most attentive consideration.

[1] MS. recollections, communicated by one of Emmet's officers, Bernard Duggan.

How Marsden and the Attorney-General settled the difficulty, no letters exist to show; but the London 'Courier' of December 5, 1803, while ignorant of the deception, lucidly reveals the facts:—

On Friday last, Samuel Turner, Esq., barrister-at-law, was brought to the bar of the Court of King's Bench, in custody of the keeper of Kilmainham Prison, under a charge of attainder, passed in the Irish Parliament, as one concerned in the Rebellion of the year 1798; but having shown that he was no way concerned therein, that he had not been in the country for a year and seven months prior to passing that Act—*i.e.* for thirteen months prior to the rebellion—and therefore could not be the person alluded to, his Majesty's Attorney-General confessed the same, and Mr. Turner was discharged accordingly.[1]

The 'Dublin Evening Post' of the day states that Turner's arrest was due simply to his indiscretion in visiting Ireland on business arising from the death of his father.[2] But as the 'Post' in 1803 had been subsidised by the Crown, this account was probably meant to mislead. The Castle archives bulge with the brimful letters of its editor, H. B. Code. Turner's committal to Kilmainham was only another act in the great drama, one scene of which Mr. Froude has so powerfully put before us. 'Samuel Turner, Esquire,' of imposing presence and indomitable mien, a veteran in 'the cause,' the man who had challenged the Commander-in-Chief, the envoy to France, the exile of Erin, the friend of Lord Edward and Pamela, the disinherited by his father, the victim of State persecution, now stood before his fellow-prisoners the 'Ecce Homo' of martyrdom, commanding irresistibly their confidence.

Of his detention in Kilmainham Dr. Madden knows no-

[1] This Attorney-General was Standish O'Grady, afterwards Lord Guillamore. The author of *Ireland and its Rulers* states of him (i. 126): 'He was a quaint joker; a shrewd wit, with a vein of dry humour. As a judge he enjoyed a plebeian popularity, for he took great sport in baffling the Crown lawyers.'

[2] 'Mr. Turner only returned to this country within the last few weeks on account of the death of his father, who left his property to younger children thinking the elder could not return, or that, if left to him, it would be laid hold of by Government by virtue of the Act of Attainder.'—*Dublin Evening Post*, November 29, 1803.

thing; but he mentions that Turner accompanied the State prisoners—nineteen in number—to Fort George in Scotland, the final scene of their captivity. Here Turner's work was so adroitly performed that we find a man of incorruptible integrity suspected instead. Arthur O'Connor told John Patten that Thomas Addis Emmet 'gave information of a letter which O'Connor was writing, through which means Government became acquainted with the circumstance.' A long correspondence on the subject has been published by Madden. Emmet at last challenged O'Connor. Patten,[1] the brother-in-law of Emmet, was told to bring a certain pair of duelling pistols to Fort George; but, thanks to the efforts of Robert Emmet to allay the dispute, the weapons were not used. It was Patten's impression that Turner's machinations had set the two friends by the ears. Although O'Connor apologised, and both parties shook hands, it is painful to add that half a century after, when the upright Emmet had been more than twenty years dead, O'Connor, in his book 'Monopoly,' stigmatised him as a man of bad faith. A suspicion more baseless was never uttered. In this book the name of his fellow-prisoner, Turner, is not once mentioned. Indeed, the inference is that he thought well of Turner; for O'Connor, after criticising the Catholic members of the Directory, declares that he had much greater reliance on the *Northern* chiefs. O'Connor, Emmet, Neilson and others were detained at Fort George until the Peace of Amiens, and then enlarged on condition that they should expatriate themselves for ever.[2]

In 1807 Sir Arthur Wellesley, afterwards Duke of Wellington, entered on his duties as Irish Secretary. A letter, dated Dublin Castle, December 5, 1807, and addressed to the Admiralty, recommends a midshipman in the navy, Francis Turner, for promotion. 'He is the son of a Mr. Turner in this country, who has strong claims to the favour of the Govern-

[1] John Patten, librarian to the Royal Dublin Society, survived until the year 1864. He furnished me with many facts, duly noted at the time. Some appear in the *Sham Squire*.

[2] For a curious poem which O'Connor distributed *en route* to Fort George, see Appendix.

ment for the loyalty and zeal with which he conducted himself during the rebellion in Ireland.' [1] Doubtless the new hand merely wrote in this letter what the permanent officials prompted.[2]

Downshire, although a staunch Tory of the old school, uniformly supported the Catholic claims. This example probably influenced his *protégé*. O'Connell, while inculcating moral force in his struggle for civil and religious liberty, was fond of enlisting in his bodyguard men who in more troubled times had staked their lives and fortunes for Ireland. He had himself been a 'United Irishman,' as will be shown. The rebel General Clony presided as chairman at the Catholic Association. Rowan, Teeling and 'Con' MacLoughlin sat at the Council board, or stood on the National platform. What confidence must not O'Connell have reposed in the man who, as will appear, avowed himself ready to die for his chief!

An aged gentleman, Patrick O'Byrne, who was born at Newry, almost under the shadow of Turner's patrimonial gable, but who never once doubted his fidelity to the cause in which O'Byrne himself has been no silent ally, supplies a fact of sufficiently curious import:—

When the Orange ascendancy faction resolved to put O'Connell out of the way [he writes], and their champion, the unfortunate D'Esterre, horsewhip in hand, was ostentatiously parading the streets of Dublin, accompanied by leering friends, to compel O'Connell to fight him, Mr. Samuel Turner took up his position in a hotel where it was known D'Esterre would go to seek O'Connell. He had not been there long before D'Esterre and his staff entered and inquired for O'Connell. Immediately Mr. Turner advanced and stated that his friend Mr. O'Connell was not there, but he—Mr. Turner—was there to represent him. No: they did not want

[1] *Civil Correspondence of the Duke of Wellington* (*Ireland*).

[2] The promotion urged by Wellington would seem to have been made, and merited. *The Gentleman's Magazine* for July, 1813, under the head of 'Admiralty, May 30,' records the capture by some boats, under the command of Lieutenant Turner, of a French privateer, after a severe conflict and loss of life. I am bound to say, however, that the Turner mentioned by Wellington as having strong claims on the Government since 1798, is not satisfactorily shown to be Turner who gave important information during the Rebellion.

Mr. O'Connell's friend; the Liberator himself was the object of their search. Mr. Turner, with the same spirit that he had challenged Lord Carhampton, now declared that he adopted Mr. O'Connell's words, publicly uttered, and made himself responsible for his actions. In vain; none but O'Connell himself would serve their purpose, and Mr. Turner was denied the opportunity of doing battle for his friend.[1]

All this time it cannot be said that, though undiscovered, Turner was still a happy man. The dread spectre of assassination ceased not to haunt him. 'After long experience of the world,' says Junius, 'I affirm before God I never knew a rogue who was not unhappy.' Nor was Turner's presentiment surprising. MacSkimmin, in his 'History of Carrickfergus,' states that the pistol and the dagger were no uncommon means of dealing with informers; and he supplies a list of men who thus suffered.

Books which treat of 'Ninety-eight' often mention Byrne of Dundalk. In 1869 the late Mr. John Mathews of that town gathered from Byrne's representative, Mr. P. J. Byrne, Clerk of the Crown, several facts, and, in enclosing them to me, styled his informant 'the highest authority on the unpublished history of the County.' Two days later Mr. Byrne was no more. The inquiries I then made had no reference to Samuel Turner, but some passing notices of this man which occur in the manuscript are useful in now supplying missing links. Mr. Mathews was an ardent patriot, and he described, not without emotion, how Turner died. Regarding him as a rebel true to the end, he writes:—

[1] Letter of Mr. Patrick O'Byrne to W. J. F., Dublin, September 6, 1880. D'Esterre was a practised duellist. He and O'Connell at last met in a field near Naas, and D'Esterre fell January 31, 1815. Lord Whitworth, the famous diplomat, was then Lord Lieutenant. The *Sentinel*, an independent newspaper, declared that the most memorable event which occurred in his Viceroyalty was this duel. It had engrossed the attention of all Ireland, and ought to engross that of Parliament also. Everyone asked why the outrage which led to the catastrophe, being so public and protracted, had not been restrained by some one of the many members of his Government who had observed it. But vainly the friends of peace inquired why D'Esterre had not been placed under arrest.

Turner went to the Isle of Man, and having quarrelled there with a Mr. Boyce, agreed that the dispute should be settled by an appeal to arms. Both, with their friends, repaired to the field of honour, and as Turner was preparing for the struggle his adversary shot him through the head; and [adds Matthews] thus terminated the career of a man whose only regret was that his life was not lost in the service of his country.[1]

Was the vengeance wreaked by Boyce meant as a tardy retribution? Was the John Boyce, who with five other prisoners was consigned in 1797 to Carrickfergus Gaol, connected with the Boyce who shot Turner? What Boyce had against Turner was a secret which died with both. No proceedings seem to have been taken against the man by whose hand he fell. And possibly this forbearance was not uninfluenced by the fact that the Crown had need no longer for their informer's services, but, on the contrary, gained by his death. Turner was a clever man, troublesome to deal with, haughty, touchy, and resentful; and, like Maguan,[2] Bird and Newell, he might at any moment publicly turn upon his employers and betray them with as little compunction as he had already sold his comrades.

A word as regards Lord Downshire, through whom Turner's disclosures were at first conveyed. This peer, who at one time had wielded potential influence at Whitehall, and had the ear of Pitt, lived to fall into deep disfavour with Government. He steadily opposed the Legislative Union, and helped to form a joint-stock purse with the object of outbribing Dublin Castle. In chastisement he was dismissed from the Lord Lieutenancy of Down, deprived of his rank as colonel, expelled from the Privy Council, and threatened with a parliamentary inquiry into his conduct. These blows told, and on September 7, 1801, he breathed his last.

[1] Turner was very treacherously served by his impulsive foe. Perhaps Boyce thought that had O'Connell accepted Turner's services in that lonely field in Kildare, he might have been tempted, like Iago, to deal a stealthy stab.

[2] Maguan of Saintfield is not to be confounded with Magan.

CHAPTER X

EFFORTS TO EXCITE MUTINY IN THE ENGLISH FLEET

Of Duckett, an amateur rebel envoy, mentioned in connection with the arrest of Napper Tandy,[1] something remains to be said. He was a man of very active habits, and if less impulsive would have had more friends. Tone, already the victim of misplaced confidence, viewed many men with suspicion, and let them see it. In 1796 he was passing as a French officer, and mentions in his diary that, when waiting to see De la Croix, the minister of war at Paris, Duckett, who chanced to be also in the ante-room, sought to enter into conversation with Tone by handing him an English newspaper. Advances of this sort, though natural in an exiled Irishman meeting another, were not without effect in making Tone distrust and avoid him.[2] Duckett no doubt had projects connected with the enterprise in hand to which the chivalrous Tone would not stoop; but of these Tone knew little, and his prejudice was formed on quite different grounds. These suspicions were shared by Madgett, an official in the French War Office. Duckett, it appears, told Madgett that two expeditions were to proceed to Ireland. 'Madgett said that he had endeavoured to put Duckett off the scent by saying he did not believe one word of the story, but that Duckett continued positive.' Tone adds that the information was probably true; but that it was terribly provoking it should be known to

[1] *Ante*, p. 72.

[2] Many men recoil from affable persons who seem over-anxious to know them. Sir Gavan Duffy in *Young Ireland* states that Davis had been prejudiced against the subsequently most distinguished Darcy Magee, because he had 'obviously determined to transact an acquaintance with him.'

Duckett, 'to whom, by the by, De la Croix revealed in confidence all that he knew, for which he ought to be damned.' Tone later on admits that he knows nothing against Duckett unless by report.[1]

Tone's unhealthy impression Dr. Madden caught contagiously. In the first edition of his book, published forty years ago, he conveys that Duckett was a spy subsidised by England.[2] Innuendo grew at last into accusation, and a more recent edition records that Duckett, 'there is good reason to believe, was not employed by the Irish Directory, but by the British Minister, Mr. Pitt.'[3] Again, we are told that Duckett was '*assuming* the character of an agent of the United Irishmen at Paris, and continually dodged Tone in all his movements.'[4]

I cannot endorse this imputation. In no pension list, or account of secret service money, is the name of Duckett to be traced; nor is there one line to criminate him in the archives of the Home Office. Nay more. Open the 'Castlereagh Papers,' and there Duckett is found denounced as a sworn enemy to England. These valuable State papers were published ten years previous to the issue of Dr. Madden's revised edition; but, uninfluenced by their revelations, he renews the charges against Duckett.

Guillon, who has had access to the Government archives in France, says that Truguet, Minister of Marine, had thrown himself heart and soul into the projected invasion, and proposed to land 30,000 men in Ireland, under Hoche; and 60,000 later on in England; but the Directory deemed the plan too daring, and threw it aside; until Tone's memorials made their thoughts recur to invasion, and they then adopted a portion of the rejected scheme of Truguet.[5] An interesting letter from Duckett to Truguet, Minister of Marine, turns up among the intercepted despatches. This functionary had just been succeeded by a new hand.

[1] Tone's *Journals*, ii. 141. (Washington, 1847.)

[2] *United Irishmen, their Lives and Times*, 1st ed. i. 40–75.

[3] *Ibid.* 2nd ed. ii. 37. [4] *Ibid.* iv. 603.

[5] *La France et l'Irlande.* (Paris, 1888.)

Is the Government still resolved to prosecute the same plans and the same projects [Duckett asks]. Can my country rely on its promises? Let me know, I beseech you in the name of Liberty, what is to be done? Shall I go home to accelerate the period for the arrival of which we are all solicitous? Consider that it is only patriots and enemies of England who risk anything—it is their blood that will flow.

The fears I had lest I should not be able to convert your bill into money are unfortunately realised. I have presented it to Citizen Reinhard, explained to him who I was, and what I was going to do. I showed him how necessary it was that I should leave Hamburg. He replied that his personal means did not permit him to comply with my application, adding that he could not act, because I had not a particular letter for him.

A mysterious task and goal are glanced at.

I am grievously mortified that I am not at this moment at the place of my destination. You know how deeply I interest myself in this cause; my presence will be conducive to the success of our friends. I wait for nothing but your answer to set out. I would merely request you to speak about me to your successor, to explain to him my situation and my necessities, in order that he may take into consideration the expenses which I shall be absolutely obliged to incur; for, when once arrived at my post, it will perhaps be impossible for me to receive assistance from him. I therefore beg of you to make him put me beyond the reach of accidents, by causing a sum that will afford me the means of subsisting and acting to be remitted to Hamburg. It does not belong to me to fix it. It is for him in his wisdom to see what sum will be necessary and indispensable for the expenses of six months. It would be superfluous to assure you of my attachment to the cause, and of the high consideration which I have for you personally.

P.S.—Address your answer to Citizen Reinhard: it is he who undertakes to forward this letter to you.[1]

It will be remembered that the betrayer whom Mr. Froude dramatically pictures as unbosoming himself to Downshire was the confidant of Reinhard at Hamburg, had access to his house, and used that fact to prove that his services, as an informer,

[1] *Castlereagh Papers*, i. 294–5.

were worth purchase by Pitt. I have elsewhere shown that the letters headed 'Secret Information from Hamburg,' which have crept into the 'Castlereagh Papers' to puzzle the world,[1] can only have been written by 'Lord Downshire's friend'—*i.e.* Turner. One appears at page 306 of the first volume of that work. *There* the objects vaguely broached by Duckett are revealed as plainly as though Reinhard himself had whispered the word. The spy, having furnished other items of news, writes:—

> Duckett is at Hamburg; he has denounced Stone at Paris as a traitor.[2] I hear he [Duckett] has got money from the [French] Government for the purpose of renewing the mutiny in the English Fleet.'[3]

Obstinately hostile winds, as in 1796, once more saved England. Tone, whose untiring energy had accomplished the organisation of the invading forces, soliloquises in his diary of 1 August, 1797:—

> I am, to-day, twenty-five days aboard, and at a time when twenty-five hours are of importance. There seems to be a fate in this business. Five weeks—I believe six weeks—the English Fleet was paralysed by the mutinies at Portsmouth,[4] Plymouth, and the Nore. The sea was open, and nothing to prevent both the Dutch

[1] The puzzle is increased by the noble editor's arrangement of the letters—made without regard to chronological order.

[2] Stone is the man who had been tried in 1795 for high treason, and found guilty. But Duckett, though a staunch rebel, may have had good reason for denouncing Stone three years later. Madame de Genlis, in her *Mémoires*, upbraids Stone with having treacherously retained some money which had been entrusted to him for Pamela. See tome iv. 130–1.

[3] Clarke, when giving Tone his commission in the French army, asks him (*Journals*, i. 151) if he knew one Duckett: 'I answered I did not, nor did I desire to know him.' Clarke replied that Duckett was 'clever.' Clarke, afterwards Duke de Feltre, stooped to ignoble tactics from which Tone recoiled. Clarke was a strong advocate for *chouannerie* (see Tone, ii. 96–9), and probably encouraged Duckett in his scheme for destroying the English dockyards and exciting mutiny in the fleet.

[4] At Portsmouth, when Lord Bridport gave orders to put to sea, every ship at St. Helens refused to obey. The marines fired and five seamen were killed. The crew of the 'London' turned the guns, and threatened to blow all aft into the sea. The officers surrendered; the marines laid down their arms, and Admiral Colpoys and Captain Griffiths were put in confinement.

and French fleets to put to sea. Well, nothing was ready; that precious opportunity, which we can never expect to return, was lost; and now that at last we are ready here the wind is against us, the mutiny is quelled, and we are sure to be attacked by a superior force. At Brest it is, I fancy, still worse. Had we been in Ireland at the moment of the insurrection at the Nore, we should beyond a doubt have had at least that fleet, and God only knows the influence which such an event might have had on the whole British Navy.

Much that Tone privately penned is found confirmed by a secret committee which sat while Parker's[1] corpse hung in chains at Sheppey. It appeared that the crews were largely sworn to espouse the Irish cause; 'to be faithful to their brethren who were fighting against tyranny;' to carry a portion of the fleet into Irish ports, hoisting, instead of the Union Jack, a green flag emblazoned with *Erin-go-bragh.*[2]

Dr. Madden's suggestion that Duckett was a spy of Pitt's is reiterated with cruel consistency. Part of the grounds of his suspicion was Duckett's intimate relations with Reinhard, also suspected by Madden, but who is now shown conclusively to have been true. Madden frequently quotes from the 'Castlereagh Papers,' but overlooks the following letter from Sir J. Crawford to Lord Grenville, one wholly inconsistent with his hypothesis that Duckett, like Turner, was a spy for Pitt. Crawford was, of course, the British representative at Hamburg.

October 23, 1798.

I shall abstain from any measures against Duckett, continuing, at the same time, to have him narrowly watched, which I hitherto have so completely, that there is scarcely a single step which he has taken since he has been at Hamburg with which I am unacquainted. His views for the present seem to be turned principally towards his Majesty's dockyards, and not choosing to venture in England himself, he is very desirous of getting over hither some one of those evil-disposed persons whom he knows to be employed in the dockyards, for the purpose of concerting with him the means of setting them on fire. . . . He is in very little esteem in France,

[1] Leader of the mutiny.

[2] *Report of the Secret Committee of Commons, England,* 1799.

and is particularly ill with Talleyrand.[1] His principal supporter is Bruyes (*sic*),[2] brother to the deceased admiral, and who was Minister of the Marine. He pretends that, in case of a successful attempt on the part of the French to land in Ireland, his object would be to get over to that country; but I have not hitherto been able to learn any particulars respecting his commission. He affects much secrecy, even with those with whom he lives in the greatest intimacy.[3] He has of late been in correspondence with Holt,[4] the rebel chief, who, through him, has been pressing the French for assistance. He says that there are 3,500 land troops on board the squadron which lately sailed from Brest, but that they have French uniforms for 7,000 men, with the view, as he pretends, of clothing the first bodies of Irish that might join them in the same way as their own troops, and thus, a numerous body appearing in French uniforms, of impressing the Irish nation at large with an idea that they had landed a considerable force.[5]

This letter explains the more ambiguous despatch written two months before. Wickham transmits, by direction of Portland, for the information of the Irish Viceroy, a copy of a secret note,

which had been confirmed by the arrival of Mr. D—— [*i.e.* Duckett] under a feigned name in Hanover, on his road to Hamburg, and I have little doubt of the truth of the rest from my intimate knowledge of the writer. D., by the extreme vigilance and activity of Sir James Crawfurd, has been discovered and arrested on his road; but, as he has been acknowledged as a person attached to the French Mission at Hamburg, and claimed as such, I fear there are no hopes whatever of his being delivered up, or even of having his papers examined.[6]

[1] As Tone suspected Duckett to be a spy, he doubtless cautioned Talleyrand against him. These misgivings spread from bureau to bureau.

[2] Tone's *Diary* of June 16, 1798, praises the talents and activity of Bruix; 'but what could he do? In the first place, he had no money,' &c.—ii. 501.

[3] Turner's instructions from the Home Office were, if he would not prosecute, to open a correspondence, at least, with leading rebels.

[4] Joseph Holt, a Wicklow Protestant, published his memoirs in two volumes, but does not mention Duckett.

[5] *Castlereagh Papers*, i. 263-4.

[6] Duckett was secretary to Leonard Bourdon, who voted for the death of Louis XVI., and by his energy overthrew Robespierre, July 27, 1794. He headed the Conspiracy of the Faubourgs in 1795, and doubtless applauded Duckett in his scheme.

Your lordship, who will be aware of the extreme delicacy of this business, will no doubt feel the necessity of keeping the whole of it as secret as possible. In the mean time it is a point of no slight importance that this man should have been discovered on his road, and his journey so much delayed as that the object of it will be, in all probability, defeated.[1]

Tone's prejudice against Duckett influenced Macnevin. 'Mr. Duckett is still here,' writes Reinhard to De la Croix in another intercepted letter. 'I proposed to Mr. Macnevin to reconcile himself with Mr. Duckett. He has refused to do so.'

It is remarkable that while the usually clear-sighted physician suspects Duckett of being an English spy, he praises '*the zeal and talents of* TURNER.'[2] Nor is there one line in Tone's Diary to indicate distrust of Turner; but the wrong man, in true dramatic style, incurs suspicion and blows. On September 21, 1797, Tone called on General Hoche at Rennes. Hoche spoke of Duckett, and Tone destroyed him with an expressive shrug, adding that he had boasted at Paris of his acquaintance and influence with General Clarke, and even with Hoche himself. Two days later Colonel Shee, the uncle of Clarke, and who accompanied the expedition to Bantry Bay, also inquires if Tone knew Duckett. 'I answered that Duckett was a scoundrel. I besought him to put Hoche on his guard.' It appeared that Duckett had made two or three advances to Shee, who, however, had consistently avoided him. Tone's gorge is raised, and he ends some remarks of asperity with 'I'll Duckett him, the scoundrel, if I can catch him fairly in my grip.'[3]

Duckett, according to the Hamburg spy, now shown to be Turner, was employed by the French Government to excite mutiny in the British fleet. Its first outburst was at Portsmouth; it was renewed at the Nore. As historians, who might be expected to treat largely of such incidents, barely

[1] *Castlereagh Papers*, i. 263.

[2] *Vide* Dr. Macnevin's memorial relative to a landing in Ireland.—*Ibid.* i. 305.

[3] Tone's *Journals*, i. 208. (Washington, 1827.)

notice that mutiny, a few remarks here are perhaps admissible; the more so as it will be necessary to recur again to Parker, who led the revolt. It assumed so formidable a front that Truguet thought it might prove the death-blow to England's greatness. Parker, who possessed wonderful powers of persuasion, was soon joined by a large portion of Lord Duncan's squadron, and became the *soi-disant* admiral of the fleet. He blockaded the Thames, and threatened to starve London. His mutinous force now consisted of twenty-four sail of the line. Each ship was governed by a committee of twelve, together with two delegates and a secretary, and all assembled by beat of drum. The pulse of public feeling was shown in three per cent. Consols falling to forty-five. The Board of Admiralty visited the scene of the mutiny, but failed to effect an arrangement. Lord Northesk, R.N., waited on Parker to hear his terms. These were so exacting that Northesk hesitated. The following is culled from the (London) 'Courier' of June 8, 1797, and it will be seen how much Parker's letter differs from the mild version of it given in Campbell's 'Lives of the Admirals':—

They persisted that the whole must be complied with. . . . Lord Northesk was now rowed on board the 'Duke of York' Margate packet, under a flag of truce, with three cheers from the 'Sandwich,' and with the following paper to ratify his credentials.

To Captain Lord Northesk.

You are hereby authorized and ordered to wait upon the King, wherever he may be, with the Resolutions of the Committee of Delegates, and are directed to return back with an Answer to the same within 54 hours from the date hereof.

R. Parker, President.

Northesk, furnished with a passport from Parker, returned to town, while Pitt and Dundas were hanged in effigy at the yard-arm. It was even debated to surrender the fleet to the French. Thereupon Sheridan suggested that all the buoys and beacons should be removed. A paper of the day states that the troops, ordered to fire on the fleet from the batteries at Gravesend, broke out into mutiny themselves, declaring that fratricide formed no part of their duty. The biographical dictionaries say that the popularity of Northesk and the firmness of Lord Howe caused the utter collapse of this great mutiny; but such history is misleading. The 'Repulse' was the first ship to abandon the cause, and becoming stranded was mercilessly cannonaded by the fleet. Its foremast and rigging were shot away; its decks were red with blood. Two more deserters, the 'Agamemnon' and 'Vestal,' escaped better. In slipping their cables and entering the Thames it was supposed that they were carrying into effect an already debated plan of bombarding Gravesend. The rest of the fleet followed and found themselves snared into the hands of the Government. When this fact became apparent, the mutineers were filled with fury. The ships separated, turned the great guns on each other, and fought furiously for hours, until at last Parker succumbed. In reading the trials of the delegates one is struck by such Celtic names as Sullivan, Donovan, Walsh, Hughes, Brady, MacCarthy, Maginnis, Coffey, and Branon. Strange reports were current.[1] The 'Courier' of June 6, 1797, records that

when he [Parker] was carried before the magistrates, he took two

[1] The *Courier*, describing the execution of the delegates, states that the inextinguishable vitality of one man named Lee presented a striking spectacle, and that extra balls had to be poured into his head before he was despatched! A letter from the Irish Under-Secretary of the day, now preserved in the State Paper Office, reveals that Lee was discovered to have been a most determined United Irishman, and had joined the fleet for the sole object of helping the cause he had at heart. Lee and Duckett seem to have acted in concert. How largely the British navy was composed of Irish sailors, and under what circumstances their discontent originated, appear from an amusing anecdote. Shortly before Trafalgar, the first lieutenant of a man-of-war, when making his rounds to see that all hands were at their guns, observed an Irish sailor kneeling in prayer: 'What! are you afraid?' exclaimed the officer. 'Afeard, indeed! replied the tar, contemptuously. 'I was only praying that the shots of the French might be distributed like the prize money—the lion's share among the officers.' Tone assured Carnot that England had recently raised 80,000 Irishmen for her navy and marines. Carnot did not tell him in reply to reserve that statement for the marines themselves, but took it as strict truth. The compu-

letters out of his pocket, saying, 'These are my authorities; it was on these I acted.' From this it has been inferred [adds the 'Courier'] that he was set on by 'higher powers,' as the lower class call them: they say that Parker has declared he will not die till he has garnished Temple Bar with heads.

However, he made no distinct revelation. He was subjected to a number of interrogatories, 'dans lesquels,' observes a French authority, 'on chercha vainement à découvrir les secrets moteurs de l'insurrection.'

Duckett's letter to Truguet, minister of marine, and the information of the Hamburg spy, help to throw light on this stirring episode. The mutiny is commonly ascribed to some harsh regulations of the Admiralty. A deeper design underlay it. Parker was at first committed to stand his trial before a civil court; but a court-martial was suddenly substituted. This deprived him of the forensic services of Erskine, whose powerful eloquence had successfully defended Horne Tooke against the Cabinet of Pitt. It was desirable that so dangerous a man should be got rid of without delay. His application for an adjournment was refused; and on June 30, 1797, he suffered death.

These mutinies were largely the work of Duckett, acting under the instructions of La Croix, the French minister of war. Tone, as we have seen, hated Duckett, whom he constantly snubs and denounces. Had there been a co-operation, the event would doubtless have been different. However all moderate men rejoiced at the issue. The mutiny formed part of a scheme to sever England's right arm; but the chivalry of Tone recoiled from a manœuvre of which he finally saw the importance while hesitating to approve of it. Dutch and French fleets for the invasion of Great Britain and Ireland had been nearly ready to start at the time of the mutinies.

Pitt used a powerful engine in subduing the mutiny. He

tation, however, will not stand historic scrutiny. According to an official return, it appears that Ireland had furnished 11,457 men for the navy, and 4,058 for the marines.

despatched to the Nore a Roman Catholic priest, who impressively preached the doctrine of submission.[1] This was probably the same priest who, Father O'Coigly complains, worried him in the condemned cell in the hope of persuading him to inform. Meanwhile Duckett kept severely aloof from Saxon soil, and closed his career writing poems at Paris.[2]

[1] Of course with the sanction of Bishop Douglas, whose name is often mentioned in the *Castlereagh Correspondence*.

[2] Mr. O'Donoghue, in his *Poets of Ireland*, claims (p. 65) Tone's Duckett as identical with William Duckett who wrote Odes on Greek and South American Independence. Mr. O'Donoghue says that he died at Paris in 1841; but Dr. Madden, in 1846, pointing at Duckett as a pensioned spy, adds 'he is still living.' See *United Irishmen*, 1st edition, 3rd series, i. 75.

CHAPTER XI

THE BETRAYER OF LORD EDWARD FITZGERALD [1]

Another man there was of the same type as Turner, who posed in impenetrable disguise, but unlike Reynolds and Armstrong, spied in secrecy and on the express condition that he should not be asked to give public evidence and thus damage his social status.

An historian often quoted in these pages is not safe in suggesting that we may find behind the mask of Lord Downshire's visitor the betrayer of Lord Edward Fitzgerald. The utterly distinct quarter to which the Geraldine's arrest is due will presently appear. Lord Edward had the command of Leinster. Turner had mainly to do with Ulster. Guiltless he was of Lord Edward's betrayal in Dublin, for the simple reason, no doubt, that living abroad himself he knew nothing of his hiding-places. All other sensational incidents of that stirring time paled before the sorrow by which Lord Edward's arrest and death oppressed the people. A Dublin ballad expressed the fierce anxiety felt to discover and destroy the veiled betrayer—

May Heaven scorch and parch the tongue by which his life was sold,
And shrivel up the hand that clutched the proffered meed of gold.

Whilst, on the other hand, ballads inspired by loyal ardour did not hesitate to regard as a holy work the annihilation of Lord Edward Fitzgerald.[2]

[1] I leave unchanged some of the circumstantial evidence which had convinced me of Magan's guilt, adding in brackets the criminatory letters subsequently found (January 1891).

[2] Thus, in 'Croppies lie down,' to the tune of which, as Moore says, 'more blood had been shed than often falls to the lot of lyrical ballads'—

'The ruthless Fitzgerald stept forward to rule,
His principles formed in the Orleans school.'

In 1830, when continental thrones trembled and others fell, Moore published his interesting 'Life of Lord Edward'—a work which, however popular and opportune, will not bear a critical scrutiny as regards historic exactness. 'From my mention of these particulars respecting Neilson,' writes Moore, 'it cannot fail to have struck the reader that some share of the suspicion of having betrayed Lord Edward attaches to this man.' Moore's book attained a wide circulation, and the descendants of Neilson naturally felt the wounding words. A letter of his daughter strongly protests against them, and expresses a hope that allowance will be made 'for the indignant feelings of a child who has always been proud of her father's character.' Colonel Miles Byrne, a shrewd head which narrowly escaped the axe in '98, failed to endorse the imputation on Neilson, but hesitated not to declare that Lord Edward had been 'betrayed, and discovered by Reynolds, a United Irishman, to the agents of Government.'[1] In this random shot the Colonel missed his mark. The flaming patriot, Walter Cox, often states in his magazine that Laurence Tighe had shadowed to death the Geraldine chief. Thereupon Dr. Brennan, in the 'Milesian Magazine,' broadly charged Cox with the perfidy. Murphy, an honest, simple man, in whose house Lord Edward was taken, has not been exempted from suspicion. 'Lord Edward's concealment,' observes Patrick Brophy, 'became known through a soldier who was courting Murphy's servant girl;' forgetting that Thomas Moore, in his account of the arrest, incidentally remarks: 'an *old* maid-servant was the only person in Murphy's house besides themselves.' Maxwell, in his 'History of the Rebellion,' said of Neilson, 'Thou art the man.' Mark O'Callaghan, in his 'Life of O'Connell,' brands John Hughes as having received 1,000*l.* for Lord Edward's blood, thus endorsing the indictment previously framed by Dr. Madden.[2] The son and biographer of

[1] *Memoirs of Miles Byrne*, iii. 247. (Paris: Bossange, 1863.)

[2] 'Dr. Madden,' writes the Rev. James Wills, 'mentions a train of circumstances which seems to fasten the imputation on Hughes.'—*Lives of Illustrious*

Reynolds flings suspicion on Murphy; while Murphy, in his own account, says: 'I heard in prison that one of Lord Edward's bodyguard had given some information.' Again, Felix Rourke was suspected, and narrowly escaped death at the hands of his comrades. Suspicion also attached to Mr. Ogilvie, who, as a near connection, visited Lord Edward in Thomas Street a few days before the arrest, and transacted business with him. Interesting as it is, after near a century's speculation, to know the name of the real informer, it is still more satisfactory that those unjustly suspected should now be finally acquitted.

'On the 18th of May' [1798], writes Mr. Froude, 'Major Sirr received communications from a quarter unhinted at in the most secret letters of the Viceroy, telling him where Lord Edward could be found.'[1] I proceed to point out 'the quarter.'

In 1841 Dr. Madden obtained access to a book in which Mr. Cooke, formerly Under-Secretary at Dublin Castle, had made secret entries of various payments to informers. Amongst these items is: 'June 20, 1798, F. H. discovery of L. E. F. 1,000*l.*' Although Cooke disclosed merely the initials 'F. H.,' he gave the name in full when recommending the informer for a pension. Writing to Lord Castlereagh in 1799, Mr. Cooke says: 'Francis Higgins,[2] proprietor of the "Freeman's Journal," was the person who procured for me all the intelligence respecting Lord Edward Fitzgerald, and got —— to set him, *and has given me much information*, 300*l.*' This 300*l.* was an annual stipend.

Irishmen, vi. 51. Years after, in his new edition, Madden suggests suspicion against one Joel Hulbert (i. 85; ii. 443). Eventually, however, Dr. Madden wrote: 'And now, at the conclusion of my researches on this subject of the betrayal of Lord Edward Fitzgerald, I have to confess they have not been successful. The betrayer still preserves his incognito; his treachery, up to the present time (January 1858), remains to be connected with his name, and once discovered, to make it odious for evermore. . . . Nine-and-fifty years the secret of the sly, skulking villain has been kept by his employers, with no common care for his character or his memory.'—See *Lives of the United Irishmen*, by R. R. Madden, ii. 446, 2nd ed.

[1] Froude, iii. 342.

[2] *Cornwallis Correspondence*, iii. 320.

The 'Freeman's Journal' at this time was the organ of Dublin Castle, and it is stated in a memoir of Secretary Cooke that he had written for that paper. Hence a frequent intercourse subsisted between Cooke and Higgins; and the evidence is conclusive as to Higgins having received the Government reward. But the person of whose good name Cooke is so careful that in writing to Castlereagh he considerately puts a blank for it, was not so easily traced when first I took up this inquiry. Mr. Ross, editor of the 'Cornwallis Papers,' who was allowed to ransack the archives at Dublin Castle, writes: 'The man who gave the information which led to his [Lord Edward's] arrest, received 1,000*l.*, *but his name has never transpired.*'

The point is now to prove that Francis Magan, M.A., barrister-at-law, a man traditionally described as one of the most unsociable of men, was the private friend and political ally of Higgins.

Thomas Magan, of High Street, Dublin, was the father of Francis. The leading journal of that city, in its issue of June 30, 1787, records how, on the previous evening, 'Mr. Magan, of High Street, entertained Mr. Francis Higgins' and others. 'The glass circulated freely, and the evening was spent with the utmost festivity and sociality.' The editor concludes by styling him '*Honest* Tom Magan.' On November 5, 1789, he returns to the charge:—

Mr. Magan, the woollen-draper in High Street, in conjunction with his friend Mr. Higgins, are preparing ropes and human brutes to drag the new Viceroy to the palace. It was Mr. Magan and the Sham Squire who provided the materials for the triumphal entry of Lord Buckingham into the capital.[1] . . . Mr. Magan is really clever, and never has flinched in his partiality and attention to the

[1] The Viceroy, whose carriage Magan and Higgins hired a mob to draw triumphantly through the streets, was Lord Temple, afterwards Marquis of Buckingham, twice Chief Governor of Ireland, and of whom Mr. Grattan writes: 'He opposed many good measures, promoted many bad men, increased the expenses of Ireland in a manner wanton and profligate, and vented his wrath upon the country.'

cause of Mr. Francis Higgins—Mr. Magan has the honour, and that frequently, to dine Higgins.[1]

From an old Directory it appears that Tom Magan's loyal zeal was acknowledged about this time by his appointment as 'Woollen Draper and Mercer to His Majesty'[2]—one of the few paltry boons to which, in penal days, a slavish Catholic trader dare aspire. In 1793 a Catholic Relief Bill passed, and the bar was opened to Papists—a concession due to the menacing attitude of the United Irishmen and the boom of the French Revolution. Tom Magan's son, Francis, entered Trinity College, Dublin; graduated in 1794; and became a member of the bar—probably on the suggestion of Higgins, who was an attorney. In 1795 Francis Magan left the parental roof-tree in High Street and took house for himself at 20 Usher's Island, where he continued to live until his death in 1843. This house having been the residence of the Catholic Archbishop of Dublin, Dr. Carpenter, who died there a few years previously, was regarded reverentially by the survivors of his flock.

'Will no one urge Lord Edward to fly—I pledge myself that every port in the kingdom shall be left open to him'—said Lord Chancellor Clare. But money was to be made of his blood; and vampire instincts must needs be sated. The arrest was not effected until Saturday, May 19, although a proclamation promising 1,000*l*. as its price had been out since March.

[1] *Dublin Evening Post*, No. 1767. The same journal adds:—'It was in Mr. Magan's house in High Street that the creditable certificate of the clergy of Rosemary Lane Chapel was written and obtained.' It may be explained that when the moralist, Magee, denounced Higgins as one who had defied the laws of God and man, an advertisement, purporting to come from the priests of Rosemary Lane Chapel, said that they had no official or other knowledge of an imposture alleged to have been committed twenty-three years previously by Mr. Francis Higgins, and adding that, during his residence in Smock Alley, his conduct had been marked by benevolence. 'This sprig of Rosemary,' commented the *Post*, 'may serve to revive the fainting innocence of the immaculate convert of Saint Francis!' Magan, as a leading Catholic parishioner, had much weight with the clergy.

[2] *Dublin Directory*, 1790.

Higgins, who constantly transmitted the result of his espionage to Dublin Castle, was now more than ordinarily on the *qui vive*. At Moira House, Usher's Island, Pamela, wife of Lord Edward, sometimes stayed. In March, Leinster House, Kildare Street, was searched by soldiers—on which occasion Major Swan said to Lady Edward: 'This is an unpleasant duty for any gentleman to perform.'—'It is a task which no gentleman *would* perform,' was the reply.[1] She little dreamed that men whose friendship she valued were playing a part still more ungentlemanly. On this occasion Lord Edward narrowly escaped; thenceforth he avoided both Leinster House and Moira House, unless for stealthy visits, and for weeks he remained hidden at Portobello near Dublin.

Thomas Moore, when engaged on the 'Life of Lord Edward,' had an interview with Major Sirr, and learned from him that on May 17,[2] 1798, 'he received information that a party of persons, supposed to be Lord Edward Fitzgerald's bodyguard, would be on their way from Thomas Street to Usher's Island that night.' Their destination, Moore adds, he had failed to discover. I am in a position to show, however, that the party were on their way to the house of Francis Magan and his sister, in Usher's Island. Mr. James Moore, of 119 Thomas Street, had given Lord Edward shelter when 1,000*l*. lay on his head; but a carpenter named Tuite—who worked in Dublin Castle, and knew Moore—having overheard Cooke say that Moore's house should be searched, gave a timely hint to Moore, who therefore fled to Meath, previously telling his daughter to provide for Lord Edward's safety. Francis Magan and his sister were well known and respected by Miss Moore. She conferred with Magan on the subject, and an arrangement was made that Lord Edward should move that night from Moore's in Thomas Street to Usher's

[1] It was during this anxious period that Lord Edward, venturing out at night, had an interview with Pamela in Denzille Street, when their little child was taken from its cot to see its father, and a servant suddenly entering the room found the parents in tears.

[2] It should be Friday, May 18, as appears from Sirr's original memorandum.

Island and occupy a bedroom in Magan's house.[1] But it was suggested that, as two or three people knocking at his hall door on Usher's Island might attract attention, it would be safer to admit them by his stable in Island Street, which lay immediately at the rear. The biographer of Lord Edward knew nothing of Miss Moore's arrangement with Magan; but he casually mentions that the Government received information of his lordship's intended visit to Usher's Island. Major Sirr, attended by a guard, proceeded to the quarter pointed out; a conflict between the parties took place; 'and,' adds the biographer, 'Sirr in defending himself lost his footing and fell; and had not those with whom he was engaged been much more occupied with their noble charge than with him, he could hardly have escaped. But their chief object being Lord Edward's safety, after snapping a pistol or two at Sirr they hurried away.'[2]

Several volumes containing the original correspondence of Major Sirr are now preserved in the library of Trinity College, Dublin. Amongst them is the following letter:—

Lord Edward will be this evening[3] in Watling Street. Place a watch in Watling Street, two houses up from Usher's Island,[4] another towards Queen's Bridge;[5] a third in Island Street, at the rear of the stables near Watling Street, and which leads up to Thomas Street and Dirty Lane. At one of these places Lord Edward will be found, and will have one or two with him. They may be armed. Send to Swan and Atkinson as soon as you can.[6]

EDWARD COOKE.

[1] Statement of Mr. William Macready, the grandson of Moore, furnished exclusively to the present writer.

[2] *Life and Death of Lord Edward Fitzgerald*, by Thomas Moore. Paris ed. p. 160.

[3] May 18, 1798.

[4] Lest he should arrive at the hall door.

[5] Dirty Lane, now Bridgefoot Street, was another route by which Lord Edward could come from Moore's. The Queen's Bridge is at the foot of Dirty Lane. Island Street runs parallel with Usher's Island, a suburban quay; and Magan's is the second stable from Watling Street.

[6] Major Swan was the assistant town major. Atkinson will be remembered as the chief constable of Belfast. See *ante*, p. 8.

Cooke, with due consideration for the feelings of Magan and Higgins, does not tell Sirr from whom the information came; but the plot now thickens, and will be soon made clear.

Miss Moore—afterwards Mrs. Macready—died in 1844. To her son, she said:—'The Government got timely information that we were going to Usher's Island. Now this intention was known only to Magan and me; even Lord Edward did not know our destination until just before starting. If Magan is innocent, then I am the informer.'

On the day after Magan's apparently humane arrangement with Miss Moore he called at her house, anxiously inquiring if aught had happened, as he had waited up until the small hours, and yet Lord Edward did not come! Miss Moore, not suspecting Magan, replied: 'We were stopped in Watling Street; we hurried back to Thomas Street, where we providentially succeeded in getting Lord Edward a room at Murphy's.' Mr. Magan, satisfied by the explanation, leisurely withdrew, but, no doubt, quickened his gait on reaching the street. That evening, at four o'clock, Murphy's house was surrounded by soldiers, and Lord Edward, after a desperate resistance, was secured, and conveyed in a sedan-chair to the Castle.

Higgins claimed, and received, 1,000*l.* as the price. How much was given by him to the 'setter,' or what precise agreement subsisted between them, I have no document to show. A pension was bestowed upon Magan, and I find in the Secret Service account the following entry: 'September 11, 1800—Magan, per Mr. Higgins, 300*l.*'

The name of Thomas Magan, the father of the betrayer, disappears from the Directory in 1797—from which I, at first, inferred that his death occurred about that time. But it now appears that he subsided into bankruptcy. On May 2, 1798, the assignees of Thomas Magan, woollen-draper, a bankrupt, grant to John Corballis, for the consideration of 690*l.*, some house property belonging to Magan.[1] This date is worthy of

[1] The premises were on Wood Quay (then known as 'Pudding Row'), Wine Tavern Street, and Fisher's Alley; they also included the 'Dog and Duck' inn,

attention; it is one fortnight before the arrest of Lord Edward Fitzgerald. The difficulties of the Magan family had been gathering for some years. They commenced in 1793, when Higgins lent Thomas Magan 1,000*l.*; and three years later, as will be seen, another thousand. 'The borrower is servant to the lender,' saith the proverb. Further search in the Registry of Deeds Office, Dublin, discloses two additional mortgages from Thomas Magan, senior, to Francis Higgins —one for 2,341*l.*, another for 1,000*l.* The 'witness is Francis Magan.'[1] Their date is July 7, 1796, when very serious embarrassments threatened the family. How closely Shamado's toils[2] grasped father and son is now clear; and let us hope that when Francis Magan was persuaded by his tempter to sell Lord Edward's blood, he muttered, not without emotion, 'My poverty, and not my will, consents.'[3]

The name 'James Dixon' appears in the private list, supplied by Mr. Froude, of those who constituted the executive Committee of the United Irishmen in 1795, and 'by whom the whole organisation was managed.' Dr. Madden does not seem to know this, and says merely[4] that 'James Dickson hospitably treated and succoured on all occasions the families of the State prisoners.' The late Mathias O'Kelly told me that one of the few persons with whom Magan lived, in early life, on

north side of Thomas Street, with a rear extending to Marshalsea Lane.—*Registry of Deeds Office.* Traces of other property held by Thomas Magan crop up in unlooked-for places. By the settlement of Philip Whitfield Harvey with Miss Frances Tracy, dated September 16, 1802, it is recited that Thomas Magan, having become a bankrupt, his properties at Blackstaheny and in Britain Street were sold by auction to Samuel Dick and a Mr. Halpin for the sum of 4,830*l.* Higgins had property of his own at Blackstaheny, for I find a conveyance of lands there in 1806 from the Harveys and Tracys to Andrew Rorke of Clonsilla; consideration, 1,084*l.* 12*s.* 6*d.*

[1] Magan's seal displays a boar's head, with the motto 'Virtute et probitate'!

[2] A nickname by which the popular journalist, John Magee, satirised Higgins.

[3] It was whispered that Francis Magan may have been the godson of Francis Higgins, and baptised Francis in compliment to him. The Catholic baptismal registries of the parish do not go back sufficiently far to throw light; but, inasmuch as Thomas Magan married, in October 1770, the daughter of *Francis* Kiernan, merchant, their son would be very naturally called after the grandfather.

[4] *United Irishmen*, iv. 25.

terms of intimacy was 'James Dickson, of Kilmainham,' and that he had repeatedly met Magan at Dixon's house. 'Dixon was deeper in the confidence of the rebel party than many more prominent leaders,' adds O'Kelly. 'He took the chair at the meeting of United Irishmen which had been convened to thank Napper Tandy for challenging Attorney-General Toler, afterwords Lord Norbury; and he was twice imprisoned for alleged complicity in the rebellion.' But the Government treated him with a consideration extended to few others; and, on the grounds of ill-health, he was permitted to leave Kilmainham Gaol daily on short riding excursions.[1]

Undemonstrative in his habits, it is not easy to trace him in the scanty reports of contemporary newspapers. On May 17, 1797, a meeting of barristers was held urging the Government to 'yield to the moderate wishes of the people, and thereby defeat the designs of any party dangerous to the country;' and amongst the seventy-three signatories, with Francis Magan, were T. A. Emmet, H. Sheares (afterwards hanged), Robert Orr, B. B. Harvey (commander at Vinegar Hill in '98, and also hanged), W. Sampson, Robert Holmes, J. Philpot Curran, L. McNally, and many other popular men, some recognised as members of the United Irish Society, such as Joseph Huband, and W. Newton Bennett, afterwards a chief justice.[2] The subsequent Baron, Smith, is there too with Robert Johnson, dismissed from the bench in 1806, and George Ponsonby, afterwards Lord Chancellor. In 1797 they stood upon a pitfall, but by a miracle escaped.

Francis Magan posed through life as the pink of propriety. Before the last century closed he had strong claims for secret service; but I cannot doubt, knowing his quiet and somewhat nervous nature, that whatever information he gave must have been communicated through Higgins. The latter owned a newspaper, which was the openly subsidised organ of the Government. He constantly assailed the popular party with

[1] This would give Magan an opportunity of meeting and discoursing with his old friend.

[2] *Dublin Evening Post*, Tuesday, May 23, 1797.

invective; so that, unless through Magan, he could have had no opportunity of approaching the patriots, much less sucking their brains.

My contention as regards Magan was first expressed in a 'Note on the Cornwallis Papers' printed thirty years ago,[1] and it is with no small interest that I now find all my suspicions confirmed by Magan's own letters. The letters of Higgins to Cooke claiming blood-money for Magan form the crowning proof of that which at first was mere theory. Magan was an informer of the most mercenary type—constantly tendering his services, and withholding information when coin ceased to clink.

The earliest mention of Magan by name is in 1797; the reports of Higgins are specially full at that date, no doubt the fruit of intercourse with Magan, who was completely his creature. One, undated, says: 'On Wednesday last, Jackson, Dixon, Magan, and a large party dined at McKinley's, opposite Kilmainham Gaol. The two first went into the prison, and distributed money which the prisoners had wrote for.'

Many letters follow. Higgins told enough to show how important a spy Magan could become if betrayal were made

[1] Dublin: W. B. Kelly. Long out of print. The Rev. Dr. Stokes, Professor of Ecclesiastical History, Trinity College, Dublin, in the *Mail* of October 14, 1885, stated that this pamphlet 'may be found in the library of Trinity College, Dublin, Gallery H. 10, vol 92.' The brochure had been printed mainly for the purpose of correcting a mis-statement made by the *Athenæum*, when reviewing the *Cornwallis Papers*. The *Athenæum*, then edited by W. Hepworth Dixon, far from resenting my correction, reviewed the book in terms which stimulated further efforts, and, if any excuse for them were needed, it is supplied in that too favourable judgment. See No. 1649 p. 744. 'This biography reads like so many pages out of Mr. Lever's *Con Cregan, or the Irish Gil Blas*; but Mr. Fitzpatrick quotes several legal and literary documents to authenticate his text. Facts in abundance are produced. As illustrative of the state of Irish political society in those days, this tract is extremely curious. With extraordinary power of social research, an intimacy is established between the hateful Higgins and Magan; . . . most curious circumstantial evidence, to criminate Magan. This tract merits preservation. The mass of social and personal knowledge accumulated by Mr. Fitzpatrick is very striking. He writes like an *ex post facto* Boswell, and the research with which he amasses minute particulars is a speciality with him. It is for want, heretofore, of detailed and accurate domestic knowledge, that Irish history is so crude and colourless; and works like those of Mr. Fitzpatrick have value.'

worth his while. On December 29, 1797, he writes: 'You have not, dear Sir, determined as to M. At such a momentous and critical period . . . every intelligence should be obtained for Government.' [1]

But is the proof certain that 'M.' means Magan? Higgins four days later returns to the charge, adding: You have said nothing about Magan, and will let his information slip through your hands, as he is about to go down to Belfast, and thence to England.' [2]

Higgins and Magan, strange to say, did not know that the democratic barrister, McNally, was already in pay as a spy. Part of the information furnished concerns McNally's movements, which may have made Cooke indifferent as regards some of the letters. Higgins, on January 3, 1798, reports that at the pillorying of Finnerty, Lord Edward, O'Connor, Bond, Sheares and McNally attended the rebel as a mark of sympathy. Magan was hungry for Lord Edward's blood; and Cooke must needs be brought at once to business. On January 5, 1798, Higgins says he will 'fix Magan to meet Cooke at dinner,' and 'shall in the course of to-day or to-morrow give you a hint of his terms.'

The dinner did its work. The ill-fated priest O'Coigly—or Quigly—was now 'wanted,' but meanwhile other wants must needs be satisfied.

M. wants money, and I am sure will serve your intention [Higgins writes]; let him have it, and I will bring you his receipt. I shall also send him in quest of Quigly.[3] Permit me, however, to mention that you have not half sufficiently examined M. I shall, therefore, set down an outline for you, or obtain him to attend when you can be more particular.[4]

Four days later he writes:—

M. dines with Jackson,[5] etc., to-morrow. He promises to have many particulars. Two days before O'Connor sailed for England,

[1] Higgins to Cooke, December 29, 1797. [2] *Idem*, January 2, 1798.

[3] O'Coigly left for London on his luckless mission, and Magan lost sight of him. [4] Higgins to Cooke, January 12, 1798.

[5] Henry Jackson, a very active member of the Rebel Directory, and father-in-law of Oliver Bond.

M——, Emmet, and Lord Edward Fitzgerald dined with Fallon on settling a plan as to Galway. Fallon is a man of property.[1]

A bundle of letters covering six weeks follows. Magan feigned to be the attached friend of his victims, and was so entirely trusted that they resolved to give him higher office in the rebel executive.

M. wishes you to send wt [what] was promised on the 28th. He is to be elected into office.[2]

A letter dated March 7, 1798, contains a long account from Magan, through Higgins, regarding persons from Belfast and Wexford, recently forming deputations from their committees. 'He is to be with me at 12 o'clock to-morrow. I request you will be so good as to recollect sending to me for him as promised.' Magan was duly pumped, and Higgins, on March 15, writes: 'M. was with me this day, and seemed as if I had received a second 100*l.* for him. For God's sake send it, and don't let me appear in so awkward a situation.' And on March 23, 1798, Higgins writes:

M. became quite offended that I did not send wt was promised. He has not communicated anything to me for the ten days past, tho I know he must have much information to give in.

The money was sent, and Magan's tattle was resumed.

This night there is to be a meeting at Lawless's.[3] I shall learn to-morrow the nature of it. I would wish to put you in possession of something M. knows of, that you may ask and interrogate him about them, and let him agree to come to a fixed point of information. I know it is (or will be from his late election) in his power.[4]

Raised to a post of trust and authority in the organisation, Magan's power of betrayal became, of course, largely increased. He had hitherto communicated solely through

[1] John Fallon, Esq., J.P. and D.L., born April 6, 1767. Higgins to Cooke, January 16, 1798.

[2] Higgins to Cooke, February 26, 1798.

[3] Lawless was Professor of Physiology in the College of Surgeons; but, on finding that a warrant was out for his arrest, got safely to France, where he rose to the rank of General, and lost a leg at Leipzig.

[4] Higgins to Cooke, March 28, 1798.

Higgins. Stimulated by reward, he now addressed Cooke direct, but anonymously. Cooke, however, has endorsed the letter 'Mag.' It is dated not from Usher's Island, where he lived, but from Higgins' house in Stephen's Green, and the handwriting is the same as that in a later document with an acknowledged signature.

I did not receive your promised favour till Easter Monday last, and on reading your letter requested Mr. H. to know your leisure for an interview. . . . He wrote me a most pressing letter not to leave town. . . . At the risk of my personal safety I accompanied him in a carriage to your door. . . . I have *all along* had in contemplation to put you in possession of some act that would essentially serve the Government as well as the country, and it may not be very long till such is effected. At present perhaps you may not know that Lord Edward lurks about town and its vicinity; he with Nelson was a few days ago in the custody of a patrol in the neighbourhood of Lucan, but not being known and assuming other names, they were not detained for any length of time.[1] Nelson is now the most active man, and affects, if he really does not hold, the first situation. For my part I sometimes imagine he is the person that communicated with Government; however, suspicion has not pointed at him.[2] His absence, I know, at the present moment would be considered as very fatal to the cause in Dublin. I have just this moment heard Lord Edward has been mostly in Thomas Street.[3]

On May Day 1798, when boys and girls were rejoicing, and the May-pole at Finglas was the scene of a festivity in glad welcome of the coming flowers, Higgins writes in great fuss to Cooke that a more formidable rising was at hand, adding: 'If you can see M. this night, you can bring out where Lord Edward is concealed.' 'What hour shall I bring M. this night, if your leisure will permit? Remember to bring him to a point—I mean about Lord Edward.' But his lordship's

[1] Moore mentions that Lord Edward and Neilson were stopped, at midnight by the patro. at Palmerstown; but the former having personated a doctor hurrying to the elie of a patient, both were suffered to resume their journey.

[2] The accurate nformation on other points which daily reached Cooke convinced not a few United Irishmen that treachery was at work.

[3] Magan to Cooke, April 22, 1798.

frequent change of abode baulked the projected capture. Mr. Lecky considers that the search must have been made with singular languor to produce such little fruit. It should be remembered, however, that no police force deserving the name existed in Dublin; and that arrests were usually made, as in Lord Edward's case, by soldiers.

On May 15 Higgins wrote to Cooke:—

M. seems mortified that when he placed matters within the reach of Government the opportunity was neglected. . . . Lord Edward skulks from house to house—has watches and spies around who give an account of any danger being near. It is intended he shall go into the country (it is thought Kildare) and make a rising. Give me leave to remind you of sending to M.

Magan is shown to have met Lord Edward at council at this time, but it was not easy to seize the chief on such occasions. Higgins was the Castle journalist, and could throw off letters with ease. Mr. Lecky says that his missives to Cooke would be found most useful material in illustrating the history of his time; and, no doubt, they are destined some day to see the light. Higgins uniformly writes of Lord Edward as a monster of evil, but it is due to the ill-fated Geraldine to say that men whose testimony ranks far higher record a different estimate.[1] Lord Holland, a Cabinet minister, thus writes of him:—

More than twenty years have now passed away. Many of my political opinions are softened—my predilections for some men weakened, my prejudices against others removed; but my approbation of Lord Edward Fitzgerald's actions remains unaltered and unshaken. His country was bleeding under one of the hardest tyrannies that our times have witnessed.[2]

[1] It is also due to Lord Edward's memory to remind the reader that Higgins was a man of leprosied reputation. Nearly thirty years ago, I gave some account of him in *Ireland before the Union*. Meanwhile, the reader might see what an English historian, Mr. Plowden, says of him, *vide* p. 266 *infra*. I printed in the *Sham Squire* the original informations against Higgins for the basest fraud, the true bills found against him by the Grand Jury in 1766, and the records of his committals to Newgate.

[2] *Memoirs of the Whig Party*.

If he had personal ambition to gratify, the powerful influence of his family could easily have fed it to repletion. His life was one of sacrifice and attests the sincerity of his soul.

Higgins thought that Cooke was not sufficiently alive to the importance of Magan's hints. He now tells Cooke that an attack on Dublin Castle had been proposed and adopted, but this information may have been embellished to rouse the Irish Government. 'M. thinks it is on the ensuing Tuesday or Wednesday, but will be certain for your information,' he writes. 'He says the 300*l.* promised should have been given at once. . . . However, I have given him leave to draw upon me, and fully satisfied him of the honourable intentions of Government where service was actually performed, and of your kind attention if he would go forward among the meetings, communicate what is transacting, and, if found necessary, point out the spot where they may be seized, etc. This he has at length agreed to do.'[1]

The reader will remember Magan's arrangement with Miss Moore that, for Lord Edward's greater safety, the noble fugitive was to shift his quarters from James Moore's house to Magan's. The latter, to screen himself from suspicion, felt anxious that Lord Edward's capture should be made in the street.

> . . . I also mentioned your kind promise of obtaining 1000*l.* for him (without the mention of his name or enrolment of it in any book) on having the business done, which he pointed out before the issuing of the proclamation. He, therefore, puts himself on your honour not to admit of any person to come and search his house (which I ventured to promise you would have observed), but to place watches after dusk, this night near the end of Watling Street or two houses up in that street from Usher's Island . . . [here the pith of Mr. Cooke's letter, see p. 122 *ante*, is given], and at one of these places they will find Lord Edward disguised. He wears a wig and may have been otherwise metamorphosed, attended by one or two, but followed by several armed banditti with new daggers. He intends to give battle if not suddenly seized.[2]

[1] Higgins to Under-Secretary Cooke, May 18, 1798. [2] *Idem.*

The 'armed banditti' consisted merely of Mrs. and Miss Moore, Gallagher, a clerk in Moore's employ, and a man named Palmer.[1] This is the account furnished to me in a most circumstantial statement by the late Mr. Macready, the son of Miss Moore. She had been educated in Tours; Lord Edward always conversed with her in French, and he usually passed as her French tutor. The hour was 8.30 in a lovely May evening. Palmer and Gallagher walked some yards in advance, and were the first to come in contact with Sirr's party at the corner of Island Street. Sirr gave Gallagher an ugly wound which afterwards favoured identification. The latter, a powerful man, made two or three stabs at Sirr, who fell in the struggle, but, as he wore a coat of mail, he was able, after a few moments, to regain his feet. Lord Edward was also in handigrips with one of Sirr's guard; both came to the ground, but with no more ill result to his lordship than some unsightly daubs of mud on his coat. In the confusion the ladies hurried back with their noble charge to Thomas Street, leaving Palmer and Gallagher to hold Sirr at bay. The party abandoned their design of going to Magan's, though not from any distrust of his fidelity, and obtained shelter for Lord Edward in the house of a faithful adherent named Murphy with whom he had previously stayed. Miss Moore told Magan next day the whole adventure, and how the retreat had been safely effected. Lord Edward was lying on his bed in Murphy's attic, after having drunk some whey to relieve a bad cold, when Major Swan and Captain Ryan peeped in at the door, exclaiming that resistance would be vain. At once Fitzgerald started up like a lion from his lair and rushed at Swan. Revolvers were as yet unknown and his pistol missed fire; he then drew a dagger. The account furnished by Swan to a Government print states:—

His lordship then closed upon Mr. Swan, shortened the dagger, and gave him a stab in the side, under the left arm and breast, having first changed it from one hand to the other over his shoulder (as Mr. Swan thinks). Finding the blood running from him, and

[1] Afterwards known to Turner at Hamburg, p. 14 *ante*.

the impossibility to restrain him, he was compelled, in defence of his life, to discharge a double-barrelled pistol at his lordship, which wounded him in the shoulder: he fell on the bed, but, recovering himself, ran at him with the dagger, which Mr. Swan caught by the blade with one hand, and endeavoured to trip him up.[1]

Here Captain Ryan came upon the scene, but his flint lock missed fire; and thereupon he lurched at Lord Edward with a sword-cane, which bent on his ribs. Sirr had been engaged in placing pickets round the house, when the report of Swan's pistol brought him upstairs.

On my arrival in view of Lord Edward, Ryan, and Swan [writes Major Sirr, in a letter addressed to Ryan's son], I beheld his lordship standing with a dagger in his hand as if ready to plunge it into my friends, while dear Ryan, seated on the bottom step of the flight of the upper stairs, had Lord Edward grasped with both his arms by the legs or thighs, and Swan in a somewhat similar situation, both labouring under the torment of their wounds, when, without hesitation, I fired at Lord Edward's dagger arm, and the instrument of death fell to the ground. Having secured the titled prisoner, my first concern was for your dear father's safety. I viewed his intestines with grief and sorrow.

Lord Edward, in fact, had completely ripped him open. Although Sirr had lodged several slugs in his lordship's right shoulder, he continued to fight furiously until the soldiers, of whom more than 200 were present, overwhelmed him by pressing their heavy firelocks across his person. They had brought him as far as the hall, when he made another desperate effort to escape, and a drummer from behind stabbed him in the neck.[2] Previous to this scene Higgins plied Cooke with gossip from Magan, as the case about to be cited will show.

The nickname applied to Pamela in the following extract was due to a popular rumour that her parents were Madame de Genlis and Philippe Egalité, Duke of Orleans: 'Lady

[1] *The Express*, May 26, 1798.

[2] Mr. Froude says that 'Lord Edward was naturally a powerful man' (iii. 343). This impression is not accurate. Jasper Joly, LL.D., son of Lord Edward's godson, tells me that 'he was a small, wiry man.'

Egality complains dreadfully about Lord Castlereagh ordering a short passport. She will have letters sewed or quilted in her clothes, and goes to Hamburg. I shall send you particulars.'[1]

Lady Fitzgerald was at this time at Moira House, within a few doors of Magan; and the concluding words go to show that he had access to the house, and was entirely conversant with its domestic doings; the status, politics and attainments of so near a neighbour would facilitate access to its gilded salons.[2] Lord Edward probably sent, through Magan, messages to Pamela. Magan acted his part so plausibly that on the very night Lord Edward lay a bleeding captive in Newgate, he was raised by the votes of United Irishmen to a still higher post in the organisation.

Lord Edward had been arrested in Murphy's house; and Mr. Lecky remarks[3] that there is no mention of the place in the letters of Higgins. The latter, to save time, may have given the hint orally. Higgins resided within twelve minutes' walk of Cooke's office. Mr. Lecky states:[4] 'He [Higgins] was accustomed to go openly and frequently to the Castle.' Cooke told Sirr that if he would go on the following day, between five and six P.M., to the house of Murphy in Thomas Street, he would find Lord Edward there.[5]

On May 20, when Lord Edward was dying of his wounds in Newgate, Magan furnishes through Higgins fresh hints, and promises further information 'to-morrow.' 'He was elected last night of the committee,' adds Higgins. 'I had a great deal of exertion to go through to keep him steady, and was obliged last week to advance him money.' On June 8 Higgins writes: 'I cannot get from M. a single sentence of who

[1] Francis Higgins to Under Secretary Cooke, May 18, 1798.

[2] John Wesley visited Moira House in 1775, and has described the splendour of its rooms, one of which was inlaid throughout with 'mother-of-pearl.' The spiritualised philosopher adds, 'and must this pass away like a dream?' But he did not live to see, as Magan did, Moira House the *refugium* of hunger, rags, and dirt—a 'Mendicity Institution.'

[3] Lecky, viii. 44.

[4] *Ibid.* vii. 211.

[5] *Life of Reynolds*, by his Son.

assumes a Directory. I have so frequently put him off about the payment of the 1,000*l*. that he thinks I am humbugging him.'[1]

It will be remembered that, according to a secret entry of Cooke's, 1,000*l*. was paid on June 20 to 'F. H.' for the discovery of 'L. E. F.,' and he observed the compact that Magan's name should not appear. Magan thought that there was an effort to 'humbug' him as regards the blood-money which he earned, but he knew how to 'humbug' a little himself. Higgins, setting forth his own claims, tells Cooke, later on: 'By your interference Mr. M. obtained 300*l*. for expenses; give me leave solemnly to assure you that I paid every possible expense he was at, and more than I can mention.'[2]

Magan was one of the first Catholic barristers called after the Relief Bill of 1793, and wore an aspect highly demure and proper. He was a trump card in the hands of Higgins, which, if adroitly played, could not fail to clear the board. But with what a small share of the winnings Magan was content is consistent with all we know of his crawling career.[3] Arthur O'Connor, writing to Dr. Madden in 1842, says: 'So far as I could learn, no one betrayed Lord Edward'—a striking testimony to the secrecy with which the thing was done.[4]

Magan, the better to cloak his treachory, and to command that confidence the fruit of which was distilled into dainty

[1] Francis Higgins to Cooke, Stephen's Green, June 8, 1798. Quoted by Lecky. For curious facts about Higgins, see chapter xiv.: 'Father O'Leary.'

[2] Higgins to Cooke, June 13, 1801.

[3] The writer will be excused if he seems to linger on this theme; but from childhood 'Magan' has been to him a familiar household word. His grandfather, John Brett, lived next door to Magan's house at Usher's Island. Voices, long since hushed, often described their strange, silent neighbour, of whom it might be said, 'still waters run deep.' Brett, though not a rebel, had popular sympathies, and several patriots, including James Tandy, visited at his house. One day Major Sirr created a great scare at Brett's by instituting a search for pikes and papers. The hysterics of the young ladies and the protests of their brothers served only to stimulate his ardour. No nook was left unexplored, no stone unturned. The intruders even uprooted the flower-beds in the garden, hoping to make a discovery, but all in vain; and Sirr, with drooping plumage, at last withdrew.—See James Tandy's arrest, Appendix, *infra*.

[4] *United Irishmen*, ii. 234.

drops for Cooke's ear, continued to manifest popular sympathies. He went further, and on December 9, 1798, is found taking part against the Government in a debate and division, where his feeble voice could carry no influence, unless to deceive democratic friends. It was on the occasion of the bar meeting, in Dublin, convened to discuss and oppose the Legislative Union. The name of Francis Magan appears on the patriotic side, in company with Charles Kendal Bushe, B. Burton, Jonah Barrington, Peter Burrowes, John Philpot Curran, William Fletcher, W. Conyngham Plunket, George Ponsonby, and Leonard McNally.

Passing on to 1802, we find a round sum of 500*l.* slipped into the hands of Francis Magan on December 15 in that year, as appears by 'an account of Secret Service money applied in the detection of treasonable conspiracies.' This is the same amount which was given in 1848 for the discovery of Smith O'Brien, and again in September 1865 for Stephens, the Fenian head centre; while in 1798 only 300*l.* was offered for Neilson and General Lawless. The discovery which earned the reward of 500*l.* in December 1803 must have been esteemed of importance. What that discovery was has been hitherto involved in mystery; but the succeeding chapter, devoted to William Todd Jones, may help to make it clear. The 500*l.* is given to Magan direct, nearly eleven months after the death of Higgins, through whom Magan's information had been previously conveyed to Dublin Castle. He was now thrown on his own resources, and seems to have been less squeamish than of yore. Were Higgins then living the refresher might have been less, for 'Shamado' had no objection to a lion's share.

Magan continued successfully to preserve his mask. A great aggregate meeting was held on December 18, 1812, to protest against acts of the Irish Government, and among the signatures convening it are those of Daniel O'Connell and Francis Magan. This fact is brought out in a memoir of the Liberator by his son, who, however, does not suspect Magan.

It was a national crisis. Meetings in aid of Catholic Emancipation had just been forcibly dispersed. Lords Fingall, Netterville, and Ffrench were dragged from the seats in which, as chairmen, they presided. Other signatories who, with Magan, convened this meeting, were the three Catholic peers just mentioned, Dr. T. Dromgoole, Bernard Coyle, Sylvester Costigan, Con McLoughlin, and Fitzgerald of Geraldine—the latter five having been, as well as O'Connell, United Irishmen.

I was not surprised to hear from Mathias O'Kelly,[1] an old member of the Catholic Board and at one time secretary to the Catholic Association, that Magan possessed the respect and confidence of those bodies. He seemed to prove the sincerity of his sympathy in the most practical way, and rarely gave less than ten pounds as a subscription to their funds. It is, no doubt, to Magan that Wellington refers in his letter to Dublin Castle, dated London, November 17, 1808: 'I think that, as there are some interesting Catholic questions afloat now, you might feed —— with another 100*l*.'[2]

Dr. Dirham, who from his boyhood had resided on Usher's Island, heard it rumoured, he told me, that Magan during the troubled times kept frequently open the door of his stable in Island Street to facilitate espionage.[3] Moira House, now the 'Mendicity Institution,' is situated within a few doors of No. 20, Usher's Island, the residence for half a century of Francis Magan. As already mentioned, Pamela, the beautiful wife of Lord Edward Fitzgerald, received in the stormy period of '98 hospitable shelter from Lady Moira. To my surprise I find, in a manuscript life of Dwyer the outlaw, by the late Luke Cullen, a Carmelite friar, that two of Emmet's most active emissaries, Wylde and Mahon, lay concealed in Moira House

[1] O'Kelly held, from a close personal knowledge of the man, that he would be incapable of treachery.

[2] *Correspondence of the Duke of Wellington (Ireland)*, pp. 485–6.

[3] Two gardens belonged to Moira House: one in front of Island Street, the other at its opposite side. These gardens are separated by Island Street, which runs parallel with Usher's Island. A subterranean passage under the street communicates with both pleasure grounds. Usher's Island was formerly called Usher's Garden.

while a proclamation offering 500*l.*[1] for their capture was being widely circulated. Before this curious fact came to my knowledge, it will be seen, from a former work of mine dealing with informers, that on utterly distinct circumstantial evidence I sought to trace Magan as on the track of Wylde and Mahon at Philipstown during the same eventful year.

Major Sirr made a private note, which remains duly on record[2] that the retreat of Wylde and Mahon 'is sometimes at the gaoler's in Philipstown, who is married to Wylde's sister.' The following entry appears in the 'account of secret service money employed in detecting treasonable conspiracies per affidavit of Mr. Cooke': 'April 2, 1803. Francis Magan, by post to Philipstown—100*l.*'[3]

In the State Papers of the time I can find no letters bearing on this transaction, and therefore I must seek to trace it on circumstantial evidence.

Who can doubt that Magan, when a refresher reached him at Philipstown, was in hot scent after Wylde and Mahon? Later on, during the same year, we find Captain Caulfield and a party of military laying siege to the house at Philipstown in which Wylde and Mahon were thought to be concealed. An account of a skirmish is supplied by Captain Caulfield in a letter, dated December 17, 1803, also preserved in the Sirr papers: 'Captain Dodgson was killed, and,' adds Caulfield, 'we were obliged to retire, while the villains made their escape.'[4]

Luke Cullen, the Carmelite already referred to, spent his later life gathering from the peasantry their recollections of the

[1] The monk names this figure, but I think overstates it.

[2] The Sirr MSS., Trin. Coll. Dublin.

[3] In library of the Royal Irish Academy, Dublin.

[4] The Sirr MSS. This letter is quoted by Dr. Madden, who thinks that the information on which Dodgson and Caulfield acted came from Kildare; but it appears by the letter he himself prints (i. 522) that it came from Dublin. Caulfield's letter, addressed to Major Sirr, says, 'In consequence of *your* information, I reached Philipstown.' On the two previous occasions when Major Sirr had laid hands on Lord Edward Fitzgerald, the information as we see came from Magan. Dr. Madden, in printing the letter referred to above, erroneously assigns to it the date 1798; but the original MS. displays 'December 17, 1803.'

troubled times. His manuscript life of Dwyer has been placed in my hands by the superior of Clondalkin monastery. Folios 595 to 597 describe Wylde and Mahon's refuge at Philipstown, the abortive efforts to catch them there, and afterwards their concealment at Moira House, Dublin. The governor of Philipstown Gaol, we learn, was a near connection of both. They are stated by Cullen to have at last effected their escape from Moira House, Usher's Island, in a boat which rapidly passed out of the bay. Having reached the United States, Wylde and Mahon joined the army, and found speedy promotion. The statement that two proscribed men, most active propagandists of Emmet's plans, lay under Lord Moira's ægis seems startling; but this statesman and his countess had very popular sympathies, and liked to succour rebels. The late Mr. Thomas Geoghegan, solicitor, informed me that two uncles of his named Clements, who were United Irishmen, obtained refuge at Moira House while warrants were out for their arrest, and finally succeeded in escaping all pains and penalties owing to the precautions taken by Lady Moira.

It is not a little singular that General Lord Moira, who, later on, was offered the Viceroyalties of Ireland and of India, and who in 1812, on the death of Percival, sought to form an administration, should have performed the perilous task of harbouring men who loved Ireland 'not wisely, but too well.' Portland, in a letter to Camden, dated 11 March, 1798, classes with 'the disaffected,' 'Lord Moira and his adherents.' This impression was partly due to his indignant protest in Parliament against that policy of torture by which the people had been daily goaded to rebel.

Magan's life involved some strange contradictions. Proud, and even haughty, he yet hesitated not to commit base acts; with the wages of dishonour he paid his just debts. An interesting letter, in reply to a query, was addressed to the present writer by the late John Fetherstonhaugh, of Griffinstown, Kinnegad. His grandfather, Thomas Fetherston, of Bracket Castle, was, he states, in the habit for years of lodging in High Street, Dublin, at the house of Thomas Magan, a draper, 'and departed this life in his house.'[1] Fetherston's son, on inspecting his papers, found a joint bond from the draper and his son, Francis Magan, for 1,000*l.*, and on speaking to the former respecting its payment, he declared that he was insolvent.

So my father [adds Mr. Fetherston] put it into his desk, counting it waste paper. Some years elapsed and the son came to Bracket Castle, my father's residence, and asked for the bond. 'For what?' said my father. To his astonishment, he said it was to pay it. I was then but a boy, but I can now almost see the strange scene—it made so great an impression on me. Often my father told me Magan paid the 1,000*l.*, and he could not conceive where he got it, as he never held a brief in court; and he was always puzzled why the Crown gave him place and pension.[2]

James Dickson of Kilmainham has been more than once mentioned in these pages. As soon as he had been discharged from gaol, in the absence of evidence to convict him in a court of law, he opened his house for the entertainment and solace of the families of the State prisoners. But his guests were not confined wholly to the United Brotherhood. My informant, the late Mathias O'Kelly, often met there William Todd Jones, of whose arrest in 1803, on suspicion of complicity in Emmet's treason, pamphlets were published; Lord Kingsland,

[1] How Mr. Fetherston came to patronise Thomas Magan's lodgings, and otherwise to befriend him, was partly due to the fact that Magan had descended from a once opulent race in West Meath. *Vide* wills, in Irish Record Office, of Thomas Magan, Togherstown, co. W. Meath, dated 1710; and another, probably of his son, dated 1750. By a deed, dated May 2, 1798, it appears that James and John Fetherston had been trustees of the will of Mary Magan, the grandmother of Francis. The property of Papists in penal times was liable to discovery and forfeiture, and the help of friendly Protestants as trustees sometimes became a necessity. The first mention of the Magans, and of the Fetherstons as their trustees, is in 1763.

[2] Mr. Lecky has been kind enough to say (*History of England*, viii. 45) that I have 'thrown more light than any other writer on the career of Magan;' and he quotes the above as 'a very curious fact,' adding that it would be interesting to know if 'the transaction took place shortly after the death of Lord Edward.' As satisfaction of the bond might possibly have been 'entered,' I searched the records of the Four Law Courts, term after term, from 1798 to 1808, but no trace can be found. The above letter was addressed to me by the late Rev. John Fetherstonhaugh in 1860. The branch of the family which he then represented is extinct, and Griffinstown House is now occupied by strangers.

famous for a career of marvellous vicissitude; Mrs. Neilson, wife of the rebel leader, then imprisoned at Fort George; and Plowden, the popular historian, who gathered at Dickson's table much valuable information. The house was quite a centre of liberal opinion in Dublin, and no man shared Dickson's confidence more fully than Magan. Mathias O'Kelly greatly respected Magan, and thirty years ago, when I first started my suspicion, he laboured hard to convince me that I was entirely wrong. Magan told O'Kelly that he had been a member of the Society of United Irishmen, but withdrew from it when he saw it drifting into dangerous courses. The reverse is the fact. He played his part so well that at the time of his betrayals he was promoted to a high post in the rebel executive.[1]

In 1832 a brochure was 'printed for the author by William Shaw, Dublin,' which must have quickened the sluggish pulse of Mr. and Miss Magan. It was 'An Impartial Enquiry respecting the Betrayal of Lord Edward Fitzgerald,' by Joseph Hamilton. No charge was preferred against the Magans in this pamphlet. But conscience makes cowards; the probing given to a sore spot, and Hamilton's mention of 'Mr. Magan and his sister,' with others who knew of Lord Edward's movements previous to the arrest, proved distasteful at 20 Usher's Island.

Hamilton's labour was undertaken with the avowed object of clearing Neilson from a suspicion which Moore, in his Memoir

[1] The deliberate and mercenary way in which the respected 'counsellor' set himself to spy could be shown by fifty letters. Father Quigley, or O'Coigly, who, it will be remembered, was arrested at Margate in February on Turner's information (see chap. iii. *ante*), and suffered death soon after, escaped by a hair's breadth the net which Magan had been weaving for his capture in Dublin. A letter from Higgins to Under-Secretary Cooke, dated 'Stephen's Green, 12th January, 1798,' goes on to say: 'When I saw M—— this day and just mentioned Quigly's name, he gave me instantly a description of him. Met him before he went abroad often, and *was sheltered in Dixon's house.* Will, he is convinced, find him out. But I beg to recommend a strict watch on Dixon's and you will instantly discover him.' Four days later, *i.e.* January 16, 1798, Higgins tells Cooke, 'M—— went several times to Dixon's, but found no trace of Quigly at his former residence. Neither has he been at Dr. McNevin's. The only place that he can be sheltered among the party is at Bond's, and which will be known by Thursday.' Two previous letters, dated October 17, and October 30, 1797, report very fully Dickson's conversations with Magan.

of Lord Edward, ventured to start. Whether Moore, in gathering facts for his book, had been referred to the Magans, I know not, but he certainly returned to England strongly prejudiced against the incorruptible Neilson, and straightway framed an indictment bristling with innuendos.[1] Hamilton prints, with other vindicatory papers, letters from Hamilton Rowan and Dr. McNevin, also a touching protest from the daughter of Neilson. Hamilton knew Lord Edward well.

Dearer to me was Edward's life than Neilson's memory [he writes]. Dearer to me is Ireland than are Neilson's children and his friends. If I thought he was the man who could betray his generous friend and noble chieftain, I would leave his memory and his bones to rot together. I took up his vindication, not as a partial advocate; and in thus conducting his defence I will not endeavour to suppress a single fact which might go to justify the accusing passage in Lord Edward's 'Life.'

Mr. Hamilton proved Neilson guiltless, but he fell into the error, which a man blindfolded at play commits, in very often making a grasp in the wrong quarter. He suspects Reynolds; Captain Armstrong, who betrayed Sheares; 'a Mr. Hatton, one of the rebel Executive, *who unaccountably escaped*.'[2] Even Sir Jonah Barrington; nay, the estimable philanthropist, Mathias O'Kelly, who lived with his father at Galway's Walk, near the scene of Lord Edward's tussle with Sirr, was also mentioned in a suggestive way. 'On the 17th May,' writes Hamilton, 'Armstrong met both the Sheares, and on that evening Major Sirr was seen looking towards the rear of Miss

[1] Magan, to divert suspicion from himself, may have been the first to set the story going that Neilson was a base informer. Thomas Moore, after making inquiries in Dublin, returned home strong in suspicion that Neilson had betrayed Lord Edward. Magan, in his secret letters of 1798, sometimes seeks to convey that Neilson was giving information at Dublin Castle. One letter, dated April 22, 1798, says: 'I sometimes imagine he (Neilson) is the person who communicated with Government; however, suspicion has not pointed at him.' Higgins writes (May 15): 'M. says Neilson is playing a double game.' So faithful did Neilson prove, that Major Sirr discovered him organising a plot to rescue Lord Edward.

[2] P. 19. The italics are Hamilton's. Hatton was one of the rebel executive at Wexford.

Magan's house from Mr. O'Kelly's stable door in Galway's Walk. I know five different places where Lord Edward was concealed,' he adds. The secret which, like the sword of Damocles, had long hung over the heads of Francis Magan and his sister, now seemed on the point of falling; but their names were not used in this pamphlet more freely than those of Miss Moore, Murphy, and a few other persons amongst whose haunts the Geraldine flitted during his last days in this world. Hamilton thus closes the first stage of his inquiry:—

> My documents and anecdotes are every hour increasing. I have received communications from the wife and son of him with whom the Major had the struggle near the house of Miss Magan. I call on Mrs. Moore, Mrs. Dixon,[1] Mrs. Rowe, and Miss Magan; I call on Mr. Magan, Mr. Murphy, their families, and all those individuals who either visited or served them or their noble guest, to tell all Ireland all they are acquainted with respecting the last week Lord Edward had his freedom. I know what some of them can say; I know what more of them might say; and I pause for their full and faithful declarations.

A promised second part never appeared; but it were almost better for the feelings of Magan and his sister had the dreaded charge been boldly fulminated, than the agony of suspense to which they were doomed. I had not seen this scarce pamphlet when I first expressed my suspicions of Magan.

When the present century was in its teens, the aristocratic section of Irish Catholics sought to give the Crown a 'veto' in the appointment of their bishops, and started in opposition to O'Connell, who had been demanding unfettered emancipation. In the ranks of this troublesome schism, the records of which would fill a library, I find Francis Magan, Lords Fingall,[2] Trimleston, Kenmare, Gormanstown, and Southwell,

[1] James Dickson, at whose house Magan had been a constant guest, died a few years previously, and was buried beside the Round Tower at Lusk.

[2] Fingall before his death expressed deep regret for this policy. See Fagan's *Life of O'Connell*.

Wolfe,[1] Shiel,[2] Bellew, Lynch, Donellan,[3] Wyse,[4] Ball[5] and others anxious to reach by a short cut the good things of the State.

The gentleman into whose hands Magan's papers passed tells me that he found a letter addressed to him in 1834 by Sir W. Gossett, Assistant Secretary of State at Dublin Castle, asking under what circumstances he claimed a pension from the Crown, and requesting information as to a small office he held. A copy of Magan's reply was appended, saying that the Viceroy of the day had promised him a county chairmanship —or, as it would now be called, a county court judgeship; but, owing to the disabilities then affecting Catholics, he was found to be not eligible for appointment, and the emoluments in question were given as compensation.[6] Gossett had succeeded Gregory in 1831, and having come in with the Whigs sought to administer a more liberal form of government. Cornwallis, Castlereagh, Cooke and Marsden had been long gone to their account, and dead men tell no tales. Whether Gossett viewed Magan's reply as quite satisfactory does not appear. In 1835 Earl Mulgrave deprived Watty Cox of his pension, but I cannot say whether the same high-handed course was extended to Magan.

[1] Afterwards Chief Baron.

[2] Afterwards Master of the Mint and British minister at Florence.

[3] Bellew, Lynch, and Donnellan had pensions; not for secret service, but to restrain them from clanking their chains.

[4] Afterwards a Privy Councillor, and British minister at Athens.

[5] Afterwards Mr. Justice Ball.

[6] The papers which set forth Magan's real claims to his pension were not then accessible, even to the Irish Government. One of the many letters addressed by Higgins to Cooke, dated June 30, 1798, refers to the original intent of the United leaders to rise on May 14. 'Lord Edward was then with Magan, who found means to prevail on him to postpone his purpose.' The postponement would give time for the capture of Lord Edward Fitzgerald and others. This letter was written after the death of the chief, and informs Cooke that 'the plan *was* to rise Garretstown, Naul, &c., and circuitously round the metropolis to Dunleary, &c. Lord Edward insisted on his Kildare men and those of Carlow being brought in, and he would take the field at Finglas, and march into the city, which was his great object to carry.' The above is curious as showing how much Lord Edward's views had changed since Reinhard described him as one 'of the moderate party.'

Magan was said to have filled some small legal office long since abolished, though of its precise character even his relatives could afford no information. A gossiping missive is subjoined, the less reluctantly because Magan, having often stood in misanthropic isolation, it is pleasant to find any person who came in frequent contact with him. Moreover it is one of the last letters of a not undistinguished man. Sir W. Gossett, who wrote to Magan for information as regards the sinecure he held, might have been glad of the dates which are now supplied. The late Huband Smith, M.R.I.A., served with Magan as a Commissioner for Enclosing Commons. This was rather an unpopular appointment. The disturbances of 1766, ending in the execution of Father Sheehy, all originated in the resistance offered to a similar measure. From 1821 to 1827 Mr. Goulburn filled the office of Chief Secretary for Ireland, and he was a very likely man to have recognised the claims of any person who had rendered secret service in '98. The same remark applies to the Premier, Lord Liverpool, who provided so munificently for the family of Reynolds the informer. On the death of that peer in 1827 his successor, Mr. Canning, earned popularity by refusing to employ in his departments any of the spies of '98, or even to ratify the appointments of Lord Castlereagh or Lord Liverpool.

Huband Smith's letter runs:—

I deferred replying to your note and queries till I could lay my hands on some documents which I had preserved respecting the Commission for inclosing Waste Lands and Commons in Tallaght, Killsillaghan, &c. The Act was passed in the 2nd of George IV. session of 1821. The original Commissioners were Morgan Crofton, James Clancy, and Francis Magan, all barristers. The lands to be inclosed were:—In Tallaght, 783 acres; Killsillaghan, 150 acres; Luske, 320 acres exclusive of the racecourse. The Act recited the owners of the adjoining lands, lords of manors, and also the General Inclosure Act of 43 George III. The earlier meetings of the Commissioners were held in the Royal Exchange, and the later ones at the house of William Duffield Rooke, an eminent solicitor, in Molesworth Street, well known also in the musical world as an accomplished violinist, and member of the 'Beef-Steak Club.' Mr. Morgan

Crofton having died in 1830, it became necessary for the surviving Commissioners under the Act to appoint a third in his place, and in February 1831 I was sworn in as a Commissioner at the meeting held on March 11, 1831, and this was the first time I met Magan. Mr. James Clancy was a barrister of some eminence well known to the profession by able legal treatises, amongst them one of considerable authority on the law of husband and wife.

In regard to your query, what was the average amount of the fees which constituted Magan's salary—he was entitled to receive three guineas *per diem* for every day on which the Commissioners sat in furtherance of the Act. Magan and his brother Commissioners were armed with large powers, such as examining witnesses on oath, awarding costs, and enforcing payment by distress warrant, &c. In point of fact they held a sort of court, and constituted a tribunal from which the appeal lay to the Superior Courts by action at law, under certain restrictions. The Commissioners were directed to hold perambulations, and authorised to sell such parts of the lands as, in their opinion, were necessary to defray the expenses of passing the Act and of carrying it into execution, and to execute conveyances of the fee-simple.

It is on the commons at Lusk that the admirable Irish convict system, which has worked so well, has been fully carried into operation.

With regard to Magan's manner, it appeared to me very unobtrusive, and, as one would say, undemonstrative. He was then an elderly man sufficiently gentlemanlike in appearance, tall, yet rather of plain, and even coarse exterior; perhaps a little moody and reserved at times, and something may have been pressing on him of which he said little.[1] As to his private income, there were no data

[1] Some said of Smith that he was 'cracked with larnin',' and his chat deserved that Irish compliment. 'Your phrase "Still waters run deep" seems happy,' he writes, 'in its application to Magan. There is also an Irish proverb of which it reminds me:—

Mi'as maíṫ leat síocain
Cair dear agas molaḋ
Eisd faic ís fan balḃ

Well rendered by the Latin, seemingly a mediæval rhyme—

"Audi, vide, tace:
Si vis vivere in pace.'

and almost literally translated by the French—

for coming to any conclusion. . . . He resided at Usher's Island, near the Four Courts, a neighbourhood at that time inhabited by a better class than now, and it formed no part of the Commission to inquire more minutely into his affairs.

Mr. Magan was socially described as a person who 'held his head high,' and with a nice sense of honour. In later years he seemed unduly sensitive and, at times, retiring. Possessing few friends through life, he continued staunch to these few, beginning with Francis Higgins and ending with 'Master' Clancy. 'I hold Magan in such esteem,' the latter said, 'that only for his advanced age I should like to appoint him my executor.' Some other men who remembered '98, its horrors, and its gossip, rather recoiled from Magan without knowing well why. There was something of a 'Dr. Fell' about him. He occasionally went the home circuit, but got no briefs. When hailed by juniors with a deference which put to flight all misgivings on his part as to whether acquaintanceship was likely to be valued, his *hauteur* softened into a dignified affability, and this relaxation was often taken as a gracious condescension. His white locks made him venerable, and by some he was regarded as a father of the Bar.[1]

Another man who viewed him with respect was the late Judge Corballis, who in reply to a letter wrote:—

I never, directly or indirectly, heard anything of the alleged

---

"Oys, vois, et te taise,
Si tu veux vivre en paix."

Magan was not dumb, but he knew well probably when to hold his tongue.'—Letter of the late J. Huband Smith, M.R.I.A., June 5, 1866.

[1] The only sense of humour that he is recorded to have evinced was in reference to Con Leyne, a wit often named in Moore's *Diary*. The late Rickard O'Connell, of the Munster Bar, and satellite of the Liberator, wrote, in reply to some questions, that he had been introduced to Magan at the Four Courts in 1831 by Maurice King, who said: 'Our young friend can tell you some good ones as to how Con got on at Darrynane' (Dan's seat); and from time to time after, as I met Magan in the 'Hall,' there was generally some allusion to Con, and a chuckle if any fresh story or point against the renowned gastronome turned up. 'The only members of the Munster Bar I ever saw speaking to Magan were King, O'Loghlen (Sir M.), Con Leyne, and Howley—all men of high honour, who would shun him as a black sheep if they had even a strong suspicion that he was the character you assume him to be. Usually, he was rather starched and formal in manner.'

charge against Frank Magan during his life. I was on habits of intimacy with him to the day of his death, and was with him on his death-bed. He always bore a high character, as far as I could ever learn, either at the bar or in society.

Mr. Corballis lived in the country and knew not what Magan's neighbours said. In their eyes a black cloud seemed to hover over his house.

For forty long years, as the neighbours declared,
His abode had ne'er once been cleaned or repaired.[1]

But in personal appearance he was neat enough, and might be daily seen, in the stiff high cravat of the Regency, emerging from its precincts. Dr. Atkinson and Charles Kernan say that, though Magan was a familiar object to them all the year round, they never saw him accompanied by mortal in his walks. He never married, would sit in solitude, or stalk from room to room like Marlay's ghost. Perhaps the voice of conscience muttered, 'You are said to have sought the confidence of men in order to betray it; show the world by your frigid attitude that such is not likely to be true.' He was reported to have wealth: how he acquired it seemed a mystery.

In 1842, Dr. Madden, when engaged on his 'Lives of the United Irishmen,' had interviews, as he tells us, with Mrs. Macready, who, as Miss Moore, had been with Lord Edward the day before his arrest;[2] but her son informed me that as Magan was then alive and residing near at hand, she did not mention his name to Dr. Madden. Magan, however, cannot fail to have heard of the inquiries being instituted around him by Madden, and his nervous temperament was not calmed by that knowledge. He died in 1843, during a period of great popular excitement and when fears prevailed that the events of '98 were about to be renewed.

'Magan's remains lie in our vaults' writes a local priest.[3]

[1] William Allingham.

[2] See *Lives and Times of the United Irishmen*, 2nd ed. ii. 408.

[3] Canon O'Hanlon, author of *The Lives of the Irish Saints*, then attached

'By his will he requires a perpetual yearly mass to be celebrated by all priests of this church for the repose of his soul, so that I have been praying for him once each year since I became attached to this parish, without knowing anything of his antecedents.'

Dr. Dirham had been residing within a few doors of Magan's house, and on the death of that gentleman it occurred to him to move to the more ample accommodation it afforded. His account, though wholly unimportant, is curious in its way. For years Miss Magan kept constantly promising to vacate in his favour, stating that a small cottage in some rural spot would be much more suitable to her lonely life; but an irresistible fascination bound her to the dingy rooms in which she had vegetated since the dark days of '98. Francis Magan, by a will of ten lines, had left all his property to Elizabeth, his sister, and directed that his funeral might be private. The rooms were now all shut up, and Miss Magan herself eat, drank, and slept upon the landing. For twenty years the drawing-room had not been opened, owing to the fact that a younger sister had died there; and the other apartments of the house were locked up for reasons equally odd. A strange indisposition to permit the humblest visitor to enter the place, was shown in various ways. A quarter of a century seemed to have elapsed since the dust-pit had been emptied, and boards were erected round it which enabled the Magans to add daily *débris*, until at last they became dust themselves. When Dr. Dirham came into possession of the place[1] he found the garden covered from end to end with some feet deep of cinders, through which rank nettles struggled like the stings of the self-consciousness that made life with Magan the reverse of roseate. In a retired nook stood a bottle drainer, the wooden bars of which had fallen in from decay, smashing in its descent the emblems of conviviality it once enshrined, and

to the church of SS. Michael and John. The vaults referred to were once the pit of Smock Alley Theatre. The coffin, inscribed 'Francis Magan,' reposes close to that of the sainted Betagh.

[1] This was written in 1866, though not published until now.

through the aid of which profitable secrets may erst have been gained. The sewers and gratings had become choked; and the deep area at the rear of the house was filled with eight feet of stagnant water. A subterranean cell, adjoining this fosse, and by courtesy styled the 'coal-vault,' opened on another dark chamber; and a feeling of awe crept over the Doctor when, impelled by curiosity to gauge its depth, he cast a stone into the pit, and listened until its descent terminated in the sound of splashing water below. The hinges of the hall door were so stiff during Miss Magan's tenancy, that Dr. Fleming, who as a cousin once ventured to visit the moneyed recluse, had to call at a neighbouring chemist's for sweet oil ere he felt safe in crying 'Open Sesame.' Seated on the cold landing, in the midst of chests of mysterious treasure, this 'unprotected female,' trembling in every nerve lest friends should wrest it from her grasp, gloomily passed the closing years of a hidden life. Once, on a false alarm of fire, her anguish was pitiable, and, to the surprise of everybody, she relinquished the custody of some chests to a neighbour,[1] Mr. Cotton, who, however, detained them only a few hours. At another neighbour's, Miss Flanagan's, who kept an old established bakery, Miss Magan always got her bank-notes changed; but, fearful of being waylaid between the covered car she occupied, and the door at which it stopped, Miss Flanagan was always obliged to get into the vehicle and place in the hands of its shrinking occupant the metallic equivalent for the crisp new note. Some arrears of rent had accumulated at the time of Miss Magan's death, and a term of years in the lease remained unexpired; but her property was so left that the landlord's claim could not be satisfied. The house was in such a ruined state that the landlord, Colonel King, was glad to accept half the former rent. Although an extremely old house, only one tenant, Archbishop Carpenter,[2] occupied it before Magan. In

[1] Secretary to the Mendicity Institution.

[2] Dr. Carpenter preceded Dr. Troy in the see, and by great prudence guided the suffering Church through the quicksands which in penal days encompassed it. He deprecated public agitation on the part of his flock, lest the very

its back parlour had been ordained Dean Lube and many other old priests well known in Dublin during the struggle for Catholic Emancipation; and so searchingly severe was the operation of penal law, that students for ordination had to be smuggled into the Archbishop's house by the stable in Island Street, afterwards turned to ignoble purposes. An altar stood in a recess of this parlour, which the Magans changed into a cupboard.

William Allingham would seem to have had the house in his eye when, some years later, he wrote:—

Outside, the old plaster, all spatter and stain,
Looked spotty in sunshine and streaky in rain;
The window-sills sprouted with mildewy grass,
And the panes from being broken were known to be glass.

Within there were carpets and cushions of dust;
The wood was half rot, and the metal half rust;
Old curtains—half cobwebs—hung grimly aloof:
'Twas a spider's Elysium from cellar to roof.

But they pried not upstairs, through the dust and the gloom,
Nor peeped at the door of the wonderful room
That gossips made much of, in accents subdued,
But whose inside no mortal might brag to have viewed.

Full forty years since turned the key in that door:
'Tis a room deaf and dumb 'mid the city's uproar.
The guests, for whose joyance that table was spread,[1]
May now enter as ghosts, for they're every one dead.

On consulting the records of the Probate Court early in this inquiry, I was puzzled to find that the sum which Miss Magan appeared to have died worth was quite nominal. This discovery disturbed, and for some time retarded, the completion of the chain of evidence. On inquiry, however, it was stated that, in order to save the legacy duty, she transferred,

clanking of the chains should arouse their keepers to renewed activity and vigilance.

[1] The brother of Mathias O'Kelly was betrothed to Miss Magan; but he broke away. Whether the bridal feast had been absolutely spread, is not stated.

when almost *in extremis*, a considerable sum to the late Very Rev. Dr. Taylor and a respected physician [1] still living; and she made a will ratifying that act. Orally, she expressed a wish as to its bestowal for some useful purpose, but leaving details entirely to their discretion. With the bulk of this money a refuge for penitent females and an asylum for the insane were built.[2] Miss Magan died worth 14,000*l.*, not to speak of a fee-farm property known as Hartstown, held under Lord Carhampton, and not far from the Devil's Mills, near Dublin, which, local tradition states, his lordship built in one night by demoniac aid.[3]

[1] The late Dr. Fleming of Merrion Square, one of the next-of-kin, sought by legal proceedings to foil this arrangement, but failed. Mr. H. Fetherston, his attorney after the case had been decided against his client, said to the gentleman who partly represented Miss Magan: 'According to Canon Law you are now free to keep this money, and none but a fool would reject it.' Mr. Fetherston was right; but the other replied that there was also a law of honour and of conscience.

[2] Hartstown being a freehold, it could not go towards the endowment of the institution, and the executor says that this fee-farm has cost him more trouble than all the worry attendant on her complicated affairs.

[3] By a deed, dated December 10, 1797, Lord Carhampton, commander-in-chief, a leading terrorist of his time, grants to Francis Higgins part of his estate of Hartstown and Barnageath; but without mention of trusts or considerations of any kind. During a law suit which took place in 1802, as Mr. James Curran, great-grandnephew of Higgins, informs me, it transpired that Higgins, in this transaction, had been merely trustee for Magan. The freehold conveyed by Carhampton to Higgins is now in the hands of Magan's legal representative. I long suspected, but, on full inquiry, have failed to satisfy myself, that Carhampton's grant to Higgins, in trust for Magan, was part of an arrangement cunningly devised to baffle suspicion, and meant as an acknowledgment of private information regarding rebel doings, which Magan, it is certain, was giving to Higgins; but at least, it proves Carhampton's friendly wish to promote the interwoven interests of both. On pursuing the labyrinths of the Registry of Deeds Office, Dublin, I find that the Magans had connection with the property so far back as 1780. On February 20, 1793, 1000*l.* was lent by Higgins to Thomas Magan, the father of Lord Edward's betrayer, charged on Blackstaheny and Clonsilla, the adjoining lands. Three years later Higgins tightens his toils, and, as already stated, seeks to further secure this 1000*l.* charged on the same property. 'Shamado,' doubtless, well knew how to make his creature work. The consent to harbour Lord Edward, and the whispered information as to place and hour would be an easy way of wiping out the debt for 1000*l.*, and of currying favour with the lender. I may add that the fore-

It seems strange that Magan, who was insolvent before the rebellion, could amass so much money. His secret pension was merely for 200*l.* a year[1] (a sum insufficient to pay the rent of his house), give good donations to the Catholic Board, pay off Fetherston's bond, and support himself, his sisters and his horse—for in early life Mr. Magan did indulge in that luxury. His pension, there is reason to think, from the letter of Sir William Gossett in 1834, ceased to be paid about that time. His fees as a Commissioner for enclosing commons were enjoyed by him for a few years only; and as but three payments to him are officially recorded viz., on September 11, 1800, April 2, 1802, and December 15, 1802—it is evident he must have derived income from other sources. There are payments of secret service money to the informers of '98 and their representatives which obtain no record in the book ostensibly devoted to that purpose. Captain Armstrong, who betrayed the Sheares's, is known to have received, throughout sixty years, about 29,000*l.* in recognition of that act; and yet no trace of his name appears in the book of Secret Service Money expenditure. Money was also obtainable under a clause in the Act of 39 George III. cap. 65, by which a sum of 2,910*l.* was allocated to the Under-Secretary in the Civil department (Dublin Castle) for the time being, in trust for payment of secret annuities. A letter from Dr. Ferris suggests another source. He states, on the authority of a clerk in Gleadowe Newcomen's Bank, then dead, that an annuity had been paid from that house to Francis Magan, and that the clerk had seen Magan's receipts. Dr. Ferris suggests that

going note was written long before I had found the criminatory letters of Higgins and Magan.

[1] Some of Magan's receipts have been preserved. On these receipts the letters 'S. A.' are marked, a cipher implying that he belonged to a class of informers who, by special agreement, were never to be called upon to give public evidence. His pension was paid quarterly, and here is one of his receipts:—

'Received from Wm. Gregory, Esq., by Wm. Taylor, Esq., fifty pounds sterling, for the quarter to December 24 last.

'Dublin, January 22, 1816. F. MAGAN.'

the books of the bank might be still accessible for examination.[1]

An Act of Parliament provided that the Secret Service Money placed at the Viceroy's disposal should pass confidentially through the hands of the Chief Secretary; but this arrangement has not always been adhered to, as is evident from the fact that the 1,000*l* reward for the discovery of Emmet was lodged to the credit of the informer in Finlay's bank. The hint of Dr. Ferris is not uninteresting, but the books of Newcomen's bank do not seem to have been preserved. Barrington states that Sir W. Gleadowe Newcomen, who voted for the Union, received a reward of 20,000*l* with a peerage, and the patronage of his county. It is a strange irony of fate that Lord Newcomen died poor. For years he lived alone in the bank, gloating, it was wildly whispered, over ingots of treasure, with no lamp to guide him but the luminous diamonds which had been left for safe keeping in his hands. Moore would have compared him to 'the gloomy gnome that dwells in the dark gold mine.' Wrapped in a sullen misanthropy, he was sometimes seen emerging at twilight from his iron clamped abode. La Touche's bank stood on the opposite side of Castle Street and Dublin wags compared the street to a river because it ran between two banks. Jokes soon gave way to sobs. One day Newcomen's bank broke,[2] and prosperous men perished in the collapse. Lord Newcomen had previously retired to Killester, where he died by his own hand. No claimant appeared for his coronet, and the line became extinct. This was the twenty-seventh Irish peerage which had failed since the Union. Gleadowe had been M.P. for Longford when he voted for the extinction of the Irish Parliament. Richard Lovel Edgeworth, a betrayed

[1] Letter of Edward Ferris, M.D., Athy, June 21, 1867. He died, March 25, 1877.

[2] A run had been made on La Touche's Bank, and great fears were expressed lest it should break. At last Lord Limerick, who as Sexten Pery had been popular, took his stand at the counter, and when people saw him paying out the gold, confidence became restored.—His kinsman, Aubrey de Vere, to the Writer.

constituent, regarded this vote as an act of treason, and in anger shot forth the following bolt :—

With a name that is borrowed—a title that's bought,
Sir William would fain be a gentleman thought ;
His wit is but cunning, his courage but vapour,
His pride is but money—his money but paper !

What was a pointless sarcasm in 1800 became a stubborn fact in 1825—Newcomen's notes were waste paper. The Hibernian Banking Company soon after began business within the walls.

CHAPTER XII

WILLIAM TODD JONES. EMMET'S REBELLION

Todd Jones, Wolfe Tone, and Hon. Simon Butler were three Protestants to whom, Mr. Froude says, the Catholic Committee voted 1,500*l.* each, as a reward for their cordially rendered aid. This was in 1793, and we hear no more of Todd Jones from Froude. His subsequent history is not without interest, and seems interwoven with that of Francis Magan.

John Philpot Curran's writing-desk remains exactly as he left it when quitting Ireland in 1817 to die. A long and cautiously written letter,[1] without signature, dated August 13, 1803, but known to be from Lady Moira, reposes in this desk. It was written three weeks after Emmet's rebellion, and a month prior to his execution. The letter begins mysteriously, 'Read, reflect, but do not answer. Time will unfold the intentions.' She complains of information which had been sent to the Government, regarding a trunk, assumed to be full of papers, reaching Moira House, Usher's Island, and presumably from Todd Jones. She declares that her rooms were ransacked, under a warrant from the Secretary of State, and how letters addressed to Todd Jones at Moira House had been carried to Dublin Castle. In writing to Curran, whom she wishes to be her counsel if the matter should come to trial, she makes light of these letters, and prudentially describes her correspondence with Jones as mainly of an antiquarian and picturesque interest.

Magan, who resided within a few doors of Moira House,

[1] The full text of this long letter will be found in the Appendix.

possessed peculiar facilities for 'setting'[1] the movements of its *habitués*.[2] It must have been in 1802 when he was found by Mathias O'Kelly[3] associating with Todd Jones, and that date merits attention. 'I had been absent from Ireland for *ten* years, from the year 1792,' writes Jones in his petition to the king, 'during the whole of which period I was uninterruptedly a resident in England, and in May 1802 I was indispensably compelled to return to Dublin, by an affair of honour.'[4] Soon after he proceeded to Munster, 'which I had never beheld, and had long entertained an inclination to see.'[5]

At what date can we trace the first arrival of Jones on his mysterious mission to Clonakilty, where with several of his friends he was arrested on a charge of high treason in July 1803? To that question the answer is, December 1802. The 'Account of Secret Service Money, applied in detecting Treasonable Conspiracies,' contains the following entry:— '1802, December 15th, Francis Magan, by direction of Mr. Orpen, 500*l*.'

There is but one family named 'Orpen' in Ireland; and the only Orpen who could possibly be authorised to direct the payment of 500*l*. to Magan at this time was the High Sheriff of Cork, in whose bailiwick Jones was tracked and caught.[6]

Emmet, in his speech from the dock, denied that he was the life and soul of the conspiracy, as alleged by Mr. Solicitor-General Plunket; declared that men of greater mark than he were deep in it; that on his return to Ireland he found the organisation formed; he was asked to join it; he requested time to consider; they invited him again, and he embarked in

[1] 'Setting' is the phrase used by Mr. Secretary Cooke (see *ante*, p. 118).

[2] *Ibid*. p. 134.

[3] See previous chap. p. 140.

[4] Mr. Jones's 'Petition to the King,' dated 'Cork, March 9, 1808'; printed in Plowden's *History of Ireland*, iii. 624.

[5] *Ibid*.

[6] The records of the Chief Secretary's Office show that in 1802 Richard Thomas Orpen, of Frankford, was High Sheriff of Cork. I have seen in the Irish State Papers a letter dated 'Cork, March 24, 1802,' from the above Mr. Orpen, in his capacity of high sheriff, regarding a correspondence he had with General Myers as to a small assistance of cavalry.

the enterprise. And yet, so carefully was the secret kept, that nothing transpired to show that he had any colleagues of good position. Lord Norbury, who tried the case, and the Attorney-General stigmatised the plan as contemptible from the fact that Emmet's allies were of no higher rank than 'ostlers, bakers, carpenters, and old-clothes men,' and, notwithstanding the solemnity of Emmet's dying words, history has since given him the exclusive credit, or discredit, of the rising of 1803.

Among others to whom suspicion attaches, although there is no absolute evidence to show his guilt, may be mentioned William Todd Jones, a Protestant of good family and some means, a barrister and writer, and a member of the late Irish Parliament. The Viceregal organ, the 'Dublin Journal,' in its issue of August 6, 1803, after noticing the arrest of Jones, adds: 'This gentleman has been many months on a tour through the provinces of Leinster and Munster, making speculations on the state of the country through which he passed.' He remained eight months in Cork, and it is a question whether, during that prolonged stay, he may not have sought to foment revolution. All memoirs of Emmet have hitherto been silent as regards the complicity of Cork in his designs. Kildare is the county of which mention is chiefly made. The following from the 'Courier' (London) of August 5, 1803, furnishes a glimpse into the then state of Cork:—

A Dublin mail arrived this evening, and brought us letters and papers of Monday last. . . . Though there has been no rising in Cork, yet very unfavourable symptoms of disaffection have appeared there, and to the south of that city we are sorry to hear that the malignancy of the former rebellion is by no means extinguished.

The same journal, of August 16, 1803, contains a letter 'written by a gentleman of distinction in the county of Cork,' possibly Mr. Orpen himself, who commanded a corps of Yeomanry. The writer, after stating that he had spread yeomen in all directions to prevent the embarkation of persons charged with treason, goes on to say:—

Todd Jones has been at Dr. Callanan's, Clonakilty, the last eight months: H.,[1] by order of Government, arrested him for high treason, as also the Doctor and his son. . . . These measures have been attended with alarm; but I think we are at present quite safe; and a strong fleet at Beerhaven relieves me from all apprehension of an enemy.

The entire of the Yeomanry of this kingdom is now on the permanent establishment. Our corps is strong, and without vanity a good one. I have applied for an addition of infantry: with this augmentation, I shall feel very little apprehension for any attack made upon us without the aid of foreign force.

It appears from this letter, dated August, 1803, that Jones had been then eight months at Clonakilty in the county Cork: therefore his arrival would have been in December 1802—the very date of the payment of 500*l.* to Magan by direction of Mr. Orpen, high sheriff for the county. Meanwhile the locality in which Jones pitched his camp became, from some cause, decidedly heated. A letter in the London 'Courier,' dated 'Cork, August 21,' after recording the arrest of Todd Jones, Donovan, and Dr. Callanan, states, 'The peasantry in the neighbourhood of Ross, near Clonakilty, go armed to their chapels, and mount a regular guard over their arms while they perform their devotions.'

We have seen that Magan—traditionally described as an unsociable person, possessing few friends—maintained most intimate relations with James Dickson of Kilmainham, in whose house Jones was also a constant guest. About the same time as the arrest of Jones in Cork, the 'Courier' of August 30, 1803, announces in its Dublin news: 'Yesterday Mr. James Dickson, of Kilmainham, was arrested at his house by Messrs. Atkinson[2] and Carleton, chief peace-officers, and his papers searched. The superintendent magistrate had him conveyed to the Castle, where he underwent examination, and was afterwards committed to Kilmainham Gaol.'[3]

[1] Probably Dr. Hardinge of Cork, an active agent in those troubled times.

[2] Atkinson was desired to be on the alert in Cooke's letter to Sirr, written on the day of Lord Edward's intended move, of which Magan gave notice.

[3] Mr. Justice Day, writing to the Irish Government on September 27, 1803

Todd Jones, writing at the time, warmly details the circumstances of his arrest (the italics are his own) :—

My person has been assaulted in my bed at daybreak, in the respectable mansion of a venerable friend, Doctor Callanan, near Clonakilty, and I have been conveyed, very strongly guarded by Troops, to an ignominious common Gaol: in reaching which, at the moderate distance of twenty-two miles, I have been wantonly exhibited, *like an already convicted Felon*, for two long summer days, the first and second of August, in *Orange Triumph*, to the gaze of a very crowded Bandon rabble; and thence paraded, with like ostentation, *through all the streets of Cork*, as if *in progress to Execution*.—My venerable friend and hospitable entertainer, Doctor Calanan, a Physician of the age of seventy, with his only son, *on my account*, have been dragged from the same mansion to Prison, after a similar triumphant exposure of two days, to gazing multitudes, in the short distance of twenty-two miles: a Man eminent for a long professional life, dedicated to the Poor, and to the Peasants, whose tears kept pace with his progress.

He then goes on to request that all concerned in his detainer, including the Sheriff of Cork, may be summoned to the Bar of Parliament. An account of his shattered health is sent to the Secretary of State—'It is my liberty which I pray for—a trial—liberation—or death! I have been a close prisoner for eleven weeks, without even having been shown my indictment, or been told the names of my accusers.' [1]

These complaints were made in October, 1803, but entirely failed to obtain redress. His petition to the king, dated 1808, resumes the story: 'Within this prison I continued confined from 23rd July, 1803, until the latter end of October 1805, when I was unconditionally discharged by the High Sheriff of the County of Cork—untried—unbailed—unexamined and unredressed.' [2]

(eight days after Emmet's execution), suggests that Lord Bantry, who got his peerage for reporting the arrival of the French in '96, would be a good man to make inquiries regarding Jones.

[1] *Curious Correspondence of William Todd Jones with the Secretary of State.* Dedicated to Lord Moira and Mr. Fox. (Cork: Odell, 1804.)

[2] Plowden's *History of Ireland since the Union to* 1810, iii. 626 *et seq.*

When the High Sheriff of Cork liberated Jones it may be assumed that the same authority was instrumental in his committal. Formerly, high sheriffs took much more active part in such proceedings than now. No organised system of police then existed, and the high sheriffs seem to have been duly impressed with the responsibility of their position. On March 18, 1800, we find in the Secret Service Money Book, 100*l.* handed to Mr. Archer, High Sheriff of Wicklow, for the detection of treason, and on April 27, 1801, a further sum. But these exertions were dignified in comparison with the acts of Sir Judkin Fitzgerald, High Sheriff of Tipperary, who, with his own hands, flogged the peasantry to extort confession.

Emmet's insurrection burst forth in Dublin on the night of July 23, 1803; that same morning, and at a distance of 150 miles, Jones is arrested.

The connection of Todd Jones with Irish politics was apparently of a graver and more subtle sort than might be inferred from Lady Moira's letter to Curran, or even Plowden's account of him in his History. Plowden, a Catholic—the guest, with Jones and Magan, of James Dickson—says that the persecution which Jones underwent at the hands of the Government was due solely to his powerful advocacy of Catholic Emancipation and Parliamentary Reform. He defends Jones with all the warmth of friendship; his 'History of Ireland' enters most largely into the case, and quotes various orators who sought to vindicate Jones in Parliament.[1] But the reply of the ex-Secretary of State, Mr. Wickham, finds no place, contrary to Plowden's usual honesty and fulness in that work. Wickham, as appears from Hansard, rose from the bed of sickness to reply to Fox, who had taken up the case of Jones, and addressed the House sitting. He said:—

For some time after the arrest of Mr. Todd Jones, which the Irish Government was induced to order upon information—the particulars of which he could not with any propriety describe, but which were satisfactory to their minds as to the measure. Mr. Jones remained in prison without any particular inquiry having

[1] Plowden's *History of Ireland since the Union to* 1810, ii. 36, 216-220, 623-632.

M

been instituted in his case. As soon, however, as the trials which followed the insurrection of 1803, and which so much occupied the attention of the Irish Government, had terminated, an inquiry into the case of Mr. Jones took place. . . . He had already stated the impossibility of giving a full explanation to the House without acting unfairly towards the character of the Petitioner. After the trial of the rebels, and the fullest investigation of the charge against Mr. Jones, his case became much more serious than it appeared at the outset. Willing, however, to act with every possible mildness, his case was submitted to the Crown lawyers accompanied by this question, 'whether it would be proper to liberate Mr. Jones,' and their unanimous opinion was decidedly in the negative. The Irish Government transmitted the case of Mr. Jones to his Majesty's Ministers in this country, requiring their advice; and their answer was, that it would be extremely unadvisable to allow such a person to be at large in Ireland![1]

Of how Jones's alleged guilt was hushed up, and why the vengeance of the Attorney-General preferred to fall on 'ostlers, bakers, carpenters, and old clothes men,' as he said, an idea may be perhaps formed from a letter addressed by the Right Hon. William Saurin to Jones, proposing that he should secretly, and as if of his own accord, exile himself from Ireland. This letter was enclosed by Wickham to Jones on October 11, 1803. Saurin, Jones states, had been his schoolfellow.[2]

Dr. Madden professes to supply a list of all persons of substance connected with Emmet in his attempt; also of persons who were cognisant of his plans, and were supposed to be favourably disposed towards them; but Todd Jones obtains no place,[3] and therefore the less excuse is needed for this effort to embrace a long neglected figure, and one not uninteresting for 'Auld lang syne.'[4]

[1] *Hansard's Parliamentary Debates*, v. 793–5.

[2] *Curious Correspondence.* (Cork: Odell, 1804.)

[3] *United Irishmen*, iii. 329.

[4] The *Annual Register* and other usually well-informed sources fail to record the death of Jones. A full obituary of him appears in the *Ulster Register* for March 1818, iv. 186–8; and a fine monody on 'Immortal Jones,' probably by Drennan, in the same serial, pp. 224–5.

CHAPTER XIII

THOMAS COLLINS. PHILLIPS THE SACERDOTAL SPY

A RECENT letter from the ex-Crown and Treasury Solicitor for Ireland quotes the following from Mr. Lecky's notice of an unnamed spy, and asks me 'Who is he?'[1] 'He was a Dublin silk merchant,' writes Lecky, 'and can be identified by a letter from Cooke to Nepean, May 26, 1794, in the Record Office, London.'[2]

I may now state that his name was Collins. Cooke's letter mentions that 200*l.* a year had been settled on the informer of 1794, and that he was recommended for office in the West Indies—his future residence in Ireland, after Rowan's arrest, being unsafe.

Mr. Joynt's query comes not amiss, for John Keogh, also a silk merchant, was broadly branded by Walter Cox as an informer, and the plausible indictment is transcribed by Dr. Madden and enshrined in his *magnum opus*.[3] The charge against Keogh, who, by the way, preceded O'Connell as leader of the Irish Catholics, is, however, baseless.

Mr. Cooke does not give the Christian name of this Collins, but later official records describe it as Thomas. Collins was the first of the systematic informers. Some sheaves of his letters are still preserved at Dublin Castle, addressed to 'J. G.,' and heretofore supposed to imply 'Gregory,' a highly distin-

[1] William Lane Joynt, D.L., to W. J. F., Grange Abbey, June 29, 1891.

[2] Lecky's *England*, vii. 8.

[3] Madden's *United Irishmen*, iii. 331–2. Again, at p. 41, Dr. Madden says that so early as 1793, the very time that Collins is now shown to be at work, Keogh was suspected of infidelity. Mr. Lecky, in reply to a private query, agrees with me that Keogh was thoroughly true.

guished secretary to the Lord Lieutenant. But Gregory's name was William, and 'J. G.' stands for 'Jack Giffard,' whom Curran and Grattan, in often-quoted philippics, denounced. The reports furnished to Giffard were regularly passed on to Cooke, and two letters [1] from Collins to the latter speak of his confidant 'Mr. G——d.'

The daily reports extend almost unbroken from 1792 to 1795. All are without a signature, while the official endorsement usual on such letters is confined, in this case, to 'U. I. M.,' meaning, of course, the rebel brotherhood. On December 15, 1792, he writes to Cooke: 'Implicitly depend upon my being totally unknown to mankind in this business, save and except to you and J. G.' [2]

Collins—at each conclave—feigned to be an advanced republican, and was regularly invited to attend. New members, on being admitted, repeated 'a test.' In an early letter to Giffard he writes:—

> It is contemplated to abolish the Test, as it is found by experience that it prevents a number of very warm friends to a Reform from joining us; but I shall oppose it, as we have no business with any of your *lukewarm fellows* who may hesitate at going as great lengths as ourselves.[3]

In advance of every meeting a list was sent to Collins of the new candidates for election. Scores of his secret letters enclose these lists, and announce the results of the ballot, with the names of the rejected, and it is curiously illustrative of the precautions taken to ensure secrecy, and as showing how little Collins was himself suspected, that men much superior to him were refused admission. Carefully prepared reports of the proceedings, with the names of the speakers and of the number present, exist in endless evidence. In one

[1] Notably that of November 26, 1793.

[2] Anonymous to Cooke, December 15, 1792. One letter only, dated three years later, appealing to Dublin Castle for money and place, and in the same handwriting as the others, lays aside his disguise and is boldly signed 'Thomas Collins.'

[3] To 'J. G.' April 13, 1792. MSS. Dublin Castle.

letter he encloses, for the Viceroy's satisfaction, the receipt given to him for his annual subscription to the Society, signed by Oliver Bond, but the part which names Collins is first blotted out, and finally cut clean away.[1]

In August 1792, Cooke deputed Collins to extend his secret inquiries to a wider area than the Hall in Back Lane where the United Irishmen met; and the result is found in the subjoined letter. Its stealthy style contrasts with the boldness of later missives.

Sir—I have made every possible inquiry and I have reason to think that there now are Foreign agents here who have frequent conferences with a noble Viscount and his Brother,[2] who is a lawyer; also with J—hn K—gh, Ed—d B—re and Richard McC—m—k.[3] For your Information you have a list of such U—— I——men as I think really dangerous from abilities. As to Inclination, the whole of the Society are nearly *alike*.

You may be assured that whatever steps Mr. Tandy has for some time past taken, or is now pursuing, are by the advice of the before-mentioned noble Viscount[4] and Mr. Gr–tt–n; and also, that let the pretentions (*for the present*) of the R–m–n Ca—— be ever so moderate, the real design of their *leaders* is to effect a separation between this country and Gr—t B—t—n.

I remain, &c. &c.[5]

---

[1] The date of this receipt is November 1, 1793.

[2] The Hon. Simon Butler, K.C., was brother of Edmund Viscount Mountgarret, a peerage dating from October 1550. At a meeting of the Society of United Irishmen in February 1793, Butler in the chair, and Bond acting as secretary, a declaration was proposed and adopted, pronouncing as illegal certain proceedings of the Secret Committee of the Irish House of Lords, in compelling witnesses to answer on oath questions compromising themselves, and directed to the discovery of evidence mainly in support of prosecutions already commenced. For this act, Butler and Bond were sentenced by the Lord Chancellor to be imprisoned for six months and to pay a fine of 500*l.* to the King. (See Madden, ii. 244.) Simon Butler was fortunate in not living to witness the sad scenes of '98.

[3] John Keogh, Edward Byrne, and Richard McCormick.

[4] Diplomacy sought to paralyse the more influential arm of the movement This same Viscount Mountgarret was promoted to an earldom on December 20 following!

[5] Anon. (Thomas Collins) to Cooke, August 27, 1792.

Collins had the same liking for dramatic mystery as Turner; many of the letters to 'G.' ask him to call at night to hear things that could not be put on paper, to tap at a certain door in a dark passage, and 'no one would be the wiser.' In the graphic sketch he daily furnished, special attention is paid to the chief 'sitter,' Hamilton Rowan, who presided as chairman until his arrest; while Tone, Tandy, Emmet, Drennan, Bond, Lewins, the Sheares, and B. B. Harvey (the last three afterwards hanged) stand forth in bold outline from a crowd of minor faces grouped in the background. Sometimes they all dined together. 'When Paine's health was given his picture was introduced and received a general embrace. Several French songs were sung by Mr. Sheares, with proper explanations for those ignorant of the language.' [1] Glimpses of further feasts are caught, revealing the same familiar faces: men who had not yet begun to realise the gruesome fact that the handwriting was on the wall.

John Keogh is not often mentioned as present; and never after 1793. In October '92 Collins furnishes an abstract of a spirited speech delivered by Keogh. This led to queries, and in reply Collins tells Cooke: 'The leaders are Hamilton Rowan, Tandy, Jackson, Bond, Dowling, McCormick, Warren, and some others. But Keogh and Drennan are the *grand movers*;' [2] and on the following day he writes: 'Keogh is the principal performer behind the scenes—as the fellow's art is such he does not appear amongst us, but has a set of fellows to constantly attend and broach his sentiments.' [3] Keogh, a man of rare sagacity—whose life has yet to be written—took the course described in consequence of having recognised in his audience a person whom he did not fully trust. Turning to Richard McCormick, in the hearing of 'Billy Murphy,' the subsequent millionaire, he said, 'Dick, men's lives are not safe here,' and glided quietly away. John Keogh is the only man of mark who passed unscathed through the crisis of '98;

[1] [Collins] to 'J. G.,' November 20, 1793.
[2] [Collins] to Cooke, November 29, 1792.
[3] *Idem*, November 30, 1792.

and Cox, mistakenly believing that this immunity was due to treachery towards his colleagues, sought to brand him as a spy.

In 1793, John Keogh, Sir Charles Ffrench and several other Catholic delegates,[1] waited on George III. at St. James's and presented a petition craving relief from the disabilities by which their order was oppressed. The loss of America had preached the wisdom of concession; and the tempest of the French Revolution roared within measurable distance. While Pitt and Dundas were not indisposed to grant a full emancipation to the Irish Catholics, they were constantly opposed in this policy by Dublin Castle. The often sensational reports of Collins seem to have had due effect. A long letter to Cooke regarding the Catholics begins by saying that

There are few individuals better acquainted with the views and dispositions of those people than I am. If they are gratified the day is not far off when High Mass with all its mummery will be performed in Christ Church [2]—the auditors to be a popish Lord Lieutenant, a popish Chancellor, &c. &c., unless the use of the former be preceded by an entire separation from Honest John Bull, which is the grand object of the disaffected of every description in this country.

Where Government has *resisted*, the good effects have been found; when it has *relaxed*, demands have increased. . . . To come to the point: give the Papists all they *want* or *nothing*. Without the former the sword must be drawn at one period or another; and the query is, whether it's not better to try the *event* when they are *unprepared*, than to contirue going on to give the *adder* time to strengthen with the heat of *summer*: not that I think there is the smallest danger of any *war* but *wordy* ones from them—unless time and the interference of their *Gallic Friends* may embolden them to acts of desperation. [He then proceeds to advise the em-

[1] As in the case of Lord Mountgarret subtlety was employed in the hope of moderating the tone of Sir Charles Ffrench. He had much influence with the Irish Catholics; and in 1798 a peerage was conferred on his aged mother, who, in her simplicity, said to a cousin, 'I don't know what I have done that they should make a Lord of me.' In point of lineage few had higher claims.

[2] A Protestant Cathedral in Dublin used by the Catholics until the Reformation.

bodiment of military corps in Dublin, well officered. The pay to be such as to induce respectable Protestant tradesmen and others to enlist.]

Suppose the whole to be mounted and appointed as dragoons, this small corps will be found of as much use as any Regiment of Cavalry in the Kingdom.

If a *friend* of yours [1] should be thought of, I think there would be an end to all *illegal meetings*,[2] associations and combinations, and I will answer for his compleating and arraying the number in 10 Days.[3]

A small measure of Catholic Relief was at length offered by Pitt. Collins, a month later, courageously writes: 'If you think it prudent to have me examined by the Secret Committee, I may give some useful information previous to the Catholick Bill going to the Upper House.' [4]

It is not surprising that, from the regularity and general accuracy of the spy's reports, Giffard in his conversations more than once revealed a knowledge that fluttered the Inner Circle. On February 15, 1794, Collins reports, in the *précis* of proceedings that had taken place that night:—

A notice by Mr. John Sheares that he will on Friday next propose a new Ballot of the whole of the Society, or else the total dissolution thereof, in order, as he says, to get rid of some suspected Members, who, he says, are in the habit of betraying the Secrets of the Society to Government. At the time he gave this notice there were not more than fifteen members present and the proposition seemed to meet their approbation. The fact is they are all cursedly frightened by the examples made of some of their friends. Fear only can keep them in order; gentleness will only encourage their audacity.

Three months elapsed: they met and deliberated; the reports went regularly to Dublin Castle; arrests were made; the Society wondered; but Collins, though a loaded mine lay beneath his feet, stood his ground. On Saturday, May 10, 1794, he announces:—

Surgeon Wright proposed appointing a commission of inquiry to inspect into the character and conduct of not only the members

[1] Himself.
[2] Italics in original.
[3] Endorsed by Cooke, 'U. I., Jan. 29, '93.'
[4] [Collins] to Cooke, February 28, 1793.

of the Society, but of all other persons in this city who profess patriotism, as he had reason to suspect that Mr. Pitt's system of having spies in all company and in all Societies, had made its way into this country.

Collins, no coward like Turner, maintained his character as one of the most regular attendants at the meetings, played his part, opposed some minor propositions,[1] and continued his carefully framed reports.[2] These reports perturbed Dublin Castle quite as much as the United Irishmen had been scared by the leakage of their plans. On April 28, 1794, Marcus Beresford writes to his father, who had long been regarded as the virtual governor of Ireland :—

Government are determined to hang Rowan if possible; but they have not yet shown any suspicion of any person here being concerned in the plot, in order to lull them into security. No person knows as much as I now tell you except Lord Westmoreland, the Attorney-General, and Sackville Hamilton.[3]

Judging from Cooke's letter to Nepean, Collins' chief enterprise was in bringing Hamilton Rowan within the meshes of the law. In 1792, as we learn from his Autobiography, Rowan was arrested on a charge of distributing a seditious paper. Informations were filed against Rowan, difficulties supervened, and he was not brought to trial until January 1794. Rowan offered proof that two of his jurors had declared 'Ireland would never be quiet until Rowan and Napper Tandy were hanged.'[4] The challenge, however, was not allowed. Curran acted as his counsel, and delivered a speech reminding one of Cicero's defence of Milo. Rowan was found guilty, fined, and committed to Newgate, but, by bribing his jailer, escaped; and, after various romantic

[1] Letter of January 4, 1793.

[2] The zealous subserviency of Collins, as in the case of Reynolds and Magan, originated in pecuniary straits. A letter of January 24, 1792, to Giffard, speaks of the accommodation he had received at his hands; and addressing Mr. Cooke (June 26, 1793), he dilates on his 'embarrassments.'

[3] *Beresford Correspondence*, ii. 26 (unpublished).

[4] *Autobiography of Archibald Hamilton Rowan*, p. 183.

adventures, reached France in a boat manned by two fishermen of Howth.[1]

A proclamation offering 1,000*l.*[2] reward for his capture was read by the men, but they told him not to fear. This remarkable escape took place on May 4, 1794. Cooke's letter, saying that Collins's further residence in Ireland would be unsafe, is dated May 26 following. An amusing proof of the general distrust which then prevailed is shown in the fact, recorded by Rowan, that on reaching France he was arrested as a British spy, sent under a strong guard to Brest, and lodged with galley-slaves.[3] Judging from Beresford's letter, written two days before the escape, however, it cannot be said that he got out of the frying-pan into the fire, as Rowan seems to have thought.

Some few letters from Mr. Douglas, who filled a Government post in London, are intermingled with the Collins MSS. The Right Hon. John Beresford, in a letter dated May 13, 1794, writes: 'Douglas called upon me this day; we had a great deal of conversation about Rowan. He told me that, as Rowan had escaped, Tone was the next guilty person, and ought to be hanged.' This, however, it was not so easy to do. Neither Turner nor Collins would prosecute openly. Meanwhile some friends of Tone entered into negotiations with Government, and he was at last allowed to expatriate himself beyond the seas.[4]

[1] Rowan, until the willing hands were found, remained in Mr. Sweetman's house, now known as Rosedale, Raheny.

[2] Mr. Froude says that the proclamation named '£2,000 for Rowan's apprehension' (*Hist.* iii. 119). The proclamation, dated May 2, 1794, offers '£1,000 to any person or persons who shall apprehend the said Hamilton Rowan, wherever he may be found, or to so discover him that he may be apprehended or committed to prison.'

[3] *Autobiography of Hamilton Rowan*, p. 220.

[4] In December 1796 Tone accompanied the French fleet to Bantry Bay. Mr. Froude and other historians think that it was Grouchy who failed to attempt a landing. 'Then, as twenty years later, on another occasion, no less critical,' he writes, meaning Waterloo, 'Grouchy was the good genius of the British Empire' (iii. 205). In point of fact, Grouchy was not at Bantry. M. Guillon, in *France et Irlande*, written with full access to the papers of the French Admiralty, makes it clear that Bouvet, and not Grouchy, was the man who ought to have been named.

Mr. Collins[1] did not get the post for which he was recommended until the year 1800. It was Dominica, one of the West Indian Islands, as we learn from the 'S. S. Money Book.' The first entry of his name is on November 23, 1797: 'Mr. Collins.—Sent to him, in London, 108*l*.'[2] Here he remains for two years—no doubt one of the gentlemen 'recommended by Mr. Cooke,' and mentioned in the 'Castlereagh Correspondence' as qualified to 'dot' the movements of Lord Cloncurry in London.

In more than one of the secret letters sent by Collins to Cooke, he offers his services for fields in other countries, where he thinks he could be even more useful than at home. A large sheaf of papers regarding troubles in the West Indies is preserved at Dublin Castle. Dominica—the site of his first appointment—had been captured by the British in 1756, but in 1771 the French, after a hard fight, once more became its masters. In 1783 the island was again restored to the English, but its executive felt far from secure. Intrigue was at work; French emissaries were not few; and the presence of Collins, a practised spy, came not amiss. The French, however, again effected a landing in 1805; Roseau, the chief town, was obliged to capitulate, and pay the enemy 12,000*l*. to quit. In 1890, after the cession of Heligoland to Germany there was talk of surrendering Dominica to France.

What was Collins' later history I have been unable to discover. 'Sylvanus Urban' tells of a Thomas Collins who was hanged; but this is a mere coincidence of name. It is within the possibilities that our spy may have posed as Governor Collins, and even received at his levees Hamilton Rowan, who,

[1] Several persons named Collins, and described as silk mercers, appear in the Dublin Directory between the years 1770 and 1800. Thomas Collins vanishes in 1793; and 'Samuel Collins, silk and worsted manufacturer, 35 Pill Lane,' is also found for the last time in the Directory for 1793. They seem to have been brothers. A bill of Samuel, duly receipted, for goods supplied to Dr. McNevin, a leading rebel, is enclosed by Thomas in one of his secret missives to Cooke.

[2] Other entries follow: 'Thomas Collins' bill, from London, 54*l*. 3*s*. 4*d*.' is entered on September 22, 1798. These payments continue to be made until 1799, when they become very frequent.

during the travels by which his exile was beguiled, would pay his devoirs, as he says, to the British resident.[1]

An informer of a novel type was a priest named Phillips. Describing the events of the year 1795, Mr. Froude writes:—

Lord Carhampton went down and took command in Connaught. Informers offered their services, provided their presence was not required in the witness-box. A Priest named Phillips 'caused himself to be made a Defender with a view of giving information.'[2] Others came whose names the Viceroy dared not place on paper. With the help of these men, Carhampton was able to arrest many of the Connaught Leaders;[3] and legal trials being from the nature of the case impossible, he trusted to Parliament for an Act of Indemnity, and sent them by scores to serve in the Fleet. Thus, amidst the shrieks of Patriots and threats of prosecution, he succeeded in restoring some outward show of order.[4]

Among Mr. Froude's startling passages, none created in Ireland a more painful sensation than this. That an Irish priest—the *Soggarth Aroon*[5] of the people—should be selling the lives of his friends, flock, and penitents, was indeed a novel incident. Interest in the episode has recently been revived by Mr. Lecky, who describes Father Phillips as having given the Government some really valuable assistance in detecting Rebel Leaders.[6] For all we know to the contrary, this Ecclesiastic might have gone on to the end undiscovered, posing and pontificating as a solemn hierarch. But, in point of fact, Phillips, though in orders, had been degraded and suspended by his Ordinary. Dr. Madden, long before the publication of Froude or Lecky, casually notices Phillips[7] as an 'excommunicated priest from French Park, co. Roscommon.'

[1] *Autobiography of Hamilton Rowan*, p. 318.

[2] Camden to Portland, July 29, 1795.

[3] The late Colonel the Right Hon. Fitzstephen French, whose brother became Lord De Freyne, informed me that his father, Arthur French, M.P. for Roscommon from 1785 to 1820, had been threatened with arrest by Lord Carhampton. French lived at French Park, where 'Priest Phillips' also resided.

[4] *The English in Ireland*, iii. 161.

[5] *Anglicè* 'darling priest.' John Banim has given to the ballad poetry of Ireland a well-known piece under this title.

[6] Cooke to Pelham, Dec. 4, 1795.

[7] *United Irishmen*, i. 537.

His end was involved in some mystery which it may be well to penetrate. McSkimmins' 'History of Carrickfeargus' records, under date January 5, 1796 : 'The body of a stranger, said to have been an informer, of the surname of Phillips, was found in a dam, near the paper mills, Belfast.' How he came there we learn from James Hope, a Protestant rebel of Ulster. After the excommunicated priest, Phillips, had betrayed a number of the Defenders in Connaught, he proceeded to Belfast, only to find, however, that his character had cast its shadow before him. A party of Defenders seized Phillips, tried him on the spot, and sentenced him to death. 'They gave him time to pray,' adds Hope, 'then put leaden weights into his pockets, and drowned him.'

Punishment of informers by death was not of the frequency that McSkimmin supposed and Turner feared. Hope, who is always truthful, adds, that at a meeting of the Craigarogan Branch, 'they came to a resolution: "That any man who recommended or practised assassination of any person whomsoever, or however hostile to the Society, should be expelled."'

There is another informer whose name Mr. Froude undertakes to disclose. In April 1797 Camden sends Portland 'A statement which had been secretly made to him by a member of the Military Committee of the United Irishmen,'—and we learn that the informer in this instance was a miniature painter named Neville. Due inquiry has failed to find any man named Neville in the Society of United Irishmen, though a respectable wine merchant, Brent Neville, appears as the uncle of Henry Sheares's wife; 'Neville' has been reprinted in every succeeding edition of Mr. Froude's book. But it is now quite certain that Neville is a misprint for Newell. The 'Life and Confessions of Newell (a Spy),' written by himself, and undoubtedly genuine, was published in London in 1798; and in it (pp. 13–15) he describes his calling as that of a miniature painter.

CHAPTER XIV

LEONARD MCNALLY

THIRTY years ago I published in 'Notes and Queries'[1] an *exposé* of McNally, so far as it could then be done on circumstantial evidence. His secret letters to the Irish Government were not accessible when I first touched the subject, but these have become very familiar to me of late, and it will be seen that all I sought to show is proved by the revelation of McNally's own testimony. Before I come to these letters, some of the remarks with which I had long previously prefaced my doubts may perhaps be allowed to stand.

It is an object with Mr. Froude to show—and evidently as pointing a moral—that men who posed as the greatest patriots were secretly betraying the plans of their colleagues. But although Mr. Froude mentions McNally more than once, it does not appear that he was an informer. When describing the arrest and death of the Rev. Wm. Jackson in 1795, he mentions McNally as 'a popular barrister,' and further on his name is given with that of Curran, Ponsonby, Emmet, and Guinness, as constituting 'the legal strength of Irish Liberalism.' This remark is made in connection with an episode told with such dramatic effect by Mr. Froude that it remains merely for a minor pen to unmask 'the popular barrister.'

Charles Phillips, although he had made the lives of famous Irish barristers his study, as shown in 'Curran and his Contemporaries,' refused to believe any tale to the pre-

[1] Vide *Notes and Queries*, October 8, 1859.

judice of McNally. In the last edition of his popular book Phillips declares that

The thing is incredible! If I was called upon to point out, next to Curran, the man most obnoxious to the Government—who most hated them, and was most hated by them—it would have been Leonard MacNally—that MacNally, who, amidst the military audience, stood by Curran's side while he denounced oppression, defied power, and dared every danger![1]

In this impression he was supported by W. H. Curran, afterwards judge—a man who, unlike his illustrious father, was of the hardest and coldest nature. He travelled out of his path, in tracing that father's life, to pronounce a panegyric which is quite a curiosity to exhume:—

Among many endearing traits in this gentleman's private character, his devoted attachment to Mr. Curran's person and fame and, since his death, to the interests of his memory, has been conspicuous. The writer of this cannot advert to the ardour and tenderness with which he cherishes the latter, without emotion of the most lively and respectful gratitude. To Mr. McNally he has to express many obligations for the zeal with which he has assisted in procuring and supplying materials for the present work. The introduction of these private feelings is not entirely out of place—it can never be out of place to record an example of steadfastness in friendship. For three and forty years Mr. McNally was the friend of the subject of these pages; and during that long period he performed the duties of the relation with the most uncompromising and romantic fidelity. To state this is a debt of justice to the dead. The survivor has an ampler reward than any passing tribute of this sort can confer, in the recollection that during their long intercourse not even an unkind look ever passed between them.[2]

These remarks were elicited by a scene which occurred at Finney's trial[3] in '98. John Philpot Curran, embracing

[1] *Curran and his Contemporaries.*

[2] *Life of Curran*, by his Son, i. 384.

[3] McNally had spoken against time for an hour and three-quarters, as he states in an autograph note. This has been enlarged into 'three hours and a half' by Dr. Shelton Mackenzie in his *Life of Curran*, p. 228, while professing to quote from McNally's note given by Davis in *Curran's Speeches*, p. 365.

McNally, said, 'My old and excellent friend, I have long known and respected the honesty of your heart, but never until this occasion was I acquainted with the extent of your abilities. I am not in the habit of paying compliments where they are undeserved.' Tears fell from Mr. Curran as he hung over his friend."[1] Emotion spread to the Bench, and Judge Chamberlain, and Baron Smith warmly complimented McNally. Poor Curran! He

> loved to recall the past moments so dear
> When the sweet pledge of faith was confidingly given,
> When the lip spoke in voice of affection sincere,
> And the vow was exchanged and recorded in Heaven.[2]

In 1817, when Curran died in England, Burton—afterwards judge—singled out McNally, as the attached friend of the illustrious dead, to tell him the sad news.[3]

It does not surprise one that Phillips should have expressed the scepticism he puts on record. No man was more deeply versed in Bar traditions. He loved to question its oldest members about their contemporaries; and amongst all their ana he never heard, as regards McNally, a dark doubt started. 'Dr. Madden in his "Life of Robert Emmet,"' writes Phillips, 'broadly states the fact [that he was in Government pay], but does not give, as he usually does, his grounds for so stating it.'[4] Madden, replying to Phillips, said, 'I acknowledge I am ignorant of the time when the pension of 300*l*. was conferred.'

We now know not only the date, but the nature of the service by which the pension was earned.

Under-Secretary Cooke, in the year 1800, drew up for Castlereagh's information a confidential memorandum respecting 'Secret Service Pensions' for those who had given important assistance during the Rebellion. 'Mac,' for a

[1] *Life of Curran*, v. i. 397.
[2] From Curran's lines, 'The green spot that blooms on the desert of life.'
[3] *The Freeman's Journal*, October 13, 1817.
[4] *Curran and his Contemporaries*, p. 376. (Blackwood, 1850.)

pension of 300*l.* a year, is the first name recommended.[1] On the following page, Mr. Cooke—obliged to be explicit—writes the name *Leonard MacAnally* in full, with the amount 300*l.* as his annual wages.

Major Sirr was chief of the police system in Dublin. His papers contain no letters from McNally; but Thomas O'Hara, writing to Sirr on November 11, 1800, proffers his services as a spy, and requests Sirr to address his answer to 'Leonard McNally, Esq.'[2] McNally, irrespective of the knowledge he possessed as counsel for the rebels, was himself a 'United Irishman.' An organ of that body, the 'Northern Star,' on March 3, 1797, proudly describes him as such in connection with the fact that he challenged and fought Sir Jonah Barrington for having used disparaging language towards the United Irishmen. In this combat[3] he seriously suffered. The two Sheareses and Bagenal Harvey—all hanged the following year—escorted McNally to the ground.

A number of receipts for quarterly payments of Secret Service money were stolen from Dublin Castle during the thirties, and came to the hammer at a literary sale-room. Among them is the following:—

Received from William Taylor, Esqr., Seventy-five pounds, due the 25th June last. J. W.

Endorsed (by Mr. Taylor)—5th July, 1816, 75*l.* L. M'N.

S. A.[4]

McNally seems to have been the only recipient who was permitted to use false initials. The handwriting in the above is identical with some acknowledged autograph lines of Leonard McNally; but 'trifles light as air' at first encouraged my suspicions. For instance: there appears in the 'Cornwallis Papers,' some five hundred pages away from the part which mentions him, a letter signed 'J. W.'[5] The able editor, Mr. Ross, cannot guess the writer; but the information given deals

1 *Cornwallis Papers*, iii. 320.

2 Sirr Papers, MS., Library, Trinity College, Dublin.

3 An account of it appears in *Walker's Hibernian Magazine* for March 1794.

4 Secret Aid. 75*l.* would be a quarter's pay.

5 Cornwallis, ii. 350.

with matters arising out of legal proceedings, and thereby points to a barrister as the spy.

In the same letter,[1] 'J. W.' states that a man named Bird is determined to 'let the cat out of the bag.' Here it may be observed in passing, that a pamphlet of the day is entitled 'The Cat let out of the Bag,' and, though published anonymously, the copy now before me displays his well-known autograph, 'By Leonard McNally, Barrister-at-law.'[2]

John Pollock was Clerk of the Crown for the Leinster Circuit in 1798. The Book of Secret Service Money[3] records frequent payments, through his hands, to 'J. W.' These entries appear from February 16, 1799, to June 16, 1801, when the words 'repaid from pension' are added. McNally, it will be remembered, received his pension the previous year. Cooke, in a confidential memorandum for Castlereagh, writes:—

> Pollock's services ought to be thought of. He managed Mac——, and MacGuicken,[4] and did much. He received the place of Clerk of the Crown, and he has the fairest right to indemnification.[5]

Thus we see how weak was the attempt made by McNally's friends to explain away his secret pension. It was plausibly alleged that McNally, having been refused a silk gown in 1808, the pension was then conferred to compensate for his disappointment. So popular was this barrister, that the refusal of the Crown to give him silk was voted a grievance. Indeed, so far as outward appearance went, he uniformly took the popular side on all questions. The Bar meeting, to denounce the proposed Legislative Union, held on December 9, 1798, includes, among the patriotic orators, Leonard McNally.

[1] This letter, signed 'J. W.,' speaks of Father Quigley, dressed *à la militaire*. The *Cyclopædian Magazine* for 1808 says that McNally had lived at Bordeaux, and spoke French well (p. 537). The proceedings of the Whig Club are reported. McNally was a member of this club.

[2] Haliday Collection, Royal Irish Academy, vol. 613.

[3] MS. now in the Library of the Royal Irish Academy.

[4] The attorney for the Ulster United Irishmen (see *ante*, p. 36).

[5] *Cornwallis Papers*, iii. 320. See Appendix to present work for some account of Mr. John Pollock, who first succeeded in seducing the once staunch patriot.

Some of the reasons given by Phillips for refusing to doubt McNally's patriotism were, that he declined to join the lawyers' corps of yeomanry in 1798, and that his was the last hand Curran grasped when leaving Ireland! These waifs and strays only prove how well McNally played his part. As a successful dramatic author, and one who had been himself upon the stage, theatrical effect was at all times easy to him.

It is now time to appeal to direct evidence, not until recently accessible. Mr. Lecky, in examining the archives of the Home Office, has found record of McNally's fall, and the virtuous historian describes it as a 'peculiarly shocking one.'[1] It will be remembered that the Rev. Wm. Jackson, a parson, came to Ireland in 1794 on a secret mission from France. He was arrested, tried, and sentenced to death. McNally now found, it is said, that if he did not become an informer the halter would soon encircle a neck previously dignified by forensic bands.

> Jackson, shortly before his death [Mr. Lecky goes on to say], found an opportunity of writing four short letters, recommending his wife and child, and a child who was still unborn, to two or three friends, and to the care of the French nation, and he also drew up a will leaving all he possessed to his wife, and entrusting McNally with the protection of her interests. He wrote at the bottom of it, 'Signed and sealed in presence of my dearest friend, whose heart and principles ought to recommend him as a worthy citizen—Leonard McNally.' These precious documents he entrusted, when dying, to his friend, and about three weeks after the death of Jackson, McNally placed them in the hands of the Irish Government.
>
> A few days later, Camden sent a copy of them to England, with a 'most secret and confidential letter.' 'The paper which accompanies this,' he said, 'was delivered to Counsellor McNally, from whom Government received it. There is so much evidence against this person, that he is—I am informed—completely in the power of Government. Your Grace will observe that the care of Mrs. Jackson is recommended by her husband to the National Convention, and that Mr. McNally is desired to assist her by every means in his

[1] Lecky, vii. 139.

power to procure her assistance from them. It has occurred to me that an excuse might be made for Mr. McNally's being allowed to enter France for the purpose of attending to this woman's fortunes, that he should go through London, and in case your Grace should wish to employ him, I would inform you when and where he will be found.'

Portland replied that he was perfectly ready to make use of the services of McNally in France, if Camden thought that he might be safely trusted, but he suggested that this was very doubtful. The control which Government possessed over him depended entirely upon the conclusive evidence of treason they had against him. Would that control continue in a foreign country? Camden, on reflection, agreed that it would not be safe to try the experiment. McNally, however, he was convinced, would be very useful at home.[1]

Jackson, finding no chance of acquittal, took poison and died, just as Lord Clonmell was about to sentence him to be hanged. Shortly before his death in the dock, seeing McNally pass, he grasped his hand and is said to have whispered, 'We have deceived the Senate!' This was true of McNally, but Jackson did not suspect him; nor did Curran, or the many other shrewd scribes who have chronicled the touching incident.

Mr. Lecky thinks that McNally's fall dates only from 1794: my belief is that he had previously evinced some frailty. In 1790, when counsel for Lord Sherborne, Beresford Burston accused him of 'doing dirty work,'[2] and McNally thereupon challenged Burston. Dr. Madden says that, in 1792, at the time of Napper Tandy's action against the Viceroy, some of Tandy's legal advisers were suspected of having disclosed their ingenious case to the Crown. McNally was certainly counsel in this cause. St. John Mason, first cousin of the Emmets, broadly charges McNally with perfidy committed in 1792.[3] Previous to this date Collins the spy calls McNally 'one of us,' in a secret letter to the Government agent, Jack Gifford.[4]

[1] Lecky's *England*, vii. 140. (Longmans, 1890.)

[2] *The Grand Juries of Westmeath, from* 1727 *to* 1853, by J. C. Lyons, p. 200.

[3] Madden, iii. 37.

[4] This letter reports an early meeting of the rebel conclave, and is dated March 30, 1792. (MSS., Dublin Castle.)

Who Gifford was is shown by Curran, who complains to the Chief Secretary for Ireland, that 'Gifford, a note-taker for your Government, had the daring to come up to me in the street and shake his stick at me.'[1]

Mr. Lecky says that McNally would betray to the Crown the line of defence contemplated by his clients, and other information which he could only have received in professional confidence, and that the Government archives contain briefs annotated in his own hand. Mr. Lecky finds that

he was also able, in a manner not less base, to furnish the Government with early and most authentic evidence about conspiracies which were forming in France. James Tandy[2] . . . was his intimate friend; McNally, by his means, saw nearly every letter that arrived from Napper Tandy, and some of those which came from Rowan and Reynolds. The substance of these letters was regularly transmitted to the Government, and they sometimes contained information of much value. Besides this, as a lawyer in considerable practice, constantly going on circuit, and acquainted with the leaders of sedition, McNally had excellent opportunities of knowing the state of the country, and was able to give very valuable warnings about the prevailing dispositions.[3]

Among the earlier victims to the severe legislation of that time was Laurence Conner, a poor schoolmaster of Naas, charged with Defenderism, whose case has been invested with interest by Sir Jonah Barrington, Dr. Madden, and others. A moving speech from the dock failed to avert his doom, and his head, for years after, grinned from a stake at the top of the gaol. McNally, who had defended him, stated in his secret report to Pelham that a provision had been offered for Conner's family if he would make discoveries; but his reply was, 'He who feeds the young ravens in the valley will provide for them!'[4] It is strange that McNally should report

[1] *Life of Curran*, by his Son.

[2] For a notice of James Tandy, afterwards stipendiary magistrate for Meath, see Appendix.

[3] Lecky, vii. 141.

[4] Dr. Madden assigns Conner's death to the year 1796, but McNally's report is dated September 17, 1795.

to his employers this chivalrous speech, which places in marked contrast his own frailty and disgraceful fall. But corrupt as his heart had now become, he could not help admiring magnanimity wherever he met it. The man who sought to make Conner inform was, doubtless, McNally himself, at the instance of Crown Solicitor Pollock, who, as the 'Cornwallis Papers' record (iii. 320), 'managed Mac.'

This is the man whose name Earl Russell erased from Moore's Diary of February 27, 1835, leaving merely the initials 'L. McN.,' because some doubts of his honesty had been expressed post-prandially by Plunket, a man more clear-sighted, it appears, than Charles Phillips. Succeeding chapters will show Plunket associated with McNally during the State trials of '98.

Lord Holland amused with my saying how much I used to look up to this L—— McN—— [writes Moore], on account of some songs in a successful opera which he wrote, 'Robin Hood.' 'Charming Clorinda' was one of the songs I used to envy him being the author of.

'Your profession should have taught you principles of honour,' McNally writes in the piece which first roused the muse of Moore. With such fine sentiments it must have caused him a struggle to betray. All will rejoice that he who sang

> Let Erin remember the days of old
> Ere her faithless sons betrayed her—

escaped the blight of McNally's breath. Moore was the bosom friend of Emmet, sympathised with the 'cause,' and wrote for the organ of the United Irishmen. Shortly after '98, however, he entered at the Middle Temple, London, and saw McNally no more. Plunket told Moore that it was in a duel McNally received the wound in the hip that lamed him, and on a subsequent occasion, when he was again going out to fight, a friend said, 'Turn the other hip to him, and who knows but he may shoot you straight.'[1]

[1] Moore's *Journal*, &c., vii. 75. Edited by Lord John Russell.

McNally was indeed a brave man. If anyone seemed to doubt him, he would be called out and perhaps shot. In early life he practised at the English Bar. It is recorded in the 'Cyclopædian Magazine,' for 1808, that during the Gordon Riots, when the mob had smashed down the Bishop of Lincoln's coach, had dragged him out, and were beating him with bludgeons, McNally, at the risk of his life, rescued Dr. Thurlow, on whose forehead, he heard them say, they meant to cut the sign of the cross. This prelate, who somewhat favoured Catholic Relief, was the brother of Lord Chancellor Thurlow; and the young barrister may have had an ulterior object in thus exposing himself to danger. McNally himself evidently supplied the account, of which but a few details are here borrowed, and we learn that 'the Bishop required, and received, the address of his protector, but never after acknowledged the obligation.'[1] Some pamphlets on the Regency struggle, and the 'Claims of Ireland' vindicated on the principles of the English Whigs, introduced him to Fox, for whom he acted as counsel at an election for Westminster. 'By whatever right England possesses Liberty,' he said, 'by the same right Ireland may claim it!'

McNally as an orator was declamatory, and at times theatrical. His outward man has been often caricatured, but John O'Keefe tells us that he had 'a handsome, expressive countenance, and fine sparkling dark eyes.'[2] Sir Jonah Barrington recognises the same features. Contemporary memoirs of him supply a long list of his dramas, farces, comic operas, touching lyrics, prologues and masques, all produced at Covent Garden. But while in England he was a genuine, thoroughgoing Irishman, very unlike the sham which he afterwards became; and why he resigned a dramatic for a forensic career is curiously shown by 'Sylvanus Urban.'

[1] *Cyclopædian Magazine*, 1808, p. 539. A sensational and detailed account of the rescue, evidently supplied by McNally, is culled from a contemporary newspaper, and, in response to the present writer, appears in *Notes and Queries*, of May 19, 1860, p 293.

[2] *Recollections of John O'Keefe*, ii. 45.

The opening of Covent Garden Theatre, on September 23, 1782, was commemorated by a prelude from McNally's pen.

The author, with a partiality to his own countrymen which we know not how to censure, has drawn the character of an Irishman as one possessed of qualities which he had rather imprudently denied to the other persons of the drama—English, Scotch, Welsh, and French. This circumstance gave offence, and before the conclusion of the piece the clamour became too great for anything to be heard.

Few names seem to have been more popular with the pit and galleries, and the admiration of his countrymen for him showed itself in odd ways. Kemble somewhere describes an Irishman at Drury Lane indignantly claiming one of Shakespeare's plays for McNally: and when a spectator, duly challenged, replied that he did not want to dispute the point with him, his tormentor said, still trying to foster a quarrel, 'but perhaps you don't believe me?' Again the man received a polite assurance which seemed quite satisfactory; but five minutes later 'Pat,' observing Kemble whispering to a companion, came over in an attitude still more menacing—'Maybe your friend doesn't believe that the play is written by Leonard McNally?' and to avoid a scene both were glad to decamp. Those were the days when the voice of national predilection made itself heard and felt in dramatic criticism. Home scored a success with 'Douglas:' 'and where be your Wully Shakespeare noo?' was shrieked by some clannish Scots that night. McNally's friends regretted more than once that he ever left London. A book called 'Five Hundred Celebrated Authors of Great Britain now living' was published here in 1788, and it is amusing to find McNally's name included with those of Burke, Gibbon, Walpole, Crabbe, Burns, Cowper, De Lolme and Mackenzie, who at the close of a century were helping to educate the minds which were to adorn its successor. The extraordinary fact is stated that McNally was then editor of a newspaper called 'The Times.'

One day Lord Loughborough, finding McNally ill prepared in a case which came before the Court, advised him to abandon the Muses and study Blackstone; but love for letters predominated, and his 'Sentimental Excursions to Windsor' appeared. On rejoining the Irish Bar he produced 'The Irish Justice of the Peace,' for which 2,500*l.* was paid by Hugh Fitzpatrick, the Catholic publisher; but Charles Phillips says 'it contained so much bad law,' that it proved a treasure not to the J. P's., but to the country attorneys. Magistrates sadly soon had practical experience of a writ; and Michael Staunton told me, that if McNally's law points often served culprits, they hanged as many more.[1] 'In Dublin,' records a contemporary scribe,[2] 'he has now very considerable law business.'

'He had a shrill, full, good bar voice,' writes Barrington, in bestowing other praise. Sir Jonah occupied the judgment seat, and was famous for his power of discerning character; but, although he impugns the good name of many men, he does not distrust McNally. According to Barrington, 'Mac' was 'good-natured, hospitable, and talented.'[3] It is to be feared that hospitality with the popular barrister was but a means to an end. 'Will you walk into my parlour? said the spider to the fly.' McNally, in some of his letters to the Crown when requesting money, urges the necessity of entertaining friends in order to get at new information.

Without money [he writes] it is impossible to do what is expected. Those Spartans wish to live like Athenians in matters of eating and drinking. They live so among each other, and without ability to entertain I cannot live with them, and without living with them I cannot learn from them.

[1] Mr. Lecky thinks that, had not McNally become a spy, he might have risen to the judgment seat. This, with the testimony of Phillips and Staunton before us, is doubtful: but I am bound to say that many contemporary Irish judges were bad lawyers, who owed their promotion solely to political claims. Higgins does not seem to have known that McNally was also a spy. He often reports him to Cooke: 'Counsellor McNally told me this night at Parisoll's, that Government had offered a sinecure employment, which he rejected. I offered to hold him 100 guineas that his services were never sought for, which completely put him down.'—Francis Higgins to Cooke, November 18, 1797. MSS. Dublin Castle.

[2] *Sketches of Irish Political Characters*, 1799.

[3] *Personal Memoirs.*

McNally knew human nature quite as well as Bishop South, who says of the bacchanal that his 'heart floats upon his lips, and his inmost thoughts proclaim and write themselves upon his forehead;' and he adds that, just 'as a liar ought to have a good memory, so a person of guilt ought to be also a person of great sobriety.'[1] McNally's dinner in honour of unfortunate 'Parson Jackson' and of the man who shadowed him to the grave, suggests that it was not the only occasion when death sat at the table.

In midsummer 1798 the clangour of battle filled the air. 'Fear prevails, and all jovial intercourse has ceased, so far as my experience goes,'[2] he writes; but when hostilities stopped, amenities were renewed.

After he had ceased to produce 'masques' at Covent Garden, and entered on his new career of a barrister and a spy, one great effort of his energetic life was to divert suspicion and puzzle posterity. He saw the wisdom of the proverb, 'Show me your company,' and thus he had a double object to gain by cultivating touch with patriotic men. In 1790 he was admitted a Freeman for—as the address to him said—his services to his country. In 1802 he published 'The Rules of Evidence, or Pleas of the Crown.' It is dedicated to John Philpot Curran, 'from an affectionate attachment,' writes McNally,

> and from a proud wish to make known to posterity that a reciprocal and an uninterrupted amity subsisted between the Author and the man whose transcendent genius and philosophic mind soar above all competition—whose honest and intrepid heart was never influenced in the Senate, nor intimidated at the Bar, from exerting, with zeal, independence, and spirit, his love to his country and his duty to his client.

The 'authorised' memoir of McNally in the 'Cyclopædian Magazine' quotes the above, adding, 'The relatives of Mr. Curran may extract from this dedication an epitaph worthy of his memory.' The whole object of the memoir, one evidently inspired by McNally himself, is to foster a feeling of respect

[1] Sermon on Concealment of Sin.
[2] J. W. to Cooke, June 5, 1798.

for and confidence in his own pretensions. No wonder that, in the eyes of Young Ireland one hundred years ago, a halo encircled McNally's head. Some of the spirited efforts which roused the Muse of Moore and Drennan are found in the organ of the United Irishmen. The 'Northern Star' of November 10, 1792, contains a rebellious song signed L. M. N., beginning—

Muse of energy and fire,
Stretch abroad thy boldest wing:
Freedom calls—assume the Lyre;
Freedom calls—arise and sing!

Mr. Lecky has not examined McNally's secret reports after the year 1800, and his impression is that he 'did not wish to implicate "persons."'[1] It would appear, however, on Mr. Lecky's own showing, that McNally was not squeamish—even during the reign of terror—in pointing to men by name.

In September and October 1797 he told them [writes Mr. Lecky] that Bond was the treasurer of the conspiracy; that the chief management was now transferred from Belfast to Dublin and confined to a very few; that Keogh, McCormick, Lord Edward Fitzgerald, Arthur O'Connor, Sweetman, Dixon, Chambers, Emmet, Bond, and Jackson were in the secret.[2]

On February 5, 1797, McNally warns the Government that O'Coigly (hanged the following year) was in Ireland on a political mission, and reports the pith of his conversation.[3] 'O'Connor, Macnevin and Lord Edward Fitzgerald,' he whispers, 'are the advocates of assassination,'[4] which, indeed, there is great reason to doubt.[5] On November 19 Grattan is put in jeopardy.[6] Next month 'a most circumstantial and

[1] Lecky, vii. 142, 401.

[2] All these men, Keogh alone excepted, though never brought to trial, underwent a prolonged term of imprisonment. Keogh was the highly influential leader of the Catholics, and the Crown, probably, wished to make an exception in his favour.

[3] Lecky, vii. 55.

[4] *Ibid.* p. 337.

[5] See O'Connor's letter (*United Irishmen*, ii. 234), saying that in 1797 he expressed abhorrence of the Union *Star*, which had urged assassination; whereupon Cox, its editor, instantly discontinued it. Then, as regards Macnevin and Lord Edward, they are described by Reinhard as 'of the moderate party.' See the *Castlereagh Papers*, i. 283.

[6] Lecky, p. 423.

alarming story,' writes Lecky, had come from McNally. 'It was, that Lord Edward received, some days since, orders from Paris to urge an insurrection here with all speed, in order to draw troops from England. In consequence of it, there was a meeting of the head committee, where he and O'Connor urged immediate measures of vigour;' and thereupon their plans are laid bare: but how Emmet, Chambers, etc., opposed. McNally lived in Dominick Street, near the Dominican Fathers. In letters to Cooke he points to MacMahon and other of his reverend colleagues; and I learn from the present custodian of the 'Dominican Records' that Fathers MacMahon, Bushe,[1] and Mulhall were arrested in '98, but at last suffered to leave Ireland for America. On May 24, 1798, J. W. mentions that MacMahon had called on him the previous day. But so early as June 14, 1797 the falcon eye of McNally had become fixed on this friar. He and other priests, he states, meet weekly at Herbert's tavern, Clontarf. 'Reilly, an officer who served in Germany, is often with them. Individually, no doubt, they are all concerned in the politics of the day, and they act when together with a caution certainly suspicious. Vernon, of Clontarf, offered the waiter 100*l.* to make discoveries, which he refused.'

'Troy may be up,'[2] McNally reports, meaning that the Catholic archbishop had been probably enrolled a United Irishman. Henceforth his Grace's letters were regularly opened at the Post Office.[3] Minor names are often breathed, and who can doubt that, with the Habeas Corpus Act suspended, advanced men stood upon the brink of an abyss? Carhampton, Commander-in-Chief, sent numbers of untried men out of the country,[4] and threatened to do the same with the Rev. Edward Berwick,[5] and others. Hundreds were seized on bare suspicion and expatriated without even knowing their accusers, or hearing the charge for which they suffered.[6]

[1] Walter Cox's *Irish Magazine* for December 1814 states (p. 570) that Fr. Bushe was flogged in Beresford's Riding School.

[2] Lecky, p. 331.

[3] *Ibid.* p. 462.

[4] Plowden's *Historic Review*, ii. 537.

[5] Berwick to Grattan. See *Life of Grattan*, vol. v.

[6] 'Trials, if they must so be called, were carried on without number, under

The acts of no member of the Directory are more regularly reported than those of Arthur O'Connor. McNally seems to have been in his confidence as political ally and legal adviser. In turning over his letters I met one much more voluminous than the rest, furnishing a complete list of all the witnesses to appear at Maidstone for O'Connor's defence, and the facts to which they were prepared to testify.[1] These witnesses included Erskine, Fox, Grattan, Sheridan, Whitbread, Lords Moira, Suffolk, Thanet, and Oxford.[2]

Throughout the State Trials men stalked who, as Curran said, measured their value by the coffins of their victims, and gloom was relieved by forensic *persiflage*. McNally had been lamed in a duel, and another limping barrister one day asked Parsons in 'the Hall' of the Four Courts, 'Did you see McNally go this way?' 'I never saw him go any other way,' was the reply.

Ned Lysaght had his skit, too :—

> One leg is short which makes him lame,
> Therefore the legs don't tally;
> And now, my friends, to tell his name,
> 'Tis Leonard MacAnally.

He had been urged to join a Volunteer corps; but Curran told him that serious trouble might result, for, when ordered to 'march,' he would certainly 'halt.'[3] When writing to

martial law. It often happened that three officers composed the court, and that, of the three, two were under age, and the third an officer of the yeomanry or militia, who had sworn, in his Orange lodge, eternal hatred to the people over whom he was thus constituted a judge. Floggings, picketings, death, were the usual sentences, and these were sometimes commuted into banishment, serving in the fleet, or transference to a foreign service. Many were sold at so much per head to the Prussians. Other less legal, but not more horrible, outrages were daily committed by the different corps under the command of Government. The subsequent Indemnity Acts deprived of redress the victims of this widespread cruelty.'—Lord Holland's *Memoirs of the Whig Party*.

[1] This despatch is dated merely 'Tuesday, 25th'; but a second on the same subject bears 'April 27, 1798.' (MSS. Dublin Castle.)

[2] See *Appendix*, 'James Tandy and McNally.'

[3] In 1810, Sir William Stamer, who seized John Keogh's papers in 1803, gave a masquerade. McNally went as Æsop, but scorned to wear a mask. Huband, whom he often reports, went as Pan; Dogherty, afterwards Chief Justice, as Jeremy Diddler; Wolfe, afterwards Chief Baron, as a hair-dresser; Sir Jonah

Cooke on the subject of the Lawyers' Corps, J. W., in a secret letter of June 12, 1798, introduces his real name, no doubt to puzzle outsiders into whose hands it might fall: 'It would be well perhaps if some of the judges would institute a Corps of Invalids. McNally might lead blind Moore to battle.'

Mr. Lecky thinks that McNally after his fall 'retained all the good nature and native kindness of his disposition.'[1] I fear that this redeeming virtue cannot be safely assigned to him. A careful sketch of the man appears in a local publication of the year 1806; and we learn that among his characteristics are—

Satire—oft whetted on ill-nature's stone,
Which spares no other's failings, nor his own.
But well may Leonard wield that branch of trade
Where cunning comes to penetration's aid;
— No logic closer—strong his declamation,
But his best leg is cross-examination.[2]

This, as we now see, was done quite as much in the privacy of his study as in the forensic arena.

Curran's great speech in Hevey *v.* Sirr contains a passage which has often been quoted:—

A learned and respected brother barrister had a silver cup; Major [Sandys] heard that for many years it had borne an inscription of 'Erin go bragh'—which meant 'Ireland for ever.' The Major considered this perseverance for such a length of time a forfeiture of the delinquent vessel. My poor friend was accordingly robbed of his cup.

This 'learned and respected barrister' was none other than McNally himself. I have read his secret letter to Cooke on the subject, endorsed 'June 2, 1798,' and it makes him less a hero than he would publicly convey. He complains of the seizure of his cup, notwithstanding that, as he assured his military visitor, he had already erased the offending inscription. 'Mac,'

Barrington as a friar; and 'Doctor Turner' (no doubt Samuel, LL.D.), as Punch. For a full account, see *Hibernian Magazine* for 1810, p. 125.

[1] Lecky's *History of England*, vii. 142.

[2] *The Metropolis* (Dublin, 1806), p. 43. Written by Counsellor Wm. Norcott. See *Dublin University Magazine*, vol. lviii. 725, also p. 331.

in conclusion, says that the cup was value for 22*l.* 10*s.*, 'hardly earned,' and encloses a separate paper distinctly naming that sum as his due. Four days later he writes to Cooke: 'Major Sandys returned a *sterling* answer to *my friend's* note,' which means a full money remittance for the amount claimed.[1]

Below we have McNally's version of this transaction, as supplied to Curran's son for historic and popular purposes: —

A sergeant waited upon him, and delivered a verbal command from Major Sandys to surrender the cup. Mr. McNally refused, and commissioned the messenger to carry back such an answer as so daring a requisition suggested.[2] The sergeant . . . respectfully remonstrated upon the imprudence of provoking Major Sandys. The consequences soon appeared: the sergeant returned with a body of soldiers, who paraded before Mr. McNally's door, and were under orders to proceed to extremities if the cup was not delivered up. Upon Mr. MacNally's acquainting Lord Kilwarden with the outrage, the latter burst into tears and, exclaiming that 'his own sideboard might be the next object of plunder, if such atrocious practices were not checked,' lost not an instant in procuring the restitution of the property. The cup was accordingly sent back with the inscription erased.[3]

Arthur Wolfe, Lord Kilwarden, was the Chief Justice of the King's Bench, and his alleged intimacy with McNally is probably exaggerated. The biographer says that Curran repeatedly told this episode of '98, and quotes a touching peroration regarding Kilwarden's alleged interposition: that,

[1] McNally always describes himself, in his secret letters, as 'my friend.'

[2] Spy as he was, McNally trembled throughout the troubles, and is not likely to have delivered the defiant reply which he claims to have done. On May 24, 1798, he describes his family as 'all females—all live in terror.' He has moved them a short way from Dublin. He hopes that Cooke's interest will prevent the impending evil of free quarters on his house. It was astutely felt at Dublin Castle, however, that the more McNally seemed to suffer persecution for justice sake, the more freely would popular confidence be reposed in him. On June 27, 1798, he writes to Cooke, bitterly complaining that his house had been attacked by soldiers, who refused to respect Castlereagh's protection.

[3] *Life of Curran*, by his Son, ii. 148-9. Compare Lecky, viii. 24, where MacNally seems humanely to lament the theft by soldiers, from a Dublin barrister, of a stand inscribed 'Erin go bragh.'

in fact, great was the odour of its memory and precious the balm of its consolation!

McNally's account of the robbery of his silver cup was part of his stock-in-trade, and I am sure that for twenty times the price he would not have been without it.

William Henry Curran knew not very much of his father, whose biographer he became. John Philpot Curran had excluded him from his domestic circle, and the letters to his son which appear in the book were addressed to Richard. Who can doubt that much detail which lends interest to the ever popular 'Life, by his Son,' was supplied to the youth by the practised old scribe Leonard McNally? Curran's gratitude to him for help afforded is freely expressed. McNally wrote a style clear as rock water and full of classic strength. Nothing can be finer than his secret letters to Pelham and Cooke—three of which he often despatched in one day. The wonderful anecdotes which made Curran's Life, by his son, almost a classic have been quoted over and over, including the dinner scene at McNally's, when the ill-fated Rev. Mr. Jackson was entertained. Curran's son tells how the talk had been getting imprudent, when the butler, beckoning his master to the door, warned him to be careful; 'for, sir, the strange gentleman who seems to be asleep is not so, but listening to everything said: I see his eye glistening through the fingers with which he is covering his face.'

Cockayne was, of course, a spy of Pitt's; but some of the sensational anecdotes which McNally told of him, as also of Reynolds and Armstrong, may have been overcharged to divert suspicion from himself. These are not the only instances in which the embellishments of the professional advocate seem traceable. As regards Jackson's death in the dock, we are told that he made an effort with his cold and nerveless hand to squeeze McNally's, muttering a quotation from Otway's 'Venice Preserved'; but the lines and the adjuncts would be more likely to occur at such a moment to an old playwright than to the dying clergyman.

Emmet's revolt took place on July 23, 1803, but was soon

quelled. He remained in concealment at Harold's Cross, and chose that position in order that he might see Sarah Curran, with her father, pass daily to Dublin. On August 25 he was arrested by Major Sirr. Popular confidence in McNally had now reached its height. A special commission for trying the insurgent leaders began on August 24, 1803. 'Most of the prisoners chose Mr. McNally as their counsel, and Mr. L. McNally, junior, as their agent,' records the 'Evening Post' of the day.

McNally had long had his eye on the gifted young orator Robert Emmet: 'Emmet, junior, gone on business to France—probably to supersede Lewins,'[1] he writes to Cooke three years previous to the insurrection of 1803. On September 3, in the latter year, McNally sends one of his secret letters to Cooke, saying that he is authorised to treat on behalf of a person privy to the whole conspiracy.[2]

The remainder of McNally's letters during these troubles of 1803 are yet wanting. No doubt they remain among Wickham's papers of the period which are still a sealed book.[3] Among the sensational incidents of the hour was the outrage of searching Curran's house, and the capture of Emmet's love-letters to Sarah Curran—to whom the youth had been secretly engaged. Curran himself, we are told, though aware of Emmet's visits, was ignorant of the attachment. But there was a seemingly dear old friend, having access to Curran's domestic circle, whose eagle eye could penetrate still deeper secrets. In the absence of McNally's private reports of that month there is, however, no absolute proof against him on this point.

Mount Jerome,[4] the seat of John Keogh, the great Catholic leader, was also searched, and his papers seized. Dr. Madden

[1] J. W. (secret), September 19, 1800.

[2] Wickham seems to allude to this fact in the *Colchester Correspondence*, i. 456.

[3] Mr. Ross, in his preface to the *Cornwallis Papers*, states that Wickham's papers are destroyed. His grandson tells me that the papers are safely in his possession.

[4] Now the cemetery at Harold's Cross, Dublin.

mentions that, in 1802, Emmet had dined at Keogh's in the company of John Philpot Curran, when the probability of success in the event of a second rebellion was debated with great animation.[1] Whose was the whisper which betrayed this information never transpired. But Curran, the great depository of popular secrets, maintained, as will be shown, no reserve with McNally. So far back as 1797 McNally writes :—

Grattan and Curran are compleatly in the secret. Everything that's done or intended is communicated to them.[2]

A quantity of information follows, and the letter ends with these pregnant words :—

Curran gives a dinner at his house. *Will be there.*

This is the man whom William Henry Curran describes as having been 'from his youth to his latest hour the most affectionate, unshaken and disinterested friend' of his father.[3]

Before and after the conviction and death of Robert Emmet, the initials 'L. M.' peep from the 'Secret Service Money Book.' On August 25, 1803 (the very day on which Emmet was captured), we read: 'Mr. Pollock for L. M., 100*l.*' Pollock, Clerk of the Crown for Leinster, is the same man through whom the bribes for 'J. W.' (McNally) are paid.[4] The 100*l.* cannot have been for the actual capture of Emmet, for I know that in November following a bulk sum was paid for that service. The *douceur* to L. M. was in acknowledgment of useful information.[5]

McNally appears as counsel for Emmet in the State trial

[1] Madden's *United Irishmen*, iii. 330.

[2] J. W. to Mr. Secretary Cooke: endorsed 'November 1797.' McNally adds, of a subsequent Whig Lord Chancellor, on whom he had his eye: 'Geo. Ponsonby is not of the private meetings at Grattan's or Curran's.'

[3] *Life of Curran*, by his Son, ii. 385.

[4] The same manuscript further records, under the respective dates, March 16, 1803, and November 26, 1803, two sums of 100*l.* each, paid to 'J. W.'

[5] Mr. W. B. Kelly, who held the copyright of a book of mine called *The Sham Squire*, got it reprinted in Edinburgh many years ago. I had no opportunity for revising the proofs, and I am anxious to correct the strange misprint at p. 250, of '1,000*l.*' instead of '100*l.*' to McNally. The original edition, at the same page, states the amount correctly.

on September 19, 1803. Four days previously, namely, on September 14, 100*l.* is set down to 'L. M.' On the morning of Emmet's execution an affecting scene took place between the rebel chief and McNally, the only friend allowed to see him. Emmet's mother had just died, but he did not know it, and desire to see her filled him—'Then, Robert, you shall meet her this day,' replied McNally, pointing to Heaven in his accustomed dramatic style. A long account of the interview, doubtless supplied by 'Mac' himself with his usual itch for writing, and evidently designed to promote Lord Hardwicke's popularity as Viceroy, appears in a Ministerial journal, the London 'Chronicle,' on September 24, 1803.

> Emmet [we are told] observed that, had he not been interrupted by the Court in his address, he would have spoken as warm an eulogium on the candour and moderation of the present Government in this kingdom as his conception or language were adequate to.

After Emmet's arrest Curran was examined by the Privy Council, when Chancellor Redesdale sought by a tone of intimidation to extort the truth; but the scowl of contempt he encountered gave his own nerves the shock he designed for another's, and made him sink back into his chair, abashed by the failure of his rash experiment. Curran's son speaks of the wonderful intrepidity of McNally's language in his addresses to the Court; but it is easy to be defiant when one knows he is safe. Contemporary critics record his marvellous power of penetration in cross-examining witnesses on the State trials. A shrewd man, deep in the secrets of both sides, would not find it hard to create this impression.

Lord Cloncurry complains, in his Memoirs, that after his liberation from gaol in 1801, and for many subsequent years, no man suffered more from petty worries at the hands of the Irish Government. McNally was in the coterie of which Cloncurry formed the central figure, and it cannot be doubted that he consistently reported his fervid sentiments. The 'Press' was the Rebel organ, its tone distinguished, as Lord Camden said, by 'an unheard-of boldness,'[1] and a friendly offer made by Lawless, afterwards Lord Cloncurry, to McNally is thus reported. After mentioning when the private committee of United Irishmen met, McNally[2] announces—the underlining his own:—

Lawless, principal proprietor of the 'Press': *he has offered a share to J.W.*[3]*—a £50 share. . . . .* Nothing save rebellious toasts at the dinner; *McNevin was there.* Lawless gave 'Cut the Painter' [*i.e.* Separation from England].

An accurate and dayly [sic] *account will be given.* Lawless sails for London to-morrow night. It is his turn of duty,—perhaps to meet some people at the Head. He ought to be watched from George's Quay every hour till his return.[4]

A later letter assures Pelham: 'The fellow-travellers of Lawless shall be found out if possible.'[5]

Higgins and Magan knew nothing of Cloncurry's movements, but between Turner and McNally he had a warm time of it. Lord Holland compared his long detention in the Tower, untried and unaccused, to the operation of the *lettres de cachet* in old France. In 1803, on secret but, he declares, erroneous information, that Emmet's wounded rebels were concealed there, 'a large military force' searched Lord Cloncurry's house in Kildare, and robbed it of a quantity of papers, some fowling-pieces, armour, and even plate.'[6]

No details are forthcoming as regards the intercourse which subsisted between McNally and Cloncurry throughout

[1] Camden to Portland, December 2, 1797.

[2] Most of McNally's letters are endorsed by Cooke. This is marked by Pelham, 'November 8, 1797.'

[3] McNally himself.

[4] Cloncurry did not see Ireland again until his liberation from the Tower. The object of his mission to England was mere surmise. Pelham assumes that he carried a despatch to the French Republic (Froude, iii. 287); but Cloncurry, ignorant of the above letters, tells his law adviser: 'No papers on politics were found on me, for I never had such' (*Memoirs*, p. 138). Previously, he casually mentions that his father 'insisted upon my going to London to keep my terms at the Temple, which I accordingly did *in November*, 1797,' the very date of McNally's letter. (*Memoirs of Lord Cloncurry*, p. 57.)

[5] Endorsed, 'M. secret. November.'

[6] *Personal Recollections of Lord Cloncurry*, p. 219.

the eventful period subsequent to their friendly relations in '98; but the cordiality of that intercourse may be seen from a waif or two. The 'Correspondent,' a Dublin journal, reports on August 27, 1817, a speech of the patriot peer, Cloncurry, in which the epithet 'dear' is applied to his old friend McNally. 'There is no gentleman,' he adds, 'for whom I have a higher respect or esteem, and of whose knowledge, talent and elocution I am more sensible.'

Sometimes McNally travelled as a spy, probably in disguise, through remote rural districts. On August 28, 1805, he announces Tipperary as 'ready to rise.' In September he goes up the Dublin mountains, 'Emmet's line,' and the result of his inquiries was that no rising need be apprehended.[1] I do not find that McNally's secret letters exist at Dublin Castle beyond the year 1805; I must, therefore, seek to trace from other sources the close of his career. Pecuniary need drew its toils tighter round him every day, making him, no doubt, more energetic in his effort to cast them off.[2]

Readers of the 'Wellington Correspondence' from 1807 to 1809 will be able to identify McNally. The subjugator of Tippoo Saib, then Chief Secretary at Dublin Castle, found Catholic Ireland galled by various disabilities. One letter, dated November 21, 1807, encloses a paper headed 'Information received this evening from a very intelligent Priest.'[3] This, on being quoted by the reviewers of the Wellington Papers, excited disgust that a priest should be in secret correspondence with Dublin Castle; but it is quite clear to me that the letter came from McNally, and embodies merely the responses of a gossiping priest to the pumping of a practised

[1] Not one of McNally's letters is dated beyond the day of the week; but many have a correct date endorsed. Some conjectural dates, supplied in late years by an official pencil, are often wrong.

[2] In 1807–8 he appears as a defendant in several judgments 'marked' by the King's Bench. To Benjamin Bradley, 38*l*. 4*s*. 9*d*.; to Thomas Shaw, 56*l*.; to the administrators of Hatch, and others; and the search, if continued, would show the same results in after years. Curran frequently accommodated him, as well as William Godwin and others.

[3] *Wellington Correspondence* (*Ireland*), p. 192.

hand—the same, I may venture to add, to whom McNally, upon dying, will be found making his own confession.

The Whig Duke of Bedford took office with Fox, Lansdowne, and Grey in the administration of 'All the Talents,' and ruled Ireland for one year. Curran became Master of the Rolls, and McNally thought that he himself, as the leading popular barrister, had claims for promotion. All the men who will be remembered as voting with him at the bar meeting in 1799 had got snug berths. His appeal to Bedford was referred to Wellesley, whose common sense appears in the following reply:—

I agree entirely with you respecting the employment of our informer. Such a measure would do much mischief. It would disgust the loyal of all descriptions, at the same time that it would render useless our private communications with him, as no further trust would be placed in him by the disloyal. I think that it might be hinted to him that he would lose much of his profit, if, by accepting the public employment of Government, he were to lose the confidence of his party, and consequently the means of giving us information.[1]

Curiously enough, that at the time he is himself most active as a spy, Mr. T. Mulock, of Dublin, reports him, with O'Connell and Hutton, as persons who 'ought to be watched.'[2] An account of the first meeting for Repeal of the Union, on September 18, 1810, is preserved in the State Papers; and McNally spoke on that day 'with great zeal and patriotism,' as Plowden proudly[3] records. Mr. Mulock had not the knowledge of character shown by his kinswoman Miss Mulock, the novelist.

Reference has been already made to the fact that in 1811 the Irish Secretary of State, Wellesley Pole, with the object of suppressing the Catholic Committee, caused to be arrested, under the Convention Act, Lord Fingall, Lord Netterville, and the other Catholic delegates. Able counsel were retained by

[1] *Wellington Correspondence* (*Ireland*), pp. 99–100.
[2] Ireland, 1810, August to December, No. 648, State Paper Office.
[3] *History of Ireland since the Union*, by Francis Plowden, iii. 896.

them, and private conferences, attended by Burrowes, Johnson, Perrin, O'Connell, Burton, O'Driscoll, and McNally, were held in order to decide on the lines of defence to be taken. The questions involved were difficult and subtle; and although the courses decided upon were equally novel, it was observed with amazement that the Orange Attorney-General, Saurin, seemed marvellously well prepared for every point, as the delegates daily fought their ground inch by inch.[1]

An aggregate meeting of Catholics was held after the arrests of their delegates. John Mitchel describes the party then in power as a 'No Popery Administration,' and the appearance of a Protestant on the platform was hailed as a happy incident. The following is taken from the 'Correspondent,' a once influential organ of Dublin Castle:—

Mr. McNally offered himself to the consideration of the Catholic body. He was anxious that his name should be coupled to the glorious cause for which, as Irishmen, they were contending—a cause that, from his earliest youth, although a Protestant, he felt as his own. He insisted that the conduct of the Lord Lieutenant was illegal—that he had not the power of arresting an individual by his own mere authority; that, not having the authority, he could not, of course, delegate it to a Magistrate.—[Here he animadverted upon the conduct of Mr. Hare, the police magistrate, who made the arrests.] The King himself, he said, possessed not the power which the Lord Lieutenant assumed in the arrest of Lords Fingal and Netterville. He instanced the case of Chief Justice Hussey and Edward IV.—The King asked the Judge whether his own warrant would not be deemed sufficient to arrest a subject?—The Chief Justice answered in the negative. And the reason was obvious. *The King can do no wrong.*—But the subject could have no legal redress against such an impeccable magistrate. He referred to the State trials for an exemplification and authority on this point; and he showed that a power which could not be exercised by Majesty itself, could not pass through the opaque body of his Lieutenant—a moonshine and intermitting ray.

O'Connell followed, and the clear head of that great lawyer saved the Catholic body from the deeper pitfall in which the

[1] The late Michael Staunton to W. J. F.

bad law of a false adviser would have placed them. In the course of his speech he declared:—

With regard to what had been said by Mr. McNally he could not assent. The action of Mr. Hare was merely his own, as a magistrate, and the Lord Lieutenant had no concern in being responsible for it; and he [Mr. O'Connell] would not allow in that assembly anything to be laid to the charge of the Duke of Richmond for which His Grace was not in every respect accountable.

On October 19, 1811, Wellesley Pole writes from Dublin Castle to the Home Secretary regarding the proceedings of the Catholic Committee, and enclosing 'a report from,' as he says, 'one of our spies.' This document, signed 'J. W.,' is still preserved with Pole's letter in the Record Office, London. About the same time Pole announces to the Home Office that 'Young Mr. Curran, son of the Master of the Rolls, has been very active in soliciting from the Catholics subscriptions for Mr. Finnerty, and letters from persons associated in London for promoting that object have been addressed to the Catholics here.'[1] These regular reportings of Curran's domestic circle involve a degree of treachery painful to contemplate.[2]

The reports of 'J. W.' did not tend to make Curran a favourite with 'the powers.' The patriot's son, describing a prior year, records:—

A party of seventeen soldiers, accompanied by their wives, or their profligate companions, and by many children, and evidently selected for the purpose of annoyance, were, without any previous notice, quartered on Mr. Curran's house.[3]

The late Mr. Byrne, an old Petty Sessions clerk, informed me that when walking at this time with his cousin Mr. Phelan, an attorney of Liberal politics, McNally, with a significant

[1] Ireland, 1811, January to June, No. 652. Peter Finnerty, who, in 1798, had been pilloried as editor of the *Press*, was now (1811) in Lincoln Gaol for a libel on Lord Castlereagh.

[2] Mr. Lecky thinks that, so early as 1795, McNally reported to the Government a secret conference of Curran and Grattan. *Hist.* vii. 145.

[3] *Life of Curran*, i. 147.

wink, accosted him, saying: 'The people are at last beginning to read; those who cannot yet read have books and papers read to them; after they read they will think, and they won't be long thinking until they act.'

On the trial of Sheridan and Kirwan, two Catholic delegates, he spoke warmly against the sheriff and others tampering with the jury, and was checked by the bench. He excused himself by saying 'that where the heart and the understanding went together it was difficult to keep bounds,' etc. Great excitement prevailed by the effort made to crush the freedom of speech, in the midst of which Percy Bysshe Shelley came to Dublin, and largely helped by voice and pen to make the crisis historic. Mr. Pole declared in Parliament, that 'if gentlemen would read the debates of the Catholic Committee they would find separation openly and distinctly recommended.' O'Connell, on February 29, 1812, replied: 'Why, my lord, this is a direct accusation of high treason, and he who would assert it of me, I would brand with the foulest epithets. I defy the slightest proof to be given of its veracity.' The Duke of Richmond, then Viceroy, writes at great length to the Home Secretary, speaks of his 'secret information,' and flutters the Cabinet.[1]

It was during the same year that Roger O'Connor, of Dangan Castle—father of Feargus, member for Nottingham—headed a band of rude retainers and robbed the Galway mail coach on Cappagh Hill. Though somewhat daft, he had method in his system, and when, five years later, he found himself a prisoner in Newgate, pending the long averted prosecution, he directed his attorney, named Maguire, to draw up a fictitious case, including a false line of defence, and lay it before McNally, taking for granted that he would betray to the Crown the person he supposed to be his client. The prosecution strangely broke down, and O'Connor, although notoriously guilty, was acquitted.[2] This trial took place in 1817:

[1] These papers are exclusively quoted in the *Correspondence of Daniel O'Connell* (edited by W. J. F.), ii. 420.

[2] For details, see *Ireland before the Union*, p. 8. (Dublin: Duffy.)

the death of Curran followed soon. A man named Waring having been indicted for perjury, McNally is found saying: 'Oppressed by the loss of my earliest friend, I have not strength for the task. But I wish to repel the stigma thrown out against my client, though I should die in the trammels.' [1]

The letters of McNally to Curran would be curious to read; 'but,' writes his daughter-in-law, 'they were destroyed by my late husband when he became so disgusted by the knowledge of the double face McNally must have worn for so many years as the *friend* of his father.' [2]

Although McNally's are destroyed, some characteristic letters from Curran to him were supplied by the spy to Curran's biographer. It was a constant effort of McNally to engraft himself on the fame and name of Curran. A touching document in the romance of real life is the letter addressed by Curran to McNally in 1810. He exhibits a kind solicitude for the improved health of his false friend, and alludes to their future meeting where secrets and sorrow would be no more.

Godwin's, 41, Skinner Street, London.

Dear Mac,— . . . I am glad to hear you are letting yourself out at Old Orchard; you are certainly unwise in giving up such an inducement to exercise, and the absolute good of being so often in good air. I have been talking about your habit without naming yourself. I am more persuaded that you and Egan [3] are not sufficiently afraid of weak liquors.[4] I can say from trial how little pains it costs to correct a bad habit. On the contrary, poor nature

[1] *The Correspondent*, a Dublin journal, November 4, 1817.

[2] Letter of Mrs. John Philpot Curran, dated 'The Priory, Rathfarnham, September 14, 1872.'

[3] John Egan, a member of the Irish Parliament, lost a judicial office he held by voting against the Union, and died in poverty. A staunch patriot to the end, he belonged to the set which numbered Curran and McNally. Curran's first acquaintance with him was in an affair of honour. Egan, a large man, complained of the great advantage which Curran's diminutive figure gave him. 'I scorn to take any advantage of you, whatever,' replied Curran. 'Let my size be chalked out on your side, and I am quite content that every shot which hits outside that mark should go for nothing.'

[4] It is a question whether 'Mac,' in society, drank as much as he may have pretended to do. See *ante*, p. 185.

—like an ill-used mistress—is delighted with the return of our kindness, and is anxious to show her gratitude for that return by letting us see how well she becomes it.

I am the more solicitous upon this point from having made this change, which I see will make me waited for in Heaven longer than perhaps they looked for. If you do not make some pretext for lingering, you can have no chance of conveying me to the wherry; and the truth is, I do not like surviving old friends. I am somewhat inclined to wish for posthumous reputation; and if you go before me, I shall lose one of the most irreclaimable of my trumpeters. Therefore, dear Mac, no more water, and keep the other element, your wind, for the benefit of your friends. I will show my gratitude as well as I can, by saying handsome things of you to the saints and angels before you come. Best regards to all with you.

J. P. C.

'Mac' stuck to him like a leech to the end. 'As he walked through the grounds of his country seat with Mr. McNally,' writes Curran's son, 'he spoke of the impending event with tranquillity and resignation:—

I melt (said he) and am not
Of stronger earth than others.

'"*I wish it was all over.*"'[1]

'Curran's will, which I have in the house,' writes his daughter-in-law,[2] 'is dated September 14th, 1816, and the codicil the 5th September, 1817; it bears the signatures (as witnesses) of Richard Lonergan and Leonard McNally. Lonergan was editor of 'Carrick's Post,' a popular organ. The first of a series of papers on the Dublin Theatre, signed 'L. M. N.,' appears in this journal of December 16, 1817:—

A moral, well-acted play [he writes] is of more real benefit to Society at large than all the inflated harangues of puritanical declaimers. To men of letters the drama affords a most delightful recreation, after their understandings have been absorbed in perplexities, or their intellectual powers strained by continued study.

[1] *Life of Curran*, 1820, ii. 380. Italics in original.

[2] 'I have heard that a cheque for 300*l.* to McNally's order and signed by Curran was returned by the bankers with many other cashed cheques.'—Letter of Mrs. Philpot Curran, May 12, 1890.

The elder Farran began his career in Dublin, and McNally's criticism helped to make it a success. Mrs. Edwin, Miss Walstein, Fullam, Williams, Young, all were cleverly reviewed. It was not necessary, he said, for a tragedian to roar like a lion, or for a comedian to grin as through a horse-collar. Two letters signed 'L. M. N.' espouse the part of Mrs. Edwin, who had met with some unkindness. The concluding sentence is characteristic : 'Allow me, madam, to inform you, that while I continue your Panegyrist, you shall never know me. All old men are more or less eccentric. I have my whims, and one of them is a dislike to being thanked for doing what I think to be my duty.'

Friendly relations were established between the popular journalist and his contributor, but at last they seem a little strained. The paper got into trouble with a very formidable enemy to popular principles, Jack Giffard, known as the 'Dog in Office.' The officiousness of McNally, if he had no deeper design, is shown by Lonergan in a hurried leader of September 17, 1818—the italics are his :—

We did not and could not anticipate that an attempt would be made to induce the Recorder to fix on a day for the trial, so early as Thursday (this day !). Now, it is certainly not our intention that one hour's unnecessary delay should take place on the part of the proprietor of this paper, in meeting the Corporators face to face in Court, or elsewhere. It was, however, extraordinary, that a day so very early should be sought for, and that the motion should be made at a time when we could have no notice of even the Bills being found ! This prosecution, in other respects *unique*, is equally unprecedented, we believe, in this *extreme* anxiety to hurry the business forward. The Recorder did not countenance this very suspicious haste. Like an upright judge, he guarded the interests of the absent.

He said it was of little consequence whether a day was fixed or not, as he supposed the case would be put off until next sessions.

Mr. M'Nally—'I understand, My Lord, they do not intend to traverse in *prox. Suppose your Lordship says Thursday next.*'

Recorder—' No, Mr. M'Nally. *I cannot fix a day for the trial of an indictment only just found; especially as there is not any reason, that I can perceive, for such haste.'*

We have made this extract from one of the newspapers. If it be correct, may we ask Mr. M'Nally *who instructed him to speak for us?* We had no counsel or agent present—how then could the worthy gentleman, with all his shrewdness and sagacity, *understand* what was our intention? Mr. M'Nally, finding that nobody present was authorised to speak in our behalf, as *amicus curiæ*, we suppose, states to the Court our intention; but how Mr. M'Nally discovered that intention, it puzzles us to find out, for Mr. M'Nally, with all his legal knowledge and abilities, is no conjuror. We wait then to hear from this gentleman by what authority, he, employed on the other side, in the absence of counsel or agent for the proprietor of this paper, did undertake to state to the Recorder what were our intentions? We think the conduct of Mr. M'Nally, in this instance, of a piece with the rest of this curious proceeding.

Some legal proceedings are reported by the Dublin papers of September 18, 1818, as having been instituted by the histrions of Crow Street Theatre for the recovery of their salaries. McNally's swaggering pretensions to pose as an honourable man are amusingly marked. He was counsel for the lessee, Frederick W. Jones.

Mr. MacNally—Now, Sir, you suppose your profession to be a very honourable and gentleman-like employment—equally respectable with my own as a barrister. Now, Sir, let me ask you, are you not a servant?

Mr. Gladstone—Most certainly. I consider myself the servant of Mr. Jones and the public. But there is higher authority than mine, for the Lord Chancellor of England declared, at an investigation of the affairs of Drury-lane Theatre, that all the performers were servants, and must be paid before any other creditor.

The Lord Mayor instantly ordered Mr. Gladstone his money.

The last important case in which McNally figured was that of the Wild Goose Lodge murderers at Dundalk. This case, highly tragic in its nature, has been invested with thrilling interest by the powerful pen of Carleton.

'From grave to gay' marked his course on circuit. A

glimpse of the 'chaff' which followed McNally at mess is shown by Charles Phillips.

It was a common practice with the juniors to play upon his vanity by inducing him to enumerate the vast sums he made by 'Robin Hood.' The wicked process was thus. They first got him to fix the aggregate amount; and then, luring him into details, he invariably, by third nights and copyright, quintupled the original. Woe to the wight, however, luckless enough to have been detected in this waggery. He was ready with his pistol.

Phillips also describes 'Mac' as ever varying in his account of how he lost his thumbs, and that one night, tired and perplexed by repeated questioning on the point,[1] he at last exclaimed, 'I don't know how I lost them!' It seems to me that 'Mac' was too cool and cunning to trip. Phillips, as a most distinguished co-operator with the Catholic Board, was a man worth McNally's while to 'draw'; and the hoary-headed 'father,' in encouraging the juniors' chaff, probably feigned features which he did not possess. We have seen how resolutely incredulous Phillips stood when the spy's real character was first impugned. Phillips is remembered by the English bar as a very cunning man. But as regards McNally's treachery he died unconvinced. The man whose seeming simplicity he loved to chaff was of deeper acumen. The 'Metropolis,' a review of the Bar, indicated among McNally's gifts—

> With all he saw or learned his memory fraught
> Acute perception of his neighbour's thought.

Phillips seemed to pity the awkward simplicity of his venerable friend; but it was clearly McNally's game at times to pose as a 'butt,' and Charles adds no more than the truth in saying, 'his eyes and voice pierced you through like arrows.'

[1] He seems not to have been so badly maimed as he gave Phillips to believe. John P. Prendergast, an octogenarian, remembers McNally saying at the Trim Assizes in 1817, 'I have a finger and thumb to tweak the nose of any man who dares to question my acts.' Luckily the present writer did not live in those days. How one thumb went, see p. 177.

Howell's 'Trials' should be consulted by those who care to trace the forensic career of McNally—

> 'L' stands for Lysaght, who loves a good joke ;
> 'M' for MacNally, who lives by the rope !

sings 'the Alphabet of the Bar.' But it is McNally's speeches as a democratic orator, delivered on all great national occasions, in which he appears to best dramatic effect.

The mission of General d'Evereux to Ireland, with the object of raising troops for Bolivar—the South American patriot—took place in 1819, and with it is involved McNally's last important acts of espionage. A military passion had seized on the popular mind. For many weeks the streets of Dublin, gay with plumage, reminded one of Paris during the Napoleonic fever. The city swarmed with stalwart, ruddy youths, clad in uniforms of green and gold, their swords clanking at every step. Levées were held by D'Evereux with all the pomp of a court; public banquets sought to do him honour. At first these things caused alarm at Dublin Castle; but, finally, it was decided that the statute which forbade foreign enlistment might be suffered to lie dormant: after all, the opportunity was not a bad one to rid the land of those military spirits whose presence could never conduce to its repose. In this connection Dr. Scallan has something to say :—

The badge of the United Irishmen worn by Lord Edward Fitzgerald, and taken from his remains when he lay dead in Newgate, was given by Leonard McNally to General d'Evereux, who recruited a number of Irishmen and drilled them, and formed a regiment with which he sailed to Venezuela, and there attacked the Spaniards and drove them from the country and freed the Venezuelans from the Spanish yoke, which had grown into an intolerable tyranny. The badge has attached to it a paper on which is the following inscription :—

'From Leonard MacNally, Barrister-at-law, to General d'Evereux of the Irish Legion, raised by him for emancipating the oppressed inhabitants of South America, and punishing their Tyrants. 20 July, 1819.'

This presentation would appear to be one of the, no doubt, many acts of McNally done for the purpose of concealing his perfidy and gaining his ends.

My father-in-law, Laurence Esmonde White, of Scarnagh, exerted himself very much in assisting to procure men and officers for the Legion; and very successfully, as he had much influence with the people of the County Wexford, in which he always resided, and where his family had extensive estates. General D'Evereux gave him several tokens of his gratitude, of which the badge of Lord Edward was one. He also gave him a deed of gift, witnessed by his military secretary, of 200,000 acres of land in Venezuela. Which deed I have; but no one went there to take possession of the land, and it would seem to be lost through neglect. An old friend of mine (now deceased) who travelled much in that country, told me that the land was worth at least 50,000*l*.

I never could understand how the badge could have got into the possession of McNally, until his perfidy was revealed by Mr. Fitzpatrick. Then all was made clear. He, no doubt, obtained the badge from his paymasters in order that he might use it as he did.[1]

During the passage from Dublin to Venezuela dissensions arose among the officers, and some came back complaining that they had been misled in the business. D'Evereux returned to justify his conduct, and a committee, consisting of Lord Cloncurry, with Counsellors Curran, McNally and Phillips, was appointed to inquire and report.

In 1820 Ireland lost her Grattan.[2] The man who had long shadowed him vanished at the same time. Catholics may care to know, though they will hardly attach much importance to the accession, that Leonard McNally, 'after life's fitful fever,' sank into the bosom of Rome. Father Smith, of Townsend Street Chapel, on February 13, 1820, gave him the last rites. This priest, having got word that 'the Counsellor' wished to see him, went to his house in Harcourt Street,

[1] Letter of J. J. Scallan, Esq., M.D., to the author. Black Rock, April 23, 1890. The Doctor may not be quite right in his assumption.

[2] Mr. Lecky says that 'McNally had specially good opportunities of learning the sentiments of Grattan' (vii. 284). Grattan died May 14; McNally on February 13.

where Mrs. McNally informed him that her husband was then asleep, and must not be disturbed. McNally's son, who happened to be coming down stairs at the moment, reproved his step-mother for the indisposition she evinced to admit the clergyman, adding, 'Can't you let him go to the devil his own way?'[1] He then conducted the priest to the sick man's room. Father Smith put on his stole, and heard muttered from the parched lips of Leonard McNally a general confession, embracing the frailties of his youth and the sins of his manhood. Contrition was manifested, and the priest gave him absolution.[2] Within an hour McNally was dead. In life he had been no coward, but the death-bed was no place to show old instincts. His funeral *cortège* wended its way to the old grave-yard of Donnybrook, where his bones now lie, near those of Madden, the historian of the 'United Irishmen.'

McNally had married Miss Janson, the heroine of his famous lyric, 'Sweet lass of Richmond Hill;' but it was his second wife, *née* Edgeworth, who appeared to Father Smith. The son had acquired a rough reputation, and having been once robbed near Rathcoole, his father asked Parsons, 'Did you hear of my son's robbery?' and received for reply, 'No, whom did he rob?'[3]

[1] Rev. John Kearney, P.P., to the author, February 10, 1860.

[2] McNally and Father Smith seem to have been old chums. So far back as 1805, 'J. W.' writes, in one of his undated letters: 'Smith, the priest whom I have before mentioned, informed me last night that a person arrived here from France within these few days. The intelligence he brings is an assurance of a Descent by the French, and that the Fleet is now in the Atlantic with this object. I do not give credence to his Information. I found it impossible to extract particulars or names, but I am to see him to-morrow (Sunday).'

Smith, suspecting McNally to be a spy, is likely to have charged his news with sensationalism, and 'Mac,' no doubt, found him useful as a scout. That he was an open-mouthed gossiping man, his account of his very solemn mission to the deathbed of the spy shows. He never received promotion, and in the end became so deaf that when officiating in his confessional he always reiterated audibly the character of the sin disclosed, so as to be sure he heard it correctly, and the result was very painful embarrassment to such neighbouring worshippers as could not fail to become *en rapport* with the conscience of the penitent. Compare *Wellington Correspondence* (*Ireland*), pp. 192–3, and the 'Information of a Priest regarding threatened Invasion.'

[3] See Appendix for a letter of Leonard McNally, junior.

No will of McNally's exists, but there was certainly an administrator.[1] An action was brought by this person regarding the house in which he died. 'I was present at the trial,' writes 'Rebellion Smyth,' an aged correspondent. 'Judge Burton gave McNally a high character for legal learning and worldly simplicity. "In the affairs of the world," said Burton, "he was as simple as a child."'[2] The eminent judge for once was mistaken.

Grattan's name has been mentioned by McNally as privy to the plans of 1798. What truth may be in the assertion that Grattan would join in an appeal to arms is a point which may never be fully determined. It is certain that in 1782 he would not have hesitated to employ physical force. His friend Mr. Justice Day records of him that 'Grattan was resolved to assist, even by arms, if driven to it, the liberties of Ireland.'[3]

> Neither Grattan[4] nor Curran were United Irishmen [writes Macnevin shortly before his death]. It was known in the event of success Grattan would have accepted an important appointment in the new Government; but Curran was continually consulted by them, knew everything that was going on, and his whole heart was in the cause.

[1] Lyons, in his *Grand Juries of Westmeath*, records, deprecatingly, that Leonard McNally's people were engaged in trade; but, according to their tombstone at Donnybrook, they once owned the castle and lands of Rahobeth. Like other Irish gentry of the proscribed faith, they sank during penal times, and the name of Leonard McNally is found in the official list of 'Papists' who 'conformed' early in the reign of George III. How this came about is traceable in Sheil's notice of McNally in 1820: 'His grandfather made a very considerable personal property, which he laid out in building in Dublin; but having taken leases liable to the discovery of this property, in consequence of a bill under the popish laws, he was stripped of it. His father died when he was an infant, at which time the bill of discovery was filed, and little attention was paid to his education.' The 'will of Leonard McNally, Dublin, merchant,' who died in 1756, is preserved at the Record Office.

[2] William Smith, B.L., died at Torquay, April 29, 1876.

[3] See *Life of Grattan*, by his Son, ii. 272.

[4] One of the more voluminous of the secret reports signed 'J. W.' is dated March 24, 1797, and details twenty-three propositions of a plan, through which the United Irishmen were to act with Grattan. The proceedings took place at a meeting at Chambers's, one of the Rebel Directory. (MSS. Dublin Castle.)

CHAPTER XV

FATHER ARTHUR O'LEARY

SEVERAL years ago an influential journalist posted at Melbourne the following letter. He was the mouthpiece of many. It is rather late to answer his question publicly; but, in truth, the subject was not an inviting one to touch, especially as, not having studied it, I felt unable to reply in a way which would be deemed satisfactory by the querist. On the other hand, the application having come from the antipodes, I am encouraged to think that the subject possesses an interest not confined to a hemisphere. 'No one was more generally loved and revered than Father O'Leary,' writes Charles Butler. Yelverton, speaking in the Irish Parliament, said: 'Unattached to this world's affairs, Father O'Leary can have none but the purest motives of rendering service to the cause of morality and his country.' He was the subject of a grand panegyric from the pulpit. Two biographies of him have been written by anointed hands. Idolised while living, his memory was cherished by thousands. His name wore a halo! Now, according to recent writers, it seems not free from that light which floats over unhealthy places. Let it not be denied that at different times O'Leary did good work for his creed and country. As a religious [1] he continued true to the end;

[1] When in 1787 Dr. Butler, Roman Catholic Bishop of Cork, and the Rev. Walter Blake Kirwan, the eminent Franciscan preacher, conformed to Protestantism it was falsely reported that Father Arthur O'Leary had also changed. But he wrote a public letter declaring that he had no intention of swerving from his vows as a Capuchin friar.

but if we accept the high testimony of Froude and Lecky, the same cannot be said of him as a patriot and a gentleman.

Mr. Morgan McMahon to Mr. Fitzpatrick.

38, William Street, Melbourne, December 1, 1875.

Sir,—Knowing you from your published writings to be intimately acquainted with the secret political history of Ireland at the close of the last century, I venture to trespass on your courtesy, with a query relative to a celebrated character of those times, whose name, long gratefully and affectionately remembered by his countrymen, must in future, if the statements of a recent historian are deserving of any credit, be associated only with the names of the wretches whom, in the pages of 'The Sham Squire' and 'Ireland before the Union,' you have held up to the scorn of posterity!

I allude to the famous 'Father O'Leary,' who, according to Mr. Froude, was a spy of Pitt's, systematically employed in betraying the secrets which his sacred calling and influence as a trusted patriot enabled him to become possessed of; and, with unparalleled audacity and baseness, publicly receiving the encomiums of his most distinguished contemporaries, such men as Grattan and Curran, for virtues which he only assumed, and for talents which he so basely prostituted! Is it possible that this man could have played such an odious part? Do you consider, sir, that the evidence produced by Mr. Froude in support of so terrible an accusation is sufficiently conclusive; or, has that sensational writer in this, as perhaps in other instances, accommodated his facts to his theories? [1] With tantalising reticence Mr. Froude gives only a few meagre lines from the correspondence in which he claims to have found the proofs of O'Leary's guilt. The subject has been much discussed in Australia, as no doubt it has in every country in which Irishmen are to be found. You have yourself, in one of your . . .[2] volumes, referred to a mysterious connection between O'Leary and William Pitt. Was it an honourable, or an infamous one?

May I ask you to favour me with your opinion upon it, judged by the light of Mr. Froude's revelations? By kindly complying

[1] Mr. Froude, with the letter before him which he found, could adopt hardly any other impression. Mr. Macdonough, in *Irish Graves in England*, follows Froude, and speaks of O'Leary's 'traitorous conduct.' He, however, errs in assigning 1811, instead of 1802, as the date of his death. See *Evening Telegraph*, February 6, 1888.

[2] The omitted matter is merely a compliment.

with my request, you will oblige many anxious inquirers at the 'Antipodes.'

I am, Sir, etc.,
MORGAN MCMAHON.

Mysterious relations certainly existed between O'Leary and the Government, but there is not evidence to warrant the very sensational picture drawn by Mr. McMahon.

People always knew that O'Leary became entitled to a pension, though how he acquired it was not so clear. Perhaps it is only fair to give him the benefit of the version which his intimate friend, Francis Plowden, placed on record eighty years ago.[1] His information was, doubtless, derived from O'Leary himself; but O'Leary seems to have told him no more than it was convenient to reveal:—

O'Leary's writings on toleration had removed from the minds of many Catholics the difficulties which up to that time prevented them from swearing allegiance to the House of Hanover, and abjuring the House of Stuart. That Rev. Divine so happily blended a vein of liberality and original humour with orthodox instruction, that his writings became popular even with Protestants, and induced so much toleration and cordiality between them and the Catholics, that created a serious alarm in those who studied to perpetuate their division and consequent weakness. With much art they endeavoured to stop the progress of this terrifying liberality and harmony among Irishmen of different religious professions. The Rev. Arthur O'Leary was thanked by the British minister for the services he had rendered to the State, by frightening away the bugbear of Jacobitism, and securing the allegiance of the whole Catholic body to the House of Hanover. A pension of 200*l.* was granted to him for his life in the name of a trustee, but upon the secret condition that he should for the future withhold his pen, and reside no more in Ireland,—in such dread was holden an evangeliser of tolerance and brotherhood in that country. Two or three payments of this hush-money were made. Afterwards an arbitrary refusal for many years threw the Rev. Pensioner upon the voluntary support of his friends for subsistence. After a lapse of many years,

[1] Plowden's *Ireland since the Union*, i. 6. (Dublin, 1811.)

by importunity and solicitation, and repeated proofs of his having complied with the secret conditions, he received a large arrear; and, in order to make himself independent for the rest of his days, he purchased with it an annuity for his life from a public office, and died before the first quarter became due.

It was, in fact, entirely by Plowden's intervention that the arrear was paid. So we learn on the authority of the Rev. Thomas England, who in 1822 brought out a life of O'Leary. Plowden was a friend of Pitt's, and undertook to write a History of Ireland under the auspices of that statesman. He had previously published in defence of the British Constitution, and received in acknowledgment the D.C.L. of Oxford. When writing eighty years ago of so popular and respected a priest as O'Leary, Plowden—himself a Catholic—made his revelation cautiously. It would now seem that some greater service was rendered than the public service to which Plowden refers. It will be shown on high contemporary authority that the object of the Castle in 1784 was to divide the two great parties. This policy later on was boldly avowed as *Divide et impera*.[1] The service, therefore, for which O'Leary accepted secret pay cannot have been for promoting cordial co-operation between Catholics and Protestants.

Mr. Lecky, in the sixth volume of his 'History of England,' has brought to light a letter, from which he draws the conclusion that in 1784 O'Leary 'consented, for money, to discharge an ignominious office for a Government which despised and distrusted him.'[2]

On studying O'Leary's public life there seems no doubt that the secret pension of 100*l.* a year, which in 1784 he agreed to accept, was merely supplemental to a larger subsidy previously enjoyed. How he earned the first pension is now to be shown.

[1] Mr. Lecky, who examined the State Papers, tells us that seven years later, *i.e.* 1791, 'The chief members of the Irish Government made it their deliberate object to revive the religious animosities which had so greatly subsided, to raise the standard of Protestant ascendency, and to organise through the country an opposition to concession.'

[2] Vol. vi. 369.

A volume, 'Sketches of Irish Political Characters,' was published in 1799. The writer, Henry McDougall, commanded sources of information which gave his book value. Speaking of O'Leary, he says (p. 264) :—

During the most awful period of the American War, he addressed his Catholic countrymen, upon the subject of what ought to be their political conduct, in a manner that merited the thanks of every good citizen, and for which, it has been said, Government rewarded him with a pension; if so, never was a pension more deservedly applied.

McDougall doubtless refers to a publication of O'Leary's, largely circulated and often reprinted, *i.e.* 'An Address to the Common People of Ireland on occasion of an apprehended Invasion by the French and Spaniards in July 1779,[1] when the united Fleets of Bourbon appeared in the Channel.' On April 12, 1779, Spain had concluded an alliance with France and America, whereupon Vergennes, the French Premier, divulged to the Spanish minister, Blanca, that an invasion of Ireland was meditated. To promote this design, an American agent was instructed to foster the interests of the allies amongst the Presbyterians of Ulster; while the task of winning over the Irish Catholics was to be entrusted to Spanish agents.

America was all but lost at this time, and England found herself in a position of great difficulty. Ireland was drained of its garrison; the people much discontented; the Catholic middle classes, grown rich by commercial success, had established branches of their houses in France and Spain. A letter of warning, which alarmed the Cabinet, and probably led them to ask O'Leary's help, still exists. At the same time, hurriedly and with a bad grace, they conceded a measure of Catholic Relief. Lord Amherst, writing to Lord North from Geneva on June 19, 1778, says :—

I have acquired a piece of information here, concerning a plot for a revolt in the West of Ireland among the Roman Catholics, with a view to overturn the present Government, by the aid of the

[1] *Vide* Lecky, iv. 491.

French and Spaniards, and to establish such an one as prevails in this country, I mean the Cantons, by granting toleration to the Protestants.[1] You may depend on its authenticity.

And again:—

My intelligence comes from Rome, and I am pretty certain these Acts have been brought in from the ministry receiving the same intelligence, which I know they have been in possession of for some time; as the measures for preventing the mischief proposed by the person who gives the information are exactly those that have been adopted.

O'Leary by his address aroused not only Catholic loyalty, but awakened the apathy of many Protestants on whom the report of invasion had previously made no impression. The Volunteers sprang into vitality, and though they at first numbered merely 8,000, the force swelled ere the year was out to 42,000 armed men, and without the cost of one shilling to the Crown. Years after, the Government dreading, like Frankenstein, the heaving mass it had helped to create, sought to suppress the Irish Volunteers; but in 1778 their feeling was very different, when O'Leary's inspiring address fanned the spirit of volunteering, and conduced to preserve the country. It was then that Lord Buckinghamshire officially declared that Ireland was prepared to offer a determined resistance to invasion.

A link or two of the heavy penal chain had now been struck from Papist limbs. The relaxation, however, was hampered with a new test oath, drawn up in terms even more subtle than that which, when handed to O'Connell fifty years later in Parliament, he withdrew rather than take. Dr. Carpenter[2] ruled the R. C. see of Dublin at this time. His flock included a considerable number who, from timidity of conscience, expressed doubts as to the propriety of taking the oath. Dr. Carpenter, though himself no great friend to the temporal

[1] 'If 30,000 men under the denomination of French troops landed in Ireland,' writes O'Leary, '15,000 Protestants from France, Germany, Switzerland, &c., would make up half the number. Neither are you to confide in their promises of protection.'—O'Leary's *Tract*, p. 104.

[2] Dean Lee, the grand-nephew of Dr. Carpenter, tells me that a smart apostate priest had been deputed to frame the new oath.

power of the Pope, felt that to deny on oath a power already claimed by some famous theologians would seem rash and arrogant. Bishop de Burgo, author of the 'Hibernia Dominicana,' opposed the oath in terms still stronger; lay orators described as a poisoned cup the proffered measure of Catholic relief. Again O'Leary came to the front. A pamphlet of eighty-six pages was thrown on the country, entitled, 'Loyalty asserted, or a Vindication of the new Test Oath of Allegiance, with an impartial inquiry into the Pope's Temporal Power [a strong attack upon it] and the claims of the Stewarts to the English Throne: proving that both are equally groundless.' O'Leary examined the oath sentence by sentence, and with logical precision showed its conformity to Catholic teaching. 'The work was widely circulated,' writes Father England, the first biographer of O'Leary, and called forth as well the acknowledgments of the friends of the Government as the warm gratitude of his Catholic fellow-countrymen. In November 1778 we read that the Catholic Archbishop Carpenter, at the head of seventy of his clergy, and several hundred Catholic laymen, attended at the Court of King's Bench in Dublin and took the oath prescribed.[1]

The dreaded invasion never took place; but O'Leary's address was scattered broadcast, and during subsequent years it reappeared again and again. It reads more like the argument of a paid advocate than the disinterested appeal of a poor Franciscan.

All this—not to speak of O'Leary's tracts on Toleration, and his exertions, written and oral, in support of law and order—furnishes sufficient claim to a pension, without assuming that it must have been earned in the dark field of espionage. However, we now approach the time when overtures to discharge an ignominous task are alleged to have been made to him.

On August 26, 1784, the Viceroy, Rutland, addressed a '*most secret*' letter to Pitt's brother-in-law, Lord Sydney:—

[1] *Annual Register*, xxi. 208. See also a fine panegyric on O'Leary, published in the *Irish Quarterly Review*, vii. 686.

I have discovered a channel by which I hope to get to the bottom of all the plots and machinations which are contriving in this metropolis. As I always expected, the disturbances which have been agitated have all derived their source from French influence. There is a meeting in which two men named Napper Tandy and John Binney, together with others who style themselves free citizens, assemble. They drink the French King on their knees, and their declared purpose is a separation from England and the establishment of the Roman Catholic religion. At their meetings an avowed French agent constantly attends, who is no other than the person in whose favour the French ambassador desired Lord Caermarthen to write to me a formal introduction.[1] . . . One of this meeting, alarmed at the dangerous extent of their schemes, has confessed, and has engaged to discover to me the whole intentions of this profligate and unprincipled combination.[2]

This is a glowing picture, one more than realising the pleasant vision of Davis :—

The mess tent is full, and the glasses are set,
And the gallant Count Thomond is president yet.
The vet'ran arose, like an uplifted lance,
Crying : 'Comrades, a health to the monarch of France ! '
With bumpers and cheers they have done as he bade,
For King Louis is loved by the Irish Brigade.

The first mention of O'Leary's name in the State Papers is under date September 4, 1784, when Sydney writes to the Lord-Lieutenant :—' O'Leary has been talked to by Mr. Nepean, and he is willing to undertake what is wished for 100*l*. a year, which has been granted him.'

On Sept. 8th [writes Mr. Lecky] Orde thanks Nepean for sending over a spy, or detective, named Parker, and adds : I am very glad also that you have settled matters with O'Leary, who can get at the bottom of all secrets in which the Catholics are concerned, and they are certainly the chief promoters of our present disquietude. He must, however, be cautiously trusted, *for he is a Priest*, and if not too much addicted to the general vice of his brethren here, he is at

[1] This is, no doubt, M. Perrin, of whom some particulars will be found, *infra*, p. 246.

[2] Rutland to Sydney, most secret, Aug. 26, 1784.

least well acquainted with the art of raising alarms for the purpose of claiming a merit in doing them away.[1]

Thus, as it would seem, O'Leary had already not been slow in claiming from the Government the merit, if not the wages, of allaying the causes of public alarm. Plowden and England admit that O'Leary had a pension of 200*l.* a year. He must have been in receipt of at least 100*l.* for his writings at the time that, for an extra hundred, it was proposed to him to undertake a new task. The promptitude and facility with which Sydney, in September 1784, made the proposition shows the close relations that had previously subsisted.

A curious letter from Weymouth, a previous Home Secretary, addressed to Dublin Castle, is printed in Grattan's 'Life' (vol. i. p. 369). In great panic he expresses fear that the Catholic colleges of France and Flanders would despatch their *alumni* as secret agents to Ireland. These were among the reasons that made the Government anxious to secure O'Leary's aid.

Dr. England—his earliest biographer—lived comparatively near the time, and heard from O'Leary's publisher, Keating, a few interesting incidents which, to some extent, tally with the revelations of the State Papers. The biographer knows of an interview between O'Leary and Nepean on behalf of Sydney and Pitt, but England and his informant are deceived as to the conditions which accompanied the pension. Their memory is also at fault as regards the year. Instead of 1784, they set it down as 'soon after O'Leary had fixed his residence permanently in London,' which, of course, was in 1789. O'Leary had been a good deal in London previously, as we know from other sources. Froude states that Orde in 1784 asked Sydney to send him over confidential agents, and in September 1784 he writes, 'your experts have arrived safe.'[2]

[1] Rutland's letter, to which this is an answer, seems to have been destroyed.

[2] My first idea was that, unless it were possible to trace some of the written reports in which Froude insinuates that O'Leary kept a daily record of espionage, his guilt as a spy must be doubted. Probably on other grounds his friends might seek to explain his services. In 1786 he took a specially con-

Soon after he [O'Leary] had fixed his residence permanently in London [writes Dr. England], one day whilst dining with his attached and valued friend, Mr. Keating, the bookseller, he was informed that Lord Sydney's secretary was in the adjoining parlour, and had a communication to make to him. He immediately left the table; and when, in a short time, he returned, he related the substance of the interview. The secretary stated to him that Government had observed with much satisfaction the good effects which Mr. O'Leary's writings had produced in Ireland—peace, good order, and unanimity, amongst all classes of his countrymen, had been promoted and advanced by his exertions; and that, in consideration of the services thus rendered to the Empire, it was determined to manifest the approbation of such conduct by offering him a pension suitable to his circumstances, and worthy of his acceptance; that, with a delicacy arising from the ignorance of his means of subsistence, they had as yet hesitated fixing on any specific sum, choosing rather to learn from himself what would answer his expectations, than to determine on what might be insufficient for his claims. The secretary took the liberty of asking a question to which, at the same time, he did not insist on receiving an answer: whether, in the event of any popular commotion in Ireland, as it was dreaded would be the case from the diffusion of American republican notions, O'Leary would advocate, as formerly, principles of loyalty and allegiance? To this latter question an unhesitating reply was given, confirmatory of the known inflexibility of O'Leary's political conduct; with regard to the pension, he never had sought for one, though, at a former period of his life, something of the kind had been hinted to him; in the present instance he was grateful to the Government for the recollection of him, and suggested that the utmost of his claims would be answered by 100*l.* a year. He was afterwards informed officially that his presence in Ireland was necessary for the purpose of having the pension placed on the list of that country. He repaired thither, and, after the necessary formalities were gone through, he became entitled to 200*l.* per annum; but England adds that, 'for some unexplained

spicuous part in quieting the Whiteboy disturbances. Answering Woodward, Bishop of Cloyne, he speaks of Colonel Luttrel, afterwards Lord Carhampton, 'whom I had the honour of being with on the very scene of the commotions, and had given the most favourable account of my conduct and exertions to the Privy Council in the Duke of Rutland's Administration.' Lord Carhampton is noticed at pp. 152–172, *ante*. See also Ireland before the Union, p. 128.

cause, his pension, after one or two years, was arbitrarily withheld.'[1]

It will be seen that the point here made is not consistent with Plowden's account (*ante*, p. 213). According to him, the pension was 'hush-money:' he was to write no more, and, above all, he was not to write in promotion of good feeling and toleration. England upholds that it was given in the hope that O'Leary would continue to write in the same tone that had already earned Governmental gratitude. Sydney settled terms with O'Leary in London, and, through his secretary, told him what to do.

It was a clever thought to plan the corruption of O'Leary for the performance of a part which his employers describe with gusto. Two years previously, on February 27, 1782, popular confidence in him had reached its height when Yelverton, Grattan, and Sir Lucius O'Brien praised him with enthusiasm.

A man of learning, a philosopher, a Franciscan [said Grattan] did the most eminent service to his country in the hour of its greatest danger. He brought out a publication that would do honour to the most celebrated name. The whole kingdom must bear witness to its effect by the reception they gave it. Poor in everything but genius and philosophy, he had no property at stake, no family to fear for; but descending from the contemplation of wisdom, and abandoning the ornaments of fancy, he humanely undertook the task of conveying duty and instruction to the lowest class of the people.[2]

How he qualified for these praises Mr. Froude professes to show. After O'Leary arrived in Dublin he saw Orde, and was told what he was expected to do. The following letter is dated September 23, 1784:—

Your experts have arrived safe [wrote the Secretary, reporting their appearance]. At this moment we are about to make trial of O'Leary's sermons,[3] and Parker's rhapsodies. They may be

[1] *Life of Rev. A. O'Leary*, by Rev. T. R. England, 1822, pp. 234 *et seq.* In 1788, Orde himself received a pension of 1,700*l.* a year, charged on the Irish Establishment.

[2] *Irish Parl. Debates*, i. 293.

[3] From the word 'sermons' I thought at one time, that O'Lear was sum-

both in their different callings of very great use. The former, if we can depend on him, has it in his power to discover to us the real designs of the Catholics, from which quarter, after all, the real mischief is to spring. The other can scrape an acquaintance with the great leaders of sedition, particularly Napper Tandy, and perhaps by that means dive to the bottom of his secrets.[1]

Sir Richard Musgrave was one of the alarmists who loved to purvey sensational news for Dublin Castle. His 'History of the Rebellion,' published in 1801, embodies his impressions of events for twenty years before. No wonder that Dublin Castle was fluttered by his reports. Here is clearly one of them, and it serves to show why it was that the Government were so anxious in 1784 to secure O'Leary by a subsidy:—

A corps called the Irish Brigade was raised in Dublin, of which nineteen out of twenty were Roman Catholics, and they appointed Father O'Leary, an itinerant friar, their chaplain. I have been assured that they exceeded in number all the other Volunteer corps in the city.

And again:—

In the summer of the year 1783, the Irish Brigade, with the Dublin Independent Volunteers, commanded by James Napper Tandy and Matthew Dowling, formed an encampment between Roebuck and Dublin, under the pretext of studying tactics and learning camp duty, though it was well known that they were hatching revolutionary projects. It is to be observed that the war, the only pretext for their arming, was now at an end; yet many corps in different parts of the kingdom resolved not to lay down their arms but with their lives.[2]

Musgrave's construction of the above, as in many other incidents, is not wholly correct; though in his estimate of

moned—on the re-appearance of the 'Whiteboys'—to administer the dissuasives which, some years previously, had produced good effect. I have diligently searched newspaper files and contemporary pamphlets, and I can find no letter, or reported sermon, addressed by O'Leary to the Whiteboys in 1784. Two years later, he certainly tried to reason with them. The words 'if we can depend on him,' lead to the inference that O'Leary gave Orde some personal assurance as regards his willingness to assist the Government.

[1] Froude's *English in Ireland*, ii. 413.

[2] Musgrave's *Memoirs of the Rebellion*, pp. 50–1. (Dublin, 1801.)

Tandy and Dowling, both Protestants, he was accurate enough.

If O'Leary played the part assigned and attributed to him, never did face more belie internal baseness, or was more exquisitely fashioned to command the confidence of its dupes. The 'Gentleman's Magazine' for February 1802 contains a study of 'Father Arthur' from the pen of Mr. Pratt.

His manners [he says] were the most winning and artless, anticipating his goodwill and urbanity before he opened his lips; and when they were opened, his expressions did but ratify what those manners had before ensured. And you had a further earnest of this in the benign and ineffable smile of a countenance so little practised in guile that it at the same time invited to confidence, and denoted an impossibility of your being betrayed.

Curran, addressing the Irish House of Commons in 1787, revealed a trait highly honourable to the friar: 'Mr. O'Leary was, to his knowledge, a man of the most innocent and amiable simplicity of manners in private life. The reflection of twenty years in a cloister had severely regulated his passions and deeply informed his understanding.'[1] Curran's knowledge was partly derived from the fact that O'Leary belonged to 'The Monks of the Screw,' often regarded as a convivial club; but 'whose more important object,' writes Hardy, the biographer of Charlemont, 'was a co-operation of men holding a general similarity of political principles resolved to maintain the rights and constitution of their country.' Previously, O'Leary had dedicated his Miscellaneous Tracts 'to the Dignitaries and Brethren of the Monks of St. Patrick,' addressing them, with his wonted humour, as 'Reverend Fathers and illustrious Brethren.'

[1] In 1784, the very year that Mr. Froude brings his serious charge against Fr. O'Leary, a gold medal was presented to him by the Cork Amicable Society. 'Father O'Leary is represented in the habit of his order,' writes the Rev. Thomas R. England, 'crushing with his right foot the Hydra of religious persecution; with his right hand he opens the gates of the Temple of Concord; whilst with his left he beckons his countrymen (emblematically represented by the harp) to enter the sacred edifice, forgetful of their prejudices against each other. The genius of his country is represented with extended arms over his head, each bearing a crown - the one of Science, the other of Victory.'

He had already written in denunciation of French designs on Ireland; and what more natural than that he should now be asked to track the movements of certain French emissaries which the Government heard had arrived in Dublin, and were conspiring with the Catholic leaders to throw off the British yoke.[1] This task O'Leary, as a staunch loyalist, may have satisfied his conscience in attempting, especially as he must have known that in 1784 the Catholics, as a body, had no treasonable designs, though, doubtless, some few exceptions might be found. In fact, his friend Edmund Burke, a member of the Ministry in 1783, declared, but later on, that 'the Irish Roman Catholics were everywhere loyal, save at certain points where their loyalty had been impaired by contact with Protestants.' Orde,[2] while using O'Leary, thought him a knave; yet feigned a readiness to believe his reports. The exhaustive correspondence of Count d'Adhémar, the French ambassador in London, with his Government, is now open to inquirers at the French Foreign Office; but, as it makes no allusion to any French agent in Ireland at this period, the story may be little better than one of the sensational myths so often found in the letters of informers to the Irish executive.[3] But, although no documental evidence exists of a French agent having been in Dublin in 1784, it is certain

[1] See Attorney-General Fitzgibbon's account of this scare, *infra*, p. 245.

[2] The Chief Secretary for Ireland.

[3] State papers of the present century are a sealed book; but special leave was given to search for such papers as threw light on Shelley's visit to Dublin in 1812. During this inquiry a sight was obtained of a correspondence between Dublin Castle and the Home Office, numbering many hundred sheets, and dealing entirely with the information furnished by a tipsy clerk of Mary's Lane Chapel to the effect that a general massacre of all the Protestants in Ireland had been projected! Myths of this sort have periodically scared the executive. Passing on to 1830, we find, in the Sirr Papers, informations dated December 24 and 27, and disclosing another Popish plot. Among the men alleged to be deep in the conspiracy were the late saintly Bishop Blake, Brother Syrenus, a monk, Thomas Reynolds, afterwards city marshal, W. J. Battersby, and a number of other Catholic laymen. Twenty-three officers—*i.e.* young priests from Carlow and Maynooth—are alleged to be sent by different coaches to various parts of Ireland, and all charged with secret missions of a most formidable character!

that five years later, *i.e.* in 1789, one Bancroft, an American by birth, was sent on a secret mission from France to Ireland.[1]

We hear of no important arrests during the troubled period that O'Leary is said to have been set in motion; but the Habeas Corpus Act had not been suspended since 1779, and was not until 1794 that Pitt renewed the suspension.

In analysing O'Leary's life and judging his conduct, it is not fair to ignore any remark of his tending to exculpate; but, if panegyrics are desired, the reader should consult the memoirs by England, Buckley and some others. Almost O'Leary's last public performance appeared in 1800: 'An Address to the Lords of Parliament, with an account of Sir H. Mildmay's Bill relative to Nuns.'

His loyalty was not [he said] the effect of necessity or time-serving policy, for in France, where the Penal Laws of England drove him for education, and where the Catholics of Ireland had Seminaries and Convents with full admission to all the degrees of her universities, I *resisted every solicitation to enlist any of the subjects of these kingdoms in the French King's service*, though I had then every opportunity of being appointed to superintend prisons and hospitals during the wars. It was my interest to recommend myself to the favour of people in power, and consequently more my interest to become more a courtier than a moralist. St. Paul calls God to witness when he asserts the truth: I can do the same when I assert that conscience was the rule of my conduct.[2]

This is further useful in showing that O'Leary was no admirer of the French king, and now that he was a pensioner of England would hardly object to discover the reported French agents in Dublin, who, with Napper Tandy, are said to have 'drank on their knees' the toast of 'Louis of France.'

The latter story—told by the Viceroy, Rutland, in his

[1] Lecky, *Hist. of England*, vi. 537.

[2] London, printed; Dublin, reprinted by H. Fitzpatrick, 1800. O'Leary seems to have had a pension when in France. 'I resisted the solicitations,' he adds, 'and ran the risk of incurring the displeasure of a Minister of State, and losing my pension.' 'A small pension from the French Government he retained until the French Revolution,' as we learn from a sketch of O'Leary, probably written by Plowden, in the *Gentleman's Magazine* for January 1802.

letter to Sydney—bears improbability on its face. It seems strange that Tandy and his party, who not long after were Red Republicans and the allies of Carnot and Hoche, would drink the health of Louis XVI. on their knees.[1] They were principally Protestants; and John O'Connell, in the Life of his father, says that Sheares shocked the future Liberator by exultantly displaying a handkerchief soaked in the French king's blood.

I suspect that when O'Leary returned from making, in September 1784, the inquiries which he is assumed to have done, his report was something in the spirit of Canning's knife-grinder: 'Story! God bless you, I have none to tell, sir;' and that Orde concluded O'Leary himself was in the plot. On October 17, Orde writes to Nepean, alluding to some rumour about our friar which is not stated. 'Del Campo's connection with O'Leary—or rather O'Leary's with him—may have given rise to all the report; but, after all, I think it right to be very watchful over the priest, and wish *you* to be so over the Minister. They are all of them designing knaves.'

Thus it appears that in little more than a fortnight after O'Leary is supposed to have begun to spy, Orde was far from satisfied with him.

[1] The obsolete custom of drinking healths on the knees is noticed in Brand's *Popular Antiquities*, ii. 329; and Dekker's *Honest Whore*, A.D. 1630.

CHAPTER XVI

ARTHUR O'LEARY IN LONDON

It is to be regretted that the State Paper naming 'O'Leary and Del Campo' should be couched in words so brief and cautious. Mr. Lecky offers no explanation of it. Not only are we uninformed as to the nature of the 'Report;' but we are left to guess who Del Campo was. One thing is evident: Dublin Castle and the Home Office put their heads together, shook them mysteriously, and then urged extreme caution in dealing with knaves. Books of biographic reference make no mention of Del Campo's name; but it is quite clear from Cumberland's memoirs that Del Campo was the Spanish minister, next in authority to Florida Blanca.

In the year 1780 [writes Cumberland], and about the time of Rodney's capture of the Caracca fleet, I had opportunities of discovering through a secret channel of intelligence many things passing, and some concerting, between the confidential agents of France and Spain (particularly the latter) resident in this country, and in private correspondence with the enemies of it. Of these communications I made that use which my duty dictated and to my judgment seemed advisable. By these, in the course of their progress, a prospect was opened of a secret negotiation with the Minister Florida Blanca, to which I was personally committed, and of course could not decline the undertaking it.[1]

While the American War still raged, and hostilities from France and Spain continued to threaten, Richard Cumberland, son of a bishop and the secretary of a former viceroy, started on his secret mission to the courts of Lisbon and Madrid,

[1] Cumberland's *Memoirs*, ii. 2–38. (London, 1807.)

bearing from England letters of accreditation, quite a boxful of instructions, and accompanied by his wife and daughters 'on the pretence of travelling into Italy upon a passport through the Spanish dominions.' Cumberland's interviews with Del Campo are described, and for a time all went well; but, owing to terrible rumours as regards the 'No Popery' riots in London, which now broke out, led by Lord George Gordon, President of the Protestant Association, the treaty[1] collapsed; Del Campo refused to appear; Cumberland was recalled, and the Government who sent him out withheld the repayment of 5,000*l.*, the amount of expenses he had incurred.

It may be said that Orde's want of confidence in O'Leary arose, not because he had furnished so little secret information, but because of some whisper that the Spanish Minister had had *pourparlers* with him. It would be strange if O'Leary, who in 1779 wrote powerfully against the hostile designs of Spain, should be suspected, within the next few years, of abetting them. The rumour, which Mr. Lecky says is not stated, may have been merely that O'Leary, the only Catholic writer of intrepidity at that day, had been asked by Del Campo, who soon after became resident Spanish minister in London, and was himself of English extraction,[2] to write an exposure of the 'No Popery Riots' and their leaders—incidents which Spain, now more than ever defiant in its pose, could not fail to turn to political account.

A postscript to O'Leary's 'Miscellaneous Tracts' mentions that he had been requested to give a history of the London riots. 'I promised to undertake the task,' he writes, 'and began to digest my materials; but afterwards reflecting that the duty of the historian bound me to arraign at the impartial tribunal of truth both men and actions—unmask the leading characters,' &c. . . . he then came to 'consider my own state exposed in consequence of the Penal Laws to the insult of

[1] Cumberland several times calls it a 'treaty.'

[2] Vide *Correspondence of Sir John Sinclair*, ii. 385–6. Del Campo's letters are written in excellent English; it appears that, though born in Spain, he had come from an English Catholic family named Field.

every ruffian, and, comparing the defenceless situation of the priest with the duty of the historian, I dropped the attempt.'

These tumults of 1780 lit a flame which did not die out even with the expiring century. During their height most of the Roman Catholic chapels of London, especially those of the foreign embassies, were gutted and burnt. Papists' houses were attacked, as well as the houses of all persons known to favour them. For days and nights the mob gained an almost complete mastery of London, which is described as like a city taken by storm. The venerable Bishop Challoner was roused from his sleep and urged to fly; he died soon after of palsy, the effects of the shock. No man's life was safe who did not mount the badge of riot, a blue cockade; windows displayed flags of the same colour; while the watchword 'No Popery' was prudentially inscribed. Broadsides were circulated under the auspices of Lord George Gordon—the unholy high priest of the holocaust—in which Englishmen were exhorted to remember 'the bloody tyranny and persecuting plots exercised on Protestants by Rome'—the Spanish Armada, of course, included. Society seemed falling to pieces. From Tyburn to Whitechapel the highway presented a frontage of mourning. Every shop was closed. Mr. Archer, a priest, deposed in court that he had paid 40*l.* to be allowed to pass through Fleet Street, and a hackney coachman refused 10*l.* to drive a papist to Hampstead. The mob, flushed with victory, now sought allies in the prisons. Newgate, then recently rebuilt at a cost of 150,000*l.*, was attacked with fury; its great gates fell before them like frail partitions; 500 felons, including those set free from Clerkenwell, were let loose upon the burning city, leaving behind them in flames, not the gaol only, but the whole street.[1] It seemed a second 1666, and the famous fall of the Bastile, nine years later, was but the mere echo.

[1] Vide *Annals of the English Catholic Hierarchy*, by W. Maziere Brady, pp. 170–4. (Rome, 1883.) 'Sketch of a Conference with Earl Shelbourne,' *The Dublin Review*, vols. xx.–xxi. Trials of the rioters, *The Rockingham Correspondence*, ii. 419. This remarkable incident has been all but overlooked by historians. Dickens was greatly struck by its features.

Storm had not as yet burst over Ireland; but the heavy air was charged with electricity. The following are the words with which Mr. Froude awakened wide-spread interest, and drew forth that missive from the Antipodes given on a previous page.

If rebellion was meditated [Froude writes], the Government required fuller knowledge; and 'a new plan of management' had to be adopted 'to obtain exact information of the conduct and motives of the most suspected persons.' 'Useful and confidential agents,' whose silence and fidelity could be relied on, 'who would write the daily history of a man's motions,' without betraying himself, were not to be found in Dublin.

The Irish Secretary applied to the English Cabinet to furnish him from their own staff of informers. Two valuable persons answering to Mr. Orde's description were sent, and the name of one of them will be an unpleasant surprise to those already interested in the history of the time.

They were both Irishmen. One was a skilled detective named Parker,[1] an accomplished orator who could outmouth the noisiest patriot, and had already some knowledge of the leading agitators. Orde welcomed this man with a twinge of misgiving. 'I hope he is discreet,' he wrote, 'for he must to a certain extent be possessed of the power of hurting us by garrulity or treachery.'[2]

The other was no less a person than the celebrated Father O'Leary, whose memory is worshipped by Irish Catholic politicians with a devotion which approaches idolatry. O'Leary, as he was known to the world, was the most fascinating preacher, the most distinguished controversialist of his time. A priest who had caught the language of toleration, who had mastered all the chords of liberal philosophy, and played on them like a master; whose mission had been to plead against prejudice, to represent his country as the bleeding lamb, maligned, traduced, oppressed, but ever praying for her enemies; as eager only to persuade England to offer its hand to the Catholic Church, and receive in return the affectionate homage of undying gratitude. O'Leary had won his way to the heart of Burke by his plausible eloquence. Pitt seemed to smile on him: it is easy now to conjecture why. When he

[1] We have no proof that Parker was an Irishman.

[2] Orde to Evan Nepean, September 8, 1784 (see *English in Ireland*, ii. 413).

appeared in the Convention at the Rotunda the whole assembly rose to receive him. Had such a man been sent over on an open errand of conciliation, his antecedents would have made the choice intelligible. But he was despatched as a paid and secret instrument of treachery, in reply to a request for a trained informer.[1] What the Government really thought of Father O'Leary may be gathered from Orde's language when told to expect him. 'He could get to the bottom of all secrets in which the Catholics were concerned,' and Catholics were known to be the chief promoters of the agitation in Dublin. But he too was to be dealt with cautiously, for he was a priest. 'They are, all of them,' Orde said, 'designing knaves;' 'the only good to be derived from them is, perhaps, to deceive them into an idea that they are believed.'[2]

Sir Jonah Barrington describes Orde as 'a cold, cautious and sententious man.[3] These letters in some respects support that impression. A few years later he was created Lord Bolton. His letter, announcing O'Leary's arrival at Dublin on secret service, is dated September 23, 1784.[4] Let us look back a little and see what the previous year was doing.

[1] In the postscript to O'Leary's letter (see Appendix) we catch a glimpse of some of the Catholic leaders in Dublin at this time, into whose secrets Orde assumes he could easily dive. They include Thomas Braughall, so often mentioned in Wolfe Tone's *Diary* as a Catholic organiser and United Irishman; Charles Ryan, a very important Catholic leader (fully described in Wyse's *History of the Catholic Association*, i. 138–9); and Mr. Kirwan, noticed at p. 177 of the same book. Sutton, 'the Brigadier,' also mentioned in O'Leary's letter, was, with Braughall, one of the thirty-three Catholic delegates who, in 1793, represented the City of Dublin (see *Vindication of the Catholics of Ireland*, p. 90.) (London: Debrett, 1793.) Edward Lewins, the two Sweetmans, Thomas Reynolds, and other afterwards very prominent rebels, figure in the said list of the Dublin delegates.

[2] Mr. Orde to Mr. Evan Nepean, October 17, 1784. See Froude's *English in Ireland*, iii. 414. But Mr. Froude will excuse me for adding that the chief passage he quotes is from a letter dated September 8, 1784.

[3] *Rise and Fall of the Irish Nation*, Paris ed. p. 319.

[4] My Australian correspondent, Mr. Morgan McMahon, was puzzled to determine how O'Leary, the scene of whose labours was Ireland, could be summoned from London in 1784, inasmuch as his biographer states that it was not until 1789 O'Leary took up his residence in that city (Buckley, p. 304). The accuracy of Mr. Froude's date is, however, confirmed by a letter in the *Life of George Anne Bellamy*, iii. 120 (Dublin ed. 1785). On August 16, 1784, Mr. W. T. Hervey writes to that celebrated actress, then living at 10, Charles Street, St. James', and expressing the 'infinite satisfaction' he felt at meeting O'Leary at dinner.

The Dungannon Convention, which won great boons for Ireland, was followed by provincial assemblies in Leinster, Munster and Connaught. Resolutions were carried, delegates were appointed, and the nation anxiously awaited the great Volunteer Convention in Dublin, on which the fate of Ireland was declared to depend. Meanwhile one hundred and sixty envoys of the Volunteer army met, electing Lord Charlemont chairman. Red uniforms fringed the streets, and the delegates, two by two, marched through the lines, amid the roll of drums and the waving of national ensigns. The Earl of Bristol and Bishop of Derry rode to the Convention with an escort of dragoons.

A distinguished corps of volunteers [writes Mr. Buckley] had conferred on O'Leary the honorary dignity of chaplain; and we are assured that many of the measures submitted for consideration at the great Convention held in Dublin had been previously placed before him for his opinion as to their prudence and utility. On that memorable day, when the delegates of a hundred thousand men met in the Rotunda, with all the pomp and power that an armed nation could concentrate for a great national purpose, it was gratifying to the assembled masses of spectators to behold Father O'Leary, as he entered the building, received at the door by the entire guard of volunteers with a full salute of rested arms. He marched up the hall amidst the deafening cheers of the surrounding delegates, and, in the debate which followed, his name was frequently mentioned with honour and applause.[1]

'Plowden's remarks, which you enclose, do not meet the specific statements of Froude, that O'Leary was employed as an informer at the period of the Volunteer Convention,' writes Mr. Morgan McMahon, my Australian correspondent.[2] Mr. Froude's words certainly tend to convey that the Convention took place at the time of Orde's application for a spy. The date of the Convention was November 1783: Orde's letter was written in September 1784. Again, it is suggested that O'Leary was despatched in reply to a request for a

[1] *Life of Father O'Leary*, by the Rev. M. B. Buckley, p. 203.
[2] See his letter, *ante*, p. 212.

trained informer. But it does not appear that though he may have been useful as a diplomatist he was already a spy. On the contrary, Sydney writes (Sept. 4): 'O'Leary has been talked to and he is willing to do what is wished for 100*l.* a year.' Orde replies (Sept. 8), 'I am very glad that you have settled matters with O'Leary, who can get to the bottom of all secrets in which the Catholics are concerned.' O'Leary had already a pension, ostensibly for his writings; but the pension for espionage must not be confounded with it.

It is certainly admitted by even O'Leary's panegyrists that at the period of the Convention of 1783 delicate overtures, which they assume he rejected, were made to him; but the magnanimous words supposed to have been used by O'Leary when parleying with his tempter rest on no authority whatever, and some will be disposed to suspect that a colour is imparted to the overtures more presentable to general readers than the naked truth, whatever it was. The pension, I repeat, which O'Leary already enjoyed, was, I think, merely for his writings; though, prior to September 1784, he may have accepted douceurs for distinct acts of diplomacy. At all events it is due to O'Leary to give him the full benefit of the exculpatory words of his brother priest. Describing the Volunteer Convention, Father Buckley writes, eighty years later:—

During Father O'Leary's visit to Dublin on this occasion, he was waited on by a gentleman who was well known to be on very close and friendly relations with the Government of the day.[1] The visit appeared, for some time, to be merely one of ceremony, and the visitor paid many handsome compliments to the Father on the style of his writings and their good effect on the public mind. Soon, however, it was easy to see that diplomacy had more to do with the visit than etiquette, for the gentleman, in courteous language, intimated that if Father O'Leary would use his pen in extolling certain measures just then brought forward by the Administration, his services would be handsomely requited. O'Leary

[1] England, from whom Buckley recast and embellished this account, calls him 'a gentleman in the confidence of the Ministry' (p. 118). Was it Sir Boyle Roche—of whom presently?

was displeased and indignant at the proposal to barter his patriotism for a bribe, and conveyed his feelings in no measured phrase. The request was therefore softened down into an entreaty that he would at least abstain from writing on those measures in terms of condemnation. But the minion of the Government knew not with what manner of man he had to deal. 'I will never be silent,' warmly exclaimed O'Leary, 'whilst my exertions can be of the least service to my religion or my country.' [1]

Thus far Buckley, the biographer of 1867. England, O'Leary's biographer of 1822, finishes the interview in less florid words: 'He was then told that a pension of 150*l.* per annum was to be offered for his acceptance, and that no condition repugnant to his feelings as an Irishman or Catholic was to be annexed to it. A change in the Administration [2] took place shortly afterwards, and the promise remained unfulfilled.' [3]

Father England assumes that O'Leary spurned the overtures at the time of the Convention, though later on his acceptance of a pension is admitted. While guiltless, no doubt, of direct betrayal, he may have been led to connive at a trick by which the Irish Government succeeded in breaking up the Convention.[4]

O'Leary, towards the close of his life, had made copious notes illustrative of the history of Ireland—notes handed by him to Plowden, who was glad to interweave them with his own when compiling 'The Historical Review.' Plowden dismisses with the following note the great incident of the Convention:—

Whilst the business of equal representation was in agitation at a meeting of the Convention in Dublin, a pretended letter from Lord Kenmare was produced, purporting to convey the general

[1] See England's account of the overtures made to O'Leary in London, *ante*, p. 220. England puts 'country' before 'religion.'

[2] In April 1783 the Coalition came into power. Pitt's administration dates from December 1783.

[3] England's *Life of O'Leary*, p. 118.

[4] O'Leary was specially weak in yielding acquiescence. Buckley states (*Life*, p. 355) that O'Leary, having been led to connive at the legislative union, he expressed remorse.

sentiments of the Roman Catholics of Ireland, in which they were made to express their perfect satisfaction with what had been already done for them, and that they desired no more than peaceably to enjoy the privileges they had obtained.

Catholics thus became excluded from the constitutional prerogatives claimed for Protestants. The proceedings of the Convention were at last adjourned *sine die*. Sir Boyle Roche invented the fatal letter, and Mr. Froude conveys that he was instigated to this course by the Viceroy. Sir Gavan Duffy states—as a common belief in Ireland—that 'had the Convention not been betrayed by its leaders, the Union would never have taken place.'[1]

O'Leary, though his name, and that of Sir Boyle Roche, are not mentioned in the printed abstract of the proceedings, was certainly present when the fictitious letter was read. Dr. England, describing the demonstration by which O'Leary's arrival was hailed at the Rotunda, adds that it 'occurred on the same day on which the message said to be from Lord Kenmare was read at the Convention,'[2] but no fault is found with O'Leary by England, who is his invariable eulogist.

Lord Kenmare was a fast friend of our friar,[3] and is uniformly praised by him.[4] It was when on a visit to this peer that O'Leary, seeing a wounded stag approaching Yelverton, wittily said: 'How naturally instinct leads him to come to you to deliver him by a *nolle prosequi*.'[5] Kenmare, this leader of the higher class of Catholics, was falsely represented as announcing at the Convention that his co-religionists were satisfied with the concessions they had got. I find that O'Leary had privately expressed, very much to his honour, but a short time before, an opinion diametrically opposite; and urging the Catholics not to cease agitation till every link

[1] *Bird's-eye View of Irish History*.

[2] England's *Life of O'Leary*, p. 105. (London, 1822.)

[3] See *Life* by Buckley, pp. 212–213, 237, 277. See also England, pp. 133, 134, 176, 179.

[4] See *Mr. O'Leary's Defence, in reply to the Lord Bishop of Cloyne*, pp. 41–42. (Dublin, 1787.)

[5] Thomas Moore's *Diary*, iv. 112.

in their fetters had been struck off;[1] but he now held his peace, and thus wittingly, or otherwise, aided the base schemes of the Viceroy. O'Leary himself had long been recognised as the most prominent exponent and mouthpiece of the Catholic demand; and, from his intimacy with Lord Kenmare, he could hardly fail to have known his sentiments on a question in which both were naturally most interested; the forged letter, however, claiming authority to speak for the Catholics of Ireland, was allowed to pass unchallenged, to the ruin of the Convention and the exultant triumph of a faction.

O'Leary and Sir Boyle Roche are not persons likely to have been intimate; and yet it can be shown that an intimacy did exist. A letter from O'Leary, written a year before the Convention, and to be found later on, avows that he was the friend and political correspondent of Roche.[2] The forged letter—in which were travestied the opinions and aspirations of the Catholics of Ireland—was read on November 11, 1783.[3] Not until a fortnight after was the fraud exposed by the popular Earl-Bishop of Derry, who read a letter from Lord Kenmare,

[1] See letter to Mr. Kirwan in Appendix. After 1783, no such bold tone is traceable in O'Leary's expressions.

[2] See Appendix. Their intercourse may have been strengthened by clannish claims. O'Leary was a Cork man, and Roche is described as 'a branch of the ancient baronial family of Roche, Viscount Fermoy.' See obituary in *Gentleman's Magazine* for 1807, p. 506. His wages comprised the baronetcy bestowed in 1782; a pension of 300*l.* a year, with a separate annuity of 200*l.* for his wife; and, later on, the miserable post of Gentleman Usher, or Master of Ceremonies, at Dublin Castle. It is remarkable that in all the contemporary reports of the discreditable transaction, as regards Lord Kenmare, the name of Sir Boyle Roche is suppressed, and George Ogle, afterwards a P.C., put in his place. Ogle and O'Leary were both 'Monks of the Screw.'

[3] The Rev. Dr. Wills, when writing his *Lives of Distinguished Irishmen* (v. 243), gathered curious facts from survivors of those times. Of Sir Boyle Roche we learn that 'it was usual for the members of the Irish Cabinet to write speeches for him, which he committed to memory, and, while mastering the substance, generally contrived to travesty into language, and ornament with peculiar graces, of his own. On many of these occasions he was primed and loaded for action by the industry of Mr. Edward Cooke, who acted during several administrations as muster-master to the wisdom of the Castle.' Sir Boyle felt that he had specially earned the gratitude of the Crown; and I find, by the Précis book of Lord Fitzwilliam, he had even applied for a peerage. In the Pelham MSS. he is constantly found worrying for honours and reward.

dated Killarney, Nov. 20, saying, 'I utterly disavow having given the least authority,' [1] &c., &c. Sir Boyle Roche thereupon addressed to several leading Catholics a remarkable note dated 'Dublin Castle, 14th February, 1784.' This document was, of course, the act of the Administration, Roche having been merely wound up and used as an automaton. His letter, seeking to entrap slavish Catholics and sink them in the mire of unpopularity, began by saying that it would flatter him in the highest degree 'if I should find that my conduct was not disapproved by yourself and friends,' and he holds out the hope that, being once more in Parliament, he would be not unmindful of Catholic interests.

I had certain intelligence [he adds] that the Bishop of Derry had leagued himself with some of the unthinking part of the Catholics, who were in town for the purpose, and that the admission of that body to the rights of voting for members of Parliament was to be the first matter agitated in the Convention. I now thought that the crisis was arrived in which Lord Kenmare [2] and the heads of the body should step forth to disavow these wild projects, and to profess their attachment to the lawful powers. . . . I therefore resolved on a bold stroke.[3]

He adds that he was elated to the greatest degree by his success, having 'entirely disconcerted the measures of the leaders of the Convention.'

The Earl-Bishop of Derry was a decided revolutionist and very eager for separation, and is alleged to have said to Lord Charlemont, 'Things are going well, my lord: we shall have blood.' O'Leary, author of 'Loyalty Asserted,' and notoriously a man of peace, would probably have felt little scruple

[1] See England's *Life of O'Leary*, p. 109.

[2] Lord Kenmare died September 9, 1795. For a careful study of his temporising character see Wyse's *Catholic Association*. He had enjoyed his title merely by courtesy. In 1798 his son was advanced to a Viscounty, and the next year to an Earldom.

[3] Mr. Lecky says that 'it is a strange illustration of the standard of honour prevailing in Ireland, that a man who, by his own confession, had acted in this manner continued to be connected with the Government and a popular speaker in the House of Commons' (vi. 368). But, in point of fact, Dublin Castle could not get on without him.

in seeking to avert by diplomatic means what Orde feared might become a bloody chaos. Burke, writing to a brother priest of O'Leary's, said, 'Do everything in your power to check the growth of Jacobinism on the one hand, and oppression, which is its best friend, on the other.' No wonder that the Irish Government blenched at the outlook. One Dublin paper, called the 'Volunteer Journal,' urged assassination; and some men had been arrested, in the previous spring, on a charge of conspiring to murder seven unpopular members of Parliament. The supineness of magistrates and the absence of any regular police force opened great facilities for crime. Riots raged in the streets owing to trade strikes; men were 'tarred and feathered' and let loose before the infuriated mob; soldiers were houghed and left bleeding on the pavement. New corps of volunteers advertised for recruits, and men of the worst repute rushed into their ranks. Meanwhile the Bishop of Derry was raising a fresh regiment of volunteers in Ulster. 'The Viceroy, at Fitzgibbon's advice,' writes Froude, 'sent down officers in disguise to watch him, with a warrant in their pockets should an arrest be necessary;' and he adds that 'this singular prelate ran a near chance of ending his career on the gallows.' The withdrawal from public life of so remarkable a figure was second only in its effect to the collapse of the Convention, of which he was the animating spirit. When, six years later, Bancroft was sent by France on a secret mission to Ireland, his report, now preserved in the Foreign Office at Paris, states, as we learn from Lecky, that the fall of the Convention had 'thrown a certain ridicule on Irish democracy, and it may be long before it is repaired.'

The Convention belongs to the year 1783. Not until the autumn of 1784 are any letters found compromising O'Leary—letters not revealing any distinct acts of espionage, or even penned by himself, but showing him to have yielded to the voice of the tempter.

In judging a man who is not alive to defend himself, one whose memory has been for a century revered, I am reluctantly led to encumber this narrative with various considerations for and against, so that readers may have the result of a conscientious study of the case, and be able to form a judicial conclusion.

The promptitude of O'Leary's arrival in Dublin impressed badly all who read it in Froude; for Orde, according to that historian, asked the English Secretary of State to send him over two trained men from their own staff of informers.[1] The letter containing this request, however, I have not seen in print or manuscript. O'Leary came over at the same time as a detective named Parker; but the alacrity of the priest's arrival, though it looks badly, may not be altogether due to his readiness to play the spy. This man, 'poor in everything save genius and philosophy,' to quote Grattan's words, was informed, according to England, one of his biographers, that his presence in Dublin was necessary in order that some formalities should be gone through ere his name could be placed on the Irish Civil List.[2] England says that a pension which, during the previous year, he was on the point of receiving, fell through because of a change in the Cabinet; and may not this consideration have been in itself enough to expedite the journey?

O'Leary had been interviewed in London by Sir Evan Nepean, a practised diplomatist, and consented, we are told, to come to Dublin to make certain inquiries. But who can tell what wily words were employed to induce him to wait on the Irish Secretary, Orde, at Dublin Castle? Orde posed as a man rather liberal for the time, and was the correspondent of Grattan and Lord Kenmare. Men of the world know that very different language is often used when writing *of* a person, than when addressing that person direct. On the other hand it should be remembered, assuming that Sydney conveys a correct impression of what passed, that O'Leary seemed willing to accept 100*l*. for services dealing, not with the special exigencies of the hour, but on condition that he continued, from year to year, and for the same annual fee, to probe to the bottom certain secrets of his party.

[1] See Froude, ii. 415.

[2] Vide *ante*, p. 220.

When he arrived in Dublin the country was rent by great and just discontent. One grievance was that Parliament possessed no adequate representation of the popular voice. In March 1784, Flood brought in a Bill for 'Reform,' and twenty-six counties petitioned in its favour.

It had been decided that the Convention[1] of the previous year should be followed up by a national Congress. This announcement brought dismay to the Castle. The loss of her American Colonies had just taught Pitt a lesson. Contemporary pamphleteers, thinking perhaps of the then fashionable melodrama, 'The Castle Spectre,' saw Dublin Castle scared by mysterious terrors.

'The letters C.O.N.G.R.E.S.S.,' writes Orellana,[2] 'are magic letters, of themselves sufficient to rise an apparition before the eyes of a guilty Minister—an apparition that will seem to draw his curtains in the dead of night, and rouse him from his pillow!'

The Congress was in fact the ghost of the Betrayed Convention.

There was to be a great meeting at the Tholsel in Dublin, on September 27, 1784, preliminary to the coming Congress. The prompt arrival from London, on September 24, of O'Leary and Parker, and Orde's confidential whisper that they were to begin operations at once, lead to the belief that both attended this meeting. Indeed, from O'Leary's prominent attitude at the previous Convention, he is almost certain to have taken part in the deliberations that followed it. No mention, however, is made of O'Leary or Parker in the

[1] The Convention had greatly alarmed the Government. In 1793, Lord Clare introduced the Convention Act, making all such assemblages henceforth illegal; but a popular leader remarked that it was the wisdom of Xerxes attempting with iron fetters to chain the sea. In 1811, Lord Fingall, Mr. Kirwan, and other Catholic delegates were arrested under the Act. It never became law in England, and about the year 1878 Mr. P. J. Smyth, M.P., succeeded in freeing Ireland from its pressure.

[2] *The Letters of Orellana*, an Irish Helot, to the Seven Northern Counties not represented in the National Assembly of Delegates held at Dublin in October 1784, for obtaining a more equal representation of the people. Haliday Pamphlets, Royal Irish Academy, vol. 482, p. 29.

Dublin prints of the day.[1] The Congress and its preliminary meeting are, no doubt, constantly referred to, but they sat with closed doors, and no reports appear. What took place must be gleaned from other sources. A letter from Orde, published in Grattan's 'Life,' and dated September 18, 1784, six days before O'Leary's arrival from London, mentions that at the coming meeting opposition would be made to putting a question upon the election of representatives for a National Congress.[2]

As this was a period full of great issues, and yet but little known, perhaps I may be allowed to cull from the local journals of the day a few remarks to show the spirit which animated both sides.

The 'Dublin Evening Post,' the popular organ, 'most earnestly recommends a numerous and respectable meeting at the Tholsel on Monday next. The occasion,' it adds, 'is great.'[3] But ere long the Castle journalist gleefully chronicles a collapse.

The weeping and gnashing of teeth among *the city Patriots* on account of yesterday's melancholy disappointment at the Tholsel is not to be described. What a damp must this falling off in the metropolis give to the yet unassembled bailiwicks. Alas! alas! that the city which laid the first stone of 'a national Congress' should now give a shock to the precious building! How are the mighty aggregate Committee fallen! ah, how are they despised! Resolutions, address, circular letters—all, all are scattered to the

[1] Besides the journals of the day, I have searched the litter of pamphlets to which that pregnant year gave birth; but the names 'O'Leary' and 'Parker' never appear. Their mission, clearly, was a secret one. Sheahan's *Articles of Irish Manufacture* (Cork, 1833) certainly speaks of Mr. Parker, 'who fell in with a Doctor O'Leary' (p. 112); but, on hunting up the pamphlet from which he quotes, *Plea for the Poor* (p. 15), it appears that the date is 1819, and the Dr. O'Leary was a physician in Kanturk.

[2] Diplomatic letters, but fulsomely servile, are addressed by Orde to Grattan (vide *Life*, by his Son, iii. 209-11). Orde must have known that Grattan was jealous—first, of Flood, with whom he constantly quarrelled, and, secondly, of a new, bold, and thoroughly honest Protestant leader, who had just made his *début*, and worked hard to make the Congress a success. This was James Napper Tandy, commander of the Dublin Volunteer Artillery, and afterwards a general of division in the service of France.

[3] *Dublin Evening Post*, September 18, 1784.

winds; and commotion, revolution, and scramble, sunk in an abyss of despair beyond all hopes of resurrection.[1]

If O'Leary attended the meeting at the Tholsel, it is easy to know what tone he took. Three years later he published a pamphlet in which he seems very familar with the incidents of that month.

I recollect the unmerited abuse given for a long time in the papers to the Catholics, because seventeen housekeepers in Dublin unguardedly signed a requisition to the high sheriff for the purpose of convening an aggregate meeting relative to a parliamentary reform, though I am confident the seventeen knew as little about the impropriety of their signing that requisition, and foresaw as little the offence it would give, as the high sheriff himself. And as to the Catholics, in their disqualified situation, they could not with either prudence or propriety follow any other line but that of a strict neutrality in a political question, on which neither the friends nor opponents of a parliamentary reform would acknowledge them competent to determine.

This tamed tone will not fail to strike on comparing it with his intrepid letter[2] written not two years before.

Meanwhile the National Congress was announced to hold its first meeting. 'Whatever underhand engines may endeavour to effect,' says the popular organ, 'we hope to see these just and constitutional deliberations re-establish the purity of representation.'[3]

One prime object of the Castle is detected and denounced by the same courageous journalist, John Magee. The 'Dublin Evening Post' of November 5, 1784, records:—

The borough-ridden Government, disappointed in its impotent attempts to prevent the laudable exertion of the people in prosecuting a Parliamentary Reform, and finding that even the venal knaves of the Castle nauseate the fulsome charges so long run on Binns and Tandy, has directed the venal writers, as the last effort of an

[1] The *Freeman's Journal*, September 28, 1784. This journal, once the organ of Grattan, Flood, and Lucas, fell into the hands of an unprincipled adventurer, named Francis Higgins, who prostituted the once virtuous print to a venal executive.

[2] See Appendix, p. 374. [3] *Dublin Evening Post*, October 23, 1784.

expiring and despairing cause, to endeavour to sow those seeds of dissension which so long desolated this divided Kingdom, and set father against son, and brother against brother, that all might become the easy slaves of foreign tyranny.[1]

These extracts do not criminate O'Leary, but are useful as illustrating the history of the time, and developing secret policy, while, moreover, they correct some strange inaccuracies. For instance: the Viceroy, writing to Sydney, as printed in Mr. Lecky's History, calls Tandy's colleague 'Binney.' Of course it should be Binns, a name frequently found in the dark records of '98.

The Castle scribe, in another paragraph, states of Binns and Tandy, both thoroughly honest men—'Fame is very busy that they have received the all-subduing touch of "aurum mirabile."' This was probably to divert suspicion from the really subsidised quarter. It will be remembered that the date of O'Leary's arrival, and that of Parker, quite tallies with the meeting on the 27th September; and it may be asked what else could have brought the popular orators to Dublin at that juncture? Parker knew Tandy, and, as Orde remarks, might be 'able to dive to the bottom of his secrets.'

While diplomacy sought to work its ends in one quarter, brute force laboured in another to disable the arm which had been upraised. The Sheriff of the County Dublin having convened his bailiwick to meet on the subject of Reform, Fitzgibbon, then Attorney-General, addressed an unconstitutional letter to him threatening to proceed by attachment against those who responded to his call. The sheriff himself was fined and imprisoned.

The subsidised journalist, Francis Higgins, writes on December 24, 1784:—

[1] The policy of creating a schism has often since been acted upon. We have already seen Lord Northington's approval of such a scheme. The Viceroy, Cornwallis, addressing Portland, June 22, 1799, writes in reference to a public question: 'Dublin is not without material for a counter party, which I should have sanguine hope of collecting if my endeavours to produce a schism in the corporation should prove successful.'—*Cornwallis Correspondence*, i. 339.

The Roman Catholics may evidently see how wickedly intent on their ruin certain people have been, with a serious idea of extending the elective franchise, or, indeed, any other privilege to them. They endeavoured to cajole (the Roman Catholics) into a commotion.[1]

In conclusion, the old charge of venality and perfidy is brought against the incorruptible Tandy. 'Napper,' we are told, 'betrayed them.' But Barrington, and all other historians, admit that Tandy was sound to the core.

Grattan, in the Life of his father, notices as strange that the Bishop of Derry, who the previous year was so active at the Convention, absented himself from the Congress. The explanation probably is that his lordship had heard something of the detectives with a warrant for his arrest in their pocket. How the Congress crumbled, and the organisation melted away, a glimpse is obtained from Plowden, who embodied in his 'Historical Review' a mass of notes made by O'Leary. 'It is well posterity should know,' writes his biographer, 'how much Plowden was indebted to his co-operation.'[2]

Plowden had never been to Ireland until about the year 1800. The following words seem those of a man who knew the inner workings of the governmental policy in 1784.

The link of unanimity having been once severed [we read in Plowden], the fall of the armed associations into difference and contention was much more rapid than had been their progress to union. The divisions of the volunteers were encouraged by Government; and for that purpose discord and turbulence were rather countenanced than checked in many counties, particularly upon the delicate and important expedient of admitting the Catholics to the elective franchise, a question which it was artfully attempted to connect with the now declining cause of Parliamentary Reform. Through a long series of years Government had never wanted force to quell internal commotions; and it seemed to be now dreaded lest an union of Irishmen should extinguish the old means of creating dissension. The desire of disuniting the volunteers begat

[1] The *Freeman's Journal*, December 24, 1784.

[2] *Life of O'Leary*, by Rev. M. B. Buckley, p. 385. See also England's *O'Leary*, p. 289. (London, 1822.)

inattention to the grievances of the discontented and distressed peasantry of the South: that wretched and lawless rabble once more assumed the style of *White Boys*,[1] and for some time committed their depredations with impunity, particularly against Kilkenny.[2]

The Volunteer army became gradually disorganised and disbanded; and the cannon, on which the words 'Free Trade or This' were inscribed, went back to the foundry.

In 1785 things looked a little dark in Dublin, which must have given O'Leary something to do to see through. A storm signal was raised by a few alarmists, and the Attorney-General, Fitzgibbon, though he sought to make light of the outlook, admitted enough to show that the country ought to be prepared for foul weather. Mr. Lecky, in rejecting as without foundation[3] the report confided by Rutland to Sydney in 1784, that a French agent was then in Dublin, makes no reference to a man named Perrin, mentioned in a remarkable speech of the Attorney-General, Fitzgibbon, better known as Lord Clare. On February 14, 1785, he announced in the Irish Parliament that

The great majority of the original Volunteers have hung up their arms and are retired to cultivate the arts of peace: their place has been assumed by men who disgrace the name. I have seen resolutions inviting the French into this country. On the 26th April, 1784, the Sons of the Shamrock voted Mr. Perrin, a native of France, honorary member of their corps. I have seen publications inviting Catholics, contrary to the laws of the land, to arm themselves to reform the constitution in Church and State. I have seen encomiums on Louis XVI., the friend of mankind and the assertor of American liberty. . . . They may invite the French to invade our country. I have seen invitations to the dregs of the people to go to drills and form into corps; we should therefore distinguish between the gentlemen—the original Volunteers—and those sons of sedition. I have seen a summons from a Major Canier, ordering his corps to attend with nine rounds of ball cartridge, *as there might*

[1] The 'White Boys' were perpetually denounced by O'Leary.
[2] *Historical Review of the State of Ireland*, by Francis Plowden, ii. 104.
[3] Lecky, vi. 369.

be occasion for actual service, and at the same time intimating a threat to Government; and will any man tell me, that we should be overawed by such people as these? or that the Commons of Ireland should be afraid to grant a sum of money to array a militia until these people should lay down their arms? [1]

M. Perrin, the native of France, whose name Fitzgibbon mentions in connection with the resolution to invite the French to invade Ireland, was no doubt the father of the subsequently well-known judge of the Queen's Bench, Louis Perrin. Under what circumstances M. Perrin first came to Dublin is not clear. Sometimes he was styled a Professor of French; usually resided in Dublin; but would sojourn, for months at a time, in the houses of such Irish gentry as wished to acquire a knowledge of that tongue. 'Perrin's French Grammar' was at a later date very familiar in Irish circles.[2]

The tinge of disappointment which peeps forth in the later allusion of Secretary Orde to O'Leary may have been influenced by a circumstance casually noticed by his biographer. We have seen from a well-informed local journal of the day, that venal writers had received instructions to endeavour to sow the seeds of dissension. It will be shown that O'Leary was specially intimate with the proprietor of the Castle organ,

[1] *Irish Parliamentary Register*, iv. 227.

[2] 'For King Louis is loved by the Irish Brigade,' we know on the authority of Irish song, and the judge was baptised 'Louis' apparently in compliment to the French king, described as 'the assertor of American liberty.' The bias of the Perrins was always democratic, and the judge himself had been the attached friend of Robert Emmet, whom he embraced in the dock. The conduct of '*P. the Scholar*' (T.C.D.) at this time is noticed by Archbishop Magee, then a fellow, in a letter printed in Plunket's *Life*. The judge's brother, Mark Perrin, rector of Athenry, in a letter to me, states that on the night Emmet was sentenced to death, Louis Perrin came home to their house at Chapelizod, bathed in tears. In that picturesque part of the 'Strawberry Beds,' where one can cross the Liffey by a ferry, access is gained to the old churchyard of Palmerstown, in which, partly smothered in weeds and fallen leaves, may be traced the epitaph of Judge Perrin's father. When Brougham declared in 1828 'The Schoolmaster is abroad, and I trust to him armed with his Primer against the Soldier in full military array,' he used the idea in a higher sense than could apply to M. Perrin and his 'Grammar,' who, unobtrusive as he seems to have been, caused some disquietude to Lord Clare, a man of all others the most difficult to perturb.

and O'Leary would be one of the first writers on whom Orde's thoughts could not fail to fall. O'Leary's biographers say, but without giving dates, that he recoiled from the proposal to write in the organ of the Irish Government. Indeed, in a pamphlet, previously published, he records his dislike to anonymous compositions.[1] An eloquent divine, the Rev. Morgan d'Arcy, in preaching the funeral panegyric on Father O'Leary, travelled slightly out of his path to touch on this point. He said :—

The well-timed and effectual exertions of this extraordinary man, could not fail to attract the notice of Government, and, consequently, were not suffered to remain unrewarded by his gracious and beneficent sovereign ; but, though he received with all becoming gratitude this unsolicited and well-earned mark of royal remuneration, yet such was his disinterestedness, and the noble independence of his spirit, that when, soon after, a very considerable annuity had been offered him to become the supporter of a periodical publication,[2] which then was, and still continues to be, the foul vehicle of misrepresentation, slander, and calumny on the Irish people; indignant at the insulting proposal, he rejects it with becoming contempt, though by his refusal he was sure to incur the displeasure of a certain description of men, and through their influence might apprehend a discontinuance of his pension ; yet, destitute as he was of all earthly property beside, sooner than prostitute his heaven-sent talents, he leaves his native country and repairs to this metropolis, to enjoy the boasted and enviable blessings of British protection and British liberty.

The preacher's reference here would be to the year 1789, when O'Leary removed permanently to London. It was in '89 that the great struggle on the Regency Question, which will be dealt with later on, raged between the camps of Whig and Tory in Ireland.

Higgins, the subsidised owner of the Castle organ, was called 'Shamado' by John Magee, and painted in colours of

[1] 'I disclaim anonymous productions.'—Postscript to his *Miscellaneous Tracts.* (Dublin, 1781.)

[2] Buckley says that this proposition was made to O'Leary in Dublin (*Life*, p. 354).

demoniac hue. According to Dr. Morgan d'Arcy, O'Leary did not yield to the tempter, but rejected the proposal with indignation and contempt, and this would naturally incur displeasure. The statement proves too much, for Higgins, by his will dated 1791, speaks of O'Leary as his 'long and faithful friend,' and leaves him a bequest in proof of affection. Further, his journal devoted part of its very limited space to occasional paragraphs laudatory of O'Leary, and not ill-calculated to strengthen popular confidence in his name. Thus, on May 12, 1785—a few months after Orde says he had consented to work secretly for pay—we read in the subsidised organ of the Irish Government:—

Nothing can more mark the influence of wisdom and superior genius than the mention made of Dr. O'Leary in George Anne Bellamy's 'Apology' where she says the philanthropy and interference of that liberal man put an end to the scandalous conduct of Count Haslang's (the Bavarian ambassador's) chaplain on the death of that old representative of the *corps diplomatique*.[1]

[1] As service of a political or diplomatic sort might possibly be inferred from this paragraph, I thought it just to O'Leary to see the book from which 'Shamado' quotes. The incident is described by Mrs. Bellamy in the *Apology for her Life*, ii. 246–7 (Dublin ed. 1785). She complains that the remains of Count Haslang were not treated with due respect; and that a new chaplain, who had been assigned to the Bavarian ambassador, behaved towards 'the chaplains and domestics of the late count with unmanly arrogance. . . . had it not been for the timely arrival of that justly respected luminary Father O'Leary.' Her account is not very clear. In what year Haslang's death occurred is not mentioned; but the *Gentleman's Magazine* of the time throws in a few dates and facts. Count Haslang died at Golden Square, London, on May 29, 1783, after an embassy of forty-two years (liii. 454). George II. had formed an attachment for him in Hanover, and brought him to London. Haslang's son was Prime Minister of Bavaria, while his father, during a crisis in its history, filled the post of ambassador to England. On June 5, 1783, a solemn dirge, attended by all the *corps diplomatique* in London, was sung in Warwick Street (R.C.) Chapel; but 'owing to a dispute at the grave [in old St. Pancras] several of the ambassadors returned home without supporting the pall.' The dispute, which is not explained, at last obliged the Anglican chaplain to read the burial service over the deceased envoy of a Catholic power.

O'Leary, in finally adjusting the difficulties, may have discharged a diplomatic mission inspired from Downing Street. Mrs. Bellamy alludes to insults offered even to the domestics of Count Haslang. How serious it was to insult even a servant of the Bavarian ambassador is shown by the *Gentleman's Magazine*, xxv. 232–3. In 1755, we learn that 'T. Randall, late an officer to

The organ of the Irish Government does not praise O'Leary for political support. To do so would arouse suspicion whether well founded or not; but Higgins, from friendship or policy, seeks to exalt his prestige and popularity. In the 'Freeman' of November 20, 1784, we have a long account of how he put down Dr. Johnson, who had addressed him with boorishness. 'The literati,' it is added, 'consider themselves as much obliged by Dr. O'Leary's conduct on the occasion, as it has much humbled the imperious and surly behaviour of Johnson.'

The statement of Plowden, that O'Leary was pensioned on condition that he should withhold his pen in support of toleration,[1] will not bear test.[2] In 1784, O'Leary is conclusively shown to be subsidised. His dissuasive address to the common people of Ireland denunciatory of Whiteboyism, a bulky treatise, bears date 1786. It seems more likely that a subsidy would be given for writing in support of the oppressive laws of that day. This letter to the peasantry writes up that

the Sheriff of Middlesex, pursuant to his sentence for arresting a servant of Count Haslang, was brought from Newgate before his Excellency's house in Golden Square, having on his breast a paper proclaiming that he had been adjudged by Lord Chancellor Hardwicke and the Chief Justices to be *a violator of the laws of nations, and a disturber of the public repose*, and stands convicted thereof.' Randall was carried back to Newgate.

Mrs. Bellamy, in vaguely alluding to insults offered even to Count Haslang's domestics, doubtless includes herself, for Haslang describes her as his 'housekeeper' (*Life*, ii. 104). This woman, the natural daughter of Lord Tyrawley, ambassador at Lisbon, was introduced into society by his sister; became a very influential person, and shared the confidence of Fox and other Whig lights. O'Leary, she describes (ii. 8): '. . . who, with unaffected piety, is blest with that innocent chearfulness which, joined to his brilliant wit and sound understanding, makes him the admired darling of all who have the happiness of knowing him.'

Count Haslang's house in Golden Square has been, since 1789, the presbytery of Warwick Street R. C. Chapel; and its transfer to parochial uses dates also from that year.

[1] *Ante*, p. 213.

[2] The *Freeman*, the subsidised organ of the Irish Government, after extolling O'Leary, added, on May 12, 1785: 'It were sincerely to be wished that this excellent writer and Christian philosopher would once more sit down and employ his talents in the service of his country and literature in general.' In the following year, *i.e.* 1786, he reviewed a 'forgotten controversy,' including a defence of Pope Clement XIV. in suppressing the Jesuits.

grinding impost—Tithes—in reference to which Bishop Doyle afterwards prayed, 'May our hatred of Tithes be as lasting as our love of justice!'

Pray, my brethren, what right have you to curtail, to your own authority, the income of the Protestant clergy? [O'Leary writes]. If the tithes became the property of the laity, they would raise their rents in proportion. Or is it because that, from the earliest ages of the world, those who believed in the true God have consecrated to Him a part of the fruits of the earth, you will think it an heavier burthen to pay the same thing because it was in conformity to the law of God that the laws of Christian states have appointed it? You know that the rules of justice extend to all without exception, and that, to use the familiar phrase, everyone should have his own, whether he be Protestant or Catholic, Turk or Christian. It is more your interest than you imagine, that the Protestant clergy of this country should be maintained in their rights. For many ages you have been defenceless, destitute of any protection against the power of your landlords, your clergy liable to transportation or death. The mild and tolerating spirit of the clergy of the established religion has been the only substitute for all other resources. They trained up from their early days the Protestant nobility and gentry in the principles of morality and virtue. If they preached against Purgatory, they enforced charity. . . . If they denied that the Pope is head of the Church, they taught their congregation that no man is to be injured on account of his religion, and that Christianity knows no enemy. As by nature we are prone to vice of every kind, and that the earliest impressions are the strongest, had it not been for those principles which they instilled into the minds of their hearers, long before now your landed men in this country would have treated you as Turks, who think it no scruple to violate the beds of the Jew, and warn the husbands that if they come into their houses whilst they are doing them this injustice they will cut off their heads.

Is it then to gentlemen of this description, the children of the first families in the kingdom, the instructors of the most powerful part of the community, the most moral and edifying amongst them, the most charitable and humane, that a handful of poor men are to prescribe laws tending to diminish the support of their offspring, destined to fill one day the most important offices in the State? What! a Rev. Archdeacon Corker, a Rev. Archdeacon Tisdal, a

Rev. Mr. Chetwood, a Rev. Mr. Weekes, a Rev. Mr. Meade, a Rev. Mr. Kenny, who spent his time and fortune amongst you, relieving your wants, and changing part of his house into an apothecary's shop to supply you with medicines, which yourselves could not purchase, must from an apprehension of violence quit his house.[1]

In this strain O'Leary argued at much length; but the impartial historian of this very time describes 'the system of Tithes as the greatest practical grievance, both of the poorer Catholics and of the Presbyterians.'[2]

Most people have heard of O'Leary's controversy with the Bishop of Cloyne, in which, when the prelate disputed Purgatory, O'Leary retorted that he might 'go farther and fare worse.' The 'Critical Review' examined the controversy with a shrewdly penetrative eye. Lord Kenmare, in a letter dated October 2, 1787, writes: 'I read with the greatest pleasure the "Critical Review" on the Cloyne controversy. It is the best performance that has yet appeared on the subject. Grattan is violent against the Bishop of Cloyne for his publication, and thinks, with the reviewer, that Government is at the bottom of it.'[3] O'Leary's reply, which runs to 175 pages, contains many excellent truths worthy of commendation; but it is a question whether this elaborate controversy may not have been inspired and encouraged from Dublin Castle. Law and order are, very properly, inculcated throughout by O'Leary, and powerful dissuasives addressed to the 'White-boys' are printed at the end.[4] As regards the Bishop of Cloyne, O'Leary assures him, in words somewhat supereroga-

[1] The Rev. Mr. O'Leary's *Address to the Common People of Ireland*, pp. 12–14. (Dublin: Cooney, 1786.)

[2] Lecky's *England in the Eighteenth Century*, vi. 540.

[3] Edward Hay, in his *History of the Rebellion*, says that the Bishop of Cloyne's pamphlet 'was dedicated to the Spirit of Discord.' Dr. Woodward was hardly the bigot that he pretended to be; his epitaph in Cloyne Cathedral records that 'he was a warm friend to Catholic Emancipation.'

[4] A very clever, poetic version of this and other addresses of O'Leary, entitled *The O'Leariad*, appeared, and seems to have been written to direct attention to O'Leary's loyal pamphlets, and to enforce and imprint their arguments on the popular mind. (Printed in Dublin, and reprinted at Cork by Robert Dobbyn, 1787.) *Vide* Haliday Pamphlets, Royal Irish Academy, vol. 514.

tory: 'I was not sent here to sow sedition (p. 119). I returned here, not as a felon from transportation, but as an honourable exile, who returns to his native land after having preferred a voluntary banishment to ignorance and the abjuration of the creed of his fathers.'

O'Leary was a Capuchin friar who had made vows of voluntary poverty. The fact that he had long been accustomed to rest content with a little may help to explain the modest sum he was satisfied to accept for services which, if cordially rendered, were worth the amount twenty times told. And in judging the man for accepting this money it must be remembered that the bulk of it was spent in alms deeds. Bishop Murphy told Father England that when a youth he was frequently O'Leary's almoner, and that a number of reduced persons were weekly relieved in Cork to the average extent of two or three pounds.

CHAPTER XVII

THE REGENCY—STRUGGLE BETWEEN WHIG AND TORY CAMPS—O'LEARY AND THE PRINCE OF WALES

THE State Papers throw no light on what Plowden styles 'the arbitrary withdrawal of O'Leary's pension.' The following historic incident, now forgotten, and curious in its detail, may have led to that act.

In 1789, a great struggle raged between the Parliaments of England and Ireland on the question of creating the Prince of Wales Regent during the insanity of George the Third. The Prince at this time had been bound up, politically and socially, with the Whigs. Pitt, fearing that the Regency might prove fatal to his ambition and his Cabinet, resisted the heir-apparent's right to the prerogative of his father, and declared that 'the Prince had no better right to administer the government during his father's incapacity than any other subject of the realm.' An address to the Prince from the Irish Parliament requested that he would 'take upon himself the government of Ireland during the continuation of the King's indisposition, and no longer; and under the title of Prince Regent of Ireland, in the name, and on behalf of his Majesty, to exercise, according to the laws and constitution of that kingdom, all regal powers, jurisdiction, and prerogatives to the crown and government thereof belonging.'

Pelham, speaking of 'the tricks and intrigues of Mr. Pitt's faction,' adds, 'I have not time to express how strongly the Prince is affected by the confidence and attachment of the Irish Parliament.' Portland takes the same tone. The Buckingham Papers afford rich material for a history of this struggle. The noble editor admits that 'the Parliament of Ireland preserved the unquestionable right of deciding the Regency in their own way. The position of Lord Buckingham[1] had become peculiarly embarrassing. What course should be taken in the event of such an address being carried? The predicament was so strange, and involved constitutional considerations of such importance, as to give the most serious disquietude to the Administration.'[2]

Hopes were felt that the King might recover. The Viceroy receives instructions to use obstructive tactics, 'to use every possible endeavour, by all means in your power, debating every question, dividing upon every question, moving adjournment upon adjournment, and every other mode that can be suggested, to gain time!'[3] But the Viceroy did more. He openly threatened to make each opponent 'the victim of his vote.' Fitzgibbon was promised the seals and a peerage if he succeeded for Pitt. Lures and threats were alternately held out. The peerages of Kilmaine, Glentworth, and Cloncurry were sold for hard cash, and the proceeds laid out in the purchase of members. Meanwhile the King got well. Thereupon the Master of the Rolls, the Treasurer, the Clerk of Permits, the Postmaster-General, the Secretary of War, the Comptroller of Stamps, and other public servants, were dismissed. The Duke of Leinster, Lord Shannon, the Ponsonbys were cashiered. Employments that had long remained dormant were revived, sinecures created, salaries increased; while such offices as the Board of Stamps and Accounts, hitherto filled by one, became a joint concern. The weighmastership of Cork was divided into three parts, the duties of which were discharged by deputies, while the principals, who pocketed the profits, held seats in Parliament. In 1790, one hundred and ten placemen were members of the House. The Viceroy, Buckingham, during his short

[1] The Viceroy of Ireland.

[2] *Memoirs of the Courts and Cabinets of George III., from Original Family Documents*, by the Duke of Buckingham and Chandos, 1853.

[3] *Ibid.*

régime, added 13,040*l.* a year to the pension list; the names of the recipients are already on record. On the other hand, some men who had taken the Prince's side in the contest lost their pensions. O'Leary may have been in this batch.[1] Croly, in his 'Life of George IV.,' dilates on the intimate relations which subsisted between the Prince and the priest, and adds that O'Leary was no unskilful medium of intercourse between his Church and the Whigs, and contributed in no slight degree to the popularity of the Prince in Ireland. According to Buckley, the Prince patronised O'Leary to such an extent that rumour whispered it was by him the marriage ceremony with Mrs. Fitzherbert had been performed.

Barrington, describing the chastisement applied to those who, in Ireland, favoured the appointment of the Prince as Regent, says: 'Lord Buckingham vented his wrath on the country;' but what proof have we that the alleged agent of the Castle, O'Leary, incurred that Viceroy's displeasure?

In 1789, the year O'Leary removed permanently to London, he settled down, at the Spanish Ambassador's Chapel in London, as an assistant priest to Dr. Hussey, and, apparently, a most unwelcome one. An extraordinary pamphlet, not known to his biographers, was privately issued by O'Leary referring to a feud between himself and Dr. Hussey. At page 11 O'Leary writes:—

> The old clerk told me in the vestry, 'that I might now return to Ireland, as my enemy, the Marquis of Buckingham, had returned to England.' Surprised how or where the clerk of a vestry could get such an insulting information, I recollected that his master [Dr. Hussey] had told me some time before that he had seen a letter from the Marquis of Buckingham, when Viceroy of Ireland, to some nobleman or gentleman of the English Catholic Committee, wherein he depicted the Catholics of that kingdom in very unfavourable if not odious colours, and painted me as one of the ringleaders.[2]

[1] Dr. England, the first biographer of O'Leary, mentions that his pension had been charged on the *Irish* Establishment.

[2] *Narrative of the Misunderstanding between Rev. A. O'Leary and Rev. Mr. Hussey*, p. 11. (Dublin, 1791.)

This serves to explain Dr. England's remark in 1822, when accounting for O'Leary's permanent removal to London, that 'his residence in Ireland had become painful;'[1] but elsewhere in his book he assigns a different reason for the change.

It has been stated [he writes] that a secret condition was annexed to this grant, binding O'Leary to reside in England,[2] and preventing him from further interference in the political concerns of the empire. The fact, however, is that O'Leary had made previous arrangements for a permanent residence in London—not only as being more favourable to his health, which generally suffered by his visits to Dublin, but from a rational conviction that the great seat of influence and power was the proper sphere of his benevolent exertions.

This biographer did not know O'Leary personally; his conjecture, or explanation, is plausible. But few men would remove for their health to the purlieus of St. Giles and Soho, the mission with which O'Leary had most to do. Its fearful squalor at the period described is curiously shown in Clinch's recently published 'Bloomsbury and St. Giles.' It will be remembered that the preacher of his funeral sermon conveys that the migration in 1789 was caused by O'Leary's refusal to write in a venal Dublin print against the party with whom he had long been associated. Snubbed by the Viceroy, Buckingham, his usefulness at Dublin Castle was now a thing of the past; but yet, as he could not afford to give up all State endowment, I suspect that he settled down in London in some undefined diplomatic rôle, where his tact and influence would find a field for exercise. A most careful memoir of O'Leary, ending with the words 'Requiescat in pace'—written probably by his friend and co-religionist Plowden—appears in the 'Gentleman's Magazine' for February 1802. It contains some facts not noticed by his more diffuse biographers. 'This laudable conduct,' we are told, 'did not escape the attention of the Irish Government, and induced them, when he quitted

[1] *Life of O'Leary*, by Rev. T. England, p. 190.

[2] The good Priest does not quite deny the statement though seeming to do so.

Ireland, to recommend him to men of power in this country.' I believe that O'Leary's removal to London was made under Government auspices, extended in the hope that, by his diplomatic power, it might lead to useful knowledge and results.

As George, Prince of Wales, held Whig views at this time, Mr. Pitt's great career ran some risk of being cut short. The Prince gathered round him the leading Whig lights, including O'Leary, as we learn from Croly's 'Life of George IV.'[1] A good picture of life in the Pavilion at Brighton is given, and of the brilliant jokes which capped the hits of Sheridan and Curran. But O'Leary's presence had, I think, a deeper significance. With graver men his intercourse was frequent. 'Edmund Burke was very marked in the regard which he manifested to O'Leary,' writes England. 'Fox was not only Pitt's rival, but the leader of a powerful party constantly on the watch to oust Pitt from office.' It may be presumed that the men of power in London to whom O'Leary, on leaving Ireland, had letters from Dublin Castle, occupied a camp hostile to the Whig garrison of the Pavilion.

One proof that O'Leary wished to regain favour with Pitt is afforded by the casual remark of his biographer. 'When O'Leary learned that his friend Plowden was engaged at the desire of Pitt in writing the "Historical Review," he sent him his invaluable collections, as affording the best and most authentic materials for the recent history of Ireland.'[2]

I do not like that phrase of Plowden in which he says—when speaking of O'Leary's pension—that it was only after giving repeated proofs that the secret condition had been complied with, he received a large arrear.[3] Plowden no doubt thinks that the pension was meant as 'hush money;' but it

[1] With Lord Moira, too—a great Whig power in those days—O'Leary was specially intimate; and it was this peer who erected in St. Pancras the monument to his 'virtues and talents,' for which the *Tablet* newspaper, fifty years later, opened a subscription list to restore,—in such enduring honour was the memory of this marvellous friar held.

[2] England's *Life of O'Leary*, p. 289. (London, 1822.)

[3] See *ante*, p. 214.

is a question whether O'Leary was quite frank with him as to its character.

'An oak of the forest is too old to be transplanted at fifty,' said Grattan, regarding Flood's removal to London in 1784. 'Disgusted with the condition of his country,' writes O'Leary's later biographer, Buckley, 'and hopeless of doing anything by which it could be improved, he resolved on quitting it altogether and living in the free atmosphere of England, so congenial to a bounding and manly temperament like his. . . . In the year 1789 Arthur O'Leary left Ireland for ever, and took up his residence in London as one of the chaplains to the Spanish Embassy.'[1] It appears, however, from the testimony of Plowden, the attached friend of O'Leary, that it was a condition expressly made by the Crown that O'Leary was 'to reside no more in Ireland.'[2] I suspect that the appointment just described was brought about by Court intrigue. From the time of the Armada the movements of the Spanish minister were viewed with jealousy, often with alarm. In 1779, when the combined fleets of Spain and France rode menacingly in the Channel, O'Leary, as we have seen, denounced them to the Irish people, and his appointment to the Spanish embassy must have been the work of England rather than of Spain. In 1789 strained relations had again arisen between Spain and England; and a few years later war was actually declared by Spain.[3] Sydney states that O'Leary had already consented to furnish secret information.[4] His present position would enable him to acquire knowledge of, not only the designs of Spain, but of Dr. Hussey too; and without saying that O'Leary could be capable of downright treachery, it is probable that Pitt believed he would. It will be remembered that, in 1780, Dr. Hussey, chief chaplain to the Spanish embassy in London, had been sent with Richard Cumberland to effect a treaty with the Court of Spain, a negotiation not entirely successful. What was the precise nature of the

[1] *Life of the Rev. A. O'Leary*, by the Rev. M. B. Buckley, pp. 304-5.

[2] Vide *ante*, p. 213.

[3] See Alison's *Europe*, ii. 30, 203, 425.

[4] See p. 218, *ante*.

hold which Hussey, originally a Carthusian monk, acquired over the Court of England is destined to remain shrouded. Buckley says it was at the special request of George III. that Dr. Hussey accompanied Mr. Cumberland on a secret mission to Madrid.[1]

What Cumberland himself thought of his colleague is curious to see. We are told that 'the high-sounding titles and dignities showered upon Dr. Hussey by the Court of Spain outweighed in his balance English guineas;' that 'in his heart he was as high a priest as à Becket, and as stiff a Catholic as ever kissed the cross;' but yet 'had left behind him in his coffin at La Trappe no one passion native or ingrafted that belonged to him when he entered it.' So clear-sighted a man as Hussey could not fail to see the secret thoughts of Cumberland, or to have diagnosed, in his turn, the jaundiced retina through which he was viewed; for Cumberland complains of 'his singular, sudden, and capricious conduct to the author and his family, of which he was an inmate.'[2] Hussey had demanded his passports to return to England; but on Cumberland's remonstrance paused, and cancelled a letter he had addressed to the English Secretary of State asking leave to return. Mystery covers much of this mission to Spain, for Cumberland says, 'I will reveal no more than I am in honour and strict conscience warranted to make public. For twenty years I have been silent, making no appeals at any time but to my official employers, who were pledged to do me justice.'[3]

Mr. Froude tells us that Dr. Hussey[4] was in the confidence of Dundas and Portland, and had received favours from them. Both were prominent statesmen in the Cabinet of Pitt, and both eventually turned against Hussey. Dr. Hussey is described as Chaplain to his Catholic Majesty of Spain, and Rector of the Church of the Spanish Embassy in London.

[1] Buckley's *O'Leary*, p. 306.

[2] Cumberland's *Memoirs*, ii. 62–5. (London, 1807.) Dr. Hussey had died four years previous to their publication.

[3] *Ibid.*

[4] Previously, Dr. Hussey is found at Vienna, hand in glove with the Emperor Joseph of Austria. See England's *O'Leary*, p. 199.

He evidently knew something of O'Leary not revealed to the world.

At this point it may be well to open once more the pamphlet privately printed—'A Narrative of the Misunderstanding between the Rev. Arthur O'Leary and the Rev. Mr. Hussey.' Its purport, O'Leary says, is to remove the bad impressions which a late report, one which impugned his morality, might have made on some Catholic families, and the reader is requested either to burn the *brochure*, or erase altogether the name of Mr. Hussey. The latter is just the man to have muttered 'qui s'excuse s'accuse' as he read the following; and O'Leary's remark serves to show that Hussey suspected he had deeper motives.

> The desire of co-operating in the work of the ministry [writes O'Leary] was my only inducement for associating with Mr. [Hussey] in the Spanish Ambassador's Chapel. He soon began to throw some obstacles in my way—but in the most insulting and contemptuous manner. The old clerk of his vestry, who retails among the common people all the stories he hears from his employer, was commissioned by him to direct me in the choice of my theme [in the pulpit].[1]

In 1780, the Spanish ambassador to London was, we learn, 'Count Fernan Nunez, who had committed himself to a conversation from which Mr. Hussey drew very promising expectations.'[2] But in 1789 we find him succeeded by no less a person than the Marquis del Campo, whose previous attitude, as sub-Premier of Spain, had filled the British Cabinet with alarm.[3] Orde, writing to Nepean, of the Home Office, five years before, tells him to be very watchful over this minister; and O'Leary's friend, Plowden, whatever he means by it, says that it was only after giving repeated

[1] *A Narrative of the Misunderstanding, etc.* p. 7.

[2] Cumberland's *Memoirs*, ii. 2.

[3] Del Campo lived in the well-known palatial structure opposite the old chapel in Spanish Place, described by Thackeray as 'Gaunt House,' and lately occupied by Sir Richard Wallace. The defeat of the Armada in 1588 had marked an epoch in the history of the British Empire, and Englishmen uneasily regarded the feasts and intrigues in Manchester Square.

proofs that the secret conditions had been complied with, that O'Leary received a large arrear of his pension.

'A Narrative of the Misunderstanding' between O'Leary and Hussey shows that the appointment of the former as Hussey's colleague was forced upon the latter, and that Hussey distrusted and despised him, confirming the old adage, two of a trade never agree. O'Leary complains that on Good Friday, in presence of a crowded congregation numbering many Protestants, Hussey sent

> one of the boys who attend the altar, twice into the pulpit to interrupt me in the most pathetic part of my discourse by chucking the sleeves of my surplice and ordering me to come down under pretence that the ceremonies of the day were too long. Thus a scene was exhibited of which neither the congregation nor myself had ever been spectators before.

And again :—

> By the manner in which he concerted his plans, in waiting until the eve of the days on which I was to appear in public, and then sending me, on a sudden, verbal messages by his clerk, and afterwards such insulting notes as no Prelate would send to the meanest clergyman in his diocese, one would be apt to imagine that he played the part of a skilful general, who amuses an enemy the better to decoy him unprepared into an ambuscade.
>
> I was surprised at such peremptory mandates from a man who, at most, could pretend but to an equality. . . . But his view was, either to disgust me with the chapel, or to commit me with the public, in thus thwarting me in the exercise of my functions.

O'Leary was the lion of the hour; his portrait looked out from the windows of Bond Street and Piccadilly, surrounded by soul-stirring sentiments culled from his published books.[1] Then it was that Dr. Hussey sought to reduce his prestige, which he considered overcharged, and to destroy the confidence and respect usually manifested in his regard. It is certain that he felt as uncomfortable in his society as he had ever

[1] One, published in 'April, 1784, by Keating, of Bond Street,' displays the following fine sentiment: 'Let not religion—the sacred name of religion—which even in the face of an enemy discovers a brother, be any longer a wall of separation to keep us asunder.'

done in the hair shirt and enforced reserve of La Trappe. He did not brand O'Leary as a Government agent; he could not do so without offending Pitt; but he raised what lawyers call 'a false issue.' Indeed O'Leary charges the doctor, on strong circumstantial evidence, with having supplied to the newspapers paragraphs in which an unworthy innuendo is advanced, and one by no means calculated to exalt the friar's reputation for asceticism: 'In proportion as the breach widened between us, the paragraphs rose in a climax to a greater degree of asperity.'[1]

Many curious things transpire in this *brochure*, and amongst them the following: 'I got the very singular information,' writes O'Leary, 'that some years before, in a boarding-school at Hampstead, then under his (Hussey's) direction, he took my picture out of a frame, tore it in several pieces, and cast it away with disdain, saying, "One would imagine he is founder of this establishment."'[2] Here again I submit that Dr. Hussey raised a false issue, and his dislike to O'Leary, as evidenced by this strong proceeding, must have had deeper grounds than the paltry plea assigned.

> When this affair relative to the picture happened [writes O'Leary] I was in Ireland, in the full bloom of my reputation,[3] which I would have preserved unfaded to the last moment of my existence, had it not spread on the lips of a man to whom I cannot apply the Italian proverb, Whatever your mouth touches, it heals: 'La vostra bocca sana quel che tocca' (p. 14).

Dr. Hussey, as already stated, was in the secrets of the Crown. In 1784 Sydney conveys, rightly or wrongly, that O'Leary had consented to furnish private information. In 1789 O'Leary, as we have seen, removed to London and settled down in alarming proximity not only to Hussey, but to the

[1] *A Narrative of the Misunderstanding between the Rev. Arthur O'Leary and the Rev. Mr. Hussey.* (Dublin: printed at No. 75, Aungier Street, 1791.)

[2] *Ibid.* p. 13.

[3] O'Leary's comment on Hussey's treatment of his picture are amusing. 'When Constantine the Great was informed that stones were cast at his statue, he rubbed his forehead and said that he did not feel himself hurt. And I can say that my body was not lacerated when my picture was torn.'

minister of Spain. Hussey's attachment to Spanish interests, Cumberland states, outweighed his devotion to his English patrons, and of course it was highly inconvenient that a man who played fast and loose with both should be domesticated with O'Leary. 'They are all of them designing knaves,' writes Orde, and doubtless he and his colleagues, acting on the coarse prejudice thus expressed, urged the arrangement on the principle of 'set a thief to catch a thief.' The more refined Sydney probably calculated that it would be 'diamond cut diamond' between them.

The effort it must have cost so polished a person as Dr. Hussey to pursue the course ascribed to him may be inferred from the words of Charles Butler: 'He was a man of great genius, of enlightened piety, with manners at once imposing and elegant, and of enchanting conversation: he did not come in contact with many whom he did not subdue: the highest rank often sunk before him.' Cumberland, his companion in the secret mission, describes him as wearing 'a smile seductive; his address was smooth, obsequious, studiously obliging and, at times, glowingly heightened into an impassioned show of friendship and affection. He was quick enough,' he adds, 'in finding out the characters of men.'

O'Leary appealed to Bishop Douglas, and a meeting between the parties took place at his house. The result was a written statement, dated June 21, 1791, that Dr. Hussey never had any crime or immoral conduct to allege against O'Leary, and that he had left the Spanish Ambassador's chapel of his own free will. 'Mr. O'Leary and I have come to a full explanation upon all past misunderstandings, and are both satisfied with the explanation,' writes Dr. Hussey. This paper was certified by Bishops Douglas and Berington[1] and by Francis

[1] Why Dr. Berington, Bishop of the Midland District, should be called in was, clearly, because a schism threatened the diocese in consequence of the Pope appointing Dr. Douglas bishop in opposition to the strenuous efforts made by the Catholic Committee to get Dr. Berington translated to London. Several lay members of that league went so far as to maintain that the clergy and laity ought to choose their own bishops without any reference to Rome, and procure their consecration at the hands of any other lawful bishop. After the appoint-

Plowden to be conformable to Dr. Hussey's verbal declaration. The finale was worthy of an ecclesiastic who wished to avoid disedifying the laity by unseemly wrangles. But, privately, Dr. Hussey took means to prevent a recurrence of an incident which greatly annoyed him. The Castlereagh Papers contain a letter to Lord Hobart from Sir J. Cox Hippisley, in which he mentions as having been reported to Rome, 'a very offensive measure of Hussey's in a way so as to have produced a sort of censure on Bishop Douglas of London.' Dr. Hussey, it is stated, had claimed the right, as chaplain to the Spanish mission, of nominating priests to officiate at the Spanish chapel in London independently of Bishop Douglas.[1]

Frequent reference has been already made to Del Campo. The concluding words of O'Leary's 'Narrative' go on to say :—

I intended to complain in person or to write a severe letter against him to the Marquis del Campo,[2] than whom there are few

ment of Dr Douglas, they even threatened to pronounce it 'obnoxious and improper.' Dr. Berington, however, addressed a printed letter to the London clergy, resigning all pretension to the London vicariate, and soon the schismatical opposition to Dr. Douglas was withdrawn. See Brady's *Catholic Hierarchy in England*, pp. 178-9. (Rome, 1877.)

[1] On visiting this chapel, in 1888, a fine relic of the ancient splendour of Spain, I found it very much as it was in the days of Father O'Leary. A study of Dr. Hussey's face, by Gainsborough, is preserved here, as well as some maps and papers in the autograph of the former. The foundation stone of a new church to replace it, and near the old one, was laid by Cardinal Manning, on June 27, 1887, in presence of the Infanta of Spain and the Spanish minister. Canon Barry, the present pastor, mentions an interesting tradition connected with Tyburn tree, which, as is well known, stood near the Marble Arch : 'The Chapel of the Spanish Embassy was, during the dark days of persecution, a special home for Catholics. Many a martyr on his way to Tyburn received the blessing of the chaplain of the embassy and was aided by the prayers offered in the Spanish Chapel for perseverance in his conflict for the faith.' The Canon, in the course of a statistical detail, adds : 'When war between England and Spain broke out, the usual payments made by Spain for the support of the chapel fell 4,000*l.* into arrears. Diplomatic relations having been again suspended between England and Spain in 1805, the chapel was confided to the care of Don Miguel de la Torre.'

[2] Del Campo ceased, soon after, to be Spanish minister to St. James's, and was succeeded by the Chevalier Azara. The latter had great influence at the Vatican, and proposed that Dr. Hussey should be the channel of communication between the Pope and the British Government.—*Castlereagh Papers*, iii. 86.

ambassadors[1] of a more amiable disposition, or in whose train a chaplain would be more happy. But, expecting never to be disturbed by Mr. [Hussey], after leaving him in the unrivalled possession of his pulpit and controversy, I retired without the slightest murmur. Had I even been treated with that civility to which I was entitled, I would yet have quitted York Street. We were on the eve of a war with Spain, and from my peculiar obligations to my own sovereign, in case of a threatened invasion, I would have returned to Ireland, where, upon a similar occasion, the exertions in the line of my profession had been attended with the happiest results in promoting that loyalty which recommends my Religion and countrymen.

Here O'Leary, though so recently attached to the Spanish embassy, declares himself a partisan, if not a sentinel, in the English interest. It appears that, while officiating at Spanish Place, he lodged in Warwick Street, probably acting as assistant chaplain to the Bavarian embassy as well, and where, as Mrs. Bellamy records, he arrived opportunely, in 1783, to adjust angry difficulties that had arisen in that quarter. Seven years later, although ostensibly pastor of St. Patrick's, Soho, from 1790 to his death, he seems still attached in some way to the Bavarian chapel and embassy, for the preface to his sermon in denunciation of French principles is dated from Warwick Street, though the sermon itself had been preached at St. Patrick's.

In March 1797, O'Leary's desire to retain the favour of Pitt is traceable in the sermon to which reference has just been made. It was preached before a congregation mainly Irish, but including also the famous Duchess of Devonshire, and many other great personages.[2] Its aim is apparent in the

[1] An historic writer, Sir Nathaniel Wraxall, famous rather for pleasant gossip than for strict accuracy, states that the Spanish embassy in London maintained friendly relations with England. But what was the prevailing idea in Spanish diplomatic circles at this time is traceable in a despatch of Talleyrand first published in 1890 by M. Pallain. Talleyrand states, on the authority of the personal assurance of the Spanish minister, that nearly all the sailors who man the British fleet are Irish, and from love of country would turn their guns on England. The accurate number will be found set forth at p. 114, *ante*.

[2] The sermon was preached in St. Patrick's, Soho, where O'Leary mainly officiated. Last year (1891) the chapel was in process of demolition.

account given of it by the 'Monthly Review' as 'a discourse well adapted to keep alive a high degree of good, warm, Christian hatred of the French, on whom the preacher is very severe, with now and then a stroke of pleasantry, sarcasm and rough wit.' Ireland had been nearly lost to England the previous year by Hoche's expedition to Bantry Bay, but England's unsubsidised allies, the winds, had come to her aid. O'Leary's discourse, occupying fifty pages, was at once issued in pamphlet shape, and reprinted in Dublin.

As has been already observed, O'Leary maintained cordial relations with some men who bore a bad name. Francis Higgins, once a Newgate felon, became at last a most influential negotiator. Plowden exhibits fully his unpleasant character in the 'Historical Review,' vol. ii. pp. 256–9. 'This man,' he says, 'had the address, by coarse flattery and assumed arrogance, to worm himself into the intimacy of several persons of rank and consequence, who demeaned themselves by their obsequiousness to his art, or sold themselves to him. The fact that he died worth 40,000*l.* is highly illustrative of the system which generated, fostered, and pampered this species of reptile.' Higgins is shown by the 'Cornwallis Papers' to have been a spy on a great scale. There is reason to know that he wormed himself into the confidence of O'Leary; and reason to fear that he turned it to account. The man who began his career by duping a Jesuit and obtaining his co-operation in making an heiress his wife, is not likely to have failed with the genial Franciscan. Higgins early won the friendship of O'Leary; and his bequest 'to my long and faithful friend, the Rev. Arthur O'Leary,' has been already noticed.[1]

Higgins liked to utilise profitably the information he acquired from pliable Catholics like Magan.[2] Magan was a barrister, and held his head high. It will be remembered that Higgins drew from him the secret of Lord Edward Fitzgerald's hiding place, and for this service alone received

[1] Last will of Francis Higgins, Record Office, Dublin.
[2] *Vide* chap. xi. *ante*.

1,000*l*. in hand, and a pension of 300*l*. a year. The 'Sham Squire' was not the man to leave money, in 1791, 'to his long and faithful friend,' O'Leary, unless he had made more than the amount by the use of him. Higgins claims O'Leary as a dear friend; the habits of the time warrant the assumption that he was his boon companion too. In the unguarded intimacy of social intercourse, that frank and affable nature is likely to have enriched the Squire's stock of gossip. To what extent that confidence was unfolded can be now but darkly surmised.

O'Leary, if called upon to reveal political information, may have acted with reserve. In softer moments[1] much may have leaked out which was not deliberate betrayal.

It is casually stated by Mr. Lecky (vol. vii. p. 211) that Higgins, in enumerating his services to the Government, especially mentions the expense he had incurred in entertaining priests, and other persons of the higher class, for the purpose of obtaining intelligence. In one respect O'Leary's intercourse with Higgins worked for good. The newspaper of the latter, though an organ of Orangeism, advocated the Catholic claims.

In 1796 Dr. Hussey, afterwards Bishop of Waterford, seems to have accepted the post of secret agent,—probably not widely dissimilar from that which the statesmen of 1784 thought O'Leary would not object to discharge. Higgins, writing to Dublin Castle in October 1796, expresses regret that the Government had not been very judicious in their selection of

[1] Father Buckley, the biographer of O'Leary, died soon after the date of the following letter. It notices a weakness, of which a paid purveyor of news, like Higgins, would be apt to take ready advantage. Shamado is likely to have been the more successful because his own character of a brain-sucker and betrayer had not then been unmasked. On December 7, 1869, Father Buckley writes from SS. Peter and Paul's, Cork: 'The *Personal Memoirs* have arrived, and I am much pleased with them. The sketch of O'Leary I am sorry I had not seen, to embody in my book. I fear, however, it would not have tended much to enhance the esteem of the good *padre's* character, inasmuch as, in the background of the picture, there is a strong steam of whisky-punch, and the narrative affords a strong confirmation of what Michael Kelly records that Father O'Leary, like himself, was rather partial to "Saint Patrick's Eye-Water."'

an agent for acting on the Catholics.[1] 'The Roman Catholic body hold a superficial opinion of Dr. Hussey as a courtly priest. If anything was to be effected or wished to be done in the Roman Catholic body, Dr. O'Leary would do more with them in one hour than Hussey in seven years. Of this I am perfectly assured; and O'Leary not ten days since wrote me word he would shortly claim a bed at my house.'[2]

O'Leary had a nephew for whom in a recently published letter he hopes to provide a berth when some friends of his would regain their power. The allusion no doubt is to Fox and the Whigs. This is the nephew noticed by Francis Higgins, in a secret letter to Under-Secretary Cooke eight months before the rebellion. 'At a meeting at Bond's, which Lord Edward Fitzgerald and O'Connor attended, O'Connor read a letter from Fox which had been delivered to him (O'C.) by O'Leary, nephew of Dr. O'Leary, who had arrived from London with despatches from Mr. Fox, and set off in the mail for Cork the same night.' These despatches concurred with the United Irishmen as to the necessity of enforcing a parliamentary reform.[3]

The bequest of Higgins to O'Leary is noticed as strange by the priest's biographer. Was it meant by way of restitution, seeing that the compact to pay O'Leary had been broken?

The will of Francis Higgins goes on to say: 'To Andrew D. O'Kelly, of Piccadilly, London, I leave 300*l.*: declaring that if I did not know that he, my friend, was in great affluence, I would have freely bequeathed him any property I might be possessed of.' This was the man sometimes known

[1] It cannot be said that this agency was of a base character. In 1795, Dr. Hussey announces to Edmund Burke that the Catholics were loyal and ready to spill their blood to resist the French (Lecky, vii. 90). Mr. Lecky states that he was 'constantly employed by the Government in negotiations with the Irish Catholics.' In September 1794, Dr. Hussey, then an *employé* of the Crown, comes over to consult with the Catholic bishops at Dublin on new measures of education (Lecky, vii. 121). Maynooth College was the result.

[2] Higgins gave money in alms, and priests held him in fair esteem as an influential man and a friend to 'Emancipation.' John Patten—brother-in-law of Addis Emmet—told me that he once sat next him at a Lord Mayor's banquet, and rarely met a pleasanter fellow.

[3] Higgins to Cooke, September 1, 1797. (MSS. Dublin Castle.)

as Count O'Kelly, but more generally as Colonel O'Kelly. An Irish judge who once acted as advising counsel for the legatees of O'Kelly, informs me that the latter was originally a jockey, afterwards a successful blackleg, and was made colonel of a regiment that never existed, simply by the Prince Regent addressing him under that title. This explains a remark made by the 'St. James's Gazette,' that 'his military rank, whatever right he may have had to it, as well as to his Countship, could never obtain for him an entrance to the clubs of his fellow-sportsmen.'[1] He owned the racehorse 'Eclipse,' and by its aid netted 124,000*l.*

There has been much discussion by O'Leary's biographers upon Plowden's statement as to the stoppage of the pension, and they vainly try to account for so harsh a step. 'What the reason for this withholding was, it is not easy to ascertain,' writes Father Buckley; but, from an observation in the 'Life of Grattan,' by his son, we surmise that it must have been because O'Leary refused to comply with a request made by the minister, that he *would write in the support of the Union.*[2] Plowden takes care to say that the pension was 'hush money.' Buckley's argument demands, however, a fuller reply.

The agitation against the Union took place chiefly in 1799. O'Leary died in January 1802, soon after the Union became law. Plowden, through whom he got the arrears paid, says that it was 'after a *lapse of many years*, by importunity and solicitation, and *repeated proofs* of his having complied with the *secret conditions*, he received a large arrear.' Therefore there could not have been time for all this in the interval between the Union and O'Leary's death.

[1] *Vide* 'Fathers of the Turf,' in *St. James's Gazette*, January 6, 1881. The writer adds that O'Kelly is said to have held post-obits to a large amount, 'and his transactions were upon so large a scale that he might be seen turning over "quires" of bank-notes in search of a "little one," by which term he meant one for £50.' In the Registry of Deeds Office, Dublin, is preserved a document, dated February 12, 1819, whereby the Marquis of Donegal secures to O'Kelly the sum of 27,934*l.* 12*s.* 4*d.*, a gambling debt, and O'Kelly is described as Andrew Denis O'Kelly, Esq., son and heir apparent of Philip Kelly, Esq., deceased. 'Colonel' O'Kelly died in 1820, leaving no children.

[2] *Life of O'Leary*, by the Rev. M. B. Buckley, p. 357 (italics in original).

But, in point of fact, O'Leary *did* express himself publicly in favour of the Union. His 'Address to the Lords Spiritual and Temporal,' dated from O'Kelly's house, and published in June 1800, mentions that he is 'a great friend to the Union, and reconciled many to it;' and then follows much clever argument in support of the measure. This rather spoils the statement in Grattan's 'Life,' quoted by the biographer of O'Leary as proof that he spurned Pitt's proposal to support the Union.

Colonel O'Kelly [writes Grattan] related that, at the period of the Union, Mr. Pitt offered a considerable pension to O'Leary, provided he would exert himself among his Roman Catholic countrymen, and write in support of the Union; but every application was in vain; O'Leary steadfastly resisted Mr. Pitt's solicitations, and, though poor, he rejected the offers of the minister, and could not be seduced from his allegiance to his country.

The newspapers recording O'Leary's death, in January 1802, say that he died at his lodgings in Great Portland Street, London. When the Union was carried, he probably got his *congé* from O'Kelly. This man, of bad odour, became a Crœsus in wealth, and eventually a sort of Brummagem Brummell, deep in the confidence of George, Prince of Wales.[1] O'Leary is found living with O'Kelly in Mayfair, London, and some of his pamphlets are dated from 46 Half-Moon Street, Piccadilly, the 'Colonel's' house.[2] Father Buckley is puzzled 'how our worthy friar contracted so close an intimacy with a man of tastes and habits apparently so little congenial to his own.'[3] Perhaps O'Kelly[4] was the trustee in whose name O'Leary got a pension on secret conditions. Plowden is the only writer who alludes to the intervention of a trustee. He was very intimate with O'Kelly, and witnessed his will in 1820. The

[1] Vide *Ireland before the Union*, 6th ed. pp. 211–15. (Dublin: Duffy.)

[2] Grattan's *Life*, by his Son. Those who may suppose that O'Leary forgot the priest in the diplomat, should see Father Morgan D'Arcy's account of the reforms he effected in the demoralised region of St. Giles. *Vide* Buckley, pp. 397 *et seq.*

[3] *Life of O'Leary*, by Rev. M. B. Buckley, p. 359.

[4] See *ante*, p. 213.

Prince of Wales had already made O'Kelly the medium for paying a secret pension of 300*l.* a year to Chifney the jockey, in consideration of having designedly lost a race at Epsom.[1]

More than sixty years after the death of O'Leary, Father Buckley was informed in writing, by a relative of the deceased, that O'Leary, when dying, often exclaimed, 'Alas! I have *betrayed* my poor country.'[2] The informant's impression is that O'Leary's remorse was due to having, at the request of Pitt, acquiesced in the Union, notwithstanding that we have 'Colonel' O'Kelly's testimony that 'O'Leary withstood Pitt's solicitations to support that measure.' Even Irish Catholic bishops cordially encouraged the Union, as the Castlereagh Papers show—and we do not hear that Dr. Troy and his *confrères* felt much remorse—although, in addition to their support of the Union, they signed resolutions in favour of giving to a Protestant king a veto in the appointment of Catholic prelates.

But the letter of O'Leary's kinsman must not be dismissed without quoting its context. 'Pitt,' he writes, 'promised the emancipation of Catholics and repeal of the Penal Laws, if he (O'Leary) would acquiesce, &c. He did; and so silence was deemed consent. Pitt obtained the Union; then resigned his office; and tricky enough,' adds O'Leary's kinsman, 'said he could not keep his promise.'

This is slightly misleading. Pitt had given a pledge, through Cornwallis, to Archbishop Troy that he would not accept office except on condition that the Catholic claims were to be met. In 1801, owing to the fixed resolve of the King against Emancipation, Pitt went out. His conduct, therefore, was so far straight. When he returned to power in 1804, in complete violation of that compact, O'Leary had been two years dead.

Before bringing this subject to a close, it may be well to review a few circumstances. The most damaging bit of

[1] *Ireland before the Union*, pp. 211–15.

[2] *Life of the Rev. Arthur O'Leary*, by the Rev. M. B. Buckley, p. 355.

evidence is Sydney's letter to Rutland announcing that O'Leary, having been talked to by Nepean, was willing to do what was wished for 100*l.* a year.[1] These documents bear date 1784, eighteen years before O'Leary's death. No compromising letters written by him have been found. In fact there is not even a commonplace letter from him in the archives of Buckingham or Westmoreland, though he maintained friendly relations with Hobart, the Chief Secretary, as books autographically inscribed to that personage show. The voluminous papers of Pelham, the Irish Secretary, from 1795 to 1798 do not once mention his name. 'I have certainly never seen any reports from O'Leary to the Government,' writes Mr. Lecky in reply to an inquiry; 'and I have quoted in my History every passage I have come across in which he is ever mentioned.'[2] These passages are few.

O'Leary was a decided humourist: no one conversing with him felt quite sure when he meant to be serious. In the 'talk' that passed he may have played the diplomat. We have seen how Orde distrusted him. To a request blandly urged in personal converse by a statesman who had already pensioned him, this friar, existing merely by connivance, could not afford to assume attitudes of offended dignity. A glimpse of his precarious position is caught from a speech of Grattan's:—

> At the time that this very man lay under the censure of a law which, in his own country, made him subject to transportation or death, from religious distinctions, and at the time that a prince of his own religion threatened this country with an invasion, this respectable character took up his pen and, unsolicited and without a motive but that of real patriotism, urged his own communion to peace, and to support the law which had sentenced himself to transportation.[3]

Nepean and Orde suggested certain inquiries which O'Leary was to make; but who can tell at what point of these inquiries the practised casuist may have meant to draw the line? A

[1] See *ante*, p. 218. [2] W. E. H. Lecky, Esq. to W. J. F., October 28, 1890.
[3] *Parliamentary Register*, Feb. 26, 1782.

hundred pounds a year, which Nepean says he named, seems marvellously small for the magnitude and risk of the service expected. Orde writes on September 8, 1784, expressing satisfaction that Nepean, in London, had 'settled[1] matters with O'Leary, who can get to the bottom of all secrets in which the Catholics are concerned, and they are certainly the chief promoters of our present disquietude.' A fortnight later, after an interview with the priest at Dublin Castle, he adds (September 24, 1784): 'O'Leary has it in his power, *if we can depend upon him*, to discover to us the real designs of the Catholics, from which quarter, after all, the real mischief is to spring.' O'Leary must have known that, in 1784, *no* treasonable designs were harboured by the Catholics, and probably felt that he would be safe in making the inquiries prescribed. Mr. Lecky, a most patient historic investigator, a man who has searched more secret sources of sound information than any other writer of Irish history, while he considers that the letters just quoted prove O'Leary a spy (p. 369), yet, in describing this very time, doubts

whether the Catholics themselves took any considerable part in these agitations. For a long period an almost death-like torpor hung over the body, and, though they formed the great majority of the Irish people, they hardly counted even in movements of opinion. Even when they were enrolled in volunteer corps there were no traces of Catholic leaders. There was, it is true, still a Catholic

[1] A distinguished priest in reviewing this inquiry has undertaken very ably the defence of Father O'Leary. As regards the letter, of which the above is an extract, he writes: 'Might not the matter "settled" with Father O'Leary have been that he should use the arts of which he was a master, and which he had before so readily employed, to dissuade the Catholics from a French alliance? Would not this have been an excellent, as well as an obvious expedient for a viceroy who had discovered that the disturbances in Ireland "had all derived their source from French influence?" And if the Government had "subsidised" him for a service of the kind before, would there not be in the new demand made upon him a reason for subsidising him again?'—*Lyceum*, April 1892. The critic, while praising my other chapters, protests against certain inferences with respect to O'Leary, adding, however, 'We are glad to note that Mr. Fitzpatrick has generously set down the arguments that tell against his own impression.'

Committee which watched over Catholic interests; Lord Kenmare and a few other leading Catholics were in frequent communication with the Government; two or three Catholic bishops at this time did good service in repressing Whiteboyism; and Dr. Troy, who was then Bishop of Ossory, received the warm thanks of the Lord Lieutenant; [1] but for the most part the Catholics stood wholly apart from political agitation.

I do not like repetitions; but they are sometimes a necessity, as in judicial summing-up. Twelve days after O'Leary had been set to work, the Chief Secretary at Dublin Castle seems quite dissatisfied with him. The tone in which our humourist's reports were pitched may be guessed from the following passage in a later pamphlet from his pen [2]:—

Lord Chesterfield, on his return from his Viceroyship, informed George II. that he had met in Ireland but *two dangerous Papists*, of whom *His Majesty should be aware*—two [comely] ladies named Devereux, who had danced at the Castle on the King's birth-night. All the viceroys of Ireland, from Lord Chesterfield to Earl Camden, could have made a much similar answer, if interrogated, concerning what is called the *danger of Popery*.[3]

Whether from this tone, or from other causes, the Government became quite disappointed with their man; for, as Plowden states, they withheld his pension, and 'an arbitrary refusal for many years threw the reverend pensioner on his friends for subsistence.' 'The unexplained cause,' noticed by Dr. England,[4] may, perhaps, here be guessed. O'Leary, Sydney

[1] In a letter signed by Orde.

[2] *Address to the Lords Spiritual and Temporal*, p. 12. (London, 1800.)

[3] O'Leary does not tell this anecdote correctly. It was not of two ladies named Devereux, but of a famous beauty, Miss Ambrose, that Chesterfield made this joke; and it was told, not to George II., but to Lord North. Chesterfield addressed the following impromptu to Miss Ambrose at a vice-regal ball:—

'Pretty Tory, where's the jest
Of wearing orange on a breast
Which, in whiteness, doth disclose
The beauty of the rebel rose?'

[4] See *ante*, p. 220.

states, consented, in 1784, to make the secret inquiries which Orde wished—probably to offer such advice as his experience might suggest; but the idea thrown out at an early stage of this study seems likely enough,—that, after he had made due efforts to find out the truth, he pleasantly assured the Government that no French emissaries had been to Dublin at all; that the Catholics were loyal subjects; and, instead of a slumbering volcano, that Rutland had found a mare's nest! This Viceroy's letter will be remembered in which he drew a highly sensational picture of alleged secret doings in Dublin. It was he who first urged on Sydney the wisdom of securing O'Leary as a spy, and Sydney soon after reports the negotiation as successful. But we have no testimony from Nepean with whom the interview took place. When Rutland spoke, Orde spoke; the act of one was the act of the other. Both were equally fluent as correspondents; but during the three subsequent years that they held office at Dublin Castle, we find no letters from either announcing any discoveries made by O'Leary, and which, no doubt, they would have been only too glad to do as confirming their own forecast, and building up a reputation for subtle statesmanship.

More troublesome times came within the next ten years: the Society of United Irishmen spread with alarming rapidity; and if O'Leary had any wish to play the spy, he had now a grand opportunity by simulating ardent patriotism like McNally and others. His great sermon in 1797 was a declaration of war against French principles, and against all who adopted the policy of revolution. Again, when it became necessary for him to preach the panegyric of Pius VI., who died at this time, he went out of his way to run full tilt against democracy. The 'Courier,' a popular organ, thus describes it:—

Abounding with glowing imagery, classical allusion, and displaying in every sentence the energy of an enlightened and vigorous mind, the Doctor took occasion to felicitate his flock, in the most emphatic terms, on the happiness enjoyed in this country, on the constitution and state of which he pronounced a fine panegyric, applying to the extent of our dominion and national glory the line of the poet—

Imperium Oceano, famamque terminat astris.

It was by this tone, let me hope, rather than by dealing in espionage, that he sought to regain governmental favour.[1]

The sole remaining letter in the carefully preserved records of the informers of '98 which names O'Leary must not be excluded here. Things had quite changed since 1784. Higgins, in a secret letter, dated January 2, 1798, says:—

I took leave to inform you, some time since, that many Roman Catholics seem apparently sorry for the lengths they've been led, and suggested, if O'Leary, or any popular preacher, was to exert himself among them, thousands would come to swear allegiance. I know O'Leary would be a tower of strength among them. He was their first champion, and is most highly respected by the multitude. His writings and preaching prevented the White Boys and insurgents of the South from joining the rabble of Cork and rising *en masse* at the period when the combined fleets of Spain, France, etc., were in the English Channel.[2]

Higgins does not say that O'Leary authorised him to make this proposition; and even had he done so, it cannot be deemed base.

Orde's letters to the Home Office in 1784, though urging extreme caution lest he and his colleagues should be themselves betrayed, show him to be impulsive in statement, and prone to jump to conclusions. These letters, blemished by an occasional expletive, are printed by Mr. Lecky. Orde is quite sanguine as regards wonderful Catholic secrets that O'Leary would unearth, but this is not the only case in which he exhibits rashness of assumption.

My notes must now end. If their freedom and fulness need justification, it is found, perhaps, in O'Leary's own words. He had meditated a history of the political events of 1780.

[1] 'We have read that he was paid for his aid in quelling the Mutiny of the Nore by using his influence with the Irish sailors in the Fleet.'—*Catholic Times*, April 29, 1892.

[2] Francis Higgins to Under-Secretary Cooke. (MSS. Dublin Castle.)

> The duty of the Historian [he writes] binds him to arraign at the impartial tribunal of truth both men and actions; unmask the leading characters; examine into their motives; lay open the hidden springs of proceedings, whether worthy of applause, or deserving to be doomed to censure; and embellish his narrative with suitable reflections. No person is obliged to write a history [he adds], but when he writes it he must tell the truth.[1]

A word remains to be said respecting Parker, the second agent named in Orde's letter of 1784. He is not so easily identified as Father O'Leary. The Irish books which treat of the period may be vainly searched for the name of Parker. It has been said that the adventurous spirit, who thirteen years later aroused by his eloquence the British navy to mutiny, was identical or connected with Orde's agent. I do not bind myself to the truth of this theory; nor am I able to prove a negative; but certainly some circumstances support it worthy of consideration; and having promised in a former chapter to recur to Parker of the Nore, I am afforded an opportunity for doing so by Mr. Froude's account of the secret mission to Dublin. Orde's agent arrived there in September 1784, to overreach and, as we are told, outmouth noisy patriots. It is true that Parker the mutineer was finally executed by the English authorities; but Jemmy O'Brien, the spy, also swung at the same hands. The former had received a classical education, and had served in the navy during the American War. His character was bad. His irrepressible oratory and power of influencing minds got him into scrapes. He married a woman with some property, which he dissipated, and was then imprisoned for debt. Released at length, he was sent on board the royal fleet as a 'supernumerary seaman,' to quote Portland's proclamation offering 500*l*. for his arrest. 'The address, ready eloquence, but, above all,' says Rose, 'the deep dissimulation he possessed, gave him vast influence over his comrades.' If true that Parker was sent on board the fleet to counteract mutiny, the result only shows that it is possible for an extinguisher

[1] Postscript to *Miscellaneous Tracts*, 1781.

to take fire. In his written defence, read on the fourth day of his trial, he 'solemnly declared that his only object of entering into the mutiny was that of checking a most dangerous spirit of revolt which had prevailed in the different ships, the bad effects of which he had done all in his power to prevent.' How he fanned the flame of mutiny, and on its outburst was appointed 'President,' we have already seen. This was in 1797. Who is the Parker, with persuasive oratorical powers, that is sent on a questionable mission to Ireland in 1784? It may be said that this cannot be Parker who afterwards figured at the Nore, because at the time of the secret mission to Dublin he was serving in the navy at a far distant place. The following words of Gorton make it hard to prove an 'alibi' for Richard Parker.[1] After describing his service during the American War, Gorton writes: 'On peace taking place he retired from his professional duties.' American independence had been won in 1778; but the articles of peace were not signed by England until November 30, 1782. Therefore Parker could be easily in Dublin in 1784. Mr. Froude's remarks about him are meagre, but it may be gleaned that the Parker of '84 was a man qualified and ready to keep a dark diary of what he observed. Parker of the Nore had the same habit. When he was searched, an elaborate diary of the proceedings which had taken place on shipboard was found. Parker's wife testified to the fact that he was rhapsodical and eccentric, but the plea failed to save his life. Orde, in announcing the arrival of Parker of '84, speaks of his 'rhapsodies,' and avows a misgiving that he might not act discreetly. The written defence of Parker of the Nore was highly rhapsodical, and the reverse of discreet.

[1] Richard Parker is usually described as a common sailor. A statement from his widow appears in the *Courier* of July 5, 1797: she claimed Parker's corpse, and, when asked by the admiral for what purpose, she answered, 'To have him interred like a gentleman, as he had been bred.' The request was refused. Parker's corpse remained exposed for years on the island of Sheppey, hung in chains until it dropped to pieces at last. The London *Courier* of the day insists that he had been for some time a lieutenant in the Royal Navy.

But he had abundant talent. Parker of '84 is described as an accomplished orator, and a good hand at sedition. So was Richard Parker. The former was an expert in dissimulation. The same character is given of Richard Parker by Rose. It may be also noteworthy that Orde's agent hailed from London. Mr. Froude assumes that Parker was an Irishman; the name is certainly English.

The 'Courier' of October 14, 1797, records some conversations with Richard Parker which afford a sample of the rhapsodical eloquence which had so often entranced his audience. An officer on board the ship that held him prisoner expressed impatience at not getting ahead, as the winds were contrary. 'What!' said Parker, 'are you not satisfied with having an admiral of the British fleet in chains, but you must also usurp the command of the elements? Or, because you have the honour to be my executioner, are you likewise as mad as the Persian tyrant who ordered his minions to lash the waves?' Much more of his talk is given. The 'Courier' states that 'from peculiar energy of intellect, his diction, even in conversation, was bold and original.'

The 'Courier,' from which further racy citations will be found in this volume, numbered on its staff Coleridge, Wordsworth, Lamb, and Mackintosh; and even the 'Times' was below it in circulation. Coleridge in his 'Literary Biography' claims to have made the fortune of the 'Courier.'

CHAPTER XVIII

BISHOP HUSSEY

THE subsequent career of Dr. Hussey—of whom a glimpse is obtained on a previous page—affords features sufficiently curious to claim a fuller view.

A second mission of secrecy to Spain proved more successful than his first. But these missions were purely diplomatic. In 1786 London swarmed with freed negroes, made wicked by idleness, and four hundred of them, with sixty white women in bad health and worse repute, were shipped by the Government to Sierra Leone to form a colony. This eight years afterwards was attacked by the French; Spain sided against England; Dr. Hussey again hurried to Madrid, healed the rupture, and Sierra Leone is now a bishopric. For these and other services he enjoyed a pension from Pitt.[1]

The 'Wickham Papers'—published in 1870—reveal the successful efforts of Pitt to sap Napoleon's power, by paying Pichegru and other French generals on condition that they would do their best to be beaten in battle. Wickham had been sent on more than one secret mission to the Continent, and acquired a shrewd knowledge of the intrigues of men.[2] He was afterwards appointed Under-Secretary at the Home Office, in which capacity he addressed to Lord Castlereagh at Dublin Castle, many letters in 1798, but hundreds of their allusions as printed have been, hitherto, unintelligible. One,

[1] For other instances in which priests acted as secret agents see Appendix.

[2] One letter conveys the proposal of a much respected ecclesiastic 'to foment an insurrection in the Cevennes.'—*Wickham Correspondence*, i. 165.

referring to the statement drawn up by Arthur O'Connor and the other State prisoners, says:—

I observe also that they have passed very lightly over their connections with the Spanish Government, and yet we have undoubted proof that a direct communication had taken place with some Minister of that country at the time that McNevin was at Hamburg. The Duke of Portland particularly wishes that some of them should be closely questioned as to this point, and the mode now adopted of examining them separately seems to be particularly favourable for drawing the real secret from them. They certainly had audiences of the Spanish Chargé d'Affaires at Hamburg, and, I believe, also of Mr. D. C. at Paris. I have always had strong suspicions that Dr. H.[1] has sent returns of the state and temper of the Catholics in Ireland to the Spanish Government.[2]

'D.C.' must be Del Campo,[3] the Spanish minister already mentioned in Sydney's letter about O'Leary; and 'Dr. H.' can only mean Dr. Hussey, chaplain to the Spanish embassy in London. As such, he was the servant of Spain, and when a conclave of English Catholics named him as envoy to Rome, there to lay before Pius VI. a document of much importance, Del Campo refused him leave of absence. The latter had now ceased to be Spanish minister, and Lord Camden had become the Viceroy of Ireland. Mr. Froude, with warmth, writes: 'Lord Camden had brought into Ireland, as he supposed, a serpent of healing, but it turned on him and stung him.'[4] This allusion is to Dr. Hussey, who, in 1797, became Bishop of Waterford, and at once issued a pastoral charge so ultra-

[1] Hussey was residing in Ireland from 1795. Four years previously his friend, Bishop Egan of Waterford, recommended him at Rome as worthy to succeed 'the illustrious' Archbishop Butler of Cashel. See *O'Renehan Papers*.

[2] *Castlereagh Correspondence*, i. 264.

[3] It may be said that the prefix 'Mr.' disturbs this belief; but all Wickham's letters thus describe foreign diplomats. For example, he writes to Lord Grenville on October 5, 1796: 'I have had in my own hands, and read, a despatch of *Mr.* La Croix to *Mr.* Barthelemy,' etc.—*Wickham Correspondence*, i. 462.

[4] *English in Ireland*, iii. 215. As Dr. Hussey, an Irishman by birth, had been president from 1795 of the college at Maynooth, it is not quite correct to say that the young Englishman, Lord Camden, who became Viceroy in 1797, brought Hussey to Ireland.

montane that it gave quite a shock at Whitehall. He lived in a style of brilliant pretension hitherto unattempted by his brother bishops,—men who, as Shiel states, were wont to pick their steps stealthily, as among penal traps. Dr. Hussey's elevation to the See of Waterford was due to the British Crown, but may have been influenced by a desire to shelve him in a remote place where he could do scant harm by intrigue.

'It was as mischievous a performance as ever I read,' quoth Sir John Coxe Hippesley *à propos* of Dr. Hussey's pastoral, 'and ministers here took care he should know their sentiments on that subject. He was in dudgeon thereat, and the Duke of Portland told me he demanded his passport "to return to Spain;" it was made out, but the doctor thought better of it, and he remains to lend his hand to *the tranquillity* of Ireland.'[1]

It appears, however, from the Vatican archives that Hussey, in March 1798, did petition the Pope for leave of absence from his diocese, and for a coadjutor, 'as he could not obtain the consent of the Court of Spain to leave its service.' He adds that for thirty years he was head of the Spanish Ambassador's Chapel, London.[2] His *amour propre*, no doubt, revolted from accepting at Portland's hands the passport to return to Spain—if, indeed, he could desert his diocese without leave from the Pope. A coadjutor bishop was not granted, but, in reply to the request for leave of absence, it was stipulated by Rome that Hussey should appoint efficient vicars to govern the see while away.[3] Was it of this arrangement that, as Hippesley says, he 'thought better'? Between the two accounts the diplomat stands confessed. He certainly passed the year 1799 in London, where, true to his instincts, we find him busy as a bee. Writing to J. Bernard Clinch, the influential occupant of a chair at Maynooth, he says of the then mooted Legislative Union:—

Whatever my reason may tell me upon a cool inquiry, my

[1] *Castlereagh Correspondence*, iii. 89.
[2] See Brady's *Episcopal Succession*, ii. 75. (Rome, 1876.)
[3] *Ibid.*

feelings rejoice at it. I told the Chancellor of your Exchequer here, that I would prefer a Union with the Beys and Mamelukes of Egypt to that of being under the iron rod of the Mamelukes of Ireland; but, alas! I fear that a Union will not remedy the ills of poor Erin. The remnants of old oppression and new opinions that lead to anarchy (to use the words of a foolish milk-and-water letter) still keep the field of battle, and until one side be defeated, the country is not safe. Another project upon which I have been consulted is, to grant salaries or pension to the Catholic clergy of the higher and lower order.[1] The conditions upon which they are to be granted, as first proposed to me, are directly hostile to the interests of religion, and, taken in the most favourable point of view, must be detrimental to the Catholics, by cutting asunder the slender remaining ties between the pastor and his flock, by turning the discipline and laws of the Church into a mercantile, political speculation, and must end in making the people unbelievers, and, consequently, Jacobins—upon the French scale. Whether the prelates of Ireland have courage or energy enough to oppose any such project so hurtful to religion, I will not say. Indeed, the infernal Popery laws have lessened the courage of the clergy, as well as destroyed the honesty and morals of the people, and my affection for my native land is not so effaced as to enable me to say with our countryman, after he had gone to bed, 'Arrah, let the house burn away; what do I care, who am only a lodger?'[2]

Dr. Hussey had been so long condemned to observe the Carthusian rule of silence that he seemed, when freed from restraint, like an opened flask of 'Mumm.'

It has been said that only in the confessional, or in chaunting, is this Trappist vow wholly dispensed with. The desire for shrift is implied by pointing to the mouth and beating the breast. To a man orally gifted like Hussey this restraint must, indeed, have proved painful, and accounts for the wonderful reaction in which he now revelled.

[1] In 1799, it appears that Bishop Douglas of London was anxious that a provision should be made for the English Catholic clergy; in other words, that they should be pensioned. See *Castlereagh Papers*, iii. 87.

[2] In March 1799, as I find from the Pelham MSS., Dr. Moylan, Bishop of Cork, urges in the name of his colleagues a State endowment of the clergy.

As a preacher, he made a sensation in the West End second only to that subsequently awakened by Irving's sermons at Hatton Garden. Charles Butler was present at one preached by Dr. Hussey on the small number of the elect. He asked whether, if the arch of Heaven were to open and the Son of Man, bursting from the mercy in which He is now enveloped, should stand in that church and judge his hearers, 'it were certain that three or even two—nay, trembling for myself as well as for you, is it quite certain that even one of us,' thundered Dr. Hussey, 'would be saved?' 'During this apostrophe,' writes Butler, 'the audience was agonised—at the interrogation there was a general shriek—some fell on the ground—the greatest triumph of eloquence I ever witnessed.'[1]

'Dr. Hussey was no favourite at Rome—possibly through lay intrigue, to which Gonsalvi was but too open,' observes an octogenarian priest of Waterford. The Holy See, however, quite recognised Hussey's powers as a diplomatist, for one of his last acts was to draw up the *Concordat* between Pius VII. and Napoleon—in which delicate mission he obtained the thanks of both. A long account of Hussey's interview at the Tuileries is given by England; and how struck Napoleon was with his arguments and expression.

The 'Burke Correspondence' describes Dr. Hussey's resolute attitude in requiring that the rights of Catholic soldiers should be recognised. The 'O'Renehan Papers' supply further details. At Clonmel Gaol he demanded the release of a Catholic soldier who had refused to receive religious instruction from the parson. The officer in command insulted Dr. Hussey, adding that he would flog him but for his coat. 'You wear the coat of a brave man,' said the bishop, 'and no one but a coward ever uttered such a threat; I dare you to touch me.' 'You shall not remain here, sir,' cried the officer, sulkily. 'Nor the soldier either,' replied Hussey, 'for I shall report your conduct this day, and obtain his release.' He did write to the Duke of Portland, and the soldier was discharged from prison.[2]

[1] Hussey, as the friend of Johnson, is allotted a niche by Boswell.

[2] I find in the Pelham MSS. an interesting paper of eight folios, in Hussey's

People were puzzled as to how Hussey managed, in penal days, to have influence with the Home Secretary. The most secret doings of the executive were known to Hussey. Lord Cloncurry mentions in his 'Memoirs' (p. 64), that all his motions in London in 1798 were carefully watched by a spy, and he adds: 'My kind informant was Dr. Hussey, who had been private secretary to the Duke of Portland.'

How he first came in touch with the King's ministers, and even with the King himself, happened in this way. When Spain joined France in assisting America to throw off the English yoke, the Spanish minister quitted London, giving to Hussey authority to complete certain diplomatic negotiations.

Some erroneous impressions prevailed to the prejudice of this singular man. Cumberland blows hot and cold: speaks of the honours Hussey received from Spain, and that he had clearly no repugnance to those that his Church could give. 'He had no wish to stir up insurrection; but'—adds Cumberland—'to head a revolution that should overturn the Church established, and enthrone himself primate in Armagh, would have been his glory and felicity—and, in truth, he was a man, by talents, nerve, ambition, and intrepidity, fitted for the boldest enterprise.' This impression seems partly due to a Good Friday sermon, in which Dr. Hussey announced the speedy emancipation of the Catholics, and the downfall of sectarianism in Ireland. He established new schools, hospitals, and convents in Waterford, and endowed them with gold.

The widespread feeling of distrust in public men which certain incidents of the time aroused is curiously shown by the remark of Sylvanus Urban, when announcing Hussey's death. 'The enemies of administration said he was employed by Government to sow the seeds of dissension with a view to

autograph, as regards an alleged systematic interference with the religious tenets of soldiers, and handed by himself to the Government. There is also a letter from Portland, dated November 1, 1796, concerning the alleged appointment by the Pope of Dr. Hussey as Vicar Apostolic over the Catholic military of Ireland. Pitt, in giving him authority over Catholic chaplains, did so on the understanding that, as a staunch anti-Jacobin which he was, he would stamp out disaffection in the army.

bring about the Union. Others considered him an agent of France.'[1] We have seen, on the authority of Froude, that he turned on his former friends in the Cabinet, and stung them; while Edmund Burke, writing to Hussey on his famous pastoral, says:—

From the moment that the Government, who employed you, betrayed you, they determined at the same time to destroy you. They are not a people to stop short in their course. You have come to an open issue with them. On your part, what you have done has been perfectly agreeable to your duty as a Catholic bishop and a man of honour and spirit.

This was almost the last letter written by Burke.

The Pelham MSS. contain the following curious missive addressed by Hussey to Pelham, afterwards Lord Chichester, a most influential member of the Government. Hussey's informant was, no doubt, Edmund Burke:—

Waterford: April 19, 1797.

Sir,—I received this day a letter from a friend of mine who sits in Parliament, who heard you defend the meaning of some sentiments in a pastoral letter, supposed to be addressed to the Roman Catholic clergy of this diocese by the Right Reverend Dr. Hussey, against the admixture of fulsome flattery and captious malevolence of a placeman, and though the intimacy that once subsisted between us has ceased, I will not be inferior in generosity to any man, and accordingly I embrace this occasion to thank you for the justice you do me. If done some months ago it would silence some malevolent whispers and have obliged your humble servant,

THOS. HUSSEY.

An account of Maynooth College by one of its professors appears in the 'Irish Magazine' for February 1808; and it is mentioned as a fact not generally known that Burke was 'attended spiritually in his last illness by Dr. Hussey.' In the accounts of Burke's funeral Dr. Hussey's presence is recorded; and it is told by Dr. England that when Hussey approached his old friend Portland in the graveyard, the duke turned abruptly away. 'Crosses' continued to come.

[1] *Gentleman's Magazine*, September 1803, p. 881.

Pelham, replying to Dr. Duigenan on February 22, 1799, declared that the Board of Maynooth had displaced their president for non-residence.

Hussey with all his friendship for Burke was no friend to his son. A letter from John Keogh to Hussey, dated October 2, 1792, and seemingly communicated by the latter to Dundas, then Home Secretary, is preserved among the Secret Irish State Papers in London. It repudiates Burke's son, who had been sent to Ireland by his father as an agent on behalf of the Catholics, and tells Dundas that he was wholly unauthorised to speak for that body. According to Tone's journal of September 1792, Keogh regarded young Burke as a spy sent by Dundas. He was wrong, for Hobart, writing to Nepean, on October 4, 1792, states that Dundas took credit with Westmoreland for having given Burke a chilling reception on his return to England. This was the youth of whom Buckle says, 'Never can there be forgotten those touching allusions to the death of that only son, who was the joy of his soul and the pride of his heart, and to whom he fondly hoped to bequeath the inheritance of his imperishable fame.'

Hussey was succeeded as an intermediary between the Irish Catholics and the Crown by Dr. Moylan, Bishop of Cork. This prelate—who had denounced the French when their fleet lay in Bantry Bay, for which he would have lost his head had they been able to land—became a great favourite with Pitt and Portland.

The duke in a letter dated Bulstrode, July 27, 1800, states:—

There can be, and there never has been, but one opinion of the firmness, the steadiness, and the manliness of Dr. Moylan's character, which it was agreed by all those who had the pleasure of meeting him here, was as engaging as his person, which avows and bespeaks as much good-will as can be well imagined in a human countenance.

Dr. Hussey, as the first President of Maynooth, regarded it with paternal anxiety; and as he was now in deep disfavour with the Government, he asked Dr. Moylan to plead for it, and probably draughted the words. The lay seminary of Maynooth, in which Judge Corballis and other able men received their education, was threatened with suppression at this time.

Whoever was the adviser of this measure [writes Dr. Moylan] consulted more his bigotry than the welfare of his Excellency's administration, or the dictates of sound policy, for what could be more impolitic than the suppression of the only house for the lay education of the Roman Catholic youth immediately under the eye and inspection of Government, and under the direction of trustees who must have the confidence of Government—an establishment in which the principles of loyalty and attachment to his Majesty's Government and to our excellent Constitution are, I am bold to say, as strongly inculcated into the minds of the pupils as in any college or other place of education in his Majesty's dominions.

Dr. Moylan adds:—

So violent an act gives cause to suspect that it is only a prelude to other unfriendly measures, and in particular to the suppression of the college at Maynooth, of which we shall ever remember with gratitude that your Lordship has been the corner-stone.[1]

Pelham usually endorses his letters with a memorandum of his reply—but in this instance none seems to have been given. Dr. Hussey regarded uneasily the threatened downfall of the house which he had raised. The estrangement of old friends, and prolonged anxiety, preyed upon him, and in the following year he dropped down dead. This event occurred at Dunmore,[2] Waterford. He had

> Fondly hoped—his long vexations past—
> Here to return, and die at home at last.

The Bishop outlived O'Leary by eighteen months, and attended the funeral of his rival. His own was marked by a painful incident. Polemic and party spirit ran so high that

[1] Cork, January 1, 1802; the Pelham MSS. Pelham had been Chief Secretary for Ireland when Maynooth College was founded.

[2] All the memoirs say Tramore; but the records of the Christian Brothers (brought by Mr. Rice to Waterford in 1802 during Dr. Hussey's episcopate) name Dunmore.

some militia and soldiers attempted to throw the coffin into the river Suir; a disgraceful riot took place, and several lives were lost.[1] My correspondent was puzzled to account for an occurrence so painful, but it is clearly traceable to the friction which had arisen between Dr. Hussey and influential redcoats. He was fortunate in not living to see the extinction of the Lay College at Maynooth which had known his fostering care.

[1] The late Very Rev. Dr. Fitzgerald, P.P., Carrick-on-Suir, to the Author, September 19, 1888.

CHAPTER XIX

PRESBYTERIAN MINISTERS DEEP IN TREASON—PLOT AND COUNTER-PLOT

Twelve Presbyterian clergymen were concerned in the rebellion: the Rev. W. Steel Dickson, D.D, who wrote an interesting 'Narrative' of his 'Confinement and Exile,' Rev. Samuel Barbar, Rev. William Porter, Rev. Sinclair Kelburne, Rev. Arthur McMahon, and the Rev. Messrs. Stevelly, Simpson, MacNeil, Sinclair, Glardy, Birch, and Warwick. Of these men three were executed: Porter, Stevelly, and Warwick. It is to be feared that one of the twelve became a Judas.

There are two informers, McMahon and Durnin, who have never been noticed by Madden or other historians of the time. I now quote from Bourrienne, formerly the private secretary of Napoleon, and afterwards ambassador to Hamburg. Berthier will be remembered as the Minister of War and Prince of Wagram, who met a violent death during the Hundred Days.

'Previous to my arrival in Hamburg in 1804,' writes Bourrienne, Marshal 'Berthier had recommended to Bernadotte two Irishmen as spies. Bernadotte employed them, but I learned that McMahon, one of the two, rendered himself more serviceable to England than to us. I communicated this fact to Bernadotte, who ascertained that my information was accurate.' The future King replied :—

I have the honor to inform you, Marshal, that two Irishmen residing in Hamburg, MM. Durnin and MacMahon, who had been liberally rewarded by the English Government *for coming to France* to act as spies on the Irish refugees and the views of the French Government, have offered their services to assist the designs of France in the cause of the United Irishmen.

His Majesty wishes that you should accept the offer of these two Irishmen; that you should employ them in obtaining all possible information, and even furnish them with whatever money may be necessary.

For the sake of expedition, I have written on this subject to General Dessolle, who commands in Hanover during your absence, and I beg that you will transmit to him the orders necessary for following the Emperor's instructions.

I have the honor, etc.

BERTHIER.

Bourrienne says that, but for the information he had transmitted to Berthier, Bernadotte would have conceived himself bound to employ the two men recommended to him. The following was his answer:—

I have received your letter, my dear minister, and thank you for your attention in communicating to me the information it contains.

I never had great confidence in the fidelity or intelligence of MacMahon. He was never entrusted with any business of importance, and if I furnished him with the means of subsistence, it was because he was recommended to me by the war minister, and, besides, his unfortunate condition could not but excite pity. I at first allowed him four hundred francs per month; but finding him perfectly useless, I reduced that allowance to two hundred and fifty, which was barely sufficient for him to live on. He has not been at head-quarters for the last three months.

I enclose a copy of the letter which the war minister wrote to me respecting MacMahon.

T. BERNADOTTE.[1]

Bernadotte's missive, like a shell, bursts with crushing force. The fact that McMahon's movements in '98 are continually reported to the British Government would show, however, that it was not until *after* the collapse of the rebellion,

[1] Napoleon's marshals were rich men. The salary of a marshal was 1,600*l.* a year; but their emoluments were much increased by allowances made by Napoleon. Berthier had in addition 400*l.* a month as a major-general, and further received from his generous master 50,000*l.* every year.

and want stared him in the face, that he sold his information. When hunger sent its spasm remorse lost its pang.

In the report of the Secret Committee of the House of Lords, issued in 1798, it appears, from the sworn testimony of John Hughes of Belfast, that

in June 1797 he attended a meeting at Randalstown, which consisted of Teeling, Lowry, Robert Moore, and Colonel James Plunkett. He attended said meeting by the direction of Lowry and Teeling to hear the report of the Colonels of the County of Antrim. The Report was brought by Dunne, accompanied by the Rev. Arthur MacMahon of Holywood. The first resolution was that it would be imprudent to act at that time without foreign aid, but that if the County of Down would act, a part of the Antrim Colonels, who could bring out nine or ten thousand men, would act with Down. The meeting broke up in consequence of the division amongst the Antrim Colonels. The Rev. Arthur MacMahon told the meeting that he had been sent by the Colonels of the County of Down to state to the Colonels of the County of Antrim, who had met at Park Gate that day, that they (the Colonels of Down) were willing to rise, and that he had delivered such the message of the Down Colonels to the Antrim Colonels. MacMahon was then a member of the Ulster Provincial Committee, and he told him that he had been one of the seven Colonels of the County of Down who had been selected and appointed leaders for said county; and he also told him that he (MacMahon) was a member of the National Executive.

MacMahon was informed on his road home (as he heard) that he would be taken; and he, Robert Rollo Read, Hastings Mason, once an officer in the Downshire Militia, and John Magennis, took boat at Bangor and got over to Scotland, and afterwards *MacMahon got to France*, where he still is.—Pp. 28–9.

The report and appendix of the Secret Committee is known to have been edited by Alexander Knox, whom Lord Macaulay afterwards described as 'a remarkable man.' Mr. Knox was the private secretary of Lord Castlereagh; and, in compiling the report for the Government, he disclosed as much of McMahon's proceedings as was convenient for their purpose. The Government well knew that McMahon had engaged deeply in treason between the period of his taking boat at Bangor and getting to France. The second volume of Lord Castlereagh's Correspondence opens with the following secret letter. Quigley, or O'Coigly, will be remembered as the unfortunate priest who was hanged at Maidstone in May 1798:—

'McMahon, member of the executive committee, a Presbyterian parson from the County of Down, forced to emigrate in June last, came over to London, where he met with Quigley, who was likewise obliged to leave Ireland. They stayed together in London, imitating the Patriots in the mode of forming societies after the plan of the United Irish. They had heard of the expedition at the Texel being intended for Ireland, and it was agreed on that an insurrection should be attempted in London, as soon as the landing was effected in Ireland. Colonel Despard was to be the leading person, and the King and Council were to be put to death, &c. Their force was estimated at 40,000, ready to turn out. McMahon, hearing he was traced to London, resolved on going for France, and took Quigley as his interpreter; he got a subscription made to pay Quigley's expenses, and collected twenty-five guineas, fifteen of which were given by a Mr. Bell, of the City.

'McMahon and Quigley went over to Cuxhaven, thence directly to Holland, were on board the fleet, and, when the expedition went off, proceeded to Paris. They there found Lewins, but could get no satisfactory answers from him relative to his communications with the French Government. A quarrel was the consequence, and Father Quigley was despatched privately by McMahon to London, to get some one sent over to represent the Patriots of both nations, and to replace Lewins.'[1]

Seaton Reid, D.D., the able historian of the Presbyterian Church, says that in 1789 McMahon was ordained to the pastoral charge of Kilrea, and in 1794 became minister of

[1] It may have been because Lewins, the shrewd envoy of the United Irishmen, suspected McMahon, that he refused to yield information on being pumped. Hence the intrigue to oust Lewins of which we have already heard. See Appendix.

Holywood. He is described as a man of daring character, and considerable literary attainments. Dr. Reid's History has been continued by Dr. Killen, an ecclesiastical historian of rank, who found McMahon's subsequent career involved in great mystery. 'On the Continent,' writes Dr. Killen, 'he embraced the military profession, and it is said—with what truth I know not—that he became distinguished as General Mack.' Most notices of Mack, the Austrian general, say that he died in obscurity, and at a date unknown. It is almost a pity to disturb the romance with which Dr. Killen has invested this subject,—but 'truth is stranger than fiction.' An inquiry into the life of General Mack is fatal to the suggestion of the Presbyterian historian.[1]

The arrival of Arthur McMahon at Paris is specially noted in Tone's Diary on February 1, 1798.[2] Soon after the Hamburg spy announces, with other facts, that McMahon—O'Coigly's companion—is appointed colonel and aide-de-camp to Napper Tandy.[3] A later letter of secret information, no doubt from Turner—who had been a colleague of McMahon when organising treason in Ulster—says:—

MacMahon has about 300*l.* sterling, property remitted him by Charles Rankin of Belfast; this he means to employ in buying a farm. Tired of politics,[4] especially those of France, he is to write to Citoyen Jean Thomas, à la Poste restante, à Hamburg, whom he looks on as a good patriot.

[1] McMahon was in the pastoral charge of Kilrea at the very time that Mack, a native of Franconia, held high rank in the army of the Prince of Coburg, and was directing the operations of the campaign of 1793. From 1794 to 1797, while McMahon was preaching at Holywood, and representing the rebel colonels of the county Down, General Mack was serving in the Netherlands, and in command of the Army of the Rhine. Charles Mack earned notoriety by delivering over to Napoleon, in virtue of the capitulation of Ulm, 33,000 Austrians as prisoners of war. For this act he was tried at Vienna, and received sentence of death as a traitor to his country. But Bourrienne denies that any secret understanding existed between him and Buonaparte. Mack's sentence having been commuted, he was consigned to an Austrian dungeon, where for a long time his fate was lost in mystery. Even more inglorious was the final career of Arthur McMahon.

[2] *Life of Wolfe Tone*, ii. 460. [3] *Castlereagh Correspondence*, i. 306.

[4] Compare the passages 'sick of politics,' in p. 6, *ante*, &c.

The 'Castlereagh Papers' give a secret account of Tandy's expedition; and how 'Joseph Orr and McMahon the clergyman, went out in a small corvette of eight guns, to reconnoitre the Irish coast and to fire signals; but the boat turned leaky, and they were obliged to put into Flushing, being chased by the English cruisers. These two refused to go any more, and went to Boulogne, where they follow privateering.'[1]

This is the last we hear of McMahon until he turns up in the letter of Berthier, the French Minister of War.

It would have been well for McMahon's friends had the quondam shepherd entered on pastoral work of another sort, assuming that he seriously entertained the idea, and that it was not mooted by him to throw Turner off the scent. Turner —at this time—had begun to be suspected, as Reinhard shows (*ante*, p. 53). Certain it is, the *soi-disant* farmer chose dirtier work than scouring drains, or even spreading manure. But as his movements with Tandy are secretly reported to the British Government, it would seem that he had not as yet become a regular informer. Whatever proposal he made to Pitt, the bargain was apparently bungled. Unlike others, his name is not to be found in any pension list. Judging from the poverty in which Bernadotte found McMahon in 1803, his trade as a spy cannot have been very remunerative. But increased trade often brings large profits, and his opportunities for doing good work for Pitt were certainly greater after 1804.

Experience taught McMahon something. A disappointed man, willing to spy on behalf of whichever side paid best, had at least no difficulty in making a choice. How he gradually acquired facilities for plying his trade with profit now remains to be shown.

Miles Byrne—who held a command in the rebel lines at Vinegar Hill, narrowly escaped with his life, was afterwards the trusted agent of Robert Emmet in 1803, and became a colonel in the French service—supplies in his Memoirs an

[1] *Castlereagh Correspondence*, i. 408.

honoured list of 'exiled Irish whom he met in France,' including 'Arthur McMahon.' This would be about the year 1803. Matthew Dowling, Byrne's host on the occasion, had been deeply compromised in '98, and his name is often met in the autobiographies of Cloncurry, Hamilton Rowan, and Moore.

> I spent [writes Byrne] one evening at his lodgings in company with Paul Murray and Arthur MacMahon, and he made us nearly forget we were far away from our home; he made us proud of being exiles in a good cause.

The statement of the historian of the Presbyterian Church that the Rev. Arthur McMahon embraced the military profession, and became distinguished as 'General Mack,' is true in every particular, except the last three words.

In 1804 the Irish legion was formed by Napoleon, and McMahon got a commission from Berthier. Colonel Miles Byrne speaks of McMahon as amongst his 'best friends and comrades—we were happy and united.'[1] The risk he ran of a bear's hug never struck him. 'We could see the masts of the ships in the bay of Brest, from whence we expected soon to sail with an army to liberate our beloved country; this view caused sensations that exiles alone can feel and appreciate.' Byrne goes on to say that General Sarazan was 'suspected to have been in the pay of England.' Not one word is dropped to the prejudice of McMahon.

A great crisis in England's history had now arisen. Buonaparte was master of Europe. Russia joined him; Prussia and Austria were all but his serfs; North Germany was annexed to France. In 1809 the Walcheren expedition —consisting of 235 ships and 40,000 land forces—was despatched by England with the object of checking Napoleon's advance into Austria.

Never had a grander fleet left England, or great expectation been more utterly crushed. After a prolonged bombardment, Admiral Strahan and Lord Chatham evacuated Walcheren on December 23, 1809. They returned to England,

[1] *Memoirs of Miles Byrne*, ii. 17. (Paris, 1862.)

but with McMahon a prisoner.[1] This capture, however, failed to satisfy Parliament. Angry discussion rose, Canning and Castlereagh fought a duel, Burdett was lodged in the Tower, riots rent London, and Lord Chatham resigned to avoid deeper disgrace.[2]

Bernadotte, it will be remembered, while admitting that McMahon had never been entrusted by France with secret business of importance, yet complains of his inefficiency as a spy. What but disappointment could ensue? Bourrienne, the minister of France at Hamburg, learned long after, as he tells us, that McMahon gave to England information vastly exceeding in value anything he told France. England could pay well when she chose, while the fund available in France for secret service was shallow and precarious.

As regards the second spy named in Bernadotte's letter to Berthier, histories of the rebellion may be vainly searched for any mention of Durnin; nor is it surprising, when we know, as we now do, that this man had three or four aliases. Nay, more—he is sometimes described in the Government reports merely by an initial! Thus, Wickham encloses to Castlereagh a letter from Crawford, British minister at Hamburg, in which he says, 'one D——, alias C——, who murdered Pentland at Drogheda—a man much esteemed by Mr. Beresford, is now here.'[3] The usually exhaustive index to the 'Castlereagh Correspondence' includes no name resembling Durnin. However, it turns up in a letter of Wickham to Castlereagh, dated November 23, 1798, announcing that a vessel named the 'Morgan Rattler' had just arrived at Hamburg from Dublin with some rebel fugitives, and bearing letters and papers from Coll, a colonel in the rebel army at Wexford, and 'Duff, alias

[1] *Memoirs of Miles Byrne*, ii. 59.

[2] Hoche's expedition was scattered by adverse winds. How the Walcheren came to grief was partly due to fever, which decimated the troops. A long report from Dr. Renny appears in the sixth volume of the *Castlereagh Correspondence*, and, on reading it now, one cannot doubt that the 'antiphlogistic' treatment then employed thinned the ranks more effectively than Napoleon's shells. Antimony and calomel, blister and blood-letting, did their work.

[3] *Castlereagh Correspondence*, ii. 226.

Campbell, but whose real name,' he adds, 'is *Dornan*.'[1] Lower down in the letter, Wickham adds that 'Campbell, alias Duff, but whose real name is Dornan, is said to have been concerned in the murder of a person of the name of Pentland, or Portland, near Drogheda.'[2]

Here at last one gets upon a long-lost track—a track, it is to be feared, of a double-dyed villain. Dalton's 'History of Drogheda' mentions (ii. 370) that in 1796, shortly after the arrival of the French fleet in Bantry Bay, 'Mr. Pentland, surveyor of excise in Drogheda, was inhumanly and wilfully murdered.'

Officers of excise usually kept a sharp watch on the coast; and hence, probably, Durnin deemed it well to 'remove' him. Why Durnin figured under the name of Duff at Drogheda may have been because it was endeared to the people by historic tradition. D'Alton—the historian of Drogheda—often mentions the Duffs, and how for faith and fatherland they suffered attainder in 1691. I cannot find that Durnin attained any influence in the councils of the United Irishmen; but McMahon must have been a person of culture and prepossessing manners to succeed in exciting the sympathy of a stoical soldier of the Revolution, and who, moreover, had reason to doubt his fidelity. The name Arthur McMahon is found in the Fugitive Bill of 1798. But this circumstance affords no proof that he was not then a spy; for Turner also figures in the Fugitive Bill, and was afterwards subjected to the mock penalty of imprisonment. The Banishment Act includes the name 'John Dorney.' Durnin and Dorney are convertible names. A gardener named Durnin, or Dorney (for the peasantry hail him by both names), has been employed in the author's family for many years.

When one considers the heterogeneous character of the

[1] *Castlereagh Correspondence*, ii. 15.

[2] The Pentlands opposed the United Irishmen. Henry Pentland served as sheriff of Drogheda in 1799, with George MacIntagart as mayor. MacIntagart was the man who dressed up spies in French uniforms to entrap credulous peasants.

throng who joined the ranks of the United Irishmen, it is only surprising that their secrets were so well kept. The late Frank Thorpe Porter, a well-known police magistrate, gave me a personal reminiscence not devoid of interest. His father had been one of the brotherhood; but one dark night in March 1798, a beggarman having given him 'the secret sign' in the street, he musingly said, 'By Jove! if our Society includes such fellows as this, the sooner I get out of it the better.' He had been a sergeant of grenadiers in the Irish Volunteers of 1782, and his tall figure may be recognised in Wheatley's celebrated picture of the review in College Green under the Duke of Leinster and Lord Charlemont.

Many United Irishmen, whose names do not appear in history, had escapes as narrow, but on a more modest scale, as those which favoured Hamilton Rowan. Mr. Porter added a reminiscence worth preserving. The house of his father, an eminent Protestant printer, was 69 Grafton Street. The maidservant had a sweetheart in an opposite house, and one Sunday evening, while Mrs. Porter was entertaining Dignan, a proscribed rebel, the domestic left her master's door ajar, and tripped across the street for a chat. Meanwhile, who should walk up to Porter's but the city sheriff, holding in his hand the manuscript of a Proclamation which he required him to print. Finding that the hall-door gave no resistance, he proceeded upstairs. Mrs. Porter, thunderstruck, but with presence of mind, hailed him from the lobby above, exclaiming, 'Oh! *Mr. Sheriff*, I am very glad to see you.' Dignan took the alarm that she intended and, seizing a dark table-cover with which he concealed his person, flung himself under a pianoforte that stood in a corner. This had hardly been accomplished when the sheriff entered. 'Sheriff,' said Mrs. Porter, 'you probably met your friend the Town Major, who has just gone after having a glass of punch—take his seat and make yourself comfortable.' The sheriff, nothing loth, accepted the proffered hospitality. Mrs. Porter's feelings may be imagined during the *mauvais quart d'heure* of his stay, when a single sigh from the outlaw would have sealed not only his doom, but probably her husband's as well.[1]

Mr. Porter did not know what Dignan had done. But I find, among McNally's secret letters to Dublin Castle, one enclosing a copy of the 'Union Star,' a revolutionary print, which, he says, 'has been printed at Dignan's house in Grafton Street.' A later letter (endorsed May 23, 1798, the night on which the rebellion burst forth) announces 'Ferris is the informer against Dignan.' Ferris is described by Musgrave in his history (p. 176) as head of a committee of United Irishmen, who was waited upon by a blacksmith named Dunne offering to murder Lord Carhampton, the famous terrorist. Ferris warned Carhampton, and Dunne with his accomplice McCarthy was hanged. Frequent payments to Ferris through Lord Carhampton are recorded in the book of 'Secret Service Money.' Musgrave notices him as a rather meritorious man. Who Ferris was McNally tells Cooke in a letter of secret gossip. 'Ferris, forty years ago, was an attorney and stripped of his gown for perjury; lived in Green Street; at present in [Dublin] Castle.'

[1] F. Thorpe Porter, police magistrate, to W. J. F., January 1862.

CHAPTER XX

THOMAS REYNOLDS: SPY, AND BRITISH CONSUL

No greater contrast could be found to the idiosyncrasy of Magan than that of Thomas Reynolds. If the former was shy, shrinking, and unobtrusive, Reynolds had indomitable *audace*, a fondness for display and luxury, a love of society, and an effrontery which no rebuff could disconcert. After several arrests had been made, and when a suspicion of infidelity rested on him for the first time, Neilson, a powerful man, meeting him unarmed at night, grasped him by the throat, and, presenting a pistol, exclaimed, 'What should I do to the villain who has sought my confidence to betray me?' Reynolds, with perfect *sang froid*, replied, 'You should shoot him through the heart!' Neilson, struck by the reply, changed his purpose and suffered Reynolds to go.[1]

Fourteen delegates from Leinster, as they sat in council at Bond's, had been seized on Reynolds's information, and the sickening fact is told by Dr. Madden that some days after the arrests he paid a visit of condolence to Mrs. Bond, and caressed the babe she held in her arms.

But let it not be supposed that he had any share in the betrayal of Lord Edward Fitzgerald. Reynolds held an advantageous lease of lands under the Leinster family, warmed to Lord Edward, and, during the period of his outlawry, gave him money to meet a pressing call. The Geraldine little dreamed from what source it was derived. Before the payment of the 5,000*l.* to Reynolds he received from Cooke in 1798, 500*l.*

[1] This anecdote is told by young Curran in the 'Life' of his father (ii. 134), on the authority of 'an eminent Irish barrister,' doubtless McNally, to whom he tenders thanks elsewhere for valued information. See p. 192, *ante*.

Reynolds, a silk mercer, had been persuaded to inform by Mr. W. Cope, an eminent merchant, who exercised great influence over him, under circumstances that will be soon apparent. His grandson, Sir William Cope, Bart., has sent me the correspondence which attained this end. Cope, in a memorandum, dated 1799, writes:—

I exerted my influence, and, though Mr. Cooke said to me, 'You *must* get him to come forward; stop at nothing—100,000*l.*—anything,' etc., I conditioned with Government for him for only 5,000*l.* and 1,000*l.* per year, and he is satisfied. He came forward at my repeated intercession.

The 'Life of Thomas Reynolds,' by his son, was issued in 1839, with a view to whitewash a sullied memory; the biographer—not supposing that the Cope papers existed—states that, as compensation for heavy losses, a bulk sum of but 500*l.* was paid to Reynolds, 'with an annuity of 1,000*l.* Irish, with reversion to my mother, my brother and myself.'[1]

The accounts of Secret Service Money have also turned up to bear out Cope's statement and confront Reynolds junior. It appears, under date of March 4, 1799, that Reynolds received on that day not 500*l.*, but the completion of a sum of 5,000*l.* As regards the pension, it continued to be paid for near forty years and he drew altogether 45,740*l.*

The information which had been dropping from Reynolds, sometimes not as freely as had been hoped, received a stimulus by his arrest at Athy on May 5, 1798. He writes to Mr. Cope that he has been thrown into a dungeon, and demands from the Government, what they well know he merits, instant enlargement. He refers to the great and essential services he had rendered to Government, and adds that by his confinement he is totally prevented from obtaining and giving further knowledge. Then it was that Cope settled the terms with Cooke. Cope's powerful influence over Reynolds was due to the fact that the latter had gradually become his slave as a

[1] *Life of Reynolds*, by his Son, ii. 514. The latter died in 1856, after having long filled the post of stamp-distributor for the East Riding of Yorkshire.

creditor to a large extent. Sir William Cope[1] has sent me a letter from Reynolds's wife to show the falsity of the biographer's assertion that he had made no terms with the Crown for his information. It appears from a letter of Reynolds that the wife was empowered to act for him, and among the terms required were, 'that he might settle in any part of England he liked, receive from the Government letters of introduction, recommending him and family to the particular attention of the gentry of the place;' the pension to commence on June 25, 1798, with 5,000*l.* in hand; in conclusion she begs Cope to advance on loan 1,000*l.*[2]

These and other references to monetary transactions led me to search the Registry of Deeds Office, and the following result appears: '1794—Thos. Reynolds of West Park Street Dublin to Wm. Cope. Consideration 5041*l.* 14*s.* 5*d.* Lands of Corbetstown, King's Co.'

The fact that Reynolds was obliged to borrow this sum shows the erroneousness of Lord Castlereagh's statement in Parliament, 'that he was a gentleman in considerable circumstances.' Fresh proof of the wisdom of the proverb (xxii. 7), 'the borrower is servant to the lender,' is afforded by this episode. In the case of Higgins and Magan, the treachery of the latter to Lord Edward was entirely due to the fact that Higgins had bound him, hand and foot, in bonds more inextricable than those by which Mephistopheles sought to enchain his victim. Shamado got the lion's share of the blood money earned by that betrayal. Cope, though a man of great wealth, and professing to have influenced Reynolds solely from a sense of moral duty, obtained a pension of 1,000*l.* a year for his wife, with reversion to his three daughters.[3] Possibly, too, the course taken by Reynolds at his instance secured to Cope the replacement of the 5,041*l.* which he had advanced in more prosperous days. Cope survived until December 7, 1820, when he died at his house in Hume Street, Dublin. His three

[1] Sir W. Cope died Jan. 9, 1892.

[2] The full text of the correspondence I have published elsewhere. The letters of Reynolds are full of bad spelling.

[3] *Cornwallis*, ii. 375.

daughters never married. The foregoing inquiries have been invited by the son and biographer of Reynolds, who, seeking to pillory Dr. Taylor, author of the 'Civil Wars,' writes:—

'Perhaps Mr. Taylor could furnish me with the records from which he discovered that my father was distressed from want of money.' He may, perhaps, consider Mr. Moore's 'Life of Lord Edward Fitzgerald' as a record, or Mr. Moore himself as an historian, of small value; but I shall notice his work in another place, I shall confine myself for the present to Mr. Taylor. 'From what source,' he asks, 'did Mr. Taylor discover that my father had been an active member of the Union? and, above all, from what record did he receive the foul slander that he had sold the secret to Government? Could not the same record have supplied him with the price also; and, if so, why did he not name it? From what records did he learn that my father had insured to himself by his conduct even the slightest reward? The whole accusation is as false as it is malicious.'[1]

Among other damaging things alleged against Reynolds on the trials of Bond, Byrne, and McCan were that he had stolen his mother's jewellery and had afterwards poisoned her, and that he had broken several oaths; and it was sworn by five respectable witnesses that they did not believe him worthy of credit on his oath.

A small incident, that has never appeared in print, may perhaps be given here. The guard which seized the fourteen delegates at Bond's house entered by means of a password, which we shall presently hear, and Major Sirr had Reynolds to thank for the information, though the father of a late police magistrate—Mr. Porter—lay for a time under the stigma. Wm. Porter—in whose house Dignan will be remembered as having had a narrow escape from arrest—met Oliver Bond one day on Cork Hill, Dublin, and asked him, as a United Brother, for a list of the signs and passwords employed on special occasions. Bond replied: 'Call at my house on Monday evening next, making sure to ask as you enter, "Is Ivers from Carlow come?"' Porter was on his way to keep this appointment

[1] *Life of Thomas Reynolds*, by his Son, i. 103.

when he met Luke White—the founder of the Annaly peerage —who asked him to accompany him to his store in Crampton Court, where some business was transacted between the two— one being a printer and the other a publisher. An hour was thus consumed, and Porter on arriving at Bond's—it was Monday, March 12, 1798—found a cordon of soldiers round the house. Reynolds, who held the rank of colonel in the rebel organisation, was not then suspected; and it was Oliver Bond's conviction, freely expressed, that William Porter had betrayed the password to Sirr. For this suspicion he made frank atonement. Bond's trial did not come on for three months, and the interval proved one of deep anxiety to Porter. Then it was that Reynolds excited much surprise by entering the witness-box. Bond, recognising Porter in court, stretched forth his arm across the necks of his keepers, and shook the hand of the man he had wronged.[1]

Reynolds, unlike Magan, who seemed content with the crumbs which fell from 'Shamado's' hand, was less easily satisfied. In 1810 he got the postmastership at Lisbon, the emoluments of which for four years amounted to 5,600*l.*, after which he became British Consul at Iceland; but, not liking the post, he coolly returned to London without leave, when the following scene took place between himself and Mr. Cooke, formerly Under-Secretary at Dublin Castle. Reynolds's son thus tells what passed: '"You are a madman; you are an imprudent; I tell you so to your face; and you were always an imprudent man, and never will be otherwise. I tell you, you are considered as a passionate, imprudent man." "Mr. Cooke," said my father, "if I was not so, perhaps Ireland would not at this day be a part of the British Empire: you did not think me passionate or imprudent in 1798." "I tell you again," said Mr. Cooke, "you are mad. Well, what do you intend to do now?" "Really," said my father, "I intend to do nothing at all; I suppose Lord Castlereagh, on his return, will settle my resignation." . . . "Lord Castlereagh," continued Mr. Cooke, "knows you to be a very imprudent man, and he would

[1] Frank Thorpe Porter, police magistrate, to W. J. F., May 30, 1860.

certainly hesitate at allowing you to be in London, where your imprudence would give advantage to your enemies to bring you into trouble, and him too. He does not like you to be in London: I tell you fairly that is the feeling."'[1]

Lord Castlereagh then filled the critical post of Minister for Foreign Affairs. A formidable Opposition daily questioned and tormented him. The horror of Mathias on hearing 'the Bells' can hardly have been greater than that of Castlereagh whenever Reynolds's ring sounded at his door. Reynolds refused to freeze any longer in Iceland, and, after some delay, was appointed consul at Copenhagen. He soon got tired of it, and coolly installed his son there as vice-consul; but, on Canning succeeding to Castlereagh, after the suicide of the latter, he sent young Reynolds adrift. Meanwhile the sire divided his residence between Paris and London. He constantly crossed Castlereagh's path, posing before him as an ill-used man and possibly helping to drive him mad. The cupidity of Reynolds is described as insatiable. In 1817, Thistlewood, Watson, and Hooper were indicted for treason; true bills were found by the grand jury of Middlesex; but the name of Thomas Reynolds having appeared on the panel, much wrath found vent, and a feeling of disgust passed over England. The press took up the subject, and Parliament resounded with 'Reynolds, the Irish informer.' 'He should retire from public view,' said Curran, hid beneath the heap of his own carnage.'

Society snubbed him, but still his chariot went round the Row day by day. After Castlereagh's death he removed permanently to Paris, where he loved to parade his pompous person, and became as well known in the Champs-Elysées as Charles X. or Louis Philippe. Some lines scribbled at this time illustrate the feelings with which thinkers of a certain type watched his diurnal progress:—

Lolling at his vile ease in chariot gay,
His face, nay, even his fearful name, unhidden!
Uncloaked abroad, 'neath all the eyes of day,

[1] *Life of Thomas Reynolds*, by his Son, ii. 445.

Which—as he passeth—close, while breath is hushed,—
Unspat upon, untrampled down, uncrushed,
I've seen the seven-fold traitor! &c.

Reynolds had a habit of leaving his card on men the buckles of whose shoes he was unworthy to burnish. Amongst others whom he thought that by doing so he honoured, was Dr. Daniel Haliday, of Paris, who represented a family distinguished in Irish letters. In Haliday's hall there hung a fine portrait of Lord Edward Fitzgerald. Turning its face to the wall, and sticking Reynolds's card on it, he said to his servant: 'When he again comes, refer him to this picture.' Reynolds, of course, repeated the visit, and felt the rebuff the more because Lord Edward was not among the men he had betrayed. The late Charles Haliday, to whom I owe this story of his uncle, shared the rather general belief as to Reynolds having informed against the Geraldine, while the now convicted Magan, who lived close to Charles Haliday on the banks of the Liffey, failed to incur his suspicion.

One fine day in August 1836, when Paris was *en fête*, Reynolds died, and his remains were brought to England and consigned to the vaults of Wilton Church, Yorkshire. By a coincidence Dr. Haliday died at the same time, as appears from his epitaph in the picturesque graveyard of Dundrum near Dublin. When struck down by death at Paris, he had been engaged on a History of the Irish Brigade.

CHAPTER XXI

ARMSTRONG AND THE SHEARESES—GENERAL LAWLESS

Armstrong was another man who, unlike Turner and Magan, boldly betrayed, and by baring his name to popular odium, bared his breast to its penalties. He lived to old age in a district specially burrowed by agrarian crime; but, though often taunted with his treachery, never suffered a pin-scratch at the hands of the people.

Before Armstrong comes on the scene it is well to give some account of the men he so cruelly betrayed.[1] This becomes the more imperative, inasmuch as unpublished letters of Sheares, containing important explanations, were placed in my hands for historic use by the late Mr. Justice Hayes.

The father of John and Henry Sheares was a banker and member of the Irish Parliament, remarkable for having introduced a bill, that became law in 1766, for the regulation of trials in cases of treason, and under which his sons were afterwards tried. He was a person of culture, too, author of some touching reflections on 'Man in Society, and at his Final Separation from it.' Several passages seem to reveal a presentiment of the great domestic tragedy which he did not live to see. A practical Christian, he published an essay elaborating the great fact that unless man forgives, he can never himself be forgiven; and these inculcations, it is

[1] The fact that Mr. Lecky, when noticing the Sheares, tells his readers to 'see a curious anecdote about them' in a former book of mine, affords in itself an excuse for now offering something new. Vide *England in the Eighteenth Century*, viii. 191.

hoped, helped to calm the closing thoughts of his suffering sons. Mr. Sheares founded a Debtors' Charity, and an amateur performance of 'King Henry IV.,' in aid of it, introduced as its chief histrions the subsequently historic brothers. Their career was dramatic. Henry successfully competed for the hand of Miss Swete with John FitzGibbon, who, as the Lord Clare of after years, is said to have shown that he neither forgot nor forgave. Alicia Swete was an heiress, and eloped with Sheares. In 1792 he visited France to see his children at school. The Revolution was then at its height; he and John Sheares became intimate with Brissot and Rolande, and thenceforth may be dated the birth of that bias which finally made both easy prey for Armstrong. In July 1793, Henry Sheares challenged his early rival, now Lord FitzGibbon, to explain or retract what he called an 'infamous calumny,' conveyed in a speech wherein the chancellor referred to two men, agents of the French Jacobin Club, who had been disseminating its principles in Dublin. But even John Sheares was not the revolutionist which party spirit loved to depict him. The 'Castlereagh Papers' contains a letter in which the writer, Redhead York, describes John at Versailles, falling on his knees and vowing that he would plant a poignard in any heart capable of hurting one silken hair of the Queen of France. In 1792 Henry, a barrister of some years' standing, secured the house, now a bank, 128 Lower Baggot Street, Dublin, then commonly called 'Gallows Road,' and described as such on Rocque's Map of 1756. This house was at that time a corner one; but shortly before his death he assigned a plot bright with flowers whereon the two houses between Sheares's residence and Pembroke Street have been since built. The large block between St. Stephen's Green and Henry's house did not then exist. Miss Steele saw, from her father's back windows in the Green, the soldiers surrounding Sheares's home when, in May 1798, treason was deemed fairly ripe for a *coup*. John Sheares, the junior of Henry by nine years, lived with him, and the utmost fraternal love united both.

Captain John Warneford Armstrong, the descendant of a

Scotch settler in Ireland, held a commission in the King's County Militia, but acted so well the part of a flaming patriot, that Byrne, a democratic bookseller, led Armstrong to his private room and presented him to Sheares as 'a true brother on whom you may implicitly depend.' Henry declined to hold converse unless in presence of his brother John. Armstrong said he would wait until John came. Conversation, however, had commenced before his arrival; he at length appeared with Byrne, and the latter introduced Armstrong in an equally impressive way. Armstrong deposed on the trial that John Sheares said—'I know your principles very well,' and asked him to join the cause by action as he had already done by inclination. Armstrong replied—'I am ready to do everything in my power for it, and if you can show me how I can assist I will serve you to the utmost.' John, an impulsive youth, said that the best way he could help was to gain over the soldiery, and confer with him as to a plan for seizing the royal camp. Armstrong appointed to meet him at Baggot Street with this end; he did so, and on Sunday night, May 13, paid another visit—both brothers being present. On the 15th he called twice; John Sheares said he would like to introduce him to a friend of his, Surgeon (afterwards General) Lawless, with whom he might consult and advise in his absence—he [John] being obliged to go down and organise Cork. All this time Henry Sheares is found reticent, and at some of the interviews he was not present at all. However, on Thursday, the 17th, both brothers appeared to this apparently zealous convert to their cause; Lawless was also by, and (according to the approver's testimony) said: 'He had lately attended a meeting of deputies from almost all the militia regiments, at which meeting there were two of Armstrong's men.' The latter continued with much industry to buzz about the brothers, and evening after evening returned like a bee, Curran said, with his thighs loaded with evidence.

Henry Sheares, now familiar with Captain Armstrong as his constant visitor, let fall some remarks by which the betrayer succeeded in implicating him as having knowledge of the military organisation. This was not enough for Armstrong; that evening he returned to their house. Henry did not appear; John came down and obtained a written introduction from him to a sergeant in his regiment, known to be a United Irishman. The most sickening part of this story has yet to be told. Armstrong continued to worm himself into the hearts of his victims. He accepted their invitation to dinner, mingled with their family, listened to Mrs. Henry Sheares singing at the harp for his entertainment, and, as Curran declared, fondled on his knee the child of the man whom he had marked for doom!

The time was now coming, and coming fast, when the blood of the Sheares' was to be set free—a fact the more painful, when we know that two of their brothers had already given their lives in the service of the King. Armstrong in the year 1843 said, in presence of Mr., afterwards Lord, O'Hagan, that 'Lord Castlereagh encouraged him to dine with the Sheareses in order to gather further information.' On May 21 both brothers were seized. That evening, while John was a prisoner, but as yet ignorant of Armstrong's perfidy, the betrayer paid him a visit of condolence, probably hoping to acquire, during the excitation of his victim, facts which would compromise absent friends. John told his cousin Flemyng that Armstrong suggested 'giving him his keys so that he would seek out all papers which might be of importance and convey them to any friends of his he wished.' This interview took place in the Guard Room at Dublin Castle. Any evidence which could incriminate Henry was far less than that affecting John. It is surprising that the wonderful caution shown by Sheares in earlier days had not made him more guarded with Armstrong; and at this point it is curious to look back at Collins's report (p. 168, *ante*) where he describes Sheares warning the Society of United Irishmen that spies were spreading snares around.

Anyone reading this trial, with the light now available, cannot fail to be struck by a circumstance which has heretofore passed without comment. The outlook was black for the brothers when their counsel, Plunket, Curran, McNally, and Ponsonby, held a conference to see what could be done. A good point was at last detected; one of the Grand Jury who found the bill appeared to be a foreigner, or, as legally termed, an alien. Law books had to be looked up; some searching inquiries made. McNally, meanwhile, had been despatched to the Court of Common Pleas to appease the judges, who had been waiting for some time and waxed impatient. McNally explained that there was a deliberation among the counsel on a serious point of law, and, until they came in, he could say no more. The court made an effort to draw him, but he parried it with seeming firmness. The case stood adjourned, and when Plunket, Curran, and Ponsonby arrived to spring a surprise, they found Attorney-General Toler (the Lord Norbury of after years) fully prepared, not only by a written 'replication' bristling with points, but by an elaborate oral argument, and, between him and the prime-sergeant, they met the objection with a readiness quite wonderful, and which meant ruin to the brothers. The court of course overruled a plea which counsel for the Sheareses hoped would have quashed the proceedings, and no doubt the point had been betrayed to Toler by one of the counsel engaged in the conference.

The Attorney-General said he would go on with the trial of John; but at another conference of their counsel it was decided, in evil hour, that both brothers should go into the dock together and join in their challenge. The luckless suggestion is likely to have come from McNally. Curran was not a great lawyer, his *forte* lay in cross-examination and classic eloquence; he revered McNally, as has been already shown, and he was not the man to differ with him. Two witnesses, it will be remembered, were then necessary to convict for treason in England; the Irish judiciary were satisfied with one. The amazement of the brothers on beholding Armstrong enter the witness-box can be imagined. Curran drew a picture of the children of his client sitting in the mansion where Armstrong was hospitably entertained—the aged mother supported by the devotion of her son—and it was suggested that the informer 'smiled upon this scene, contemplating the havoc he was about to make.' Midnight had passed when the evidence closed. Armstrong's first cousin, Thomas Drought, testified, among other damaging facts, to atheistical expressions used by the approver.[1] Lieutenant Shervinton, an uncle by marriage, heard Armstrong say 'that if there could be no other person found for the purpose, he would, with pleasure, become the executioner of George III., and glory in the deed.' Shervinton replied that if such were his principles he ought to throw up his commission and go over to the enemy at once.

In Lady Wilde's poem, 'The Brothers,' one gains a glimpse of the court:—

' 'Tis midnight, falls the lamplight dull and sickly,
    On a pale and anxious crowd,
  Through the court, and round the judges, thronging thickly,
    With prayers none dared to speak aloud.
  Two youths, two ardent youths, stand prisoners at the bar—
    You can see them through the gloom—
  In pride of life and manhood's beauty, there they are
    Awaiting their death doom.'

When the trial had proceeded for fifteen hours, Curran, sinking with exhaustion, moved for an adjournment, but Toler opposed, and at eight o'clock next morning, when the sickly lamp had sunk and the strong summer sun shone into the black dock, a verdict of 'Guilty' was returned. At these words the brothers fell into each other's arms. Lord Carleton, who presided, was said to have been appointed by Sheares's father the guardian of John, but it is correct to say that he had been only the attached friend of their father.[2] This judge in passing sentence was much affected, and made touching reference to the past. John, with his full blue eyes and open countenance, as Maria Steele describes him, made an earnest appeal for his elder brother's life, declaring that he knew

[1] Ridgeway's *Report of the Trial of the Sheares*, p. 129.

[2] The will of Sheares senior lends no support to this often repeated statement; but he commits his children to the care of Lord Shannon, a relative of their mother. This peer had been created, in 1786, Baron Carleton in the peerage of England, and hence the confusion.

nothing of a fatal manuscript that, admittedly written by John, had been found in Henry's room; all in vain: Toler seemed impatient for the sacrifice, and both were sentenced to die next day. This indecent haste contrasted with the decorum which marked trials in England for treason. Hardy's trial lasted six days, Horne Tooke's seven.

Sir Jonah Barrington prints a painful letter addressed to him by Henry, but which by some mistake did not reach him till the fatal morning. Henry could not believe that an adverse verdict awaited him, and when at last it came, he was utterly stunned. Sheares begs Barrington to see his early rival, Lord Clare:—

> Oh! speak to him of my poor wretched family—my distracted wife, and my helpless children; snatch them from the dreadful horrors which await them. Desire my mother to go to Lord Shannon immediately, and my wife to the Lord Chancellor. . . . We are to receive sentence at three o'clock. Fly, I beseech you, and save a man who will never cease to pray for you—to serve you. Let me hear from you, my dear fellow, as quick as possible. God bless you.
>
> Newgate: eight o'clock.[1]

Sheares's wife sat for hours in a sedan chair at Lord Clare's hall-door; and when, at length, he appeared, she threw herself at his feet, clasped his knees, and implored him to save her husband, but failed. Barrington, leisurely acting upon Henry's letter, had more influence with the chancellor.

> I immediately waited on Lord Clare [he writes]; he read the letter with great attention; I saw he was moved—his heart yielded. I improved on the impression; he only said 'What a coward he is! but what can we do?' He paused. 'John Sheares cannot be spared. Do you think Henry can say anything, or make any species of discovery which can authorise the Lord Lieutenant in making a distinction between them?—if so, Henry may be re-

[1] Barrington, in his *Memoirs of the Union*, gives a facsimile of this letter. Armstrong detached the facsimile from the caustic text, and pasted it into a sort of scrap-book inscribed with his autograph—thus confirming a fact, already known, that, like Bellini's Pollio, he would 'look again, and look exulting, at the ruin he had made.'

prieved.' He read the letter again, and was obviously affected. I had never seen him amiable before. 'Go,' said he, 'to the Prison, see Henry Sheares, ask him this question, and return to me at Cooke's office.' I lost no time, but I found on my arrival that orders had been given that nobody should be admitted without a written permission. I returned to the Castle—they were all at Council. Cooke was not at his office: I was delayed. At length the secretary returned, gave me the order. I hastened to Newgate, and arrived at the very moment the executioner was holding up the head of my friend, and saying, 'Here is the head of a traitor.' [1]

Barrington says nothing of Lord Shannon, who was related to the Sheareses, and it is certain that the message for him miscarried. This peer, with the object of offering condolence, called upon their mother [2] the day of the execution, and was greatly distressed when she threw herself upon her knees to beg the favour of his intervention for John; she did not know that Henry had been implicated, and, of course, was ignorant that either had already suffered death. Lord Shannon, in an agony of mind, and unable to explain, rushed from the room.

There was a butchery displayed in the immolation of the brothers which, if employed at the present day on a beast in the shambles, would evoke angry protest. The 'New Cork Evening Post' of July 23, 1798, while supplying some painful details, bears out Barrington's recollection:—

They requested that they might not continue long exposed to the gaze of the multitude, and, having each an halter fixed round his neck, and a cap drawn over his face, holding by each other's hand, they tottered out upon the platform in front of the prison. In making the rope fast within, John Sheares was hauled up to the block of the tackle, and continued nearly a minute suspended alone before the platform fell. After hanging about twenty minutes,

[1] *Rise and Fall of the Irish Nation*, p. 365. (Paris, 1833.)

[2] She did not long survive the great shock, but a prolonged purgatory was reserved for Henry's widow. She never raised her head, loved to occupy a darkened room, and always spent in fasting and prayer the anniversary of his death. Like her husband she was a Protestant.

both were, at a quarter after three o'clock, let down, when the hangman separated their heads.[1]

Much feeling was roused by this sanguinary act. Classic students who lived in the past started excitedly, comparing the Sheareses to 'the hapless victims' described by Gibbon: 'the two brothers of the Quintilian family whose fraternal love endeared them to posterity—whose bodies seemed animated by one soul—and whose union in death is due to the cruelty of Commodus.' Grattan loudly condemned the men 'whose misrule had brought Ireland to so black a crisis. 'The question men should have asked was, not why was Mr. Sheares upon the gallows?—but why was not Lord Clare along with him?' And two years later, in a speech of resistance to the Union, he declared that the treason of the minister against the liberties of the people was far worse than the rebellion of the people against the minister. But even in the latter sense, Henry Sheares must be held guiltless. John, pouring out to his sister, in an agonised letter, his most secret thoughts, writes: 'Heaven is my witness how assiduously I sought to keep aloof, in any of my political concerns, from *him*;' and there is not a line in the evidence of Armstrong to prove that Henry took any active part in the treason. Addis Emmet, Arthur O'Connor, McNevin—all the men who had been at the head of it, and its very soul, were at that hour in gaol. O'Connor declared that he and his colleagues knew nothing of the Sheareses; and it is certain that neither of them had ever intrigued with France, as O'Connor and the others had done. The names of the Sheareses find no place in the list of marked men that Turner gave Downshire (p. 7, *ante*). This omission can be easily accounted for. O'Connor, in a letter to Dr. Madden, which pointed out some inaccuracies, writes:—

You seem to think the Sheares were leading men in the Union,[2] whereas, I may say, they never entered it, so as to be known to us.

[1] The death-warrant, with written directions from Secretary Cooke, as to the troops to attend at the scaffold, is addressed to Alderman Archer, High Sheriff for Dublin in 1798, and is now preserved by his grandnephew, Rev. Thomas Gray, M.A., F.T.C.D.

[2] The Society of United Irishmen.

The fact is, they were just entering it when they were cut off. It was the younger Sheares's Proclamation, which was an act purely personal, without our knowledge or concurrence, that has misled some to think he and his brother were deeply engaged in the Union.'

The following is one of the letters, already promised, and now published for the first time. It is written by Henry previous to his trial:—

Dear Sir,—Accept my best thanks for the friendly readiness with which you consented to present my letter, which I hope has been received. I am now to trouble you on a subject more immediately relating to my unfortunate situation. I have apply'd as is usual in those cases to my different Friends to come forward on my tryal, and to give me a character such as they think I deserve, and to put it in a manner most likely to produce a beneficial effect. From my knowledge of the goodness of your heart, from a sympathy which I am sure you feel for a fond husband and an affectionate father, from the regard which I am sure you have for Mrs. Sheares, I feel a hope that in this instance you will gladly embrace this opportunity of saving us both. You know that on these occasions a general character is not admissable so that it must apply to the political character. And so far to the domestic as will go to establish the political.

Taking it this way may I hope that you can say that you know me to be a man of domestic habits, fondly attatched to my wife and children, so as to make it highly improbable that I would suffer my political conduct to endanger their happiness; that you consider me a man of liberal but not violent principles; that I go no farther in them than the first characters of opposition in the English and Irish Parliament have done, namely being an advocate for a reform in Parliament and a renovation of the ancient purity of our constitution; that I am not a friend to violent systems, and that I am not an advocate for Revolution.

This is what, from your knowledge of me, I trust you can say without going farther than will justify you to yourself. And for this friendly service I shall seize with pleasure every opportunity of showing how much I shall feel myself obliged to you for it.

As it is usual and necessary for the use of counsel to have the witnesses' names which they are to prove arranged in the brief, I have given directions to my agent to wait on you for that purpose whenever it may be convenient to you, as also to go through the form of giving you a summons.

Your very much obliged and grateful Friend,
HENRY SHEARES.

Kilmainham Gaol: July 10, 1798.

The superscription of this letter has been removed—probably by the recipient—and it seems very likely that he left his friend in the lurch, and did not come forward for his defence. The prosecuting counsel of those days loved to taunt such witnesses with a participation in the views held by the accused; they were browbeaten and bullied, and often left the court wincing under some dark innuendo, dropped with jibing leer.

John, the younger brother, wrote two letters to his sister, from which it is clear that—constituted as the jury panel was at that day—he had no hope of acquittal. The matter omitted deals with some small debts which he wished paid:—

Kilmainham Prison: July 10, 1798.

The troublesome scene of life, my dear Julia, is nearly closed, and the hand that now traces these lines will in a day or two be no longer capable of communicating to a beloved and affectionate family the sentiments of his heart. A painful task yet awaits me. I do not allude to my trial, or my execution. These—were it not for the consciousness I feel of the misery you all will suffer on my account—would be trivial in comparison with the pain I endure in addressing you for the last time. You, Julia, who have been kind to me beyond example; your solicitudes for my welfare have been unremitting, nor did they leave you a moment's happiness. As a wayward fate seems from the earliest moment of my life to have presided over my days, I will not now recapitulate the instances of a perverse destiny that seems to mark me out as the instrument of destruction to all I love. Robert—Richard—and Christopher, dear, valued brothers! If it be true that the mind survives the body, I shall shortly join you, and learn for what wise purpose Heaven thought fit to select me as your destroyer! My mother too—Oh! God! my tender revered mother, I see her torn looks—her broken heart—her corpse! What have I done to deserve this misery? I must forbear these thoughts as much as possible, or I must forbear to write.

My trial comes on the day after to-morrow, and the event is unequivocal. You must summon up all the resolution of your soul, my dear Julia; if there be a chance of snatching my afflicted mother from the grave, that chance must arise from your exertions; my darling Sally, too, will aid you; she will, for a while, suspend her joy at the restoration of her husband to her arms—for of his escape I have no more doubt than I have of my own conviction and its consequences. All, all of you must forget your individual griefs and joys, and unite to save that best of parents from the grave; stand between her and despair; if she will speak of me, sooth her with every assurance calculated to carry consolation to her heart; tell her that my death—though nominally ignominious—should not light up a blush in her face; that she knew me incapable of a dishonourable action or thought; that I died in full possession of the esteem of all those who knew me intimately; that justice will yet be paid to my memory, and my fate be mentioned rather with pride than shame by my friends and relations. Yes, my dear sister, if I did not expect the arrival of this justice to my memory, I should indeed be afflicted at the nominal ignominy of my death, lest it should injure your welfare, and wound the feelings of my family. But, above all things, tell her that at my own request I have been attended in my latest moments by that excellent and pious man, Doctor Dobbin, and that my last prayer was offered up for her. While I feared for Harry's life, hell itself could have no tortures for the guilty beyond what I suffered. I pictured you all, a helpless, unprotected group of females, left to the miseries of your own feelings, and to the insults of a callous, insensible world. Sally, too, stripped of a husband on whom she tenderly doats, and the children of their father—and all by my cursed interloping, and by my residence with them! Yet, Heaven is my witness, how assiduously I sought to keep aloof in any of my political concerns from him. My efforts, however, have kept him clear of any of those matters that have involved me in destruction. When Sally has got him back to her arms, and that I, who caused his danger, and her unhappiness, am no more, she will cease to think of me, perhaps, with reproach. This I trust she will do; she ought, for she herself could never have done more for his salvation than I endeavoured to do. But the scene is changed, I am no longer the frantic thing I was while his danger appeared imminent. A calm sorrow for the sufferings that await you on my account, and a heart-felt regret at being obliged to quit your beloved society for ever, has succeeded; yet all this will soon have an end, and with comfort I already anticipate the moment when your subsiding grief gives you back to the enjoyment of each other. Still, my dearest Julia, even when I shall be no more, your plagues on my account are not likely to cease. . . .

Good night, Julia. I am going to rest, thank God! free from the consciousness of intentional offence, and from any wish tainted with personal resentment.

I seek my bed with pleasure, because there I often fancy myself in the full possession of that domestic happiness which I always regarded as the first of human enjoyments. Pray heaven, I dream of you all night.

John when in France had been an ardent admirer of Rousseau, whose style he now unconsciously catches:—

Wednesday night: July 11.

It is now eleven o'clock, and I have only time to address my beloved Julia in a short eternal farewell. Thou sacred power! whatever be thy name and nature, who has created us the frail and imperfect creatures we are, hear the ardent prayer of a creature now on the eve of an awful change. If thy Divine Providence can be affected by mortal supplication, hear and grant, I beseech Thee, the last wishes of a heart that has ever adored Thy goodness. Let peace and happiness once more visit the bosom of my beloved family. Let a mild grief succeed the miseries they have endured, and when an affectionate tear is generously shed over the dust of him who caused their misfortunes—let all their ensuing days glide on in union and domestic harmony. Enlighten my beloved brother; to him and his invaluable wife grant the undisturbed enjoyment of their mutual love, and as they advance let their means of providing for the sweet pledges of their attachment increase. Let my Julia, my feeling—my too feeling—Julia, feel the consolation she has so often sought for others, let her soul repose at length in the consummation of all her wishes—let her taste that happiness her virtues have so well merited. For my other sisters provide those comforts their situation requires. To my mother, oh, Eternal Power! what gift shall I wish for my matchless parent? Restore to her that peace which I have torn from her—let her forget me in the ceaseless affections of my remaining sisters, and in their growing prosperity—let her taste that happiness which is best suited to her affectionate heart, and when at length she is called home, let her find in everlasting bliss the due reward of a life of suffering virtue. Adieu, my Julia, my light is just out, the approach of darkness is like that of death, since both alike require I shall say farewell for ever. Oh, my dear family, farewell—farewell for ever!

In dealing with Armstrong's conduct,[1] I regret being obliged to take a tone different from that of Mr. Lecky, who has placed his character in a somewhat favourable point of view.

The sealed chest in Dublin Castle, which was opened some years ago, contained McNally's reports, signed 'J. W.' Among them is the following, dated by him, July 14, 1798:—

Lord Cork's First Letter

Lord Cork writes: 'Mr. John Warneford Armstrong was certainly in my regiment and quitted it in a most disgraceful manner. From his conduct while there I would not pay much attention to what he did say, nor give much credit even to his oath.

'I would send a person on purpose did I not think it would be too late.'

[Dated by Lord Cork, July 9.]

Lord Cork's Second Letter, dated 11*th*

'Mr. Sheares's letter did not reach me till to-day. I lose no time to inform the Lord Lieutenant circumstances concerning Mr. Armstrong that I hope may be of service to the unfortunate brothers.'[2] ...

It has transpired [adds McNally], perhaps without foundation, that amnesty is to be held out to-morrow—chearfulness is the consequence.

The letters above alluded to are in the hands of *my friend* [*i.e.* himself]. He has kept them private.

Sheares and McNally had been old friends. Sheares stood

[1] Most writers on the period, in noticing the anomaly that in England two witnesses were necessary in cases of treason, but in Ireland only one, assume that this law continues in force. The law as regards two witnesses dates from the reign of Edward III. It received strengthening touches by the 7 & 8 Will. III. cap. 3. But in 1822 it was extended to Ireland (1 & 2 Geo. IV. cap. 24); and editors of Haydn might note this fact.

[2] General Edward Boyle, eighth Earl of Cork, survived until June 29, 1856, and was the last surviving peer who had sat in the Irish and in the English House of Lords.

by him in the hour of danger.[1] These ties were strengthened by the fact that McNally was counsel for him on the trial.[2] Assuming that McNally had the letters in his possession of which he sends copies, it seems quite indefensible to have kept back Lord Cork's, dated July 9, until the very day on which the brothers were hanged. The execution took place in Dublin at 11.45 A.M. on July 14, 1798. Sir Jonah Barrington mentions that a reprieve was granted but did not arrive in time. It cannot be assumed that McNally humanely used these letters in any other quarter, for, as he assures Cooke, he 'has kept them private.'

Sir Jonah Barrington, who was constantly consulted by the Irish Government, says, when noticing Armstrong's evidence, that, unlike Reynolds—a man of spotted fame and impoverished finances—'Armstrong had a stake and a status to lose; but he took the bold course of sacrificing openly the honour of an officer and a gentleman.' These words he would not use had Lord Cork's letter seen the light.

Armstrong, forty-five years after the execution of his victims, held, in a conversation with Dr. Madden, that Curran's statement as to taking 'baby Sheares' on his knee could not be true because he was never fond of children. An unscrupulous man, however, playing a desperate game, and in the excitement of hot pursuit, may have done things contrary to his usual habits. Armstrong's sole effort was to extort the confidence of the Sheares; and he could not forget that he who takes the child by the hand takes the parent by the heart. It is to be feared that Armstrong's oral 'pooh pooh' is untenable. The following anecdote, now told for the first time, rests on the high authority of Lawrence Parsons, Earl of Rosse. Armstrong, shortly after the death of the Sheareses, when landing from Holyhead at the Pigeon House, and anxious to avoid hostile greetings from the mob who always

[1] See notice of the duel, p. 177, *ante*.

[2] 'Anonymous letters are flying. *My friend* got two this week threatening death and destruction if he exerted himself on the approaching trials.' 'My friend' is the 'cipher' by which McNally always means himself.—J. W. to Cooke, July 10, 1798. (MSS. Dublin Castle.)

awaited the coach which brought to Dublin the usually sea-sick passengers, crossed the Strand to Sandymount, and when midway observed approaching a lady in black accompanied by two children. The latter on recognising Armstrong ran gleefully to meet him.[1] Needless to say they were the widow and orphans of Henry Sheares. Another authentic anecdote ought to be told. The grand-aunt of Mr. Gray, F.T.C.D., gave him the following curious reminiscence. Her family resided near Armstrong in the King's County, and he was intimate at their house. One evening in 1797 the lady heard angry voices in the parlour, where she had left the gentlemen after dinner, and on turning the handle to re-enter a loud smash followed. Armstrong had talked so much treason that it excited her brother to disgust; and this feeling gave place to rage when Armstrong, having left the room for some minutes, had returned dressed in rebel green. The former seized a decanter and hurled it at Armstrong, who ducked, and the panel suffered instead of his head.

The Rev. Dr. Dobbin, an Anglican clergyman who attended the brothers at their execution, now claims to be heard in a letter published for the first time. It is addressed to Captain William Flemyng, their cousin:

Finglas: July 16, 1798.

My dear Sir,—Agreeably to your desire I send the letter which Mr. John Sheares addressed to me, and which I received from his own hands on Saturday morning after his participating in the most solemn rite of our religion. However criminal I may consider his conduct to have been in other respects, of the charges from which he is so anxious his memory may be vindicated I acquit him from my soul; under this conviction I shall chearfully comply with his request, and embrace every opportunity of explaining his real intentions in writing the paper which has so much irritated the public mind. You, I trust, will exert yourself in a similar manner; when you have taken a copy of the letter you will be so good as to return it. The two unfortunate brothers, who forfeited their lives last Saturday to the violated laws of their country, were the sons of an

[1] The late Lord Rosse, a friend of Armstrong's, to Rev. Thomas Gray, M.A., F.T.C.D., who has communicated it to W. J. F.

eminent banker in Cork with whom I had lived, many years since, in intimacy and friendship. The elder brother I was but slightly acquainted with, but Mr. John Sheares I knew more intimately. I admired his uncommon talents, and still more the distinguished humanity and philanthropy which marked the whole of his conversation and demeanour. It was, therefore, with equal surprise and concern I heard of his being under confinement on a charge of high treason. With still greater astonishment, if possible, I heard a paper had been found in his handwriting, the tendency of which was to excite the people to violent and sanguinary proceedings: this was so entirely irreconcileable with the humane and liberal principles which I was persuaded had ever directed the conduct of J. S. that I ardently wished for an explanation. An opportunity soon occurred. On Friday morning I received your letter informing me of the conviction of the two brothers, and conveying an earnest request from J. S. that I should visit him as soon as possible. I undertook the melancholy office with mingled pain and satisfaction. I continued with them some hours that day. What past during the solemn interview was, I trust, suited to the awful circumstances in which they were placed, and becoming the character and situation in which I stood. I shall only trouble you, however, with what relates immediately to the subject of the letter, or is connected with it. The charge of sanguinary intentions he disclaimed as most abhorrent to his nature and repugnant to his principles, asserted his object to prevent the effusion of blood, and assigned more fully and more at large the motives and reasons contained in his letter. The whole was delivered with a serious, solemn, and unembarrassed air, such as usually accompanies truth, and must have imprest on my mind the fullest conviction of his sincerity. There is one fact he mentioned on this occasion, which I shall relate to you as nearly as I can in his own words: 'To the taking away of the life of a fellow creature where it can be prevented my nature is so abhorrent that I was called by some of my democratic friends "the Informer": assassination was mentioned, and I reprobated the idea with horror and positively declared that, unless it was instantly given up, I would myself inform against them: in consequence of my peremptory declaration it was given up, and the lives of some persons were preserved.'

On my strongly representing to him the fatal and unjustifiable part he had taken, and the miserable condition of his country, he made the following reply: 'Dr. Dobbin, many wished for reform who did not think of rebellion, but you know the progress of the human mind; where demands, just in the opinion of those who make them, instead of concession produce further coercion, discontents are encreased, and a man is gradually led on step by step to lengths he would in the beginning shudder at.'

His behaviour with respect to his near relatives was tender and affecting; resigned to his own fate, he expressed the strongest desire to save, if possible, the life of his brother. When I was parting from him at my last visit, he conjured me in visible emotion with tears in his eyes to visit his poor mother and endeavour to console her.

Adieu, my dear Sir,[1] most truly yours,

WILLIAM DOBBIN.

Finglas: July 16, 1798.

The enclosure does not seem to have been sent back by Flemyng as requested. The original of John Sheares's letter is now before me, preserved within the decaying folds of Dobbin's manuscript:—

To the Rev. Dr. Dobbin.

My dear Sir,—As to-morrow is appointed for the execution of my brother and me, I shall trouble you with a few words on the

[1] The late Dr. Ireland, a nonagenarian, who had filled official posts in Dublin Castle, knew Flemyng, to whom Dr. Dobbin's letter is addressed. Flemyng had been in the East India Company's service, but joined the United Irishmen during leave of absence from Bengal, in which place he had known Lord Cornwallis, its then Governor-General, but later Viceroy of Ireland. 'Flemyng,' says Dr. Ireland, 'attained popularity for having, with his own arm, killed the largest boar seen in India, an animal which had often ripped open horses and oxen.' One night, at Dublin, the Viceroy sent for Flemyng and surprised him by saying that all that had passed between him and the Sheares was known to the Privy Council. The Lord Lieutenant, then placing his arm on Flemyng's shoulder, said: 'Let not another day elapse, or not all my influence can save you from the gallows. Start for India at once; those fellows at Ghazapore must be put down; you are just the man to do it. You will be gazetted to your company ere you reach Bombay.' Flemyng went to India, did the work, rose, and died rich. In 1805 he again met Lord Cornwallis, on his arrival in India charged with the re-assumption of its reins of government; with gratitude he acknowledged the timely service he had rendered him in 1798. Death was written in the face of Lord Cornwallis as he landed at Calcutta: India, the grave of Europeans, folded him to its embrace, and a few weeks later the soldier-statesman was no more.—These facts I heard from Richard Stanley Ireland shortly before his death on March 13, 1875.

subject of the writing produced on my trial, importing to be a proclamation. The first observation I have to make is that a considerable part of that scrolled production was suppressed on my trial; from what motive, or whether by accident, I will not say—certain it is that the part which has not appeared must have in a great measure shewn what the true motives were that caused that writing, if it had been produced. To avoid a posthumous calumny in addition to the many and gross misrepresentations of my principles, moral and political, I shall state, with the most sacred regard to Truth, what my chief objects were in writing, or rather in attempting to write, it, for it is but a wretched, patched and garbled attempt. It was contained in a sheet of paper and in one or two pieces more, which are not forthcoming—the sheet alone is produced. It is written in very violent revolutionary language, because, as it in the outset imports, after a revolution had taken place could it alone be published—and the occurrence of such an event I thought every day more probable. The first sentence that has produced much misrepresentation is that which mentions that some of the most obnoxious members of the Government have already payed the forfeit of their lives—I cannot state the words exactly. From this it is concluded I countenanced assassination—Gracious God!—but I shall simply answer that this sentence was merely supposititious, and founded on that common remark, oftenest made by those who least wished it verified, that if the people had ever recourse to force and succeeded, there were certain persons whom they would most probably destroy. The next most obnoxious sentence—more obnoxious to my feelings, because calculated to misrepresent the real sentiments of my soul—is that which recommends to give no quarter to those who fought against their native country [unless they should speedily join the Standard of Freedom]. With this latter part of the sentence I found two faults, and therefore drew my pen over it as above. The first fault was that the word 'speedily' was too vague and might encourage the sanguinary immediately to deny quarter, which was the very thing the whole sentence was intended to discountenance and prevent—the next fault was that it required more than ever should be required of any human being, namely, to fight against his opinions from fear. The sentence was intended to prevent the horrid measure of refusing quarter from being adopted: by appearing to acquiesce in it at some future period, when the inhuman thirst for it should no longer exist. But as the sentence now stands in two parts of the sheet it would appear as if I sought to enforce the measure I most abhor. To prevent it was, in fact, one of my leading motives for writing the address: but I had also three others that are expressed on the piece or pieces of paper, which made part of the writing, but which, tho' laid all together in the same desk, have disappeared.

The three objects alluded to are these, the protection of property, preventing the indulgence of *revenge*, and the strict forbiddal of injuring any person for religious differences.

I know it is said that I call on the people to take *vengeance* on their oppressors, and enumerate some of their oppressions. But this is the very thing that enables me to point out the difference between *private revenge* and *public vengeance*. The former has only a retrospective and malignant propensity, while the latter, though animated by the recollection of the past, has ever only in view the removal of the evil and of the possibility of occurrence. Thus the assassin *revenges* himself; but the patriot avenges his country of it's enemies, by overthrowing them, and depriving them of all power again to hurt it: In the struggle some of their lives may fall, but these were not the objects of his vengeance. In short, even the Deity is said in this sense to be an *avenging* Being; but who deems him *revengeful*? Adieu, my dear sir. Let me entreat you, whenever an opportunity shall occur, that you will justify my principles on these points. Believe me your sincere friend,

John Sheares.

Newgate: 12 o'clock at night, July 13.[1]

The Proclamation which brought John Sheares to the scaffold (Henry had no part in it, and died, so far, innocent) ended with these words:—

Vengeance, Irishmen, vengeance on your oppressors! Remember that thousands of your dearest friends have perished by their merciless orders! Remember their burnings—their rackings—their torturings—their military massacres, and their legal murders. Remember Orr!

These declamatory words of a young barrister and amateur tragedian, who probably had no serious design of going red-

[1] The above letter of John Sheares, enclosed in Dr. Dobbin's communication, has, I find, been printed by Dr. Madden; but, on comparing the original document with the printed copy, no fewer than thirteen discrepancies are detected.

handed into revolution, were by no means confined to *his* mouth. In the Appendix will be found some account of William Orr. Meanwhile, the late Henry Grattan, son of the greater Grattan, writes:—

'Remember Orr!' were words written everywhere—pronounced everywhere. I recollect, when a child, to have read them on the walls—to have heard them spoken by the people. Fortunately I did not comprehend their meaning. The conduct of the Irish Government was so reprobated, that at a public dinner in London, given in honor of Mr. Fox's birthday, in one of the rooms where the Duke of Norfolk, Lord Oxford, Mr. Erskine, Sir Francis Burdett, and Horne Tooke sat, two of the toasts were,—'The memory of Orr—basely M—D—D. May the execution of Orr provide places for the Cabinet of St. James's at the Castle!'

There was very little legal evidence to show that the proclamation was in John's handwriting. It was found in an open box in a room to which many people had access.

The fate of the Sheareses was soon forgotten, but sometimes a pilgrim in thoughtful mood wended his way to their last resting place. William Henry Curran sent to the 'New Monthly Magazine,' in 1822, an account of St. Michan's, Church Street, Dublin. Here in 1795 the Sheareses had attended the Rev. Wm. Jackson's funeral. St. Michan's possesses the rare virtue of preserving human remains.[1] Curran was struck on entering the crypt to find that decay had been more busy with the tenement than the tenant:—

In some instances the coffins had altogether disappeared; in others the lids or sides had mouldered away, exposing the remains within, still unsubdued by death from their original form. . . . I had been told that they (the Sheare's) were here, and the moment the light of the taper fell upon the spot they occupy, I quickly recognised them by one or two circumstances that forcibly recalled the close of their career—the headless trunks and the remains of their coarse, unadorned penal shells. Henry's head was lying beside his brother; John's had not been completely detached by the blow of the executioner—one of the ligaments of the neck still connects it with the

[1] The soil and walls of the crypt being a compound of argillaceous earth and carbonate of lime, a singularly antiseptic property is thus imparted.

body. I knew nothing of these victims of ill-timed enthusiasm except from historical report; but the companion of my visit to their grave had been their cotemporary and friend, and he paid their memories the tribute of some sighs, which, even at this distance of time, it would not be prudent to heave in a less privileged place.

The late Richard Davis Webb, when a boy, also went to see those reliques. With a penknife he severed the ligament mentioned by Curran, and carried away the head to his own home, where it remained twenty years. He finally regretted having taken it, and offered it to Dr. Madden, at whose door the gruesome relic duly arrived.

The head was finely formed [writes this good physician], but the expression of the face was that of agony. The mark of very violent injuries, done during life to the right eye, nose, and mouth, were particularly apparent; the very indentation round the neck, from the pressure of the rope, was visible; and there was no injury to the cervical vertebræ occasioned by any instrument.

These horrible marks were doubtless caused by the brutal and bungling way in which the executioner had done his work. Madden, in good taste, restored to the shrunken trunk its long-lost head. When John Sheares, in his last letter, spoke of 'an affectionate tear shed over his dust,' he little foresaw the grim irony by which the words of the Burial Service—'Dust to dust, ashes to ashes'—were to be thwarted. He never married. Roche, in his 'Essays of an Octogenarian,' says that, happening to occupy the rooms in Dublin where John Sheares had once lived, he discovered, in a recess, a package of his letters, which, on finding them addressed to a lady, he instantly burned. Rich material for romance was thus, happily, lost.

John Sheares's last letter to his sister makes feeling reference to his natural daughter Louise, then aged seven years. Julia Sheares gave from her pinched resources what served to educate this girl. Louise married a Mr. Coghlan, but, owing to his loose habits, left him. John's dramatic dash descended to his child. She became a popular actress, and was known on the London stage as 'Miss White.' Here the gentle histrion went through many struggles, and was pursued by much adulation. But panting—like Goldsmith's hare—to the spot from whence at first she flew, Louise returned to Ireland, and died there in 1828.

Whilst the parchment features of the Sheareses wore an agonised expression, and their orphans shivered in the storms of a cold, neglectful world,[1] John Warneford Armstrong battened on his blood-money, and posed as a prosperous and popular man. Lord Cork's damaging account of his antecedents in the letter which remained near a century sealed will be remembered. The magisterial bench hailed his adhesion; he took a leading place on the grand jury of his county; Burke's 'Landed Gentry' enrolled him in its ranks.

In 1843 the name of Captain Armstrong again came before the public, in connection with the prosecution of his servant, Egan, for stealing, among other effects, a gold medal in commemoration of his discoveries in 1798. The late F. Thorpe Porter, from whose lips I had the following anecdote, was on the bench with Sir Nicholas FitzSimon as police magistrate, when the latter, recognising through a glass door the well-known figure of Armstrong approaching, said: 'Here is Sheares' Armstrong; I don't care to meet him,' and retired into a private room. FitzSimon, as former member for the King's County in which Armstrong lived, had been in pleasant touch with him, and often chuckled at his quaint conceits. Armstrong with his accustomed swagger took his seat, uninvited, on the bench. Mr. Porter said that he had not the honour of his acquaintance, and requested him to withdraw. 'I always had this privilege from Major Sirr,' replied Armstrong, unabashed; 'and I am a magistrate for the King's County.' 'This not being the King's County,' retorted Porter, 'I must only repeat my request. If you continue to sit here people in court might suppose that you were—what I should much regret—a friend of mine.'

Sir Thomas Redington, the Under-Secretary, informed this

[1] In 1860, a daughter of Henry Sheares, then seventy-two years of age, was an occupant of an almshouse in Cork.

magistrate that Armstrong had reported to the Government his withering words, but that it was decided to take no action in the matter.

Soon after a case came on for hearing before the judicial Chairman of the King's County, to whom the Clerk of the Peace, speaking in a half-whisper, said: 'Sheares' Armstrong' (a nickname by which he was well known) 'has some testimony to offer which it might be well for you to hear.' This was done, and the chairman, in summing up, said: 'I now come to the evidence of Mr. *Sheares* Armstrong'—and he then proceeded to observe upon it, innocently using—over and over again—the stigmatising nickname, to the amusement of the audience and the agony of Armstrong. All was not *couleur de rose* with this prosperous person. 'The Law Scrutiny and Attornies Guide,' a local satire, published at Dublin in 1807, notices as a judgment, a fact which can be regarded merely as a coincidence: 'Shortly after he gave his ever-memorable evidence on the trial of these unfortunate gentlemen—the Sheareses—he was afflicted with a fistula in the face, which rendered him as remarkable an object as Cain is supposed to have been after the murder of his brother.' This writer finally exclaims:—

> Unhappy Sheares—an Armstrong thus caressed
> Thy infant, hanging at its mother's breast;
> Friendship pretending, revelled at thy board,
> While round your neck he tied the fatal cord! [1]

Stings like these must have severely tried his patience. His temper was of as hair-trigger a character as the pistols which he carried for protection. Robert Maunsell, a leading solicitor, of whom Armstrong was a client, informed me that the captain, on one occasion, when entertained by Mrs. Maunsell in Merrion Square, smashed, by an awkward swing-

[1] Halkett and Laing's *Dictionary of Anonymous Literature* fails to give the author of this book; and the British Museum Catalogue is silent upon it. The *Dublin University Magazine*, vol. lviii. 725, states that the writer was Counsellor [William] Norcott. Called to the Irish Bar in 1797, he was probably present at the Sheareses' trial. See p. 190, *ante*.

ing gesture, the leg of the chair on which he sat, whereupon his exclamation was not a gallant apology, but—'D——n your chairs, madam!' This, Maunsell said, was intoned with a nasal twang—the penalty paid for the *lupus*—which ate into his beauty fifty years before.

To earn 500*l.* a year Armstrong may have done something more than merely to ensnare the Sheareses, although hitherto he has been credited with that exploit alone. William Lawless was Professor of Physiology at the College of Surgeons, Dublin, a man of mark, and very highly connected. Immediately after his interview with Armstrong at Sheares's house we find a warrant issued for his arrest, and it was not Armstrong's fault if he failed to meet the fate of the brothers. A timely hint from Surgeon-general Stewart put Lawless on the alert. By hair-breadth escapes he eluded his pursuers, and at last reached France, where he became a distinguished general under Napoleon.

Armstrong, when stealing on the Sheareses, sought to kill another bird with the same stone. He was clearly making notes for the ruin of Lawless as well, and mentioned on Sheares's trial, among other remarks alleged to have been made by Lawless, that the trees near the Royal camp would come handy in suspending prisoners captured by the rebel force. Lawless had luckily escaped at this time, but at once wrote indignantly denying that he had ever made so horrible a suggestion. Previous to his flight he had resided in French Street, Dublin, whither Major Sirr proceeded with a warrant both for his arrest and that of John Sheares, who had been in daily conference with him. While Sirr was engaged in searching Lawless's house a knock came to the door, Sheares entered, and Sirr at once said, 'You are my prisoner.'

Lawless had seen Lord Edward constantly during the period of his concealment; but Armstrong knew nothing of the chieftain's movements, and, of course, had no hand in his betrayal, though some infer to the contrary from a passing remark made by Mr. Froude.[1] But he qualified for his pension

[1] Froude, iii. 341.

by a general vigilance and activity in support of that red system and policy which John Sheares's proclamation brands. Armstrong having been questioned by Curran as to three peasants which he had taken prisoners in '98, he replied: 'We were going up Blackmore Hill, under Sir James Duff; there was a party of rebels there. We met three men with green cockades. One we shot, another we hanged, and the third we flogged and made a guide of.' [1]

The murder of a little child by a yeoman named Woolagan excited, even in those days, a feeling of abhorrence, and Plowden, in his 'History of Ireland,' notices Woolagan's acquittal by the court-martial which tried him, but does not cite the evidence. This we find in the 'Dublin Magazine' for October 1798. There it will be seen that the murderer threw the onus on the general orders issued by Captain Armstrong. Phillips and Curran, who have written of the latter, do not appear to have read this trial. The crime was proved and not denied, yet Woolagan was acquitted. But the Viceroy, Lord Cornwallis, condemned the verdict, and disqualified the president of the court-martial, Lord Enniskillen, from again presiding in that capacity.

When the troubled times had passed Armstrong smoothed his couch for repose, and on October 18, 1806, married Miss Anne Turner, by whom he had two daughters. For several years he lived on the Continent and in America. He had the courage at last to return to Ireland and settle down in the King's County. The late Maurice Leyne wrote me word that he met him—attended by two policemen, with loaded arms—on board the packet which plies on the Shannon, and that when Armstrong was landing near Clonmacnoise, a boatman, with vengeful malice, addressed him as 'Mr. Sheares,' pretending to mistake the name.

Captain Armstrong, though hot-tempered, was capable of generous acts, and his redeeming points must not be ignored. He was a bad hater, a good laugher. Affable to all, he fre-

[1] *The Trial of the Sheareses*, reported by Ridgeway, p. 129.

quently went out of his way to be civil; and with him sweet words had more than their proverbial value. In days when landlordism reigned with iron sceptre, he showed indulgence to his tenantry; but when giving leases, or using his influence with higher lords of the soil for that end, he cunningly got his own life inserted as a beneficial interest to the tenants. Thus in the hot-bed of Ribbonism he gloried to the end in a sort of charmed life. His will, witnessed by Patrick Egan and Lundy Dickenson, is dated August 21, 1856. He survived until April 20, 1858, when he died at Ballycumber House, Clara, King's County, aged eighty-seven, after having drawn from Dublin Castle 500*l.* a year, or about 29,464*l.* Castlereagh, who recommended him for a pension, and predeceased him by nearly forty years, might have deemed this sum excessive had he lived to see it paid.

Seeking to disarm prejudice and cultivate rural friendship, Armstrong maintained polite relations with the peasantry. He would enter their cabins, sit with rude hosts, and converse with their wives on various domestic points solely of interest to themselves. We must assume that, consistently with his later utterance, their children attracted from him no moving manifestation of regard. His long life had one decided advantage. It is stated that he lived down every political enemy and contemporary, becoming in the end downright popular. His face, familiar from childhood even to old men, had become at last endeared to early memories, and Captain Fuller, who attended his funeral, testifies to the almost incredible fact that he saw some well-known Ribbonmen, who were present, weep, and horny hands upraised which, in the hot blood of youth, had dispensed 'the wild justice of revenge.' [1]

[1] The late Sir Robert Peel.

APPENDIX

LORD DOWNSHIRE'S MYSTERIOUS VISITOR

(*Vide* p. 8, *ante.*)

THE following is a *résumé* of some earlier evidence which had convinced me that the informer whose name Mr. Froude says is still wrapped in mystery [1] could be only Samuel Turner, LL.D., barrister-at-law.

Speaking of Lord Edward Fitzgerald, Mr. Froude says: 'His meeting with Hoche on the Swiss frontier was known only to very few persons. Hoche himself had not revealed it even to Tone.'

But Turner knew a vast deal about the arrangements with Hoche. An intercepted letter addressed by Reinhard, the French Minister at Hamburg, to De la Croix, and written on July 12, 1797, may be found in the 'Correspondence of Lord Castlereagh,' and assigned by mistake to the year 1798. In this letter Reinhard tells De la Croix that he sent Turner to General Hoche. From Hoche [2] himself Turner most likely learned of the secret interview between Lord Edward and the French general.

But what proof have we that Lord Downshire's muffled visitor had had himself an interview with Hoche?

Mr. Froude at some pages distant from the part where he refers to Lord Edward's meeting with Hoche, when recurring to Downshire's visitor, whose identity was 'kept a secret even from the Cabinet,' states, from knowledge acquired after reading the spy's secret letters, 'He had actually conferred with Hoche and De la Croix.'

The intercepted letter in the 'Castlereagh Papers' refers at much length to the proceedings of Lord Edward Fitzgerald,

[1] Froude, iii. 277.

[2] See *Castlereagh Correspondence*, i. 285.

MacNevin, and Turner; but Turner in this letter is called *Furnes.* The general index to that work states[1] that Furnes is an alias for Samuel Turner; and further he is described as 'an Irish rebel.' Had the noble editor supposed that Turner was a spy in the pay of the Crown, this letter would doubtless have been suppressed in common with others which Dr. Madden misses. Lord Londonderry brought out his brother's correspondence in 1848, during the 'Young Ireland' agitation, and was careful to let few secrets appear.

'He had accompanied the Northern delegacy to Dublin,' proceeds Mr. Froude, 'and had been present at the discussion of the propriety of an immediate insurrection.'

John Hughes, of Belfast, an officer in the Society of the United Irishmen, was arrested immediately after Turner opened communication with Downshire, and while in gaol turned King's evidence. From the sworn testimony of John Hughes we learn that, in June 1797, he was summoned by Lowry and Teeling to attend a meeting in Dublin of delegates from the different provinces of Ireland, in order to receive a return of the strength of the United Irishmen. Whilst he was in Dublin, in June 1797, Teeling invited him to meet some friends at his lodgings, including Tony McCann of Dundalk, *Mr.*[2] *Samuel Turner,* John and Patrick Byrne, Lowry, Dr. MacNevin, and others.[3] The leaders differed as to the expediency of an immediate rising. 'He met the above mentioned persons at several other times in Dublin, in June 1797.'[4]

'The Northern delegate had been present at the discussion of the propriety of an immediate insurrection. The cowardice or the prudence of the Dublin faction had disgusted him,' writes Mr. Froude.

The Northern leader who was disgusted with the prudence of the Papist conspirators in Dublin must have been Turner. In the 'Castlereagh Papers' is a letter of Reinhard, the French Minister, stating, on the authority of Turner, 'that it was of dilatoriness and indecision several members of the Committee were accused; that the

[1] *Castlereagh Correspondence,* i. 285.

[2] Turner's is the only name in the list to which Hughes prefixes this title of courtesy, which shows that he was looked up to as a man superior to his fellows.

[3] *Castlereagh Correspondence,* iv. 504.

[4] *Report of the Secret Committee of the House of Lords,* 1798, pp. 26–8.

Northern province, feeling its oppression and its strength, was impatient to break forth.' [1]

Reinhard adds, what will surprise many regarding Lord Edward: 'Macnevin and Lord Fitzgerald are of the moderate party. Furness [Turner] is for a speedy explosion, and it is some imprudences into which his ardent character hurried him that obliged him to leave the country, whereas the conduct of Macnevin has been circumspect.' [2]

Among the men whom Hughes swears he met in June 1797, with the Northern delegates in Dublin, were *Turner*, Teeling, MacCann, John Byrne [Union Lodge, Dundalk], Dr. Macnevin, Colonel Plunket,[3] and Andrew Comyn of Galway. These men—Turner excepted—were all Roman Catholics; so were John Keogh, Braughall, MacCormick, and other influential Dublin leaders—whose names do not appear. Tone was abroad. Downshire's visitor speaks of the men he met in Dublin as 'Papists' whose prudence and cowardice disgusted him, and he came to the conclusion that the two parties could not amalgamate.

Mr. Froude, again describing Downshire's visitor, writes: 'He had seen Talleyrand and talked with him at length on the condition of Ireland.'

The 'Castlereagh Papers' contain a remarkable letter, headed 'Secret Intelligence,' and describing very fully an interview with Talleyrand in reference to an invasion of Ireland. On the third page of his letter the spy writes: 'Enclosure containing the cyphers *I sent to the Marquis of Downshire*.'[4]

To this letter I must again return.

Mr. Froude states that Downshire's visitor had discovered one of the objects of the Papists to be a seizure of property, and had determined to separate himself from the conspiracy.

Turner belonged to a family of Cromwellian settlers. This we learn from Prendergast's 'Cromwellian Settlement of Ireland,'

[1] *Castlereagh Correspondence*, i. 283. Turner was known by the *alias* of 'Furness,' partly, perhaps, in allusion to his seemingly red-hot patriotism.

[2] *Ibid.*

[3] James Hope in his narrative speaks of Colonel Plunket as at first a flaming rebel, who had been assigned to the command of Roscommon; but Lord Carleton, in a manuscript note to *Irish Pamphlets*, vol. 129 (Nat. Lib. of Ireland), says that on the eve of action he surrendered to Dr. Law, Bishop of Elphin. Plunket was tried by court-martial and hanged.

[4] *Castlereagh Correspondence*, ii. 231.

p. 417. The letter (quoted above), printed in the 'Castlereagh Papers,' and acknowledging to have spied for Lord Downshire, mentions that the writer's 'most particular friends' were men 'who feared in a Revolution the loss of their property, especially such as held their estates by grants of Oliver Cromwell.' [1]

Mr. Froude says that when the mysterious visitor threw back his disguise Downshire recognised in him the son of a gentleman of good fortune in the North of Ireland. Lord Downshire is part proprietor of Newry, where Turner lived, and Hill Street, Newry, is named after the Downshires, just as Turner's Hill, Newry, is called after the Turners.[2]

It may be added that Jacob Turner, of Turner Hill, in the county of Armagh, esquire, by his will, dated April 27, 1803, acquits and discharges his son 'Samuel from a judgment debt obtained by me against him for 1,500*l.*' [3]

'"The person" had been a member of the Ulster Revolutionary Committee,' writes Mr. Froude. This Turner admittedly was.

'He had *fled* with others,' he tells Lord Downshire when describing how he came to leave Ireland and settle at Hamburg.

James Hope, in his narrative supplied to Dr. Madden in 1846, when noticing Turner, writes, 'He *fled* and settled in Hamburg, where he was entrusted by the Directory with carrying on the correspondence between the Irish and French Executives.' [4]

Mr. Froude says that the mysterious man was intimate with all the United Irish refugees at Hamburg, received instructions

[1] *Castlereagh Correspondence*, ii. 232.

[2] Every man desiring to become a barrister is obliged to lodge a memorial describing himself and his parentage. Anxious to ascertain whether the description of Lord Downshire's friend would apply to Turner, as the son of a gentleman of property in Ulster, I applied at the King's Inns, Dublin, to be allowed to see how Turner described himself—but was refused, although the object was explained to be one purely historical. This greatly retarded my inquiries, which were begun many years ago. At last an examination of the wills and the entrance-book of Trinity College, Dublin, established all that I had surmised, and the following letter, which I find in the Pelham MSS., is further important in this connection:—'The arms belonging to Mr. Turner, senior, a magistrate near Newry, were taken from him at the time of the general search for arms in that county. I believe that his conduct has been misconceived owing to the conduct of his son, and, if you see no particular objection to it, I should be glad that his arms should be restored to him' (Pelham to General Lake, Phœnix Park, August 3, 1797).

[3] *Records of the Probate Court, Dublin.*

[4] *United Irishmen*, 1st edit. i. 252.

from the Home Office to open a correspondence with rebel leaders, and had the *entrée* to the house of Lady Edward Fitzgerald.

No wonder that Lord Downshire's friend should command these exceptional facilities for spying when we know, on the authority of James Hope, a veteran rebel of Ulster, that Samuel Turner was the accredited agent at Hamburg of the 'United Irishmen.'[1]

Mr. Froude tells us that he revealed such evidence of his power to be useful—at Hamburg—that Pitt was extremely anxious to secure his help.

As Turner is shown by Hope to have been the authorised agent of the 'United Irishmen' at Hamburg, the reason becomes clear why Pitt was so anxious to secure a man who had access at that place to all the secrets of his party.

'An arrangement was concluded,' writes Mr. Froude. 'He continued at Hamburg, as Lady Edward's guest and most trusted friend, saw every one who came to her house, kept watch over her letter-bag, was admitted to close and secret conversations upon the prospect of French interference in Ireland with Reinhard,[2] the Minister of the Directory there, and he regularly kept Lord Downshire informed of everything which would enable Pitt to watch the conspiracy.'

The first volume of Castlereagh should here be opened. At pp. 277–286 will be found three intercepted letters, addressed by Reinhard at Hamburg to De la Croix, revealing minute particulars regarding the United Irish envoys, and bearing testimony to the zealous help rendered to the conspiracy by Turner.

'I showed Reinhard Lowry's letter,' quotes Mr. Froude.

Turner and Lowry were old allies in Ireland, and had no secrets between them. The sworn information of John Hughes mentions that he saw Lowry, Turner, and Teeling engaged on a committee for conducting the defence of United Irishmen at the Antrim and Down Assizes in February, 1797.

Mr. Froude tells us that the spy who hurried to London and sought Lord Downshire was able to describe an important letter which was on the point of going over from Barclay Teeling in

[1] *United Irishmen*, 1st edit. i. 240. These references to Turner, supplied by Hope, were not reprinted by Dr. Madden in the second edition of his *United Irishmen*. 'The Cornwallis Papers' had not then appeared, disclosing the name of Samuel Turner as a recipient of a pension for important but unexplained services in connection with the Rebellion.

[2] Bourrienne's *Life of Napoleon* describes Reinhard as a Lutheran.

France to Arthur O'Connor.[1] Great confidence must have been reposed by Teeling in the man who could tell all this; and such confidence could be earned only by old intimacy and association. What proof is there that early intimacy existed in Ireland between Barclay Teeling and Samuel Turner?

The correspondence of Major Sirr, the Fouché of Dublin, with minor spies is preserved in Trinity College, Dublin. These papers contain an information in which Dr. Conlan of Dundalk denounces, as deep in the conspiracy, Samuel Turner, Barclay Teeling, Lowry, and Byrne. He describes some hair-breadth escapes of Barclay Teeling, Turner, and Lowry, and how they spent one night in a barn near Dundalk. Conlan had been a United Irishman, who finally brought to the gibbet his cousin Hoey and Marmion[2] of Dundalk.

After the betrayer had hurried from Hamburg to London to sell his secrets to Pitt, and then as suddenly disappeared, 'he wrote to Lord Downshire,' observes Mr. Froude, 'saying that he had returned to his old quarters, for fear he might be falling into a trap.'

In fact, as Mr. Froude shows, he was in mortal terror of the assassin's knife. Conlan's sworn information, describing the previous doings of Teeling and Turner in Ireland, mentions how Teeling, Corcoran, and Byrne had a password for putting informers out of the way. Whenever one was detected he was sent to some United Irishman with the password, 'Do you know Ormond Steel?' 'But,' adds Conlan, 'there never was occasion for this.'[3] Turner's treachery was of enormous magnitude, and most momentous in its results. Once a man of indomitable courage, conscience made him an arrant coward in the end.

'I feared,' writes the betrayer to Lord Downshire, 'lest Government might not choose to ratify our contract, and, being in their power, would give me my choice either to come forward as evidence or suffer martyrdom myself. Having no taste for an exit of this kind, I set out and arrived here safe.'[4]

[1] The betrayer, in his letter to Lord Downshire, states that Lowry wrote from Paris to him on October 11, 1797, in great despondency on account of Hoche's death.

[2] Mr. Cashel Hoey, grandson of Conlan's victim, an important Government official in London, decorated by the Crown, died Jan. 6, 1892. Antony Marmion, author of *The Maritime Ports of Ireland*, was the son of Conlan's second victim.

[3] The Sirr MSS. Trin. Coll. Dublin.

[4] Froude's *English in Ireland*, iii. 284.

His dread of 'Ormond Steel' is further proved by Portland's words in reply to the Viceroy Camden, who vainly begged that he might come over to Dublin—'he is convinced he would go to utter destruction.'[1]

Speaking of Napper Tandy, Mr. Froude says of the veiled informer that he 'had been naturally intimate with the other Irish refugees.'[2]

Tandy, in the chapter devoted to him, tells how he and three other Irish refugees had been invited at Hamburg by 'T.' to sup, and were betrayed. Watty Cox, a sound authority on such points, broadly states in the 'Irish Magazine' for January 1809, p. 34, that Tandy and his comrades were 'betrayed by TURNER.'

'He had come to England to sell his knowledge to Pitt,' says Mr. Froude.

It wil be seen that the price paid to *Samuel Turner* is officially reported in Dublin Castle. For centuries it had been the custom for England to charge her Pension List on the Irish Establishment. Irish spies and informers are generally of a low type. Reynolds—perhaps the most important of them—could not spell, as his letters, placed in our hands by Sir W. Cope, show. The same remark applies to the correspondence of other informers printed by Dr. Madden. The letters of Mr. Froude's spy are those of an educated man, and show that he corresponded and conversed in French. Samuel Turner was well qualified for all this and more, having graduated in the University of Dublin.[3]

These are but a few of the reasons which satisfied me that the betrayer described by Mr. Froude was SAMUEL TURNER. I arrived at my conclusions slowly—according as certain facts, 'far between,' presented themselves in the field of research. But the reader, if he cares to trace the career of this man, and does not object to meet a repetition or two, will find an array of circumstantial evidence amounting to moral demonstration. It may be added that documental proof finally came to crown these researches.

[1] Froude's *English in Ireland*, iii. 305. [2] *Ibid.* p. 281.

[3] Samuel Turner, B.A., T.C.D., 1786; LL.D., T.C.D. 1787, *College Calendar*. He claimed to have descended, I believe, from Dr. Samuel Turner, M.A. of Oxford in 1605, whose parliamentary career and daring spirit are noticed in L'Estrange's *History of the Reign of Charles I.*

GENERAL NAPPER TANDY

(See chap. viii. *ante*.)

THE late Mr. Allingham, of Ballyshannon—father of William Allingham the poet—in one of his last letters, dated April 25, 1866, recalls a strange incident. 'Should you treat of the stirring period of 1798,' he writes, 'perhaps the following little fact may be acceptable. Some forty years ago I chanced to be on a visit at the hospitable residence of the late N. Foster, Esq., in the Rosses;[1] he told me of J. Napper Tandy having put in to the Rosses, in the year 1798, with a French ship of war, the "Anacréon," and how he at once hoisted an Irish flag emblazoned with the words "Erin go Bragh." Tandy was then a general in the French service. He had with him, for distribution, a sheaf of proclamations, addressed to the Irish nation; they had been printed in France, and he left several copies at Mr. Foster's. I got Miss Grace Foster to take an exact copy of the strange document, and which now I send you.

'The French General Rey also had a grandiloquent proclamation with him, beginning "The soldiers of the Great Nation have landed on your coast, well supplied with arms and ammunition of all kinds, with artillery worked by those who have spread terror amongst the ranks of the best troops in Europe, headed by French officers; they come to break your fetters, and restore you to the blessings of liberty. James Napper Tandy is at their head; he has sworn to lead them on to victory or die. Brave Irishmen! the friends of liberty have left their native soil to assist you in re-conquering [*sic*] your rights; they will brave all dangers, and glory at the sublime idea of cementing your happiness with their blood."[2]

'Napper Tandy had a large number of saddles and cavalry appointments on board the French ship of war, but he could not procure any horses in the Rosses. So Mrs. Foster said to him, "I fear, General, you will not be able to put the saddle on the right

[1] A wild district near Gweedore, on the coast of Donegal, embracing the contiguous island of Rutland.

[2] The facsimile of this proclamation, as furnished by Mr. Allingham, is headed 'Liberty or Death!' and displays a drawing of the Irish harp and the cap of liberty; but as the text appears in the *Castlereagh Papers* (i. 407), a sample must suffice here:—'Horrid crimes have been perpetrated in your country, your friends have fallen a sacrifice to their devotion to your cause, their shadows are around you and call aloud for vengeance, etc.'

horse!" N. Tandy asked Mr. Foster: "What news?" to which Foster replied that a part of the French troops had landed at Killala, and, after winning the battle of Castlebar, had been finally compelled, near Longford, to capitulate to Lord Cornwallis. Napper Tandy seemed to doubt this intelligence, and proceeded to take forcible possession of the Rutland post-office, which was kept by Mr. Foster's sister. He opened the newspapers, and, to his dismay, found that all was over with the expedition. His descent on Rutland took place September 16, 1798. Tandy, when embarking from the island for France, wrote an official letter, signed and sealed, with a view to exonerate Foster from blame for not having despatched his mail-bags. Tandy testified that, being in temporary want of accommodation, he was obliged to put "citizen Foster under requisition," and place sentinels around the island. He and his officers paid for everything they took, including two pigs and a cow. General Rey, when leaving, removed a gold ring from his finger and presented it to Mrs. Foster, as a token of fraternity. Tandy not only discharged every obligation, but discharged a cannon as a farewell note. Foster was a staunch loyalist, and ere the "Anacréon" was under way he despatched two expresses, one to Letterkenny, in hopes that the Lough Swilly fleet would intercept them. This was not so easy, for Tandy told Foster they had met several English cruisers *en route*, but had outsailed them all. The "Anacréon" was equally successful on its return voyage, captured two English ships near the Orkneys, after a stiff engagement, and at last landed Tandy and his A.D.C.s in Norway.'

A copy of Tandy's letter, deliberately penned when leaving Rutland, appears in the appendix to Musgrave's 'Rebellion,' and seems not quite consistent with the statement in the 'Castlereagh Papers' that he got so drunk on the island he had to be carried to the ship.[1] But his grief was so poignant on finding his dearest hopes frustrated that it would not be unnatural, in days when hard drinking was the fashion, if the amateur French general had recourse to *eau-de-vie*. How he was arrested on neutral territory, contrary to the law of nations, subjected to cruel suffering, and sentenced to death, a previous chapter tells.

Fuller inquiry into the career of this quondam merchant of Dublin finds it curiously interwoven with the history of Europe

[1] These and other statements appear in a letter signed 'O.' which will be dealt with presently.

and his fate influential in its affairs. In 1793 Holland was the scene of disaster to the Duke of York; and his second campaign to that country in 1799 ended in a disadvantageous capitulation. Previously he had sent General Don into the interior of Holland to foment among the natives an insurrection against French rule. Don was seized as a spy and threatened with death for seeking to corrupt an enemy which England had failed to conquer in the field.[1] He was, however, safely restored during the negotiations of 1799, and Plowden makes the statement, as one generally believed, that in the Helder convention there was a secret article for restoring to liberty Tandy and Blackwell, in return for the delivery of Don, who, by the laws of war, had incurred the penalty of death. The Paris journals of October 1799 said that the Duke's capitulation contains some private articles which his Royal Highness did not wish to submit to the consideration of the coffee-houses in London.

Prolonged delay attended the liberation of Tandy. Brune bitterly complained of it in the Council of Five Hundred; and then it was that Buonaparte branded, as an attack upon the rights of nations and a crime against humanity, the surrender, by Hamburg to England, of Tandy, Blackwell, Morres, and Corbet.

The painful details already given as regards the severity of their imprisonment it is pleasant to relieve by some notice of the conduct of one official who, superior in gentlemanly instinct to others of higher rank, treated Tandy and his companions with a courteous consideration most acceptable to men whose hearts ached from recent persecution. This letter—unknown to Mr. Ross, the editor of the 'Cornwallis Papers'—was addressed, we believe, to a near kinsman of that writer.

To Mr. Ross, the King's Messenger.

'Dublin: November 18, 1799—*in prison.*

'Sir,—We find ourselves at a loss to know how we best can express our acknowledgments for the very polite, gentlemanly, and philosophic manner in which you have uniformly behaved towards us, ever since the period of our first getting under your care at Sheerness, during our subsequent stay in London, upon the whole

[1] From 1795 the Duke enjoyed the titles of Field-Marshal, Commander-in-Chief, and Bishop of Osnaburg.

of our journey through England, and until our arrival here; a conduct the peculiar inheritance of a man of sense, education, and honour; and which, upon all occasions in life, must leave with the feeling mind a pleasing and everlasting impression.

'All that we, sir, on our parts, can offer (and request your acceptance of as a just tribute to your merit) is our sincerest wishes for your happiness and future welfare—and to all of our fellow-citizens whom the casualties of the day may hereafter chance to place in similar circumstances with us, we wish from our hearts the superior good fortune of falling into the hands of an officer who, knowing his duty like Mr. Ross, like him also executes it in a manner that honours humanity—an idea, that, with us, while drawing a comparison between such-like conduct as we now speak of, and that which we but very recently experienced in a foreign country, restores to its pristine, but nearly lost worth, in our minds, the invaluable weight of social law, and of all generous and liberal-minded converse betwixt man and man.'

The following signatures are affixed: 'JAMES NAPPER TANDY, COLONEL BLACKWELL, HARVEY M. MORRES, GEORGE PETERS.'

The interest which continued to attach to Tandy's memory long after his death, even in quarters not likely to evince sympathy, is curiously shown in the following extract from a letter addressed in 1846 by Robert Shaw Worthington, B.L., to O'Connell, soliciting his patronage with the Whig Government: 'My Liberal opinions I inherit from my father, who, strange as it may appear, was Lord Mayor of Dublin in 1795.[1] *His* liberal opinions did not serve him in those days; he was a supporter of Catholic Emancipation, and in the year 1809, at a private dinner-party at the house of Mr. Farrell, Blackhall Street, my father proposed the memory of Napper Tandy.[2] One of the company (the perfidious name was Fanning) reported the circumstance next day at the Castle; my father received a letter from the Chief Secretary (the present Duke of Wellington) calling upon him to disprove the charge; but, being unable to do so, he was dismissed from his office of Dublin Police Magistrate, the salary of which was 500*l.* per annum.'[3]

[1] The Corporation at that time was notoriously Orange.

[2] James Farrell, though a Rebel leader during the troubles, is afterwards found entertaining at dinner H.R.H. the Duke of Sussex and Major Sirr.

[3] Letter dated 'Salmon Pool Lodge, Dublin, September 21, 1846.' (O'Connell MSS. Derrinane Abbey.) If it were not for the letter of Sir A. Wellesley, which fixes the date, I would be disposed to place this incident earlier.

'O'

The letters of secret information in the 'Castlereagh Papers,' though assumed by most readers to come from the one source, are divided between two spies. No successful attempt has been hitherto made to identify the writers. The result of Dr. Madden's inquiry went no further than to show that the letters were penned, not by spies of a low type, but by *gentlemen* of high standing.[1] It was then that I sought to draw aside their masks. 'Downshire's friend' (Turner) was traced more easily than a correspondent of the Home Office, London, whose initial 'O' is dropped once only by Wickham. The spy who contrived to accompany General Tandy's staff in the expedition to Ireland in 1798 has left us a curious account of what passed on board the 'Anacréon'[2] during their brief visit to Ireland. The perilous character of his enterprise was quite as striking as Tandy's descent on Donegal and escape from the English fleet. Wickham confides to Castlereagh merely the initial letter of this spy's name.[3] The written statement from 'O' is a curious document, and one which has been more than once quoted by historians. An old note-book of mine contains the following:— 'I have long and vainly tried to discover this man; but to Dr. Madden it will be at least satisfactory to know that "O" can never have taken any prominent part in the councils of the United Irishmen, and his name, even if discovered, would not be a familiar one. He can never have been in the Executive Directory, or on any of the baronial committees. He mentions incidentally that he has been but once in Ireland for eight years.'

Some readers fancied that the spy 'O' who accompanied Tandy was O'Herne,[4] O'Finn,[5] Ormby,[6] O'Mealy,[7] O'Hara,[8] O'Neill,[9]

[1] Madden's *United Irishmen*, ii. 391.

[2] There is an account in Musgrave of the arrival of the 'Anacréon' with notices of some of the men on board, but it throws no light on 'O.' He was lost in the crowd of French officers and adherents.

[3] *Castlereagh Correspondence*, i. 405.

[4] O'Herne, otherwise Aherne (see *Castlereagh*, i. 308). He is often mentioned in *Tone's Journal*.

[5] O'Finn (see *Castlereagh*, ii. 5). O'Finn figures in the Fugitive Bill. See p. 96, *ante*.

[6] Ormby, an Irish rebel in France (*Castlereagh*, i. 307).

[7] O'Mealy, an Irish rebel in France (*ibid.* ii. 7, 359 *et seq.*).

[8] O'Hara (*ibid.* i. 327).

[9] Colonel O'Neill (*ibid.* ii. 230).

O'Connor,[1] or O'Keon[2]; my own theory was that 'O' stood for some man whose name would prove to be Orr. At p. 309, vol. i., of the 'Castlereagh Papers,' in a report of the French fleet preparing to invade Ireland, a list is given of the Irish agents at Brest: 'Orr, *who accompanied Murphy*, was still at Paris.[3] Did not seem to like going.' The letter of 'O,' describing the crew on board the 'Anacréon' in its expedition to Ireland, mentions 'Murphy . . . and myself' (p. 407).

'O,' in his secret letter dated 1798, speaks of having been in Trinity College, Dublin, nine years before. An 'Orr' graduated as B.A. in 1789, but this proved not much. His letter shows (pp. 406–10) that he had the confidence both of the French Directory, and of the Irish envoys in France. Another anonymous letter of secret information from Paris (Castlereagh, ii. 2–7) is undoubtedly Turner's. He speaks of Orr and Murphy as together; the first as a 'relation of him that was hanged,' and 'Murphy as having been lately expelled Dublin College,' and both, he adds, were applying for passports at Altona (p. 6). John Murphy made a deposition[4] at Bow Street, dated November 2, 1798, in which he names *George Orr* and himself, proceeding to the Hague, thence to Paris, and afterwards joining Tandy's expedition, when Murphy became secretary to the General. It is curious to find Turner[5] and Orr—each ignorant of the treachery of the other—reporting their movements to the Secretary of State.[6]

'By direction of the Duke of Portland,' writes Wickham to Lord Castlereagh, 'I send for the information of the Lord Lieutenant

[1] O'Connor (*Castlereagh*, i. 374).

[2] O'Keon, who went with the French to Killala. See *Byrne's Memoirs*, iii. 164. (Paris, 1863.)

[3] At Paris 'O' had three interviews with General Lawless in reference to the invasion, which is detailed in his clever letter (see *Castlereagh*, i. 397). He is able to tell Lawless the number of men the French Directory were prepared to sacrifice in the attempt. The added statement that 'Orr did not seem to like going' is consistent with his sneering tone at all that passed on board the 'Anacréon.' Were Orr discovered to have been a spy, he would have swung from the yard-arm.

[4] MSS. Record Tower, Dublin. A narrative of the progress of Tandy's expedition, dated October 21, 1799, and preserved in the same archives, is endorsed 'G. O.'

[5] Turner (see p. 5, *ante*) announces Orr as at Paris with Tandy, Teeling, Lewins, and other arch-rebels.

[6] See p. 56, *ante*, and *Castlereagh Papers*, i. 405.

the enclosed extract from some very important communications that have been made to his Grace by a person of the name of O——.'

In this letter, describing Tandy's descent on Ireland, the relations between him and the French Directory are minutely detailed, with an account of the equipment of the expedition, and studies of the officers on board and their antecedents.[1] It is not unlikely that Orr and Murphy, especially the latter, had been at first zealous adherents of the movement headed by Lord Edward and Tone; but that after the death of these leaders and the consignment of the Rebel Directory to dungeons they considered their own position as materially changed.

When Buonaparte broke faith with Addis Emmet, and sent his legions to the Pyramids of Egypt, instead of encamping them among the Round Towers of Ireland, Orr then sought to fill his purse, and console a baulked ambition, by extracting gold from Pitt: 'To show how the finances of France are,' he writes regarding Tandy's expedition, 'and how they meant to make their Irish friends pay their expenses, three generals went out on that little expedition; and all the money they could muster among them was about thirty louis d'or. One of them, to my own certain knowledge, had but five guineas in all.'[2]

Again, in a subsequent letter, he writes: 'The grand object of the French is, as they term it themselves, London. *Delenda* (sic) *Carthago* is their particular end; once in England, they think they would speedily indemnify themselves for all their expenses and recruit their ruined finances.'[3]

England, unlike France, could pay lavishly, and it would be curious to know if Orr's increasing facilities for acquiring valuable information, according as Napoleon's power grew, were acknowledged by the '5,000*l*., and not more than 20,000*l*. within the year,' which Wellington in 1808 thought fair fees for the unnamed informer who

[1] The most trivial incidents are chronicled, including Tandy's fondness for gazing on a few laced coats that he had in his wardrobe. Tone himself was not proof against this vanity: 'Put on my regimentals—as pleased as a little boy in his first breeches' (ii. 176). 'O' announces that 'Turner refused to accompany any of the expeditions to Ireland, and went from Paris to the Hague' (i. 409. Turner had been in dread of assassination as the penalty of betrayal, and could not be persuaded to revisit Ireland while the troubles and their excitement continued.

[2] *Castlereagh Papers*, i. 408.

[3] *Ibid*. p. 410 (October, 1798).

sent secret news from France—a man who, it is added, had been paid at this rate by Pitt.[1]

Orr continued long after to discharge in France the perilous *rôle* of a vigilant spy, and, as such, was a small thorn in Napoleon's side. The Pelham MSS. contain a long letter signed 'G. O.' (33—112, folio 205), further described in a separate note as 'George Orr,' and beginning—'I much fear that the French have out-generaled the British Government with respect to what is to go forward in the West Indies.' The date would be about 1802, but it is incorrectly placed with papers of 1807. This is the only report from Orr preserved by Pelham. With complicated precautions of secrecy it is addressed 'C. W. F., Esq.,' and by this mysterious official passed on to Pelham for perusal. These initials are often met in the State Papers, both of England and Ireland; and future inquirers have a right to know something of the man who played no unimportant part during an eventful period of our history. 'Cornwallis' and 'Castlereagh' furnish no note on this point; the 'Gentleman's Magazine,' that great storehouse of facts, knows him not. At last, in 'Three Thousand Contemporary Public Characters,' published by Whittaker in 1825, I found the following notice of a career which deserves more permanent record.

'*SIR CHARLES WILLIAM FLINT*

WAS born in Scotland in 1775; and, after having finished his studies at Edinburgh, was taken, in 1793, by Lord Grenville, into the office of Secretary of State for Foreign Affairs. In 1796 Lord Grenville sent him as confidential secretary with Mr. Wickham, then going minister to Switzerland: with that gentleman Mr. Flint entered into a close intimacy. He was recalled in 1797, and again employed in the Foreign Office. Next year the Alien Bill passed, and Lord Grenville recommended Mr. Flint to the Duke of Portland, as a fit person to put it in execution; and his Grace, who was then Home Secretary, appointed him Superintendent of Aliens. In this situation he was very active, and is said to have rendered essential service to many of the Royalist emigrants.[2] When Pichegru returned from Cayenne, he confided to Mr. Flint those plans which, in the

[1] *Wellington Correspondence* (*Ireland*), p. 455.

[2] But Flint seems to have had more to do in this *rôle* than paternally to extend the ægis. Lord Cloncurry, describing his own arrest in 1798, writes (*Memoirs*, p. 68) that his Swiss valet was seized under the Alien Act, sent out of the country, and never heard of more.

end, brought on his destruction. In 1800 the Duke of Portland granted Mr. Flint leave of absence, and he was sent as secretary of legation to Mr. Wickham, then envoy to the allied armies in Germany. After witnessing the campaigns in Bavaria and Austria, he returned to England, where he was employed until 1802, and was then sent to the sister kingdom as Under-Secretary of State in Ireland. He is now [1826] agent, in London, of the Irish Department. In 1812 he received the honour of knighthood.'

It may be added that the Irish 'S. S. Money Book' records a number of payments in 1803 by Flint to minor informers, including Murphy, the colleague of George Orr. The Wellington Correspondence makes frequent reference to Flint; but readers are left without any information as to who this 'very clever fellow' was—to quote the Duke's own words. (v., p. 643.)

ROBERT AND ROGER O'CONNOR

The unscrupulosity with which spying was practised in the days of 'the First Gentleman in Europe' is not pleasant to contemplate. I find Robert O'Connor, nephew of Lord Longueville, betraying his own brother!

Pelham writes to Brigadier-General Coote on May 27, 1797:—

'I have received at different times very important information from Mr. Robert O'Connor, and indeed he was the first person who gave me information against his brother.

'I hear that you have excellent spies, and I expect great success from your exertions.'

General Eyre Coote writes ('Pelham MSS.' July 24, 1797):—

'I enclose you strong information against Roger O'Connor just received from Robert. It is very curious that one brother should be so inveterate against the other. I, however, am of opinion that Roger O'Connor has been the principal in all the treasonable practices in this part of the country.'

Roger, of whose adventurous feats volumes might be written, was noted more for backsliding than backbone. Pelham, in a letter to Coote, dated Phœnix Park, July 25, 1797, says:—

'He [Roger] declares himself to be disposed to give every information, and to render every service to the King's Government, in his power.'

No circles, however cultured, were untainted by the spy. Dr.

Madden gives a very ugly picture of Sir Jonah Barrington revealing at Dublin Castle the seditious talk that he heard at Lady Colclough's dinner-table, and how Grogan, Colclough, and Harvey, men of rank and fortune, who were present, died on the gallows ere the year expired.[1]

Mr. Pelham's Papers afford curious glimpses of social life in Ireland as presented by his correspondents. A priest, who resided near Collon in the county Louth, is described as having dined at a squire's house in the neighbourhood,[2] and a paper having fallen out of his pocket, 'curiosity tempted some of the gentlemen to read it. A copy of it was brought to England by Mr. William Beaufort, son of the Rev. Dr. Beaufort, rector of Collon, and Mr. Young, his connection, furnished a copy.' The paper, in point of fact, embodied merely secret tenets of his religious rule.

ARTHUR O'CONNOR

On his way to Fort George prison, in Scotland, O'Connor distributed some curious lines, which at first passed as an exemplary effusion, but, on being more closely scanned, they developed rebel sentiments. O'Connor intended that the lines of the second verse should be read after the corresponding lines in the first. The first lines of the two verses constituted the great sentiment which O'Connor liked to emphasise.

The pomp of courts, and pride of kings,
I prize above all earthly things;
I love my country, but the King
Above all men his praise I sing;
The royal banners are display'd,
And may success the standard aid.

I fain would banish far from hence
The 'Rights of Man' and common sense;
Confusion to his odious reign,
That foe to princes, Thomas Paine!
Defeat and ruin seize the cause
Of France, its liberties, and laws!

[1] *United Irishmen*, iv. 232–5. Sir Jonah, in his *Personal Sketches* (pp. 163–6), tells this himself, but without the elaborate colouring of Madden.

[2] Probably Foster. Some of the papers in the same volume are addressed to the Right Hon. the Speaker, Collon (Pelham MSS. fol. 205). Thomas Pelham, Earl of Chichester, whose name has been often mentioned in this book, died July 4, 1826. A pleasing sketch of Pelham appears in *Barrington's Memoirs*, i. 180.

LADY MOIRA AND TODD JONES

(*Vide* chap. xii. p. 156.)

An unpublished letter, addressed to John Philpot Curran, though anonymous, bears internal evidence to show that the writer was Lady Moira, whose daughter, Selina, had married Lord Granard. In those days it was not unusual to intercept and read letters at the post-office, and to this circumstance is doubtless due the great caution with which the noble writer describes her relations with Todd Jones. He was then in custody, and Lady Moira's great object was to exculpate him as well as herself, for 'Cæsar's wife should be above suspicion.' Enough has been already said to indicate the spy [1] who kept his eye on Moira House and the movements of Todd Jones.

To John Philpot Curran, K.C.

'Castle Forbes: August 13, 1803.

'Read, reflect, and do not answer. Time will unfold *the intentions*. But it is common prudence to watch knaves, who are playing the fool, and who may not chance to consider that others, from having hearkened to the precept to be, although "innocent as doves," induced to adopt somewhat of the "wisdom of the serpent," will scrutinise their measures. To state the case, Mr. Todd Jones is the son of a physician, who in the year 1752 I formed the acquaintance of, and attendant on the family into which I entered by marriage; he was a sensible well-informed man, and having studied abroad his profession at the same college with Doctor Aberside, a person known to Lord Huntingdon and me; as a friend to that medical poet, he became an intimate acquaintance of mine; and having for thirty years and upwards exercised his Æsculapian skill with such success as to have recovered me from dangerous fevers, and also never letting a single patient die in his hands beneath my roof, he became the intimate friend of the family, and his son was the companion of *my* sons in his early youth, and an inmate like to a relation till my sons went into the world, and since then he has regarded me with a sort of filial respect and attention, and I have shown to him the return of maternal kindness and goodwill. However, his residence for many years past being in England and

[1] Francis Magan (see p. 134, *ante*).

Wales, has confined our intercourse to correspondence; now and then a letter from me in answer to many of his, which, as he excels in letter-writing, I always received his letters as real sources of amusement, and of information on the subject they transmitted, which usually had reference to antiquities.[1] I had not seen him for several years when he came over a twelvemonth ago, to settle some pecuniary affairs with Lord Downshire's executors or agents, having sold his estates as an annuity during his life; and a sum of money, which money was to be kept for a space of time in his lordship's hands, lest any claim should be made on the estate. I saw him frequently whilst he was in Dublin, which was during that space of time that Sir Richard Musgrave and he quarrelled and at length fought. He left Dublin before I quitted it, and came here in the first week of last October. He wrote to me lately from the Lake of Killarney giving me a description of the lake and its odd traditions, mentioning his return to Dublin in a month, and from whence he was to return to Wales. I then heard from general report that he was arrested and in Cork jail, which I imputed to Sir Richard Musgrave's malice.[2] For as to any treasonable practices, Jones's indolence as well as his turn of thinking and whimsical pursuits were a conviction to me that he was neither inclined to be, or capable of being, a conspirator. However, in the course of last week I was informed from *Moira House* that a person, by warrant from the Castle, had come to search *for a trunk in consequence of their having received intelligence that Mr. Todd Jones had sent off a trunk directed to me at Moira House.* My

[1] It would be unlike Jones if his letters to Lady Moira did not deal with warmer topics than 'antiquities.' Tone's *Life* contains a letter from Lady Moira to Jones, in which she says: 'As to making a democrat of me, that, you must be persuaded, is a fruitless hope.'

[2] It has never been my habit to print only such parts of letters as are convenient to my purpose. Lady Moira would be the last to suspect her neighbour Magan; and she naturally thought at once of Musgrave, who had so recently accepted Jones's challenge. But Lady Moira was wrong in thinking that, when their affair of honour ended, Musgrave owed spite to Jones. He afforded good proof to the contrary in omitting from later editions of his book the passages which had offended Jones. The duel took place at Rathgar, Musgrave was slightly wounded, and Ned Lysaght said that his next edition would probably be 'in boards.' Jones, in a private letter, written long after, speaks of his antagonist as 'Dick Musgrave,' and exonerates him from the suspicion of having spitefully caused his arrest. An otherwise flattering paper in the *Edinburgh Review* (July 1892) assumes, but incorrectly, that I seek to impugn Jones's honesty as a patriot.

servants were examined, my house and storerooms explored, but not any such trunk had arrived nor been heard of, and orders were left that when it did, where it was to be sent to. Some English letters that were directed to him at my house were conveyed to Mr. Marsden.[1] They were opened to show their contents. One was from a Mr. Maddox, who, I think, is married to Lord Craven's sister [2] (better known by being the daughter of the Margravine); another from a young man going to India, and not conveying a trace of injury to him. I wrote to a person who was employed to execute the warrant that I could not be blind to the affront intended to be cast upon me; that, if such intimation had been given of a trunk then sent, the person that communicated the intelligence was able and would certainly inform by what coach it went, and consequently they might have had it seized when Mr. Jones was arrested. That time had now sufficiently elapsed to have had another key made for the trunk and to place in it whatever papers, &c., *might be reckoned convenient*. That if any trunk did come, the *lock* and the hinges should be well examined, before credible witnesses, before it *went out of my house*; and that I neither was awed, nor capable of being frightened, by so mean and paltry a contrivance. Thus they had taken up McCan,[3] but, I find, have liberated him, and given out that, as he was connected with Mr. Grattan, it was to get papers of Mr. Grattan's into their hands that he was arrested for that purpose; now, whether this report is to blacken the character of the famous ex-senator, or with further views, I do not decide. In respect to the insult I have met with, it is aimed against Lord Moira through me. It is, however, to me a much blacker and more artful attempt against him, in which *high and mighty ones* were blended when too many cooks spoiled the broth. The former plot, however, has made me alert, and awakened all my expectations respecting possible malevolence. But my spirit, like the palm-tree, rises by the pressure of oppressive indignity

[1] Under-Secretary at Dublin Castle.

[2] The Lady Elizabeth Craven, whom Mr. John Edward Maddox married, died in 1799.

[3] McCan, the agent of Grattan, was examined by the Privy Council; when the Attorney-General, O'Grady, is stated to have offered McCan office, and a payment of 10,000*l*. if he would criminate Grattan.—*Life of Grattan*, by his Son, v. 228. McCan, on behalf of Grattan, had remitted money to Dowdall, but only from motives of humanity. Dowdall was concerned in Robert Emmet's plot. Mathias O'Kelly told me that he met Dowdall, Magan, and Todd Jones dining at the table of James Dixon, the active rebel already noticed.

My eyes are so weak that I fear you will not be able to decipher this hasty scrawl. How absurdly are they acting! Lady G——[1] does not know that I write this. It is not in my nature to worry people with disagreeable humours, nor to humiliate myself by complaints, though I like to guard against probable evils, in which case I shall, sir, depend upon your aid if it comes to publicity.'

JAMES TANDY AND McNALLY

Any person who has read the secret reports furnished by McNally to Dublin Castle must see that the source from which he drew his more important knowledge was James Tandy, son of the arch-rebel Napper Tandy. This information, however, may have been gathered partly during the unguarded intimacy of friendship. Its accuracy, not less than the promptitude and opportuneness of each disclosure, led a very shrewd man to suspect that James Tandy was betraying his party, and not McNally who picked his brains. In the 'Cornwallis Papers' (iii. 85) is one of the many secret reports sent by J. W. to Dublin Castle. He probably chuckled when penning the following allusion to the source from which he himself mainly derived his knowledge.

'Wright, the surgeon, of Great Ship Street, has had a long conversation with J. Tandy, in which he [J. T.] urged him to send a paper from Wright to his father, Napper; and this he did in such a manner as has created in Wright's mind very strong doubts of his sincerity; indeed, *he conceives him to be a spy*, and has resolved to avoid all further conversation with him.'

Dr. Thomas Wright, M.R.I.A., secretary to the United Irishmen, was a long-headed man, still well remembered in Dublin; but I do not think that James Tandy—beyond being indiscreetly open-mouthed—can be called an informer, much less a spy.

James Tandy is found a state prisoner with others after the rebellion, but this fact in itself is not enough to exculpate him; for Turner is also found a state prisoner. During his detention he addressed a letter to the Secretary of State, solemnly declaring that while he loved Napper Tandy as his father, he abhorred his politics; and he complains of an oral slander circulated by the Solicitor-

[1] The Countess of Granard. The Dowager Lady Moira, from whom her son inherited the baronies of Hungerford and Hastings, died on April 12, 1808.

General, afterwards Baron McCleland, that he 'was guilty of high treason, and to a certainty would be hanged.' I may here remark that the manuscript list of United Irishmen, furnished by Collins the spy so early as 1793, includes James Tandy's name. Tandy with thirteen others petitioned the Viceroy on July 11, 1804, in regard to harsh treatment they had received when state prisoners, entered into a personal correspondence with Mr. Secretary Marsden, whom he holds responsible for it, and threatens to horsewhip him in case he should ever be set at liberty. James Tandy—though not his companions in durance—was liberated on bail in September following, and he states in a public letter: 'I obtained my enlargement on condition that I would relinquish my intention of horsewhipping Mr. Marsden.' [1] This statement, however, which Plowden quotes as history, must be taken *cum grano*, for Tandy in his memorial to the Viceroy Bedford says: 'Petitioner was discharged from prison when in a state of health which allowed no hopes for his life—a fact which Dr. Richards can testify, as also the surgeon-general, Mr. Stewart.' [2]

The antecedents of his family earned no gratitude from Government, and yet we find James Tandy appointed to a lucrative post. Lord Cloncurry casually mentions him exercising his functions as a stipendiary magistrate.[3]

James Tandy's arrest and imprisonment were certainly not due to McNally, who would be the last to kill the goose which laid the golden eggs; more than that, he tells Cooke that James Tandy was no republican. How McNally utilised James Tandy may be seen from his secret letters. Both are found constantly together. A hurried despatch from McNally, dated January 31 (he rarely gives the year) says: 'McNally and James Tandy went yesterday morning to Mr. Grattan's at Tinnehinch, and returned in the evening.'

A negotiation between Arthur O'Connor and Napper Tandy in France is detailed by McNally: 'James Tandy has consulted McN. on the danger of such an undertaking.' [4] On September 23, 1800, McNally writes: 'Emmet, T. assures me (and he made inquiry), is in Paris.' On September 19, 1800, McNally writes, 'my friend [5] passed yesterday morning with T., junior,' and he jots down a large amount of matter as the result of the conference.

[1] Plowden's *History of Ireland*, 1811, ii. 22.

[2] *Appeal*, p. 122; Haliday Collection, vol. 915. R. I. A.

[3] *Personal Recollections*, p. 246.

[4] J. W. Sunday evening, 9 o'clock.

[5] McNally himself.

'Mr. Pelham's answer to James Tandy is expected with anxiety,' records a previous report.

Dr. McNevin, an eminent physician of Dublin, though described by Reinhard as a moderate man, was certainly one of the rebel Directory. Cooke, writing to Pelham in London, mentions a fact which he heard from 'our friend,' who had drawn it from James Tandy. 'McNevin went for England a few days since in a wherry from Clontarf and was nearly lost. I suppose he went for Yarmouth. Will you not send after him? He is a neat made little man of 5 feet 4.'[1]

Cooke, in enclosing to Pelham the report of a provincial meeting of 'United Irishmen,' asks: 'Do you think it would be right to seize on their next Committee on the 14th January? Our friend would then come forward, and the whole might be blown up.'[2]

McNally, however, never consented to 'come forward,' and Wellington, ten years later, said in effect that this man, wearing his mask as a spy, and possessing the confidence of the rebels, would be more useful than in any other capacity.

The secret letters of Higgins to Cooke constantly point to James Tandy. On March 7, 1798, he urges Cooke 'to watch Napper Tandy's intercourse with his son, and through him with the rest of the incendiarys. His son waited on a Mr. Connell with a letter this day.' I quote this passage because of the name 'Connell' which occurs in it. The allusion is to the subsequently celebrated Daniel O'Connell. Higgins tells Cooke that 'Connell holds a commission from France (a Colonel's). He was to be called to the Bar here to please a very rich old uncle, but he is one of the most abominable and bloodthirsty republicans I ever heard of. The place of rendezvous is the Public Library in Eustace Street, where a private room is devoted to the leaders of the United Irish Society.'

The words are given as a curiosity, and not as accurately describing O'Connell's real sentiments, and the statement that this ardent youth, fresh from the mint of the French College at Douai, held a commission from France is one of the sensational myths with which Higgins loved to garnish his reports. In 1798 Daniel was called to the Bar to please, as Higgins correctly states, his rich uncle, Maurice Connell of Darrinane—traditionally known as 'Old

[1] Pelham MSS., London. Cooke to Pelham, December 26, 1797.

[2] *Ibid.*, December 23, 1797.

Hunting Cap.' Higgins is also right in regarding the future Tribune as a rebel. He had joined the United Irishmen in 1798, but escaped in a turf-boat previous to the insurrection. It will be remembered that Maurice Connell, as shown by the Pelham MSS., was the first to report the arrival of a French fleet in Bantry Bay.

It is worthy of notice, in exploring the *genus* 'spy,' that the violently incisive language used by Higgins is never employed by McNally. The latter gives a man a wound and leaves him there. Higgins poignards his victims over and over again, and kicks their dead bodies, as in the case of Lord Edward Fitzgerald.

The arrest of James Tandy was made in 1803, a year after the death of Higgins, and is likely to have been prompted by Magan, who was active (see p. 157, *ante*) at that time. In closing these notices of the Tandy family, it may perhaps be mentioned that Napper Tandy's father took an ultra-loyal part during the excitement caused by the rising of Charles Edward in 1745. A run on the Dublin Banks was made, and *Faulkner's Journal* of October 8 in that year contains a manifesto from some Dublin merchants, including Tandy, agreeing to accept their notes as cash.

A TARDY AMENDE TO LORD CAMDEN.—THE FRENCH IN IRELAND

Lord Camden, the Irish Viceroy in 1798, has been often styled a dull man; but he seems to have had his wits about him, as will presently appear.

I find, by a remarkable letter of this Lord Lieutenant, written two months previous to General Lake's retreat from Castlebar, that he saw the weak points of the somewhat overrated warrior who afterwards got a peerage for beating the Mahrattas. It may be said that the defeat at Castlebar was due to panic among the troops, but all accounts agree that Lake and Hutchinson had been outmanœuvred by Humbert.

'I remain in the opinion I originally held,' writes Lord Camden at a time anterior to the arrival of the French, 'that General Lake is not fit for the command in these difficult times, and have written to Pitt in the most serious and impressive manner I am able to make him master of the actual danger of the country. It is unfortunate that he should have lost the advantage of General Lake's services where he was really well placed, and have brought him to one which is above his capacity. He has no arrangement, is easily led, and no authority.' [1]

Passing reference has been made to the arrival at Killala, on August 22, 1798, of a small French force under Humbert; and some notice of the sequel is due. Humbert had started from Rochelle solely on his own responsibility. General Lord Hutchinson held Castlebar with 5,200 men; but Lake, as the senior officer, assumed the command. Lake arrived at dark with a large reinforcement, and next morning was surprised to see the French troops rise from a defile hitherto regarded as impassable, General Taylor having been previously sent forward to cut off their approach by road. Although the French were jaded after a forced march of fifteen hours, they advanced with much vivacity, and attacked the King's troops, who had posted themselves on a steep hill-side with nine pieces of cannon. 'They advanced in excellent style—with great rapidity as sharp-shooters,' Cooke writes.[2] Lake's line wavered, a retreat was sounded, the flight of the infantry was most disorderly, and Sir Jonah Barrington compares it to that of a mob. Lord Jocelyn's Light Dragoons (he was taken prisoner soon after by Humbert) ran like so many 'Tam o' Shanters' to Tuam, a distance of forty miles, followed by such of the French as could get horses for the chase. All the artillery, with five pair of colours, fell into the hands of the French. This disgraceful panic is remembered as 'The Races of Castlebar.' [3]

Such conduct, unlike their position, was indefensible; for Lake's men, different from the enemy, had been refreshed by a good night's rest. The French had left 200 men to garrison Killala, and Humbert's soldiers, when in action, did not exceed 800, according to the statement of Lake's secretary.[4] But it has been often said that the French, in making so successful an attack, must have been supported by vast numbers of native insurgents. Again Cooke writes, on the authority of Lake's secretary, 'he saw no peasantry.' [5]

[1] Camden to Pelham, Dublin Castle, June 6, 1798. (Pelham MSS., London.)

[2] Cooke to Wickham, Dublin Castle, September 1, 1798.

[3] Philip Crampton, afterwards the famous Surgeon-General and medical baronet, took part in the action at Castlebar, as assistant surgeon to the Longford Militia. His friends often chaffed him on having been the first man to reach Tuam.

[4] Cooke to Wickham, Dublin Castle, September 1, 1798. [5] *Idem.*

Mr. Vereker, Lieutenant-Colonel of the Limerick Militia, got a peerage for having repulsed the French at Coloony, and the motto on his arms is simply the name of that place. Lord Carleton records, in his autograph, on the margin of a book, some curious facts :—

'The skirmish at Coloony,' he writes, 'began and ended in a blunder. Vereker (who knew nothing of the rapid march of thirty-five Irish miles which the French had made from Castlebar) supposed he was attacking only their vanguard; and Humbert, equally ignorant of Vereker's force, mistook the troops which attacked him for the vanguard of a larger body, and altered his plan of marching to Sligo, which must have surrendered at his approach. When Lake, with his division, arrived at Coloony next morning, he found eighteen Frenchmen, dangerously wounded, who were left behind by their army.'

The strangest part of the story is that Vereker in this attack acted on his own responsibility, and contrary to the instructions he had received from Lake. This brief campaign was marked by a series of wonderful misapprehensions. French accounts say that Humbert, seeing the strength of the British line at Castlebar, thought of retiring to Ballina, and to cover the retreat ordered General Sarrazin [1] to make a feigned attack, which, being mistaken by Lake for an attempt to turn his flank, produced the panic, whereupon Sarrazin, changing his plan, and without Humbert's orders, charged the enemy and sent them flying. But here Humbert's triumph stopped. Meanwhile, as Lord Carleton in another note states, 'The Hompesch Dragoons were of infinite service, being chiefly Hungarians, and hanging close on the enemies' rear; the (common) Irish, deceived by their dress and foreign language, took them for the French, and came to join them in great numbers, but were immediately cut down, and their pockets rifled by their supposed friends.'

Again, as Lord Carleton notes, the French mistaking a Highland regiment for guerilla troops, sought to fraternise with them, and greatly to their cost.

It has been repeatedly stated, and is generally believed, that Lord Camden was recalled in order to make way for the milder policy of Lord Cornwallis; but it is a fact now worth recording, though somewhat late, that the appointment of Cornwallis was directly due to Camden himself.

[1] Afterwards pensioned by England.

Camden continues:—

'I return to the opinion I had entertained before, that the Lord Lieutenant ought to be a military man. The whole government of the country is now military, and the power of the chief governor is almost merged in that of the general commanding the troops. I have suggested the propriety of sending over Lord Cornwallis, whose name, with some good officers under him, will have great weight; and I have told Pitt that which I really feel, that without the best military assistance I conceive the country to be in the most imminent danger, and that my services cannot be useful to the King.'[1]

Mr. Froude quotes from a letter of Camden's 'The insurgents will be annihilated.'[2] But his tone to Pelham is widely different. He writes:—

'Unless Great Britain pours an immense force into Ireland the country is lost. . . . I cannot suffer my character and my peace of mind to be trifled with.'[3]

Pitt acted on Camden's counsel and appointed Lord Cornwallis. Camden confides to Elliot:—

'If I relinquish my situation, as I do now, merely for the public good at the risque of a false construction, it becomes doubly necessary that I should receive some mark of confidence that it may not be supposed I am recalled from any opinion on the part of the ministers that I have not acted as became me.'[4]

And in a letter of the same date to Pelham, Camden says he is the servant of the public, and ready himself 'to act in Ireland, or elsewhere, in whatever manner I might be the most usefully employed.'

Camden's counsel was followed, that the Viceroy of Ireland—in such times—ought to be a military man. Lord Cornwallis, the new chief governor, went down to Connaught at the head of 20,000 troops, and Humbert surrendered. On September 8, 1798, after a fortnight's progress through the country, 96 officers and 748 French

[1] Camden to Pelham, Dublin Castle, June 6, 1798. (Pelham MSS.)

[2] Froude's *English in Ireland*, iii. 351.

[3] Camden to Pelham, June 11, 1798. (MS.)

[4] Camden to Elliot, Dublin Castle, June 15, 1798. (Pelham MSS.) The only weak suggestion in the remaining part of Camden's letter—needless to transcribe—is that the scene in Ireland was sufficiently extensive for the Duke of York 'to assume the command-in-chief,' for York's failures in the field constitute unpleasant incidents in history.

rank and file became prisoners of war; and, according to Gordon, 500 peasant auxiliaries were put to the sword. Several sympathisers, chiefly local gentry, were hanged; including, as Lord Carleton notes, Messrs. Blake, French, and O'Dowd. Thus ended Humbert's quixotic enterprise; but the previous expedition to Bantry Bay, in 1796, was very formidable; and England had not had such an escape since the Spanish Armada. In this connection Lord Carleton has another word to say; and I do not feel warranted in omitting what serves to explain some things hitherto a puzzle. Few believed that Hoche's expedition of 1796 could have escaped the vigilance and vengeance of the English fleet which had long been watching it.

'Admiral Kingsmill (a most excellent naval officer), who commanded in Cork Harbour, was one of these sceptics. He thought it impossible so large a fleet could have escaped the vigilance of all his cruisers. Kingsmill had no intelligence of it, and repeatedly said, if the French fleet was in Bantry he would suffer his head to be chopped off on his own quarter-deck. Had not the French, when they first made the land, mistaken the Durseys for Three-Castle-Head, by which they missed their port, and were several hours beating back again, they would have got so far up the bay as to have been able to effect their purpose. It is much to be lamented that an officer of high rank in the British navy, Keith Elphinstone (afterwards Lord Keith), returning from India in the "Monarch" of 74 guns, and putting by accident into Crookhaven at the very time the two French ships and frigates were in Bantry Bay, could not be prevailed upon to put himself at the head of the ships then in Cork Harbour—the "Powerful" of 74 guns, and three stout frigates—and block up the bay till Lord Bridport's fleet could arrive. "*It was not his business.*" He got all the stores Kingsmill could send him, and sailed off to England. I assert this fact as positively true.—H. C.' [1]

The signature of Lord Chief Justice Carleton is affixed to all the

[1] The Right Hon. Shaw Lefevre, writing in the *Nineteenth Century* for October 1891 on the 'Naval Policy of France, Past and Future,' mentions, among other facts which will surprise many readers, that 'till quite recent times the professional officers in the French arsenals surpassed in the science of naval construction the same class of men in England. The French ships as a rule were swifter and carried heavier ordnance and larger crews than their opponents of the same class. The best ships in the British navy were often prizes taken from the French. The Canopus alone, captured at the battle of the Nile, served as a model for nine vessels built in the English dockyards.' This will serve to explain how it was that Hoche's expedition to Bantry Bay in 1796 eluded the English fleet.

Government proclamations of the time. His peculiar knowledge was largely derived as a member of the Irish Privy Council, and from his relations with Cork, of which he was a native.

It was not 'the Shan Van Voght' who first announced, as the old ballad has it, that 'the French were on the sea.' The news came from Darrynane Abbey, where the waves roll in unbroken from Labrador. Daniel O'Connell's people have been accused of treasonable leanings—but unfairly. Old Maurice Connell, or O'Connell, chieftain of Darrynane, made money through 'smuggling,' but he was no rebel. Opening that scantily explored mine—the Pelham MSS.—I find Maurice Connell announcing to an under-strapper of the Government, who reports it to Pelham, that a French fleet is in Bantry Bay, and he calls it 'most melancholy intelligence.' The letter is dated 'Darrynane, December 20, 1796.' 'I give you this early information,' writes Maurice from his mountain crag, 'in order that every proper measure should be pursued on an event *soe* very alarming.' [1]

This timely information had the start by two days of Mr. Richard White's, who received his peerage in acknowledgment mainly of a message of similar tenor. We learn from the old pamphlet of Edward Morgan, that 'A servant of his (White's) brought the first despatch to General Dalrymple, in Cork, of the arrival of the French, on the night of Thursday, December 22, who was but four hours going forty-two miles, Irish, on a single horse.' [2] The above is culled from Lord Carleton's copy, and it is added in his autograph, 'Mr. White, for his services on this occasion, which were very meritorious, was created Lord Bantry.'

Communication with London proved so slow in those days that reward was justly due to those who sought to mend a state of things now hard to realise. The King's messenger, when autumnal or wintry winds prevailed, had often to wait three or four weeks ere the boat could sail from Dublin to Holyhead; and on one occasion in the seventeenth century Dublin Castle was three months

[1] The Pelham MSS., London.

[2] *A Journal of the Movements of the French Fleet in Bantry Bay* (Cork, 1797). Hugh Lord Carleton's copy, with manuscript notes. It was this peer who tried and sentenced the Sheareses to death. When the Legislative Union became law in 1800, Carleton retired from the bench and continued to reside in London until his death on Feb. 25, 1826. It was lucky that he left Ireland, for Kilwarden, who fell at the hands of the rebels in 1803, was avowedly mistaken for him. Though twice married Carleton left no issue, and his peerage, like that of Bantry, is extinct.

without letters from London.[1] Even on *terra firma* a snail's pace too often marked the progress of great officials who ought to have set a better example. Carew, when going from Dublin to London, lost five days in accomplishing the 'run' between Holyhead and Chester. When the winds proved propitious, and the King's messenger was an active man, he was able to deliver in Dublin in one week the despatch from Whitehall.

J. E. LEWINS—M. GUIZOT

JOSEPH E. LEWINS—or, as he is erroneously styled in the State Papers and by all historians, 'Edward John Lewins'—demands some notice here. The 'Castlereagh Correspondence' is specially full in its attestations to his importance as a rebel plenipotentiary. In vol. i. p. 270, Wickham, writing from the Home Office on August 16, 1798, states that he had despatched a King's messenger to Dublin with a secret note from Hamburg (no doubt Turner's), and asks Cooke to lay it before the Lord Lieutenant. This document minutely details the mission and proceedings of Lewins, including his communications with Reinhard, the French minister at Hamburg. In the 'Cornwallis Papers' (ii. 342) Lewins is styled an attorney; previously his name crops up in the examination of Cockayne on Jackson's trial in 1795. Lewins' family deny that he ever was a lawyer—as Mr. Lecky, naturally following the 'Cornwallis Papers,' designates him—and the denial is supported by Dublin Directories of the day. I am the more anxious to make this correction because I myself, in one instance, followed the stereotyped designation.

Wolfe Tone's 'Journal' of June 12, 1797, and subsequent entries record a high estimate of the talents and honesty of Lewins, and it appears from his 'Journal' of April 1798 that the same opinion was held by Talleyrand, which explains that diplomat's distrust of Turner (p. 33, *ante*), Lewins finally triumphed over Turner's efforts to destroy his good name, and became a person of influence in the councils of Charles X. He died suddenly on February 11, 1828, when reading, with much emotion, Tone's 'Journals,' which had just seen the light. His son—also attached to the French ministry—was known as 'M. De Luynes,' a change in the name made at the request of his chief, the Bishop of Hermopolis, Minister of Public Instruction, who disliked the 'w' in a name which he

[1] From the first days of October to the end of December, 1605.

was constantly obliged to enunciate. I learn from the representatives of De Luynes that when Louis Philippe was forming his first Ministry, after the fall of the government of Charles X., he summoned M. Laurent de Luynes and offered him the portfolio of Public Instruction. De Luynes, however, declined the distinction on the grounds that he was a devoted adherent of the late King, and felt that he could not conscientiously serve a sovereign whom he regarded as a usurper. M. Guizot, less scrupulous, accepted the post. De Luynes had been the secretary of the Bishop of Hermopolis, and the subsequent Premier, M. Guizot, had served, it is stated, in the same capacity, under De Luynes. The latter survived until February 1884. He had married in 1815 a pretty demoiselle, who brought him a dowry of a million francs and the mansion in which he died.

BETRAYAL OF THE SHEARES—CURIOUS CORRESPONDENCE

During the months of March and April 1892 there appeared in successive issues of the 'Standard' several letters dealing with the present volume. The first was from one of the representatives of Captain J. W. Armstrong; and remarked that 'the author of "Secret Service under Pitt" has not been quite just to his memory.' This Mr. Armstrong White sought to demonstrate.

'The Sheares [he writes] had conceived the idea of enlisting Captain Armstrong's sympathies that, through him, they might seduce the King's County Militia from its allegiance. As soon as Captain Armstrong perceived their object he went to his commanding officer, Colonel L'Estrange, and it was on his advice that he consented to have a third interview with the Sheares.

'In his cross-examination Captain Armstrong emphatically denied that he ever was a friend of theirs; indeed, their acquaintance was of the slightest. The attempt to prove at the trial that any intimacy existed between them utterly broke down. No great reliance, therefore, need be placed on Curran's detailed account of their relations. The point was only introduced into the trial to blacken Captain Armstrong's character, and evoke sympathy for the Sheares. If we consider the former's position for a moment, it is to him rather that we must extend our sympathy. He had unwittingly stumbled on a widespread conspiracy. If he did not "inform," he became a traitor to his country; if he did, he ran the risk of being branded as the betrayer of two men who, whatever were their faults, were brave gentlemen. There was no middle course; there was no time for hesitation. The capital was in commotion. The defection of a regiment in the country would have been an event of the gravest moment, and one well calculated to add greatly to the crisis.

'To stigmatise Captain Armstrong as "an informer" and the "vilest among men" is puerile. As well apply those names to any chief witness in any trial for treason, or to any officer who, in similar circumstances, placed his duty to his King and country above all other considerations. Sentiment has always played a conspicuous part in the allegations against Captain Armstrong. For my own part, I cannot see that the fact that Henry Sheares was a young married man rendered him and his brother less traitors to the existing Government, or makes Captain Armstrong's conduct towards them either more or less reprehensible. A fairer account of the incident than the one Mr. Fitzpatrick seems to give is to be found in Mr. Lecky's last volume, which in many respects bears out Captain Armstrong's own narrative in his "History of the Armstrong Family."

'The Government pension was given to enable the recipient to live abroad, out of the reach of those who justly considered him as one who was principally concerned in preventing a recurrence of the miseries of '98. Captain Armstrong returned to Ballycumber House in later years, and I believe he died there. The traitor-roll of Ireland is long enough already. The name of a gentleman who, at the risk of life and honour, did his duty to his King has no place there. The attempt to include it is as idle as it is uncharitable.

'I am, Sir, your obedient servant,

'Thomas Armstrong White.

'No. 17 Conduit Road, Bedford, March 26.'

After thanking the Editor of the 'Standard' for a most attractive review of 'Secret Service under Pitt,' I went on to say:—

'The late Captain Armstrong, it will be remembered, brought to the scaffold in 1798 two barristers—the brothers Sheares. "To stigmatise Captain Armstrong as 'an informer' and 'the vilest among men' is puerile," writes Mr. Armstrong White. As a matter of fact, I did call him an "informer," and correctly. The words referring to him as "the vilest among men," and which Mr. White puts in inverted commas, are not mine.

'"The attempt to prove at the trial that any intimacy existed between them (Armstrong and Sheares) utterly broke down," continues Mr. Armstrong White. In 1843, Captain Armstrong waited upon Dr. Madden to explain his intercourse with the Sheareses. Mr., afterwards Lord, O'Hagan was present by previous arrangement. Among other remarks, Armstrong said that "he felt it was wrong to have gone to Sheares' house and to have dined with them." (See Madden's "United Irishmen," vol. i. p. 445.) Mr. Armstrong White pooh-poohs Curran's account of their relations, and says that "the point was only introduced into the trial to blacken Captain Armstrong's character."'

Curran's words are by no means wide of the truth. Captain Armstrong told Dr. Madden that at dinner at Henry Sheares' house the family gathered round a large table—'the old lady (the mother) sat at one side, the wife of Henry sat next her, the sister and the young girl at the other. Henry sat at one end, and John at the other; I sat next John' (Madden, vol. i. p. 445). It is added by Dr. Madden that the notes of what fell during the interview were read over to Captain Armstrong, and 'their correctness assented to by him.'

The next writer to address the 'Standard' was an English lawyer, Mr. H. W. Sibley:—

'*To the Editor of the* STANDARD.

'Sir,—Though Horace speaks of "*Cervius iratus leges minitatur et urnam*," and though Juvenal alludes to Matho, and thus the character of an informer has all the sanctity which can be derived from antiquity, one may be excused for observing that the part played by Captain Armstrong in '98 would not be entirely vindicated by the denial of the charge that he dandled Henry Sheares's children. It is worth observing that the denial of this charge (which has lately been renewed by a relative) was the only defence that Armstrong made of himself. He even admitted that he acted as an Agent Provocateur. In the "Speeches of the Right Hon. John Philpot Curran," edited, with a memoir and historical notes, by Thomas Davis, Esq., M.R.I.A., we read that "Captain Armstrong was accused in Dr. Madden's 'United Irishmen,' and in Mr. William Curran's 'Memoirs' of his father of having played with

Henry Sheares's children. He considered this error so important as to seek two interviews for the correction of it. The minutes of one of these meetings will appear in Dr. Madden's 'Third Series,' and will amuse or amaze the reader."

'The passage in Curran's speech for Henry Sheares, on which the statement is based, runs as follows:—"I am disposed to believe, shocking as it is, that this witness had the heart, when he was surrounded by the little progeny of my client—when he was sitting in the mansion in which he was hospitably entertained—when he saw the old mother supported by the piety of her son, and the children basking in the parental fondness of the father—that he saw this scene, and smiled at it; contemplated the havoc he was to make, consigning them to the storms of a miserable world, without having an anchorage in the kindness of a father!" In this speech, which was begun at midnight, Thursday, July 12, 1798, Curran exhibited all his matchless powers of eloquence—*suadæ medullæ*—which have so justly ranked him as the Hortensius of Ireland. As was said of him, "At the Irish Bar there is no man, not merely next him, but near him." His exordium was characterised by an earnest solemnity which makes this speech the most moving he ever uttered.

'The dramatic nature of the situation demanded the exercise of even such talents as his. Curran's brief, which was written by John Sheares, plainly told him to save Henry Sheares, at the expense of the writer. Curran did not conclude before daylight, and the accused was convicted and sentenced to death. In his peroration Curran alluded to the religious views of Armstrong. "The danger of my client is from the hectic of the moment, which you have the fortitude, I trust, to withstand. In that belief I leave him to you; and as you deal justice and mercy, so may you find it; and I hope that the happy compensation of an honest discharge of your duty may not be deferred till a future existence, which this witness (Armstrong) does not expect, but that you may speedily enjoy the benefits which you have conferred upon your country." In the course of the trial Curran had called three witnesses to prove Captain Armstrong was an Atheist, two that he was an avowed Republican and rebel.

'I am, Sir, your obedient servant,

'H. W. Sibley.

'**Caterham, Surrey, April 2.**'

Mr. Armstrong White duly replied:—

'Sir,—In answer to Mr. Fitzpatrick's letter, I beg to forward the copy of a document now in the possession of Major Armstrong, of Garry Castle. The officers of the King's County Militia were at that time men of the highest position in the county. Their opinion of the conduct of their brother officer was given in no uncertain tones —"We, who are acquainted with all the circumstances, know that your conduct was disinterested." Their decision is the decision of a Court of Honour. The value of contemporary opinion in matters affecting a man's honour is always great. He who ignores its importance must be prepared to show good reason for his course.

'John Warneford Armstrong, in his reply to this address of his brother officers, pointed out that he first met the Sheares on May 10, and that they were arrested on the 21st. All Curran's eloquence could not alter that fact. He then continues: "The only question that can admit of any doubt is, whether, under the circumstance, it was becoming a man of honour to act as I have done. I must observe that I put myself under the direction of my Colonel and my friends. I acted by their advice, and if I have done anything wrong, they are rather more culpable than I." He points out next what a dreadful conspiracy existed, together with the murders and outrages it would entail, and then concludes—

'"When I consider these points, and many more which occur to me, I have great doubt whether a man of strict honour would not be justifiable (*sic*) in seeking the confidence of those men for the purposes of detection. But mine is a much clearer case. These men made a hostile attack on me; as an officer they offered me the highest insult, and as an Irish subject they sought, in order to forward their own views, to involve me in a transaction which would have probably led to infamy and ruin."

'Captain Armstrong told Dr. Madden that he felt it was wrong to have dined with the Sheares. Would an "Informer" have felt any prickings of conscience nearly forty-five years after the event? Surely that name is not applicable to Captain Armstrong. If it is, the esteem of his brother officers, the respect of his neighbours, and the love that some still bear for his memory have been strangely misplaced.'

Here Mr. Armstrong White appended the complimentary address which certain officers of the King's County Militia had presented to his ancestor in 1798; also a letter signed 'W. W. Westenra, Lt.-Col.,' conveying 'with much satisfaction' the document referred to. As these papers are already on record, and accessible to inquirers, it is needless to reprint them here. In reply I remarked :—

'I am very familiar with the attempted exculpation of Captain J. W. Armstrong, in 1798, by his brother officers of the King's County Militia. I have never attached any importance to that well-known document. Party spirit ran high in those unhappy days, and in Dr. Madden's "United Irishmen" (vol. i., p. 446) the officers referred to are noticed—rightly or wrongly—as "Orangemen." The flattering address to Captain Armstrong from his fellow-officers first appeared in the "Dublin Journal;" it has been often reprinted since. It receives prominence in Madden's "Lives and Times," and is now honoured with insertion by the "Standard."

'Mr. Armstrong White says that the decision of certain officers of the King's County Militia, regarding Armstrong's conduct in 1798, was "the decision of a Court of Honour." I fear that Mr. White overrates the status held by Irish Militia in '98. General Lake, writing to the Viceroy on August 28, 1798, remarks: "I think it is absolutely necessary to state, for your Lordship's information, that it is impossible to manage the Militia; their whole conduct this day of action has been most shameful."—("Cornwallis," ii., p. 393).

'The military inquiries in Ireland, during the great excitement of the time—even when they attained the rank of Courts-martial—were far from being regarded as "the decisions of a Court of Honour." A yeoman soldier, named Woolagan, murdered a boy, but was acquitted by the Court-martial that tried him. The murderer, in fact, threw the *onus* on the general orders issued by Captain Armstrong. "The Cornwallis Papers" (ii., p. 422) fully details how the new Viceroy, in disgust, disqualified Lord Enniskillen from again presiding at a Court-martial. This peer was an Orange Grand Master, which shows the spirit which animated men otherwise respectable. According to Plowden, the officers in '98 went through the fields with dogs, shooting down terrified peasants, and playfully called the slaughter "partridge shooting" ("Historical Review," ii., p. 811).

'The attempt made by the King's County Militia to clear Captain Armstrong from stain was not generally endorsed. Sir Jonah Barrington was an officer in an Irish Volunteer Corps—a regiment which, in point of social status and intelligence, held a high rank, including, as it did, Judges and King's Counsel—and the emphatic testimony of Barrington is as follows:—"He (Armstrong) had the honour of an officer and the integrity of a gentleman to sustain; yet he deliberately sacrificed both, and saw two barristers executed through his treachery" ("Rise and Fall of the Irish Nation," 1833, p. 363).

'In the so-called vindications of Captain Armstrong a special prominence is always given to the flattering letter of Colonel Westenra, dated December 23, 1798. How far this letter, signed "Yours with much regard," was inspired by political instincts, and stimulated by a diplomacy not at first obvious, might be interesting to inquire. Colonel Westenra was a candidate for parliamentary honours; and, at that time, no man could be returned if Dublin Castle did not favour his candidature. Soon after an opportunity presented itself to gratify Westenra's ambition. The Viceroy, writing on August 16, 1800, as regards the representation of Monaghan, says that "the Government could on no account be hostile to Westenra." (See "Cornwallis Correspondence," iii., p. 288.)'

Mr. Hall Worthington, writing from Oxton, Cheshire, supplied a fact not generally known. He explained that Armstrong, in cultivating friendly intercourse with the Sheares, was influenced by two motives for which he deserved well. He had 'hopes of getting the names of any disloyal men in his own Regiment (a cause of great anxiety with Militia officers), and of learning something of the designs of the Rebels. He succeeded in both objects, and his information as to the imminence of the rising and the plan on which it was to be conducted was most valuable.'

The correspondence was brought to a close by a remarkable letter from Commissary-General Lieut.-Colonel Shervinton:—

'*To the Editor of the* STANDARD.

'Sir,—I have read with minute attention and care, not only the events related in connection with the betrayal of the brothers Sheares in 1798 by Captain John Warneford Armstrong, but also the correspondence and comments in your columns to which such has given rise. As the grandson of the loyal soldier and true-hearted Irish gentleman who endeavoured to save these unfortunate young men from the fate to which the treachery of a kinsman was hounding them, I emphatically assert that the facts as recorded in the painful and humiliating narrative given by Mr. Fitzpatrick are in strict accord with the family history familiar to me from childhood.

'It is beyond a doubt that Captain John Warneford Armstrong proceeded, deliberately and designedly, out of his way to associate with these confiding men, whose destruction he ultimately compassed. It is not possible to gauge or determine the motives which actuated him when adopting the dastardly part, as my side of the family think he did. Whether it was for *kudos*, or prospective money reward, or to screen and atone for his suspected relations with United Irishmen under his command, will never now be known.

'In Captain Armstrong's acknowledgment of the coat of whitewash generously provided for him by his brother officers—all naturally anxious to save the credit of their cloth and county—he recognises the doubt whether "it was becoming a man of honour to act as I have done," but having "put myself under the direction of my Colonel and my friends, if I have done wrong, they are rather more culpable than I." Judas followed the behests of his superiors and friends, but he never "rounded" on them after this fashion. When John Warneford Armstrong parted in so self-complaisant a manner with the sole guardianship of his personal honour, he could not feel compunction in accepting its proffered and estimated equivalent.

'Captain Armstrong's long years of expatriation, coupled with the successful efforts of his family to have his name inserted as one of three lives, upon the survival of either of whom would the existence of leases depend, enabled him to close his remaining years in peace. That he enjoyed "the respect of his neighbours and the love of some" would, no doubt, be gratifying. Yet he told me, when we first met in 1843, that he had never been openly welcomed but once, when, against his political bias, he voted for his cousin in the Radical interest.

'It cannot for a moment be doubted that the name and action of Captain John Warneford Armstrong will continue to be a matter of history and censure so long as Ireland has a memory. It would, therefore, be well if his name and conduct were left to the historian alone. For it is as unavailing, as it is opposed to truth and justice, for those who would wish them other than they are, to attempt to portray him either as a disinterested Loyalist, or as one who was actuated only by noble incentive, while he was doing all he knew to bring the brothers Sheares to a felon's death.[1]

'I am, Sir, your obedient servant,

'C. R. SHERVINTON, Lieut.-Colonel.

'67 Warwick Road, South Kensington, April 14.'

Major Carteret Armstrong, J.P., of Garry Castle, has addressed me direct, in a courteous letter, dated Ilfracombe, Devon, May 9, 1892. The points to which he takes exception are brought out in the following extracts :—

'As to the two copies of letters that you publish in your book (p. 321), and alleged by Mr. McNally to have been written by Lord Cork to him, I consider that coming from such a source, and asserted to be only copies of letters that never saw the light, and the copies themselves nearly a hundred years after their supposed dates, and then in connection with secret reports written by Mr. McNally when betraying his old and good friends, that it is not fair, I consider, to use them by suggesting what Sir Jonah Barrington or anyone else would have thought had he seen the letters. Had they existed why were they not used at the trial? Why did not Curran cross-examine on them, or McNally himself, who was one of the counsel for the prisoners? The reply must be either that no such letters existed, or that McNally was determined that his friends should be convicted, and I should be unwilling to believe the latter of any man, however badly he may have acted in other matters.

'The cross-examination on the subject of J. W. Armstrong's leaving the Somerset Militia was very feeble, and extracted nothing that could even insinuate that "Mr. John Warneford Armstrong" "quitted it in a most disgraceful manner," and if he had done so would not his numerous enemies have made the fact a matter of notoriety when he posed as a man of honour?

'A statement has been recently made that J. W. A. was never

[1] He was introduced to them for the first time at Byrne's store, 108 Grafton Street—for years the well-known rendezvous of leading United Irishmen. Some of Armstrong's books are now before me, inscribed with his autograph, 'John Warneford Armstrong, Ballycumber, 1792;' but the address which follows his signature from 1796 to 1798 is '100 Grafton Street.' His object in securing lodgings so close to Byrne's store may have been espionage. He admitted in his examination that he was at Byrne's almost every day. Lieutenant Shervinton deposed that it was in Byrne's house Armstrong put Paine's 'Rights of Man' into his hand, saying 'This is my creed.'—W. J. F.

openly welcomed but once. This seems to be somewhat misleading, as it appears to infer that only on the occasion of a general election, when he voted for his cousin, the late Sir Andrew Armstrong, was he welcomed. It may have been so as to a hustings greeting, and it is much in his favour that he should have had a welcome at all; but as to private intercourse in the family it was always cordial and friendly. I myself as a boy remember well the old gentleman often driving over in his yellow coach to see my father and uncle at our place at Garry Castle, and I also recollect his being friendly with my uncle of Claremount and with all the people of the county in his own rank in life.'

In conclusion Major Armstrong writes:—'I have merely thrown out these suggestions to you as to one trying to write impartially on a most difficult subject, where it is hard to be really impartial.' His remarks show acumen and are very temperately urged. It is the opinion of Mr. Lecky, however, but without reference to the letters mentioning Lord Cork, that McNally's secret missives to Dublin Castle are uniformly accurate, and that it would have been well for the Irish Government had they always acted on his reports. I may add that Lord Cork was called on the trial of the Sheareses but did not answer to his name.

Mr. Sibley, the English barrister who took part in the discussion that appeared in the 'Standard,' finally addressed me direct by putting a question not easy at once to answer. Some Queen's Counsel whom I consulted confessed to having a most limited knowledge of the Criminal Law, but suggested Mr. Constantine Molloy, Q.C., or, as they wittily dubbed him, 'Crim. Con.,' as the highest authority on such points. His published books hold a high rank, and his library embraces a collection of trials unique in its completeness. Mr. Sibley describes him as a fountain of jurisprudence; and perhaps it will be felt that the insertion in these pages of Mr. Molloy's reply will help to make them useful for future reference.

'65 Lower Leeson Street, Dublin, 15 April, 1892.

'Dear Mr. Fitzpatrick,—In answer to Mr. Sibley's question, "whether the law which existed in Ireland, and was first acted upon in Jackson's case in 1795, that one witness should be sufficient in cases of treason was purely a rule of judiciary law not based upon any statute?" I would say that the law laid down in Jackson's case by Lord Clonmel, with the concurrence of Mr. Justice Downes and Mr. Justice Chamberlaine, and in Sheares' case by

Lord Carleton, with the concurrence of Mr. Justice Crookshank and Mr. Baron Smith, to the effect that in cases of treason under the statute 25 Edward III., statute the fifth, one witness alone, if believed by the jury, was sufficient, was then the law of Ireland. A single witness was sufficient in a case of treason by the common law of both England and Ireland. When the cases of Jackson and Sheares were decided, the common law of Ireland on this point, viz. the sufficiency of a single witness to convict, was not altered by any statute. The contrary was the case in England; there the common law had then, *i.e.* in 1795, 1798, and for a long time previously, been altered, by statute, requiring two witnesses.

'In 1547 an English statute, 1 Edward VI., chap. 12, was passed, providing by its twenty-second section that no person should be indicted or convicted for any offence of treason unless the offender should be accused by two sufficient and lawful witnesses, and in 1551 another English statute, 5 & 6 Edward VI., chap. 11, was passed, which created some new treasons and provided that no person should be indicted or convicted for any of the treasons in the statute mentioned or for any other treasons which should be thereafter committed, unless the offenders be thereof accused by two lawful accusers. These two English statutes (1 Edward VI., chap. 12, sec. 22, and 5 & 6 Edward VI., chap. 11) altered the common law of England, and made two witnesses necessary in the case of treasons under the statute 25 Edward III. No such change was made in the common law of Ireland until the passing in 1821 of the 1 & 2 George IV., chap. 24.

'Three years after the passing of the two statutes of Edward VI. to which I have referred an English statute was passed, 1 & 2 Philip & Mary, chap. 10, followed by a corresponding Irish statute, 3 & 4 Philip & Mary, chap. 11, section 6. These statutes of Philip & Mary, both the English and the Irish one, enacted that all trials thereafter to be had for any treasons should be had and used only according to the due order and course of the common law.

'After the passing of the English statute, 1 & 2 Philip & Mary, chap. 10, an opinion prevailed amongst some lawyers in England, and was acted on by the courts there, that the effect of the statute 1 & 2 Philip & Mary, chap. 10, was to repeal the statutes of Edward VI. requiring two witnesses in cases of treason and to restore the common law which required only one witness. The opinion was an erroneous one. It was disputed by the illustrious Lord

Hale when at the bar and as Mr. Hale arguing as counsel on behalf of Christopher Love, see 5 Howell's "State Trials," p. 43, and Mr. East, in his "Pleas of the Crown," vol. i. p. 128, says: "It has long been settled that the true object and operation of the statute 1 & 2 Philip & Mary, chap. 10, which was intended for the benefit of the subject, and not to deprive him of any advantage which he then enjoyed, was not to repeal the statutes 1 Edward VI., chap. 12, and 5 & 6 Edward VI., chap. 11, but to restore the common law right of trial in the proper county and the peremptory challenge of thirty-five jurors which had been intrenched upon by several Acts in the reign of Henry VIII."

'Curran's argument in Jackson's case and in Sheares' case was that at common law two witnesses were necessary in cases of treason, by the common law. The only authority he had for this was the opinion of Sir Edward Coke, who in his "Third Institute," p. 25, had stated the law to be so, which he (Curran) admitted was controverted by Sir Michael Foster in his "Discourse of High Treason," and by Serjeant Hawkins in his "Pleas of the Crown." Coke's opinion is not borne out by the authorities to which he refers in his "Third Institute," p. 25. It is at variance with the opinion of Lord Hale. If Coke's opinion were correct, the statutes of Edward VI. to which I have referred would have been unnecessary. I believe the opinion of Sir Edward Coke was wrong and that the argument of Curran was not a sound one, or well founded.

'The English Act 7 Will. III., chap. 3, was not, I think, a declaratory Act or any index to the common law. It was simply an English statute having no reference to or force in Ireland. In 1708 it was followed by another English Act, 7 Anne, chap. 21 (The Union with Scotland Act), and its 14th section enacted that persons indicted for high treason should have delivered to them, in the presence of two or more credible witnesses, copies of the indictment against them, and a list of the witnesses to be produced on their trial, ten days before the trial.

'In 1765 the Irish Parliament passed an "Act for the better regulating of trials in cases of high treason under the Statute of Edward the Third," 5 George III., chap. 21. The title of this Irish Act was in almost the same words as that of the English Act, 7 Will. III., chap. 3, but its provisions fell short of those of the English Act. It only enacted for Ireland two of those provisions, viz. those with regard to delivering to the accused copies of the indictment and enabling the accused to make full defence by counsel assigned by the court, and it omitted to enact the provision contained in the 2nd section of the 7 Will. III., chap. 3, with regard to the necessity of there being two witnesses. This Irish Act Thomas Davis, in a note to Curran's speech for the Sheares, says was introduced by their father, who sat in the Irish Parliament as member for the borough of Clonakilty. It was not until the year 1821 that the provision of the English statute with regard to the necessity of two witnesses in cases of treason became the law in Ireland, when by the 1 & 2 George IV., chap. 24, that provision as well as other provisions of the 7 Will III., chap. 3, were extended to Ireland; and it was not until 1854 that the provisions of the Acts of 7 Will. III., chap. 3, and 7 Anne, chap. 21, sec. 14, were fully extended to Ireland, when the 17 & 18 Victoria, chap. 26, was passed. This last Act was introduced by Chief Justice Whiteside, who as counsel for William Smith O'Brien on his trial for high treason moved to postpone the trial on the ground of the non-delivery of the lists of the jurors and witnesses. Mr. Whiteside said (Hodges' "Report of the Trial of W. Smith O'Brien," p. 28): "It is a short question, but one of great importance, whether the prisoner is entitled, under the Act of Parliament which now applies to this country, to a copy of the jury panel and a list of the witnesses. That is the question. It is very extraordinary that living as we do, as it is said, under like laws, that there should be one law in England and another in Ireland in a matter which goes to the very root of the defence of a party accused for high treason. Looking to the recital of the Act of Parliament in England, I find that it is stated that it is absolutely essential for a party accused, in order to prepare for his defence, that a copy of the panel and a list of the witnesses should be furnished to him. Of course your Lordships cannot make the law; and it is merely a question upon the true construction of this Act whether Mr. Smith O'Brien has the same advantages if tried in Ireland that he would have if tried in England." The judges at the trial, Chief Justice Blackburne, Chief Justice Doherty, and Mr. Justice Moore, decided against the prisoner, holding that he was not entitled to the right which Mr. Whiteside claimed for him, and their decision was afterwards affirmed by the Court of Queen's Bench and the House of Lords.

'The judges who tried Jackson and the Sheareses I think laid down the law as to two witnesses not being necessary, one being sufficient, correctly. I don't see how they could pronounce it to be otherwise, having regard to the law as it then was. The blame for the Irish law being such as the judges declared it to be rests, I think, not with them, but with the Irish Parliament, which, instead of extending the English statutes of the 7 Will. III., chap. 3, and the 7 Anne, chap. 21, sec. 14, in their entirety to Ireland, only adopted a small part of them.

'I trust that the foregoing will be an answer to Mr. Sibley's inquiry. I have to regret that I was not able to let you have it sooner. The matter was one that required consideration, and I was interrupted in the writing. 'Ever yours sincerely,

'CONSTANTINE MOLLOY.'

In a subsequent letter Mr. Molloy added:—

'I omitted to mention a matter which I would now take the opportunity of supplying. There is an interesting case which I think gives a very good if not the best illustration of the injustice of the difference that formerly prevailed between the law of England and that of Ireland as to treason. It is the case of Walter Clare, who was tried and convicted of treason for having participated in Emmet's rebellion, and is reported in vol. 28 of Howell's "State Trials," p. 887. Leonard MacNally was Clare's only counsel, and his attorney was Mr. L. MacNally. Clare was a common labourer, working in Roe's Distillery in Marrowbone Lane, and he lived in Thomas Court, off Thomas Street. The sole evidence against Clare was the testimony of a single witness, John Forrest, who lived at No. 9 Thomas Court. He swore he saw Clare on the night of the rebellion with a pike on his shoulder; testimony that was open to the gravest doubts as to its accuracy and reliability, even assuming its veracity. Judge Finnucane charged the jury fairly. Clare was convicted on this testimony, and, along with five other prisoners who had been convicted of high treason for having participated in Emmet's rebellion, and whose trial is also reported in vol. 28 of Howell's "State Trials," p. 1069, he was sentenced to death. The five other prisoners were afterwards executed at Palmerstown; but Walter Clare was respited. What afterwards became of Clare is unknown; whether he was transported, or pardoned, or discharged from prison does not appear. But the respite at all events shows that the Executive Government must have had doubts of his guilt.

'If Walter Clare's case had occurred in England he could not have been put on his trial, or much less indicted, on the evidence upon which he had been convicted in Ireland. The great probability is, I think, that he had nothing to do with the rebellion, and that he was absolutely innocent, and the jury fell into an error in convicting him. His trial is interesting on other grounds, and is well worth reading. Some of the questions asked Forrest on his cross-examination by Leonard MacNally, a man of undoubted ability and large experience, whatever else he was,[1] seem to me to have been singularly indiscreet.

'The Mr. L. MacNally who acted as attorney on Clare's trial and for other of the high treason prisoners in 1803 can hardly have been the son whom you mention as having died in 1869 ("Secret Service under Pitt," p. 210). If he was, having been an attorney in 1803, he must have been at least eighty-seven when he died. Had MacNally two sons who were solicitors?—L. MacNally the attorney for Clare and another son John. In "Thoms' Directory" for 1863, in the list of attorneys and solicitors given for that year, the name of John MacNally is the only person of the name of MacNally who is given. He had his office at No. 1 Morgan Place and his residence at No. 8 Old Mountpleasant, Ranelagh, Dublin, and is probably the son who died in 1869.'

In reply to Mr. Molloy's query I may mention that Leonard McNally had been twice married: first to Miss Janson, an English

[1] McNally asked the witness Forrest if he told any person that he had seen Clare among the pikesmen. He replied 'Yes,' and mentioned three names. If he had been mistaken - as he is said to have been—the fact of telling to others what he saw would not strengthen the evidence, though it would weigh with a jury. The three names thus casually mentioned gave the Crown an opportunity of examining each of the men, provided they could be found. Within the next few minutes McNally entered into a lengthy argument with the court and law officers of the Crown in seeking to maintain an objection which the merest tyro in law would see to be untenable. At p. 899 of Howell's *State Trials*, vol. 28, we read, 'Lord Norbury said he would be very glad to have the point argued.' Much time was thus wasted, and in the end McNally withdrew his objection, amid derisive comments from the Attorney-General. The object is now clear. Time was thus gained to send for the men to whom the witness said he told what he saw. The Attorney-General—afterwards Lord Guillamore—duly produced them, but McNally again rose to object on the grounds that the case for the Crown had closed, adding (and here he imitated Curran on Sheares' trial), 'I feel extremely ill and languid, and it might be of serious consequences to my client.' *The Solicitor-General.*—'The witnesses may be examined in reply to the prisoners' case, therefore no objection can lie to their being examined.' Thereupon they were subjected to an examination as to what they heard from Forrest. Clare was found guilty and sentenced to death.—W. J. F.

lady, and secondly to Miss Edgeworth. The attorney during the trials of 1803 was Leonard McNally, junior (*obiit* 1820). John, also a distinguished solicitor, died in 1869, and is identical with the man indicated by Mr. Molloy. Old McNally's eldest son, Leonard, had been in fair practice as a lawyer. A local journal, 'Saunders' Newsletter,' confounded the son with the father, and erroneously announced the death of the latter, whereupon the offending pressman received the following letter :—

'Sir,—I am advised, from the severe injury I have received in consequence of the great circulation your paper gave of my death on the eve of the assizes, and my practice in the city of Dublin, to apply to the calm determination of a city of Dublin jury for damages against you. 'Your obedient servant,

'LEONARD MCNALLY.

'20 Cuffe Street,[1] Dublin, 6th March, 1820.'

Leonard McNally's second son, John, practised in the Insolvent Court; but not unfrequently on behalf of clients who had been accused of misappropriating assets. Old reporters describe him as the most rapid speaker that in their experience they had known. I am informed by an old 'chief' in that body that John McNally could utter nearly 300 words a minute, and that men who tried to record his speeches *verbatim* have had at last to throw down their pencils in despair. His face was like shrivelled parchment, in which two black and lustrous eyes danced. William Henry Curran presided in the Insolvent Court, and McNally—as representing the man whom, in the 'Life of John Philpot Curran,' the judge had praised (see p. 192, *ante*)—received much patronage at his hands. One day in 1869 the exhaustless orator became faint, and his death followed almost as suddenly as that of the Rev. William Jackson in the dock.

Before dismissing Leonard McNally, the prominent counsel in '98 for the rebels who had been made amenable, it remains to supply the details of a legal incident to which allusion has been made at p. 195, *ante*.

On July 14, 1802, three Orange yeomen—hot from their own celebration of 'The Twelfth'—fired on certain persons who had assembled in Kevin Street to witness some popular observances in

[1] Cuffe Street, though now in decay, and its houses let in tenements, was a place of respectable resort in McNally's time. Shelley's letters during hi visit to Dublin in 1813 are dated from Cuffe Street.

commemoration of the fall of the Bastille. A bonfire blazed, and garlands were hung on a fountain. The yeomen were not on duty, and no resistance had been offered to their presence. A man named Ryan fell riddled with balls; his employer, Alderman—afterwards Sir William—Stamer, deposed on the trial that the deceased was wholly innocent of seditious bias. One of the yeomen, when in gaol, confessed the murder. The Attorney and Solicitor General ought to have prosecuted, but Leonard McNally is made to discharge this *rôle*, assisted by an eccentric barrister named Isaac Burke Bethel. The jury were anti-popular in their sympathies, and not likely to be influenced by a prosecutor whose entire antecedents had been on the side of rebellion. 'Bully Egan' defended the prisoners. Mr. Baron George put the points very weakly, and in the end the men were acquitted. The farcical character of the performance is shown by one incident. Burke Bethel in examining a witness got out of his depth, whereupon McNally said to him, 'Tell me what you mean, and I will put the question for you.' O'Flanagan, in his 'Irish Bar,' describes Burke Bethel as a man ever ready to accept any meals he could get, or take any fee that was offered. On one occasion he said pompously, 'I appear for the Crown, my Lord,' and was met by the reply, 'Oftener for the half-crown.'

Besides the various letters addressed to the 'Standard' others appeared containing facts which ought, perhaps, to be noticed. Mr. Leonard Dobbin, of Hollymount, Cork, published a letter in the 'Irish Times' of March 12, 1892:—

'Referring to your observations respecting "Secret Service under Pitt," I have in my possession a letter dated March 15, 1797, written by one of the leaders of the "United Irishmen" then confined in Kilmainham Jail, and addressed to the State prisoners then confined in Carrickfergus Jail, which shows that, notwithstanding spies and informers, and all the power of the Government of the day, the enemies of the Government were able securely to carry on a secret correspondence even between prison and prison, and that so little were those prisoners under the influence of fear, or under effective surveillance, that they did not require to destroy that correspondence when read, showing that the Government were at that time just as little able as the rebels were to depend upon the loyalty of those by whom they were surrounded.'

The letter possessed by Mr. Dobbin, though it might, possibly, have some historic value, would not prove much as an argument in favour of his contention. It will be evident to readers of the foregoing pages that the Government were thoroughly aware of the secret correspondence which went on between the enemies of the State, and often allowed it to continue—seemingly undetected—in order to strengthen their grasp of the conspiracy. The Duke of Portland, finding that Samuel Turner shrank from prosecuting openly, told him to open a correspondence with the principal conspirators, 'by which means we shall be fully apprised of their designs, and able to baffle them.'

The next letter which appeared was from the biographer of the 'Lord Chancellors of Ireland.'

'Grange House, Fermoy, March 21.

'Sir,—I was glad to read in your influential paper of the 8th and 12th inst. some able articles dealing with "Secret Service under Pitt," which I regard as a most important historical work, and I am glad that the author's labours have penetrated the dark depths in which the gold of Pitt has so long lain hidden. What terrible odium must attach to the memory of those who were trusted and beloved while betraying the colleagues who reposed in them such misplaced confidence!

'It is ever thus. What Mr. Fitzpatrick has brought to light was repeated in our own day in 1848. Every meeting of Young Irelanders was known in the Castle half an hour after their secret plans were arranged. Mr. Baldwin, Q.C.—afterwards a judicial personage—was then Law Adviser to the Lord Lieutenant. I was living in his house, and I did not fail to warn my friends that every step they took was revealed at once to the Castle. I informed John Blake Dillon, and a not less true and trusted patriot, John Pigot, son of the Chief Baron, and they laughed and said it was "impossible." Yet they, like so many in the days of Pitt, were deceived.

'In 1848 King Louis Philippe was hurled from his throne, and his vast army to a man turned over to the Republic. Smith O'Brien had just returned from a mission to France, and upraised the standard of revolt in Ireland. He and his comrades in the Young Ireland party expected, and frequently declared, that the military in this country were disaffected. I had personal knowledge they were not so. My father, the barrack-master of Fermoy, was then dying, and he received authority for me to act as his deputy in the large barracks at Fermoy, a rather disturbed district at the time, and while serving out the stores I frequently inquired as to the disposition of the troops. They were loyal to the core, and this was shown by the alacrity with which they acted when the revolt at length took place.

'I am, Sir, very truly yours,

'JAMES RODERICK O'FLANAGAN.'

The author of the present volume, in thanking a critic for some complimentary remarks, took occasion to explain a point. 'You add that I am mistaken in thinking that I was the first to identify Samuel Turner. It is quite true that Mr. Lecky, in his seventh volume (first issued in 1890), mentions Turner in a foot-note, and it is equally true that two years previously my book had been ready for the printer, but was laid aside in order that, as the preface states, I might go to other work which admitted of no postponement. I had a correspondence with Mr. Lecky about Turner long before his final volumes (vii. and viii.) appeared, and at p. 48 of "Secret Service under Pitt" I quote from that correspondence. My hunt after Turner began so far back as 1876. No one but myself ever attempted to identify and track the mysterious betrayer who plays so important a part in Mr. Froude's "English in Ireland," and whose mask seemed to that acute thinker impenetrable.'

THE SECRET SERVICE FUND.

The following report is taken from the 'Times':—

'Mr. P. O'Brien asked the Chief Secretary to the Lord Lieutenant of Ireland whether Mr. Fitzpatrick, author of the recently-published work, "The Secret Service Fund under Pitt," had access to the State papers in Dublin Castle; and whether there was any objection to allowing Mr. Fitzpatrick to pursue his investigations in order to give the history of the Secret Service Fund up to 1886.

'The Attorney-General for Ireland.—It is the case that the gentleman mentioned had access to certain State papers under a regulation of the State Paper Department, whereby historians are granted permission to refer to certain records, with the permission of the Keeper of the State Papers. This permission is limited to records of the age of 50 years from the making thereof, and it would, therefore, not be possible to give the permission suggested in the second paragraph of the question.

'Mr. MacNeill asked whether any regulations were given to the Castle officials for the preservation of State papers.

'The Attorney-General for Ireland [now Mr. Justice Madden].—They are most carefully preserved.

'Mr. Sexton.—Then we shall have to wait for 50 years to get at the disposal of the Secret Service Fund, say, under Harcourt.

'The Attorney-General for Ireland.—I must ask the hon. member to postpone his question for 50 years. (Laughter.)'

In Parliament the title of this book was erroneously given as 'The Secret Service *Fund* under Pitt,' and every newspaper which reported the proceedings of the House echoed the misnomer. The Secret Service Fund is very different from a history of acts of Secret Service specially performed. It will be seen that the wages eventually received for the performances in question take a mere secondary place in this book. It hardly needs to be added that 'Mr. Fitz-Patrick' was in no way privy to the question asked.

JOHN POLLOCK

(See p. 178, *ante.*)

John Pollock, Clerk of the Crown, who, according to the 'Cornwallis Papers,' 'managed' the counsel and attorney of the United Irishmen (see p. 78, *ante*), deserves a note, especially as he is one of the men regarding whom the industrious editor of that work found it impossible to ascertain particulars. His services, which, Cooke says, 'ought to be thought of,' were rewarded in 1800 by the Deputy Clerkship of the Pleas of the Exchequer. Gross abuse defiled this post; but until 1816 the iniquity was not brought before Parliament. On April 29 Mr. Leslie Foster declared that 'Mr. Pollock drew 10,000*l.* out of the profits, and on which he ought to pay the salaries of the other clerks; but, instead of this, he pocketed the whole of the money, leaving them to raise the fees upon the suitors on no other authority than their own assumptions!' In 1803 Pollock's emoluments from this office did not exceed 3,000*l.* a year. Mr. Attorney-General Saurin impeached him in nine distinct charges, and as a result he was deposed.[1]

[1] William Sinclair, of Belfast, one of the founders of the Dungannon Convention, married John Pollock's sister. He afterwards took part in the battle of Antrim, where Lord O'Neil fell. He survived until the year 1864, and had

Pollock's name constantly appears in that curious manuscript known as the 'S.S. Money Book,' one of the last payments to him being on January 10, 1799, for 1,137*l.* 10*s.* The frequent payments to 'John Pollock for J. W.' (McNally) suggested that the gold which he disbursed was usually for persons connected with the law, and with this clue I am able to trace and make clear various ciphers which Dr. Madden was unable to explain when publishing a copy of the Secret Account just named. For instance, we find: '1799—16 Feb. J. Pollock for J. W.—£150—G. M. £50.' Again, on May 3 following: 'J. Pollock for G. M. I.—£50.' And on June 5 and August 3, '£150 to G. M. I.' Who is 'G. M.' and 'G. M. I.'?

George McIntagart is described in 1798 as an attorney-at-law. Benjamin P. Binns, in an autobiographical sketch, speaks of this man as his step-father. It was George McIntagart who, when Mayor of Drogheda in 1798, dressed up Orangemen in French uniforms, and sent them through the country to entrap simple peasants. He then flogged them until they revealed whatever they knew. The future Duke of Wellington, writing to the Lord Lieutenant of Ireland on March 17, 1809, observes: 'Will you have Mr. McIntagart appointed to be Collector of Drogheda?'[1]

'February 24, 1798. Mr. Pollock for J. W. H.' appears on record. Turning to the list of attorneys in that year, the name of 'J. Wright Heatly' is found. Dr. Madden also prints, 'August 23. Major Sirr for W. A. H., £68 5*s.* 0*d.*,' but offers no conjecture as to the owner of these initials. He must be the man described by Plowden who, after an interview with the Irish Privy Council, was equipped at the expense of Dublin Castle with a showy rebel uniform, including a cocked hat and feathers, and sent on a mission to Belfast to seduce and to betray. An orderly dragoon repaired with instructions to General Sir Charles Ross, who commanded in Belfast, that Houlton was a confidential agent and not to be molested. Houlton, however, having started in a chaise and four, arrived at Belfast in advance of the orderly, and the result was that, when in the act of declaiming treason at a tavern, he was arrested by the local authorities, paraded in his uniform round the town, and sent back a prisoner to Dublin.[2] The Belfast papers of the day give his name as

reached the age of ninety-eight. The Rev. Dr. Steel Dickson's 'Narrative' gives a startling picture of Pollock (pp. 65–75).

[1] Plowden's *Post-Union History*, i. 223–5.

[2] See *Wellington Correspondence* (*Ireland*), p. 612.

William Ainslie Houlton, and he is clearly identical with the W. A. H. of Mr. Cooke's cipher. It would be endless to pursue this subject. Meanwhile, those who care to follow the various ciphers in the 'S.S. Money Book,' and to know the circumstances under which each item is penned, can obtain full information from the present writer.

Pollock in his new sinecure did not cease to gratify the instincts which made him so efficient in 1798. A letter from him is found in the 'Wellington Correspondence,' dated January 12, 1809, directing attention to McNevin's 'Pieces of Irish History,' then recently published in New York. Pollock assures the future subjugator of Napoleon that, from information he received, this book is the precursor of a French invasion of Ireland. '*If you have Cox*,'[1] he adds '(who keeps a small bookshop in Anglesea Street), he can let you into the whole object of sending this book to Ireland at this time; and further, if you have not Cox, believe me that no sum of money at all within reason would be misapplied in riveting him to the Government. I have spoken of this man before to Sir Edward Littlehales and to Sir Charles Saxton. He is the most able, and, if not secured, by far the most formidable man that I know of in Ireland.'[2] This letter, from the niche assigned to it in the 'Wellington Correspondence,' calls for a distinct notice of Cox, whose name occurs so frequently in the foregoing sheets.

WALTER COX[3]

(See p. 71, *ante*.)

Mr. O'Donoghue, in 'Irish Humourists,' states of Cox and his rebel sheet, the 'Union Star,' which openly urged assassination: 'While the moderate organs of the United Irishmen—the "Press"

[1] Watty Cox, publisher of the *Irish Magazine*. Eighteen months previously, Mr. Trail, of Dublin Castle, reports to Sir A. Wellesley a long conversation with Cox. See *Wellington Correspondence* (*Ireland*), p. 121.

[2] *Civil Correspondence and Memoranda of F.M. Arthur Duke of Wellington*, edited by his Son, p. 535.

[3] The author of *Irish Humourists* describes Cox as one of the most peculiar individuals to be met with in Irish history, and expresses hope that some day the documents relating to him possessed by the late Dr. Madden, and other manuscripts that must be somewhere in existence, will be published, and a full biography given to the world of so striking a personality.

and the "Northern Star"—were being suppressed and their editors persecuted and imprisoned, Watty Cox and his sheet were left severely alone.' I am sure the author will allow me, in the interests of history, to set this point right. The Pelham MSS. contain the following letter from Cooke:—'This day I suppressed the "Union Star." Cox offered [Justice] Bell to disclose the author, and to tell what he knew to Government on condition of pardon. I accepted the terms and have seen him. He was sole author, printer, and publisher. He composed the "Star" at different printing houses with types of different printers and struck them off by a small bellows press of his own. He says he continued the publication more from vanity than mischief; says that he has been for some time against continuing the scheme of separation from England because he thought it could not succeed . . . thinks it will if there be any invasion. Lord Edward F. [*sic*] and O'Connor have been often with him; they knew of his writing the "Star." Cox pronounced Lord Edward "weak but very zealous"; O'Connor has abilities and is an enthusiast, but he thinks they want system.' Much more follows, and Cooke adds, 'he [Cox] is a clever man and deep.' [1]

The Viceroy, Camden, writing two days later, says: 'He [Cox] seems able to give much important information;' [2] but Camden assumes this merely on the strength of the fact mentioned in Cooke's letter, and Cox does not seem to have compromised his friends by any actual disclosure. Arthur O'Connor, addressing Dr. Madden in 1842, declared that Cox remained always faithful to him, and also to Lord Edward Fitzgerald. 'Whatever changes may have taken place in his conduct, it was not until after Lord Edward's death and O'Connor's exile. While there was a chance of success, he was one of the staunchest men in Ireland to their cause.' Had O'Connor—a person of great vanity—dreamt that Cox called him an enthusiast, and Lord Edward weak, his praise might perhaps have been modified.

In 1803, when Dublin Castle was dismayed by the outbreak of Emmet's rebellion within shadow of its walls, I find addressed to Cox the copy of a letter from Under-Secretary Marsden requesting him to call upon him, and 'nobody would be the wiser.' Cox replies in writing to the effect that he did not care how public

[1] Cooke to Pelham, Dublin Castle, December 14, 1797.
[2] Camden to Pelham, December 16, 1797. (Pelham MSS.)

their communications might be; and certainly at this time he cannot be called 'a spy,' if indeed he ever was.

The Viceroy Hardwicke wrote, soon after, an official vindication of his conduct; and he mentions incidentally that it had been meditated to place Cox under arrest as a dangerous democrat. His 'Irish Magazine' is a marvellous medley, and contains, intermingled with some rubbish, a good deal of valuable matter useful for future reference. Having been put in the pillory more than once for his writings, and finally been sentenced to pay a fine of 300*l.*, and enter into security himself for one thousand, with two others of 500*l.* each, to keep in good behaviour for seven years, as well as suffer one year's confinement in Newgate, Cox at last consented, on receiving a pension of 100*l.* a year, to expatriate himself to America. This Lord Mulgrave stopped in 1835, and the death of Cox occurred soon after.[1]

'*REMEMBER ORR!*'

(See chap. xxi.)

Documents previously quoted make ambiguous reference to the fate of William Orr. This unfortunate person was arraigned at Carrickfergus in September 1797, for having administered to a soldier named Wheatley the United Irishman's oath. He was found guilty and sentenced to death. Most of the inhabitants left the town to mark their horror. Newspapers of the last century did not deal much in sensational headings. The 'Courier' of December 25, 1797—that influential journal for which Coleridge wrote—affords some exception:—

'Murder Most Foul!—The Irish papers which arrived this morning contain the affidavits of the Rev. George Macartney, D.L., magistrate for the county Antrim; the Rev. James Elder, Dissenting Minister; and of Alexander Montgomery, Esq., stating that Hugh Wheatley—one of the witnesses brought forward by the Crown against Mr. Orr, lately executed in Ireland—had confessed that he had been guilty of *perjury* and *murder*!!'

Some of the jury also came forward and admitted that they were

[1] In Birmingham Tower, Dublin Castle, the box marked 'Carton 620–24' should be consulted.

drunk when they gave their verdict. These facts, duly deposed to and attested, were laid before the Viceroy, Lord Camden, by the magistrate who had caused Orr to be arrested, 'and who,' writes Dr. Madden, 'when he found the practices that had been resorted to, used every effort, though fruitlessly, to move Lord Camden to save the prisoner. Orr was executed because of his known connection with the United Irish system, but not on account of the crime legally laid to his charge.'

The date of Lord Camden's decision, in reply to the strong appeal which had reached him, merits attention. Turner, on October 8, 1797, disclosed to Downshire—for the private information of the Government—a list of men, including 'two Orrs,' who, he said, were members of the Executive Directory of the United Irishmen; and Camden, probably, thought that Orr, who then lay in jail, adjudged guilty of having administered the rebel oath, was one of them. On October 13, Camden declared that William Orr should hang, and within forty-eight hours he suffered death.[1] A painful sensation passed through the country: Drennan's fine lyric, 'The Wake of William Orr,' will live as long as 'The Burial of Sir John Moore.' '*Remember Orr*' were the last words in the manuscript which hanged Sheares. The fate of Orr had more effect in hurrying rebellion to a premature explosion than all the efforts of Tone, McNevin, and O'Connor. The latter urged that Ireland should strike without further waiting for French aid.

Dr. Madden re-awakened interest in this case of Orr by claiming to show that Wheatley, by whose tainted testimony he died, was identical with a subsequently well-known military officer. Hugh Wheatley, the informer and common soldier (Dr. Madden holds), is the same man who afterwards figured as Captain Wheatley in the West Middlesex Regiment, who served in Egypt, 'wore the Sphinx on his cap,' and in 1827 resided at Uxbridge.[2] In 1844 Dr. Madden addressed to a brother officer of this man—Captain Hester—various queries, all of which drew forth answers disparaging to Captain Wheatley, including the fact that he was remarkable for his love of money and his profligacy. 'How did he get his commission?' asked Dr. Madden: 'I cannot say,' replied Hester, 'nor could any of the officers. The commanding officers

[1] Hope, who knew most of the secrets of his party, has stated that the man who administered the oath to the soldier was not William Orr but William McKeever, a delegate from Derry, who afterwards escaped to America.

[2] *United Irishmen*, i. 486-7.

appeared always in fear of him. It was not because he had good pistols, for he never used them himself, but he would lend them—as he would his cash—on interest.'

It seems almost a pity to spoil the piquancy of an attractive page, but 'truth is stranger than fiction,' and as Dr. Madden declares more than once that justice to the dead and historic accuracy are his objects, it is right to show that in this case he has confounded two utterly different men. Even a son of the wronged officer is brought on the *tapis* as a person Dr. Madden had known in another land. The following letter confirming my doubts will help to distinguish between the two Wheatleys :—

'War Office: September 6, 1866.

'Sir,—I am directed by the Secretary of State for War to acknowledge the receipt of your letter of the 21st ultimo, asking for particulars of the service &c. of a Mr. Hugh Wheatly in the West Middlesex Militia, between the years 1799 and 1810, and to acquaint you that he regrets that he is unable to give you the information you wish for.

'I may add that a Mr. W. Wheatley was appointed to the Regiment as Lieutenant on the 21st February, 1804, and was promoted to a Company, 17th December, 1811.[1]

'A Mr. Hugh Wheatly was serving in the Tenth (Edinburghshire) Militia in 1800 as Lieutenant. His commission was dated 26th March, 1798.

'I am, Sir, your obedient Servant,

'L. Shadwell, Col.

'W. J. Fitzpatrick, Esq., J.P.,
Kilmacud Manor.'

The Hugh Wheatley who—as we are informed by the War Office—received a commission in the Edinburghshire Militia on March 26, 1798, is certainly Orr's Wheatley. One of the depositions of the Rev. George Macartney, J.P., speaks of Hugh Wheatley as a *Scotch* soldier, who confessed that he had been instigated to give false evidence against Orr. Even after he had received his commission we find Wheatley in receipt of Secret Service money; and on February 5, 1800, 115*l.* 2*s.* 9*d.*—or one hundred guineas old currency—appears on record to his credit.

Notes of a conversation with the late Dr. Verdon—a representa-

[1] This was the Wheatley known to Captain Hester.

tive of William Orr—discloses some things new to students of the time. Major Orr, son of William Orr, served with distinction in the Peninsular War; he obtained his commission at the age of twenty-three, and on his return to England the Duke of York, then Commander-in-Chief, after complimenting him upon his services, asked if there was any promotion he ambitioned. 'I hate the sword I wear,' was Orr's sullen reply; 'perhaps your Royal Highness will allow me to retire from the service.' 'Pray are you related to Orr who suffered in '98?' inquired the Duke. 'I have the honour to be his son,' the soldier replied. The Duke with reluctance accepted the resignation, and next day wrote a cheque for 1,000*l.*, and sent it to the widow of William Orr 'as some slight compensation for the loss she had sustained' twenty years before. The Duke of York was at this time heir apparent to the throne. Captain Orr retired on full pay with the rank of brevet major. Some years after, finding that his means were inadequate to meet domestic expenses, he asked the Duke for a barrack mastership. Orr filled this office in Longford, and subsequently in Dublin till his death.

'THE WEARING OF THE GREEN'

Mrs. Anastasia O'Byrne, who died in 1875, had been in the habit of sending me rough recollections of such small things as came within the cognisance of a very unobtrusive woman. Some of her letters appeared in a former book. The following is new:—

'In May, 1798,' says Mrs. O'Byrne, 'the narrator, then a comely matron of thirty, possessing a soft innocent expression and a delicate rose-hue complexion, donned her bonnet of the previous season, with intent to make some purchases in the drapery line at a flourishing mart in Thomas Street. The bonnet was of bright green silk, had often been worn without remark, was purchased for its supposed becoming effect, and had lain quietly ensconced in its bandbox throughout the winter. But during that eventful season the political atmosphere had undergone disturbance, and the storm which shattered to pieces many happy homesteads was about to sweep through Ireland. Amid other signs of the times, "the wearing of the green" came to be regarded with suspicion and dislike by the authorities of the day. Of this, however, the wearer of the green bonnet was then quite unconscious. On she went, but was rather concerned, and somewhat puzzled, to find herself attracting an unusual share of the attention of the passers-by, particularly as she was alone. As she passed out of Dame Street into Castle Street and Skinner's Row,[1] where the narrowness of the flag-way made collisions of passengers a rule rather than an exception, she was startled to hear, every other moment, a voice whispering, almost under her bonnet: "God bless your colour, ma'am!" She remarked that those who did not use this phrase regarded her with an angry scowl; but still no thought of connecting these incidents with the *hue* of her bonnet ever crossed her mind. On her return from Thomas Street her attractive power seemed to increase, the cabalistic words: "God bless your colour, ma'am!" were not uttered so frequently, but the streets were greatly crowded by men, some of whom regarded her bonnet with so fierce a glare that she thought they had a notion of plucking it from her head. She then began to perceive, with some alarm, that scarcely any women were abroad, and that military and yeomanry paraded the streets. When she reached Cork Hill she saw masses of people thronging the line of way in Dame Street, whilst the crowd about the Castle gates and the Royal Exchange seemed heaving in agitation like the waves of a troubled sea. Whilst trying to pierce the dense crowd around the Royal Exchange she heard a familiar voice shout her name twice in a loud, excited tone. She glanced in the direction of the sound, and saw the pale, eager face of a young man of her acquaintance, the husband and brother of two intimate female friends, peering at her through one of the windows of the Royal Exchange, then a receptacle for State prisoners. Entering a little by-street she turned with great difficulty from the surge of the crowd which was floating from College Green side, and soon got into more quiet quarters. By the circuitous route she reached home unmolested, but found the household in great alarm about her, for tidings had reached them that several females during the tumult of the day had been rudely insulted, and roughly treated, for wearing ribbons or garments of green hue, one most respectable lady having had a gown of the obnoxious colour sliced

[1] This narrow street—as well as the adjoining passage known as 'Hell'—was cleared away soon after, in order to form Christchurch Place in front of the cathedral.

from her body by the sabre of a loyal trooper. The excitement of the day was caused by the arrest of the unfortunate brothers Sheares. The young prisoner who called on her from the window had just recently been arrested in the street on suspicion, solely on account of having used indignant words of remark in the hearing of a loyal yeoman. His great anxiety to gain the notice of the wearer of the green bonnet was caused by his desire that his relatives, who were ignorant of his arrest, should learn it, and take measures for his release, before the tidings of it could reach the ears of a very youthful wife in a very delicate condition.

'The poor fellow was speedily released, for higher game had been bagged, and nothing beyond his warm words could be adduced against him. But the young wife, whom he soon after left a widow, always believed that his early death was caused by his arrest. He had caught a severe cold whilst in prison, his lungs became affected, and rapid decline and early death ensued.

'On the day of the arrest of the Sheareses the wearer of the green bonnet beheld the sacking and the attempted burning of the house and stock-in-trade of Patrick Byrne, the bookseller of Grafton Street in whose shop the brothers were first introduced to their betrayer, Captain Armstrong. It was a pitiful sight to behold the amount of property in beautifully bound books ruthlessly torn to pieces and tossed out of windows into the street. Byrne was arrested, but afterwards got safely out of the country, and settled in Philadelphia. His brother, a Roman Catholic priest in Rosemary Lane Chapel, followed him to America.'

The old lady's garrulousness about her green bonnet has been allowed space the more readily because the following contemporary statement comes to illustrate and explain, not only her own reminiscence, but an oft-quoted phrase which has become historic. I have culled it from the London 'Courier' of August 29, 1797. The 'Dublin Journal' to which it refers was the organ of the Irish Government :—

Ireland.

Dublin, August 24.—The 'Dublin Journal,' with base malignity, throws out the most indecent insinuations against the virtue of every female who wears *green* in her apparel. How the citizens of Dublin, and the inhabitants of the country, who are also included in this infamous denunciation, will bear to have their wives and daughters so stigmatised, remains to be seen. A more villainous libel never disgraced the Press. In case of success, it must render useless all the goods in silk, cotton, or woollen which have been dyed green, to the ruin of the manufacturers. Language is not adequate to express the abhorrence that arises at this hellish meditation to rob women of their character and working-people of bread!

A corps, called the 'Antient Britons,' attained notoriety by their cruelties in '98. Pelham, in a secret letter, recognises their activity and loyalty; but casually adds (a trait which, coming from him, will be more regarded than if told by a partisan): 'They were quartered at Newry,' he writes, 'where there was a lady as active as the Misses Gregg at Belfast, and upon her accosting a soldier on guard, she was certainly very roughly treated. . . . They tied her petticoats round her neck, and sent her home showing her garters.' [1] Pelham probably learned this fact from one of the letters of Samuel Turner formerly of Newry. The Antient Britons were usually led in Ireland by Major Wardle, afterwards famous for his attack on the Duke of York and Mrs. Clarke.

'The Wearing of the Green' has taken a strangely strong hold even on modern minds—partly due, perhaps, to the fine minor to which the words have been wedded. This enduring interest is not shown solely by Parisian journalists (p. 70, *ante*). At the Antipodes they are equally on the *qui vive.* The Sydney 'Freeman's Journal' of June 25, 1892, says:—

'It is very far from being safe to differ from Mr. Fitzpatrick even on so trifling a matter as "the truth of a song," to quote Prior's phrase; still we venture to assert that mention of Tandy is only to be found in a comparatively recent version of the "Wearing of the Green;" in fact in the one "adapted" by Dion Boucicault for his play of "Arrah-na-Pogue."'

Dr. George Atkinson, of Dublin, now in his eighty-fourth year, says that he sang the Napper Tandy verse before Dion Boucicault was born. The 'Citizen' for January 1841 contains a fine paper by Petrie on 'The Native Music of Ireland.' 'In the years which followed '98,' he writes, 'it was the solace of every peasant—of

[1] Letter of the Right Hon Thomas Pelham, Phœnix Park, Nov. 1, 1797, to the Home Office. (Pelham MSS.)

every heart, gentle or simple—which felt for the sorrows of Ireland,' and he quotes (p. 65) the verse beginning

'I met with Napper Tandy, he took me by the hand.'

FATHER O'LEARY

(See chap. xvi. p. 236.)

THE following letter—one honourable to O'Leary—has escaped the vigilance of all his biographers. It seems to have been addressed to Mr. Kirwan, a Catholic leader who held some military rank in the Volunteer army, and who at mess had been asked to drink 'The glorious, pious, and immortal memory' of William III.! '*Jungamus dexteras*' was the motto of O'Leary and Grattan at this time. The former, in his reply to the Bishop of Cloyne in 1796, states that the policy of Dublin Castle was '*Divide et impera.*' This letter is dated a year previous to Lord Sydney's effort to corrupt O'Leary. From that hour no such courageousness of demand marked his utterances.

'Cork: October 4, 1782.

'Much esteemed and dear Sir,—I am honoured this instant with your kind favour, which makes me doubly happy, in the information that you are well, and the satisfaction of still retaining a share in your remembrance. Your choice of Lord Mornington[1] for your Colonel gave me infinite satisfaction, and your design to continue him at your head until he forfeits his claim to that honour by some unbecoming and well-attested steps is equally founded in wisdom and justice. Let it be the province of bigots to censure the toast, after the reasons alleged for having given it. King William was the first who scattered the seeds of liberty in this kingdom. There is nothing in the frame of a Catholic that is averse to its growth. He never violated his engagements with the Catholics of Ireland, though often solicited to a breach of promise. There was not a Stuart, from the first to the last, but betrayed them, either from cowardice or treachery. James II. promised to repeal his Declaration, on condition of being reinstated. What could freedom expect from the resumption of his dignity?

[1] Garret, Earl of Mornington, married the daughter of Lord Dungannon, was father of the Duke of Wellington, and died May 22, 1784.

'In the very heat of action, when the alternative was death or victory, he commands *to spare his English subjects.*[1] *Poor man! he was tender-hearted and pusillanimous!* I care not. Bears are fierce, and deer are timid. It is equal to me whether I suffer by the claws of the one or the horns of the other. In my opinion, though our sufferings have been long and unmerited, it is happy for us that King William came over; for under weak kings of our own religion, controlled by laws, we would be for ever obnoxious to our fellow-subjects. Every gentleman from Dublin whom I meet here talks with admiration of the Irish Brigade.[2] Sir Boyle Roche, who wrote me a letter the other day, talks of them in a strain of rapture. I never have seen an address from the Catholics of Ireland but I spurned with indignation at, except your late address to Earl Temple. They were always couched in the cringing language of servility, and even falsehood, boasting of *common blessings*, when it was in the power of your children to strip you of your kitchen-gardens and the shoeboy of your houses. In your last address you spoke as Gentlemen, thankful for what you got, and decently intimating that you want and deserve more. I make it my humble request that, whilst one Penal Law stands upon record, except those that exclude you from the Senate and high offices under the Crown, in every address you will glance at your restraints. Were it not from an apprehension of incurring the displeasure of the Catholic Gentlemen of Dublin, I would have torn Gormanston's[3] address, and Portland's answer, to pieces. The former addressed as a contented slave, and the latter answered with the rudeness of a Batavian burgomaster who would say "*Behave always so, or else——!*" The liberal-minded Protestants themselves acknowledge that enough has not been done for us. It is what Lord Beauchamp wrote to me when I was in Dublin. I send you Mr. Hamilton's letter on the same subject. I received it here, in a letter from Sir Boyle, who applauds *the wisdom of the Irish Brigade in not adopting the violent measures of several armed societies.* There is some meaning in these words, which I here would not have communicated but to a few of the discreet of our own. You can keep Mr.

[1] The late John Cornelius O'Callaghan, the highest authority on the Jacobite and Williamite wars, assured me that this speech, attributed to James, was never uttered.

[2] O'Leary was honorary chaplain to the Irish Brigade Volunteers.

[3] A Catholic Peer.

Hamilton's letter until I pay you my respects in Dublin. I wish I knew who he is.[1] As to the Dungannonists,[2] they should be remembered with gratitude by the Catholics of this kingdom. But as the Brigade is composed of all parties without distinction but such as merit confers, whether a letter which would give them the appearance of a Roman Catholic armed society would be expedient, however merited, you are the more competent judge. Whether the sycophants of Government, averse to the Northerns, would not represent Peter leaguing with John against Martin, who once confined them to a boxing-match over a tub, but sees them now shake hands over the table when they can appear with their swords and bucklers in the hall. However, should you deem the measure eligible, considering time, place, circumstances, the sympathies of some, the antipathies of others, the clashing of interests, the factions of parties, the jealousy of Government wishing the metamorphosis of your shining blades into shepherd's crooks,—there is not one living who would sooner comply with my friend's request than I would. But from conviction, free from flattery, I affirm that he is better qualified for a similar letter. I heard of him before I knew him; known, I conversed with him. I guessed what he could do. I read the sentimental and correct Las Casas. I was convinced that I had not guessed in vain. From this motive I cannot be prevailed on, besides the time, which has grown so scanty on my hands since my arrival here that I cannot spare one hour; exhorting every Sunday, and attending to several avocations, which, though of some benefit to others, often make me regret that I ever quitted my solitude and books. I suggested once to Mr. Weldon to propose Dr. Dunn—a Dissenting minister—to the Brigade for a third chaplain. If he be proposed and elected about the beginning of March, or any time after, I shall write him a letter, in which I shall pay those of his profession the compliment they deserve without giving offence to others. Ever &c. ' ARTHUR O'LEARY.

[1] Sackville Hamilton was a confidential servant of the Crown (see p. 169, *ante*), afterwards Under-Secretary for Ireland. The fact that Hamilton's letter was enclosed in one from Sir Boyle Roche—the notorious diplomatic agent of Dublin Castle (p. 236, *ante*)—tends to identify the source.

[2] The volunteer meeting at Dungannon in February, 1782, resolved that 'the claim of any body of men other than the King, Lords, and Commons of Ireland, to make laws to bind this kingdom, is unconstitutional, illegal, and a grievance.'

'My best regards to Mrs. Kirwan, Messieurs Braughill, Ryan, Gavan, without forgetting our worthy Brigadier Sutton.'[1]

The biographer of Grattan cannot be regarded as an authority when speaking of O'Leary. A letter headed 'Dr. O'Leary to Mr. Grattan' appears in Grattan's 'Life,' vol. v. pp. 263–4. It is dated May 25, 1805; begins, 'My dear Grattan;' speaks of his (O'Leary's) little grandson, and ends, 'Believe me, with truth and affection, your sincere friend and faithful confessor, Father O'Leary.' 'I congratulate you, myself and my country on the honour your speech on the Catholic question has conferred on us,' he writes, and thanks Grattan in extravagant terms for having introduced his name with laudation.

Grattan's speech—delivered on May 13, 1805—occupies from page 914 to 940 of 'Hansard,' and O'Leary is not once named in it. Grattan's biographer inserts with all the prominence and respect due to a genuine document this transparent hoax. He adds a footnote to say that Grattan's speech in May, 1805, praised O'Leary. The biographer ought to have known that O'Leary had been three years dead in 1805, and that it is not usual for friars to rejoice in grandsons.

Old St. Pancras.

Father Arthur O'Leary died in London on January 8, 1802. The remains lay in state; a grand dirge was sung; an imposing funeral cortège followed them to Old St. Pancras, where a fine monument to his memory, inscribed with words of praise, soon marked the spot. Tradition states that Old St. Pancras was the last church in London where Mass was said after the Reformation: hence the wish felt by Catholics in penal days to sleep within its embrace. A visit to this historic graveyard in its present desecrated state awakens emotion. No ground, however, is sacred to the engineer: old St. Pancras is now traversed by two lines of railway. Passing trains ever and anon cause this resting-place of the dead to tremble violently as if by earthquake. Indeed a seismic shock, had it passed through the churchyard, could hardly have produced more wreck. Here many an old tombstone inscribed '*Requiescat in pace*'—others displaying grand heraldic sculpture—even a bishop's mitre and a shattered coronet

[1] Who these men were, see p. 231, *ante*. Gavan may have been an error of the copyist for Thomas Glanan, one of the Catholic delegates of the city of Dublin in 1793.

—proclaim the irony of fate. The scorched and begrimed soil, once green and rural, but now split into a hundred fissures—almost tends to remind one of a great Scriptural picture, where shrouded dead are seen rising in protest from the riven earth. Tablets and tombs sufficient to represent the life of a city are rudely removed and ranged far from the graves they ought to mark. 'Old Mortality' will find them piled—close as cards in a pack—beneath a dark archway, over which engines rush, their shrill scream suggesting a cruel travesty of the last trumpet. A few massive tombs are certainly spared, and amongst them that to the memory of Father O'Leary. Another part of the disused cemetery creates quite a contrast to the scene of desolation just described. Parterres smiling with flowers may be seen; also winding walks, and an occasional shaded seat, where whispering love repeats a story older even than Old St. Pancras. It has been called an historic spot—but prehistoric remains [1] also repose there.

PRIESTS AS SECRET AGENTS

(P. 289, *ante*.)

Dr. Hussey was not the last Catholic priest sent by the Court of England on a private mission to the Continent. The subsequent Duke of Wellington, writing from London to Dublin Castle on March 18, 1808, says:—

'It would be very desirable to have a person to send over to Holland and France just at the present moment, and I know nobody that would answer our purpose so well as —— ——, the Scotch priest. I wish, therefore, that you would desire him to come over to me.'

On the following day he writes:—

'As I intend to send —— to Paris, it might not be inconvenient to know the person through whom the disaffected communicate with the French Government in order that —— might watch him.' [2]

The chief blank may be filled with the name of the Rev. James Robertson. The nephew of this man, Mr. A. B. Fraser, found among his papers, 'A Narrative of a Secret Mission to the Danish Island in 1808.' The priest had been sent by Wellington to the Spanish general Romana, and the result was the transmission of

[1] See the *Standard* of April 14, 1892, on the St. Pancras Mammoth.

[2] *Wellington Correspondence* (*Ireland*), pp. 371–6.

the Spanish army from the service of France, by the British fleet, from North Germany to Spain.

Spain was the theatre of a still more important case of secret service rendered by a Catholic priest. In 1860 I wrote to Field-Marshal Lord Combermere as the only man then living likely to know of the relations which subsisted, during the Peninsular War, between Wellington and Dr. Curtis, Rector of the Irish College of Salamanca. The following is a portion of his reply:—

'Dr. Curtis had been fifty years head of the College when he left Spain to become Roman Catholic Primate of Ireland.

'He had communicated very valuable information to the Duke of Wellington while Soult held his headquarters at Salamanca.

'His connection with the Duke was suspected before the first entry of the British into Salamanca, and two days previous to this event, while dining with Soult, Dr. C. heard the General remark how strange it was that Lord Wellington seemed so well acquainted with his proceedings.

'Some of the aides-de-camp looked at Dr. Curtis pointedly on this occasion, and the next day, while at table with the same party, similar observations were made, and Dr. Curtis perceived that the suspicions of Soult had been in some manner confirmed.

'On his return home that night, he found two gendarmes awaiting him, and he was at once conveyed to prison.

'He assured Lord Combermere that had not the English arrived the next day, he would have been executed as a spy.'

It may be added that the mysterious reference in Wellington's despatch of May 8, 1811,[1] is to Dr. Curtis.

The appointment of this priest by the Pope as 'Archbishop of Armagh, and Primate of All Ireland' was directly due to influence exerted with Cardinal Gonsalvi by British statesmen, including Lord Castlereagh, Minister for Foreign Affairs. The Duke of Wellington maintained for many years a constant and cordial correspondence with the Primate, and the Duke's change of policy on the Catholic Question was not uninfluenced by it. The papers of this eminent prelate, varied and voluminous in their character, have been long in the custody of the present writer, and at a future day may be dealt with as their importance demands.

[1] Vide *Wellington Despatches*, compiled by Lieut.-Colonel Gurwood, ii. 538. (London, 1835.)

INDEX

Aberside, Dr., and Lady Moira, 352
Aboukir Bay, lost treasure in, 81
Academy, Royal Irish, 9, 86, 138, 240
Addison, Joseph, 192
Admiralty, the, 112
'Agamemnon,' mutiny of the, 113
Agar, Mr., arrested, 42
Agnew, of Larne, 7
Aherne, or O'Herne, Capt., 75
Alien Bill, 349
Alison, Sir A., 3, 258
'All the Talents' Administration, 198
Allen, Colonel, arrested, 15
Allingham, Wm., 148, 342
Altona, 96, 347
Ambrose, Miss, 274
'American Arms,' Inn, 73
American War, 215, 278
Amherst, Lord, 215
Amiens, Peace of, 101
Amsterdam, Duke of York marches on, 81
'Anacréon,' French war ship, 71, 342, 347
Annaly, Lord, 305
Antient Britons Regt., 394
Antrim, rebel colonels of, 292, 364
Archduke, the, Charles, 81
Archer, Alderman, 315
— Rev. Mr., a priest, 229
Armada, Spanish, 229, 260
Armstrong, Captain (J. W.), 153, 308, 309, 311, 312, 314, 316, 324, 365 *et seq.*, 369 *et seq.*, 393
— Sir Andrew, Bt., M.P., 374
— Major Carteret, 373
'Arrah-na-Pogue,' 394
Artillery, present at arrests, 59
— Volunteer, commanded by Napper Tandy, 241
Assassination urged, 238, 365
'Athenæum,' the, 126
Atkinson, High Constable, 122, 159
— Dr., 148
Attainder, Act of, 83, 96, 100
'Attornies Guide,' the, a local satire, 331
Austria, 81, 90, 95, 257, 295, 296, 350
Autun, Bishop of (Talleyrand), 27
Avonmore, Lord (*see* Yelverton)
Azara, Chevalier, 264

Bailey, a rebel, 16
Baldwin, Mr., Q.C., 382
Ball, Mr. Justice, 144
— Serjeant in 1803, 99
Bancroft, a secret agent, 225, 238
Banim, John, 172; lines by, 307
Banishment Act, 96, 298
Banks, run on the, 154, 357
Bantry Bay, French expedition to, 45, 170, 287, 362–3
— Lord, 368
Barber, Rev. Samuel, implicated, 290
Barrington, Sir Jonah, 142, 177, 181, 183, 185, 189, 231, 255, 313, 315, 321, 358, 368, 370, 371, 373
Barthélemy, M., 45
Bathurst, Lord, 39, 95, 290, 291
— Benjamin, 95
Battersby, W. J., 224
Bavarian Embassy in London, 248, 264, 355
Beauchamp, Lord, 396
Beaufort, William, Rev., 351
Bedford, Duke of, 198, 356
Bell, Justice, 387
Bellamy, G. Anne, 231, 248, 249
Bennett, William Newton, a United Irishman, afterwards Chief Justice, 125
Bentinck, Lord Wm., 37

Beresford, Rt. Hon. J. C., 168, 169, 170, 180, 297
— Correspondence, 169
Bergen, Tandy at, 78
Berington, Bishop, 263
Bernadotte, King, 291, 296, 297
Berthier, Marshal, 27, 90, 290-5-7
Berwick, Rev. E., 188
Betagh, Father, S.J., 191
Bethel, Isaac Burke, 381
Binns, Benjamin P., 15, 21, 31, 40, 44, 218, 385
Birch, Rev. Mr. (Presbyterian), implicated, 290
Bird, an informer, 178, 268
'Black-book,' the, 73
Blackburn, Francis, 224
Blackburne, Chief Justice, 377
Blackwell, Colonel, 71, 79, 82, 85, 344, 345
Blake, Bishop, 224
— Mr., executed in 1798, 361
Blanca (Spanish Minister), 215, 227
Bolivar, Simon, 207
Bolton, Lord (*see* Orde)
Bond, Oliver, 7, 69, 72, 127, 165, 187, 301, 304
Botany Bay, 86
Boucicault, Dion, 394
Boulogne, 90, 295
Bourdon, Leonard, 30, 72, 110
Bourrienne, Louis, 82, 290, 291, 294, 297, 339
Bouvet, Admiral, at Bantry Bay, 170
Boyce, John, 104
Brady, Maziere, 229, 282
— D. Caulfield, *preface*
Braughall, Thomas, 7, 231, 337, 376, 398
Brennan, Dr., 'the Wrestling Doctor,' 117, 309
Brest, armament at, 90, 110
Brett, John, 135
Bridport, Admiral (Lord Hood), 108, 144, 160, 362
Brigade, the Irish, in service of France, 246, 307, 396, 397
— Volunteer corps, Dublin, 396
Brissot, Jean Pierre, 309
Bristol, Earl of (Bishop of Derry), 232, 236, 237
Brophy, P., state dentist, 117
Bruix, Admiral, 32, 83, 110
Brune, Marshal, 344
Buckingham, Lord, Viceroy of Ireland, 119, 255 *et seq.*
— Papers, 255
Buckinghamshire, Lord, 216
Buckley, Rev. M. B., 231, 244, 259, 267-9
Buller, Mr. Justice, 21
Buonaparte (*see* Napoleon)
Burdett, Sir F., 197, 297, 328
Bureaud, 14
Burke, Sir Bernard, C.B., LL.D., *preface*
Burke, Edmund, 224-38, 257, 268, 286, 287
Burton, Mr. Justice, 176, 199, 210
Bushe, Chas. Kendal, 136
Butler, Archbishop, 281
— Charles, 211, 263, 284
— Lord Jas., 37
— Hon. Simon, 167
Byrne, Colonel Miles, 117, 295-7
— Pat, democratic bookseller, 373, 393
— P. J., Clerk of the crown, 103

CALLANAN, Dr., 159, 160
Camden, Lord, 17, 38*n*, 43, 58*n*, 63, 64, 117*n*, 137, 125, 179, 194, 195, 196*n*, 274, 314-66, 358, 387, 389
Campbell, Thos., 96, 297
Canning, George, 45, 77, 145, 226, 297, 306
Carhampton, Lord, 11, 78, 103, 152, 171, 188, 220
Carleton, Lord Chief Justice, 313, 375; his MS. notes, 337, 360, 363
— Ald., peace officer, 159
— William, 205
Carnot, French Minister in 1796, 113
Carpenter, Roman Catholic Abp. of Dublin, 120, 150, 161*n*, 216
Carrick's 'Morning Post,' 203
Carrickfergus Gaol, 381, 388
Carthusians of La Trappe, 257
Casey, Rev. Mr., a priest, 15, 74-5
Castlebar, battle of, 343, 359
Castlereagh, Lord, 9, 18, 20, 36*n*, 38*n*, 39, 43, 46, 47, 48, 49, 50, 65, 66, 67, 68, 69, 71*n*, 72, 73, 76*n*, 83, 92, 95, 97, 108, 109, 110, 115, 119, 191, 200, 281*n*, 282, 283, 292, 293, 294, 295, 297, 299, 303, 306, 309, 311, 333, 335, 336, 337, 400
Catholic Emancipation in 1797, 68, 161, 215
— early object of the U. I. M., 89
Caulfield, Captain, 138, 297
Challoner, Bishop, 229
Chamberlain, Mr. Justice, 176, 374
Chambers, John, 36, 187, 210

Chapman of Cork, 85
Charlemont, Lord, 223–99
Charles, Archduke, 81
Charles Edward the Pretender, 358
Charles X., 364
Chatham, Lord, 157, 296, 297, 299
Chesterfield, Lord, 272, 274
Chichester, Earl of (*see* Pelham)
Chifney the jockey, 271
'Citizen,' the, magazine, 394
Clancy, Master, 145*n*, 147
Clare, Lord Chancellor, 120, 309, 313, 314, 316
— Walter, case of, 378
Clarke, Duc de Feltre, 108*n*
— Mrs. and Duke of York, 394
Clement XIV., Pope, 249
Clements, the Brothers, 139
Clerkenwell prisoners set free, 229
Clinch, J. B., 282
Cloncurry, Lord, 7, 21, 35 *et seq.*, 94, 195, 196, 197, 203, 286, 296, 349*n*, 356
Clonmel, Lord Chief Justice 0, 374
Clony, (Rebel) General, 102
Cloyne, Bishop of, 394
Coburg, Prince of, 294
Cockayne, John, a London attorney and spy, 48, 192
Cockburn, Lord, 30
Code, H. B., 100
Coke, Sir Edward, 376
Colchester Correspondence, *preface*
Colclough, Lady, 331, 351
Coleridge, S. T., 30, 279, 388
Coll, (Rebel) Colonel, 297
Collins, Thomas, 163, 165, 166, 169, 170, 171, 181
Coloony, action at, 359
Colpoys, Admiral, confined by mutineers, 108
Combermere, F.-M. Lord, 400
Commons, enclosed, 145
Comyn, Andrew, 337
Congress, National, in 1784, 240
Conlan, Dr., 12, 340
Connor, Lawrence, hanged, 181, 182
Convention, Volunteer, in 1783, 234
— Act, 240
Cooke, Edward, Under-Sec. for Ireland in 1798, 13, 27*n*, 93, 97, 118 119, 121, 122, 123, 127, 128, 130, 131, 133, 135, 138, 141, 144, 159*n*, 168*n*, 169, 170, 171, 172, 189, 190, 191, 193, 300, 305, 314, 315, 321, 322, 358, 384, 386, 387
Coote, General Sir Eyre, 350
Cope, Sir Wm. H., 93, 302, 303, 341
Cope, Wm., pensioned in 1798, 302–3
— Misses, pensioned, *ibid.*
Corballis, J. R., 123, 148, 288
Corbet, General, 71, 72, 78–9, 81–9
Cork, proposed capture of, 85
— Lord, on the Sheareses, 321–30, 373
Cornwallis, Lord, 6*n*, 32, 63, 64, 78, 79*n*, 118*n*, 144, 178, 243, 266, 271, 325, 333, 336, 343–9, 360–3, 384
Correspondence, Wellington, 209, 364, 365, 378–9
'Courier,' the (London), 8–82, 112, 158, 276–89, 388, 393
Cox, Walter, 71–85, 117, 144, 163, 188, 191, 325*n*, 333, 341, 386, 387, 388
Coyle, Bernard, 137
Crampton, Dr., afterwards Sir P., flight from Castlebar, 359*n*
Craven, Lady E., 354
Crawford, Sir James, British Minister at Hamburg, 71, 72, 73, 77, 79, 93, 100, 109, 169, 180–297
Creevy, General, 95
Crofton, Morgan, 145, 146, 338
Croix, De la, French Minister of War, 25, 52, 53, 54, 60, 67, 69, 78
Cromwell, Oliver, 26
Cromwellian Settlers, 32 *et seq.*
Crookshank, Mr. Justice, 375
Crow Street Theatre, 205
Cullen, Luke, *preface*, 137, 138
Cumberland, R., 227, 228, 258, 285
Curran, John Philpot, 32, 36, 42, 48, 76*n*, 80, 125, 156, 161, 164, 174, 175, 176, 180, 189, 191, 192, 306, 307, 310, 312, 313, 324, 328, 333, 368–9, 373, 376
— Sarah, 193
— W. H., 192–202, 301, 328, 367, 380
Curtis, Archbishop, 400
Cuxhaven, 23–30, 31, 81, 293
Cyclopædian Magazine, 178, 183, 187

D'ADEMAR, Count, 224
Daendels, General, 75
Dalrymple, General, 362
D'Alton, John, 298
Dangan Castle, 201
Darrynane, 147*n*
Daunt, O'Neil, 159*n*
D'Auvergne, Captain, 35, 38, 39, 60
Davis, Thomas, 105*n*, 175*n*, 218, 367–377
Day, Judge, 159, 210

De Burgo, Bishop, 217
De Feltre, Duc, French War Minister, 108
De Genlis, Madame, 5, 34, 42, 45, 108, 133
De la Croix, 66, 67, 76, 78*n*, 105, 124, 125, 140, 187
Del Campo, Marquis, 52, 53, 63, 226, 227, 228, 260, 264, 281
D'Enghien, Duc, murdered, 90
Derby, the, races, 271
Derry, Bishop of (Lord Bristol), 237
Despard, Col., 293
Dessolle, General, 291
Desterre, Mr., shot by O'Connell, 102
Destinger, J., an *alias* for Samuel Turner, 97
De Vere, Aubrey, 154
Devereux, General, 207, 208
Dickson, James, 124, 143, 159, 161
— Rev. W. Steele, D.D., 13, 291, 385
Dignan, a rebel, 299
Dillon, 23*n*
Directory, French, 26, 29, 347
— Irish Rebel, Lord Cloncurry a member of, 40; French mission to, 59, 120, 389
Dirham, Dr., 149 *et seq.*
Division in the rebel councils, 292
Dixon, W. Hepworth, 126
Dobbin, Rev. Dr., 319, 323, 325, 327*n*, 354*n*
— Leonard, 381
Dodgson, Capt., 138, 170
Doherty, Chief Justice, 377
Dominica, 171
Don, General, 344
— O'Conor, *preface*
Donegal, Marquis of, his gambling debts, 269
Donellan, Councillor, 144
Douglas, Bishop, 115, 263-4, 283
Dowdall, W., 353, 354*n*, 358
Dowling, Mathew, 222, 223
Downes, Mr. Justice, 374
Downshire, Lord, 2 *et seq.*, 14, 16, 17, 18, 34, 41, 42, 43, 44, 48, 49, 51, 54, 56, 57, 58, 59, 60, 61, 62, 74, 76, 78, 91, 92, 94, 102, 104, 107, 316, 334, 335, 336, 337, 338, 339, 340, 346; pecuniary transactions with Todd Jones, 353, 358 389
Doyle, Bishop, 59, 211
Drennan, Wm., 187, 368, 389
Dromgoole, Dr., 137
Drought, George, 312
'Dublin Evening Post,' 76, 100, 120, 241
'Dublin Journal,' 370, 393
Duckett, 30, 33, 71, 72, 73, 75, 76, 105, 106, 107, 108, 109, 110, 111, 113, 114, 141, 354*n*
Duff, General Sir James, 332
Duffy, Sir C. Gavan, 105*n*, 113*n*
Duggan, Bernard, 99
Duignan, Dr. Patrick, 287, 291, 304
Dumouriez, General, 3
Duncan, Lord Admiral, 112
Dundas, L. (Lord Melville, colleague of Pitt's), 167, 287
Dungannon Convention, 232, 384, 397
Dunn, Rev. Dr., 397
Durham, Lord, 290
Durnin, 72*n*, 290, 297, 298
Dutton, Frederick, of Newry, 18; afterwards British Vice-Consul, 23
Dwyer, Michael, an outlaw, 137

Edgeworth, Miss, 89, 209, 380
— Richard Lovel, 154
'Edinburgh Review,' 353
Egan, Bishop, 202*n*, 281*n*, 330
Egan, Patrick, 343
Elder, Rev. J., 388
Eldon, Lord, 31
Elliot, Lord, 87
— Mr., of the Foreign Office, 77
Emmet, Robert, relations with Lord Cloncurry, 41, 77, 87, 88, 129, 137, 139, 140, 156, 157, 161, 162, 192, 193, 194, 195, 196, 200, 251, 256, 275, 295, 356, 387
— Temple, 356
— Thomas Addis T., 42, 65, 79*n*, 90, 98, 101, 180, 188, 316-18, 356
England, Rev. Thomas, 214, 217, 219, 220, 226, 274, 286
Enniskillen, Lord, 333, 370
Erskine, Lord, 21, 114, 189, 328
Esmonde, Dr., hanged, 77
'Exile of Erin,' the, 96

Fallon, John, D.L., 128
Farrell, James, 345*n*
Farren, W., actor, 204
Featherstonhaugh, John, 138, 152
Ferris, Dr. E., 153
— informer, 300
Ffrench, Lord, 137, 167, 361
Fingal, Lord, 137, 143, 198, 199
Finglas, Lord Edward to take the field at, 129, 144, 323
Finlay's Bank, 154
Finnerty, Peter, 200

Finney's Trial, 175
Finnucane, Judge, 378
FitzGerald, Lord Edward, 1, 34, 42, 43, 44, 45, 57, 58, 65, 67, 76, 77, 78*n*, 86, 91, 92, 124, 125, 130, 131, 132, 133, 134, 135, 136, 137, 142, 148, 159, 303, 335, 357, 387
— Lady Edward (Pamela), 33, 49, 76, 91, 121–34
— Lady Lucy, 4, 33, 44, 92
— Sir Judkin, 161
— Very Rev. Dr., 289
FitzGibbon, John (Lord Clare), 120, 254*n*, 309
FitzPatrick, Hugh, 185, 213, 221
FitzSimon, Sir Nicholas, 330
Fitzwilliam, Lord, 303
— Dr., 150, 323, 325
— Capt. Wm., 323
Flint, Sir C., 349, 350
Flood, Henry, 241
Foley, Sir T., K.C.B., 4
Forest, John, 378
Fort George Prison, 101, 351
Foster, Rt. Hon. J., Speaker, 351
— Leslie, 384
— Sir Michael, 376
— N., 342–3
Foulkes, Mr., 21
Fox, C. J., 198, 249, 268, 328
Francis, Emperor, 90
Frankfort Peerage, 77
Fraser, Mr., a suspected rebel, 49, 399
'Freeman's Journal,' 119, 176*n*, 242
French, Right Hon. FitzStephen, 172
Froude, J. A., *preface*, 1, 8, 17, 34, 39, 41, 42, 48, 49, 52, 53, 54, 57, 58, 59, 60, 61*n*, 62, 68, 72, 75, 91, 92, 107, 118, 120, 121, 122, 124, 144, 170*n*, 172, 173, 174, 176, 179, 180, 212, 239, 277, 279, 281, 286, 332, 335, 336, 337, 338, 341, 360, 383
Fry, Parson, 9
Fugitive Bill, 96
Fullam, Mr., actor, 204
Fuller, Capt., 334
Furnes (*alias* for Samuel Turner), 47, 59, 336

GAINSBOROUGH, the Painter, 264
Gallaher, 132, 151, 159
'Gentleman's Magazine,' 102, 225, 236, 248, 256, 349
George, Prince Regent (afterwards George IV.), 257, 270
— Mr. Baron, 381
Germany, North, annexed to France, 296
Gibbon, Edward, 316
Gifford, John, 163–4, 181, 204, 278, 372
Gladstone, Mr., an actor, 205
Glardy, Rev. Dr., implicated, 290
Godwin, William, 197*n*
Gonsalvi, Cardinal, 284, 400
Gordon, Lord G., 228, 229
Gormanston, Lord, 143, 396
Gossett, Sir W., Under-Sec., Dublin Castle, 144–5
Goulburn, Rt. Hon. W., 145
Gould, Baring, Rev., 96
Granard, Lord, 144, 352
— Lady, 355
Grattan, Rt. Hon. Henry, 7, 21, 94, 164, 188, 189, 194, 200*n*, 208, 210, 212, 219, 221, 270, 273, 315, 325, 327, 354, 356, 369, 394, 398
— Junior, 328
Gravesend, project to bombard, by mutinous fleet, 113
Gray, Rev. T., F.T.C.D., 315*n*, 323
Gregg, Misses, 394
Grégoire, Bishop of Blois, 29, 33
Gregory, Sir W., Dublin Castle, 144, 153, 164
Grenville, Lord, 109, 281, 349
Griffiths, Captain, arrested, 108
Grogan, Cornelius, executed, 351
Crouchy, General, 170*n*
Guillamore, Lord (*see* O'Grady)
Guillon, M., 49, 106, 170
Guizot, M., 365
Gurwood, Lieut.-Colonel, 400

HABEAS CORPUS ACT, 225
Hague, the, 75, 88, 347
Hale, Lord, 376
Haliday, Charles, 46, 86*n*, 95
— Dr., 307, 356
Halkett and Laing, 331
Hamburg, 4 *et seq.*, 14, 39, 49–60 *et seq.*, 76 *et seq.*, 81, 84, 109, 110, 290, 294, 297, 344
Hamill, Mr., 7
Hamilton, Mr., 36, 141, 142, 396
— Sackville, 169
Hamond, Mr., of the F. O., 77
Hansard, 161, 162, 398
Hardinge, Dr., 159
Hardwicke, Lord, 194, 195, 249, 388
Hardy, Francis, 223, 231*n*
Hare, Mr., Police Magistrate, 199
Harels, Nain Jaune, 27

Harold's Cross, 193
Harpe, La, Col., 30
Harvey, B., hanged, 125, 177, 351
— Philip Whitfield, legal representative of the 'Sham Squire,' 124
Haslang, Count, 248–9
Hatton, J., 142
Hawkesbury, Lord, 87
Hawkins, Serjeant, 376
Hay, Edward, 251
Hayes, Mr. Justice, *preface*, 369
Heatly, J. W., 385
Helder, the, Convention, 344
'Hell,' a lane in Dublin, 392
Hermopolis, Bishop of, 365
Hertford, Marquis of, 50
Hester, Captain, 389, 390
Higgins, Francis, *preface*, 13, 19*n*, 24, 118 *et seq.*, 127, 128, 129, 130, 131, 133, 134, 135*n*, 136, 141*n*, 149, 185*n*, 196, 266, 267, 268, 276*n*, 357
Hippisley, Sir J. C., 264, 282
Hobart, Lord, 264
Hoche, General, 4, 6, 45, 49, 111, 126*n*, 226, 297*n*, 335, 340*n*, 361
Hoey, Mr., hanged, 340
Holland, Lord, 21, 22*n*, 160, 182, 189–91
Holmes, Robert, 125
Holt, General, rebel, 110
Hood, Admiral Lord, 144, 160, 362
Hooper, conspirator, 306
Hope, James, 5, 13, 14, 57, 173, 337*n*, 338, 339, 389
Horne Tooke, 114
Houlton, W. A., 385, 386
Howe, Admiral, Lord, 113
Howell's 'State Trials,' 84*n*, 207, 378
Huband, Joseph, 125
Hughes, John, 5, 94, 292, 336, 337
Hulbert, Joel, 118
Humbert, General, 19, 83, 327, 359, 360, 361
Huntingdon, Lord, and Lady Moira, 352
Hussey, Rev. Dr., 255, 259, 264; his agency not of a base kind, 268, 280, 281, 282, 283, 284, 285, 287, 288, 289, 399
— Chief Justice, 199
Hutchinson, General, Lord, 359
Hutton, Mr., 198

Iceland, British Consul at, Thos. Reynolds, 305
Ireland before the Union, 130
— Richard Stanley, M.D., 325
'Irish Magazine,' 386, 388
'Ivors from Carlow,' a password, 304

Jackson, Henry, of the Rebel Directory, 40, 127
— Rev. W., 33, 48, 174–9, 180, 192, 375–6; funeral of, 328
Jacobin Club, 309
Jägerhorn, M., French secret agent, 59–61, 91–2
James II., 374, 395
Janson, Miss, 209
Jeffrey the democrat, 30
Jesuits, the suppressed, 249
Johnson, Dr. Samuel, 249, 284
Johnston, Judge Robert, 125
Joly, Jasper, LL.D., 133
Jones, W. Todd, 157 *et seq.*, 353*n*
— Frederick Wm., 205
Josephine's, Empress, debts, 82
'Journal des Débats,' 70
Joynt, W. Lane, D.L., 163

Keating, a publisher, 219
Keith, Admiral Lord, 362
Kelburne, Rev. Sinclair, implicated, 290
Kelly, Michael, 267
— W. B., 194*n*
Kemble, J. P., 184
Kenmare, Lord, 143, 199, 234, 235, 237, 239, 251, 274
Keogh, John, 7, 163, 166, 167, 168*n*, 187*n*, 189, 193, 337
Keon, a rebel, 141
Kernan, Chas., 148
Killen, Rev. Dr., 294
Kilmainham Gaol, General Corbet's escape from, 89, 100, 126, 159, 318, 381
Kilwarden, Lord, 191, 363
Kingsland, Lord, 140
Kingsmill, Admiral, 362
Kirwan, the Catholic delegate, 201, 231, 395
Knox, Alex., 7, 292

Lagan, General, 72
Lake, General, 13, 338, 359–60, 370
Las Casas, 32, 397
Law, Bishop of Elphin, 337
Lawless, V. B., afterwards Lord Cloncurry, 7, 35 *et seq.*

Lawless, Wm., General, 128, 136, 310, 347
Lecky, W. E. H., *preface*, 36, 44*n*, 46, 47*n*, 48, 49*n*, 62*n*, 130, 134, 135, 140*n*, 172, 179, 180*n*, 181, 186*n*, 188, 189, 190, 208, 212, 214, 215, 218, 223*n*, 227, 228, 230, 231*n*, 237, 243, 267, 272, 273, 276, 308, 320, 364, 374, 383
Lefevre, Right Hon. Shaw, on the superiority of the French Navy, 362
Leinster, Duke of, 36, 299, 301
Lewins, Edward, Rebel Envoy to France, 5, 24, 44, 54, 60, 63, 74, 75, 193, 293
Leyne, Con, 147
Limerick, Lord (Sexton Pery), 154
Lisbon, 305
Littlehales, Sir Edward, 386
Liverpool, Lord, 145
Londonderry, Lord, 336
Lonergan, Richard, 203, 204
Longueville, Lord, 43, 310
Loughborough, Lord, 185
Louis XVI., 110*n*, 226, 245
Louis Philippe, 95, 365
Lowry, a rebel, 74
Lucas, Dr., 242
Luynes, de M. (*see* Lewins)
'Lyceum,' the, 273
Lyons, J. C., 180*n*, 209*n*
— Dorothy M., 84
— (Lord Cloncurry's seat) searched, 198
Lysaght, Edward, 353
— George, 84

Macan, 14, 57–8, 61–3–4, 304, 336
Macara, Dr., 13
Macartney, Rev. Andrew, 56
Macaulay, Lord, 292
Mac Donagh, 222
MacIntagart, George, 298, 385
Mack, General, 90, 294
Mackenzie, Dr. Shelton, 175
Mackenzie, Life of Muir, 74
Mac Skimmin's History of Carrickfergus, 103–73
McCall, Hugh of Lisbon, 57
McCarthy, 300
McCartney, Rev. G., 388, 390
McClelland, Baron, 356
McCormack, Richard, 5, 7, 74, 165, 166, 337
McDougall, Henry, 215
McGucken, James, Attorney of the U. I. M., 36, 42, 58*n*, 95, 178
McKeever, 173, 389*n*
McKeon, 368*n*
McKinley, 126
McLoughlen, Con, 102
McMahon, Rev. Arthur, 74, 290, 292, 294*n*, 296
McMurdock, W., 57
McNally, Leonard, 24*n*, 36*n*, 37*n*, 85, 87, 127, 174, 175, 176, 178, 179, 180, 183, 184, 185, 186, 187, 188, 189, 193, 194, 195, 196, 197, 198, 199, 200, 201, 202, 203, 204, 205, 206*n*, 208, 224, 301, 311, 312, 321, 322, 335, 336, 356, 373–8, 384, 385
— sons of, 193, 209, 378–9
— Mrs., 208, 209, 210, 295, 300
Mackintosh, Sir J., 279
Macnevin, Dr., 58, 59, 65, 66, 67, 69*n*, 94, 142, 316, 335, 336, 337, 340*n*, 357, 386, 389
Madden, D. H., Mr. Justice, 383
— Dr. R. R., 7, 49, 68, 76, 96, 105, 106, 109, 117, 118, 120, 121, 122, 124, 125, 126, 138, 148, 162, 163, 173, 190, 193, 194, 209, 327, 329, 339, 341, 343, 346, 352, 367, 368, 369, 385, 386, 389, 390, 391
Maddox, Mr., and Lady Moira, 354
Madgett, M., 74, 105
Magan, Francis, 108, 116, 119, 120, 121, 122, 123, 127, 128, 129, 133, 134, 135, 136, 138, 147, 169, 173, 175, 196, 301, 303, 305, 307, 308
Magee, Archbishop, 246
— Darcy, 105
Mahon, 137
Maidstone (Father O'Coigly hanged at), 21
Maitland, Mr., 6, 74, 92
Maragan, M. (French Consul at Hamburg), 76, 79
Margate, arrests at, 16, 47
Marsden, Mr. Under-Secretary, 86, 89, 99, 100, 354, 387
Marshals of France, rich, 291
Mask, the Iron, referred to, 28
Mason, St. John, 98
— Hastings, 292
Mass, High, 167
Mathews, James, of Dundalk, 12, 103, 104
Matthieson, Mrs., 6, 31, 92
Maunsell, Robert, 331
Maxwell, 93, 98
— W. H., 117

Maynooth College, 224, 288
'Metropolis, The,' a satire, 190, 206
Meyer, Daniel, Consul-General at Hamburg, 70
Mignet, M., 67
Mildmay, Sir H., 225
Minto, Lord, 77
Mitchel, John, 199
Moira, Lord, 21, 139, 150, 160, 184, 189, 257, 353
— Lady, 137, 139, 156, 161, 362
Molloy, Constantine, Q.C. (to the author), 374–8
Monks of the Screw, 223
Moore F., 116*n*, 117, 120, 131, 182
— Miss, 121, 122, 123, 132, 143
— Mr. Justice, 377
— R., 290, 296, 364
— Thomas, 117, 121, 182, 235
Mornington, Lord, 40, 395
Morres, Harvey, 71, 76, 82 *et seq.*, 304, 305, 345
Morris, Gouverneur, 32
Mountgarret, Lord, 67, 165
Mount Jerome (seat of J. Keogh), 193
Moylan, Bishop, 283, 287, 288
Muir, Thomas, 74
Mulgrave, Lord, Viceroy, 144, 388
Mulock, Mr. T., 198
— Miss, *ibid.*
Murphy, 132, 347, 348, 350
— John P., 347
— Billy, 71, 166
Murray, Archbishop, 211
— John, *preface*
Musgrave, Sir R., 222, 300, 343
Mutiny in the British Fleet, 108, 113

Napoleon, 32, 81, 82, 85, 86, 89, 90, 291, 296, 332, 344, 348, 386
Neilson, Samuel, 47, 51, 55, 59, 101, 117, 136, 140, 141, 301
Nelson, Lord, 33, 81, 137
Nepean, Sir E., 163, 218, 226, 230, 231*n*, 239
Netterville, Lord, 137, 198, 199
Neville, B., 173
New South Wales, 74
Newcomen, Lord, banker, 153
Newell, E. J., 12, 114, 175
Newgate, 130; burnt down, 229; executions, 314, 388
'No Popery' riots, 228–9
Norbury, Lord, 125, 158, 312, 379
Norcott, William, counsellor, 190, 331
Nore, Mutiny at the, 111, 115, 276
Norfolk, Duke of, 21, 328
North, Lord, 7, 112, 113, 205–75
'Northern Star,' 59, 187, 387
Northesk, Lord Admiral, 112, 113
Northington, Lord, 243*n*
'Notes and Queries,' *preface*, 73, 183
Nugent, General, 18

O'Brien, W. S., 201, 278, 377–82
— Mr. Patrick, M.P., 383
O'Byrne, Patrick, 10, 102
— Mrs. Anastasia, 391
O'Callaghan, J. C., 396
O'Coigly, Father, hanged, 15 *et seq.*, 31, 37, 38, 40, 41, 44, 47*n*, 93, 115, 117, 127, 141, 178, 188, 293, 294
O'Connell, Daniel, 102, 103, 143, 147, 198, 199, 200, 201, 216, (a United Irishman) 357, 363
— John, 226
— Maurice ('Old Hunting Cap'), 357; first to announce the arrival of the French in Bantry Bay, 363
— Richard, 247
O'Connor, Arthur, 4, 5, 17, 40, 41, 42, 43, 46, 48, 49, 60, 65, 67, 101, 102, 201, 308, 309, 311, 316, 340, 350, 351, 387, 389
— Roger, 350, 351, 368
O'Conor Don, The, 89
'Octogenarian, Essays of an,' 329
O'Donoghue, D. J., 386
O'Dowd, The, hanged, 361
O'Flanagan, J. R., 381, 382, 383
Ogilvie, Wm. (connected with Lord Edward Fitzgerald), 118
Ogle, George, 236
O'Grady, Standish (Lord Guillamore), 100, 354, 379
O'Hagan, Lord, 51, 311, 345
O'Hanlon, Canon, 148
O'Herne, Captain (*alias* Aherne), 75
O'Keefe, John, 183
O'Kelly, Colonel Andrew Denis, 268, 269, 270, 271, 354
— Mathias, 136, 140–3, 151, 157
O'Laverty, Rev. Jas., P.P., *preface*
O'Leary, Rev. Arthur, 211–13, 215–28, 230–53, 255, 257, 258, 260–3, 265–76, 281, 288, 395, 397, 398
O'Loghlen, Sir Michael, 147
O'Meara, T., 353
O'Neill, Lord, killed, 384
Orangemen, 380, 385
Orde, Irish Secretary, 218, 219, 221 223, 226, 230, 231, 233, 236, 239

240, 246, 247, 260, 262, 273, 275, 276, 277
'Orellana,' Letters of, 240
O'Renahan, Rev. Dr., 284
Orkneys, Tandy's engagement at the, 342
Orleans, Duc de, 5, 133
'Ormond Steel,' a password, 341
Orpen, Mr., 157, 158, 159
Orr, George, 346 *et seq.*, 349, 350
— J. R., 295
— Major, 370, 391
— Wm., 55, 74, 328, 388, 389, 390
Osnaburg, Bishop of, 344 (*see* Duke of York)
Otto, M., 86
Oxford, Lord, 21, 189, 328

Paine, Thomas, 166
Pallain, M., 33, 265
Palmer (one of Lord Edward Fitzgerald's bodyguard), 14, 132
'Pamela,' *see* Lady Fitzgerald
Pancras, St., Old, 248, 398, 399
'Papists,' the, *pref.*, 2, 32, 62, 140, 229
Parker, 109, 112, 114, 132, 230, 239, 240, 241, 243, 265, 277, 373
Parliament, the Irish, 1, 7, 253 *et seq.*
Parliamentary Reform in 1797, 68, 161
— first object of the U. I. M., 89
Parsons, Laurence, 189, 209, 322
Patten, John, 101
Pavilion at Brighton, 257
Peel, Sir Robert, 334
Peerages sold, 255
Pelham, Right Hon. Thos., *preface*, 56–8, 13–23, 76, 86, 87, 181, 185, 192, 196, 200, 338, 349, 350, 351, 360, 361, 387, 394
Peninsular War, 390–9
Pentland, Henry, murdered, 297
Perrin, Louis, 199, 218, 246*n*
Petrie, George, LL.D., and native music, 394
Phelan, Mr., friend of MacNally, 200
Philippe, King Louis, 5, 95, 382
Phillips, Charles, 174, 176, 185, 206, 208, 233
— Friar, a spy, murdered, 172
Pichegru, General, 46, 349
'Pieces of Irish History,' by Dr. McNevin, 66, 386
Pitt, Prime Minister, 3, 4, 6, 9, 76, 77, 85, 92, 93, 95, 106, 108, 109, 114, 167, 192, 212, 240, 253, 254, 255, 257, 270, 271, 272, 280, 339, 340, 341, 349, 361
Pius VI., Pope, 275, 281
— VII., Pope, 284, 285, 400
Plowden, Francis, 130–6, 161, 188, 198*n*, 213*n*, 214, 221, 225, 242, 245*n*, 249, 259, 266, 269, 270, 275, 281, 332, 344, 348, 370, 385
Plunket, W. C., Lord, 136, 157, 169, 182, 292, 311, 312, 337
Plunkett, Colonel, hanged, 292, 337
Pole, Wellesley W., 198, 200, 201
Pollock, John, 178, 194, 201, 384, 385, 386
Ponsonby, George, 125, 254, 260, 261, 262, 311, 312
Porter, F. Thorpe, 299, 300*n*, 304, 305, 330
— Rev. Wm. (Presbyterian), hanged, 290
— William (father of F. T. Porter), in '98, 299, 305
Portland, Duke of, 20, 22, 30, 41, 43*n*, 49, 55, 58*n*, 60, 62, 63, 64, 65, 70*n*, 110, 172, 173, 176, 179, 180, 196*n*, 208, 243*n*, 250, 253, 260, 264, 277, 281, 282, 284, 285, 287, 297, 298, 341, 347, 349, 350, 396
Portobello, 121
Portsmouth, mutiny at, 108
Pratt, Mr., on Fr. O'Leary, 223
Prendergast, J. P., 33*n*, 206, 337
Presbyterians, the, of Ulster, 215
'Press,' the, organ of the U. I. M., 197, 386
Pretender, the (Charles Edward), rising of, 357
Privy Council, Lord Downshire expelled from, 104

Quigley, or O'Coigly, James, a priest, hanged, 15 *et seq.*, 293–4
Quintilian family, case of the, cited, 316

Randall, T., 248
Rankin, Charles, 28, 62
Reade, Robert Rollo, 292
Redesdale, Lord, 195
Redington, Sir Thomas, 330
Reform, Parliamentary, 68
Regency, struggle for the, 247, 253 *et seq.*
'Register, Annual,' 217
Registry of Deeds Office, *preface*, 84, 124, 269, 303
Reid, Rev. Seaton, D.D., 293
Reinhard, French Minister at Ham-

burg, 4, 5; letters of, 53–61, 65, 66, 67, 68, 69, 76, 78, 91, 107, 108, 109, 117, 118, 144, 145, 295, 335, 336, 337, 338
Renny, Dr., 297
Rey, General, 343
Reynolds, Thomas, informer, 59, 66, 93, 116, 117, 118, 142, 145, 163, 169, 231, 301, 303, 304, 305, 306, 307
'Ribbonmen,' 333
Richards, Dr. Solomon, 356
'Richardson, J.' (*alias* for Samuel Turner), 46, 50, 68, 98
Richmond, Duke of, 201, 204
Riots in London, 229–97
Robertson, Rev. J. (Secret Agent), 399
Robespierre, Maximilian, 110
Roche, Sir Boyle, 177, 232, 233, 235, 236, 237, 245, 329, 396
— James, 329
Rodney, Admiral Lord, 227
Rogers, Samuel (examination of), 33
Rolande, Madame, 309
Romana, Spanish General, 399
Rose, Rev. Mr., 278, 279
Rosemary Lane Chapel, 120, 393
Ross, General Sir C., 385
— Charles, *preface*, 10, 73, 74, 119, 193
— Mr., King's messenger, 344–5
Rossas, the, Tandy's arrival at, 342
Rosse, Lord, 323, 326
Rousseau, Jean Jacques, 319
Rowan, Hamilton, 3, 102, 163, 166, 169, 171, 183, 296, 299
Rumbold, Sir G., 97
Russell, Sir Charles, Q.C., *preface*
— Lord John, in 1798, 21, 183
— Thomas (executed), 51
Russia, ally of England, 92
Rutland, Duke of, 217, 218, 219, 285
— Island of, 343
Ryan, Captain, 133, 169, 189, 231

St. Germans, Lord, 87
Salamanca, Irish College at, 378, 400
Sampson, Wm., 59, 85
Sandys, Major, 190, 191
Sarrazin, General, 297, 360
'Saturday Review,' 184
'Saunders' Newsletter,' 380
Saurin, Rt. Hon. Wm., 162, 199, 384
Saxton, Sir Charles, 386
Scallan, J. S., 208
Secret Committee of the Irish Parliament, Report of, 17, 53, 67, 292
Secret Committee in Paris, 75
Sexton, Mr., M.P., 384
Shadwell, Colonel (War Office), 390
Shannon, Earl of, 254, 315
'Shan Van Voght, The,' 363
Shaw, W., 141
Sheares, Brothers, hanged, 127, 142, 162, 165, 166, 173, 177, 226, 309, 310, 311, 314, 315, 316, 317, 321, 322, 327, 329, 374, 375, 393
Shee, Colonel, 111
Sheehan, Mr., writer, 241
Sheehy, Rev. N., P.P., hanged, 145
Sheil, R. Lalor, 144
Shelley, Percy Bysshe, in Dublin, 201, 224, 380
Sheridan, R. Brinsley, 5, 21, 112, 210, 287
Shervinton (Com.-General), Lieut.-Colonel, 371
Sibley, Mr. N. W., 368, 374
Sierra Leone, 280
Simms, Robert, 5, 55, 57
Simpson, Rev. Mr., implicated, 290
Sinclair, Rev. Mr., implicated, 290
— William, 384
Sirr, Major, 118, 121, 122, 124, 132, 133, 134, 135, 138, 142, 159, 177, 224, 229, 305, 330, 332, 385
Smith, Father (McNally's confessor), 208, 209
— Huband, 32, 146
— Sir W., Baron, 125, 176, 375
Smock Alley Theatre, 148
Smyth, P. J., 240
Soult, Marshal, 400
South, Bishop, 186
Southwell, Lord, 143
Spain and England, strained relations between, 215, 260, 264, 276, 281
Stafford, a rebel, 98
Stamer, Sir Wm., 189, 381
'Standard,' the, 365 *et seq.*, 399
Stanhope, Lord, 94
Staunton, Michael, 199
Steele, Maria, 309, 313
Stevelly, Rev. Mr. (Presbyterian), hanged, 290
Stewart, Surgeon-General, 356
Stokes, Rev. Dr., 126
Stone, tried for treason, 30, 33, 108
Strahan, Admiral, 296
Stuart, Mr., implicated, 39, 42, 43
Suffolk, Lord, 21, 189
Sutton, Brigadier, 398
Suvarov, Marshal, 81
Swan, Town Major, 123, 132, 133

Swete, Miss (married to Henry Sheares), 309, 314
Sydney 'Freeman's Journal,' 394
Sydney, Lord, 217, 219, 220, 224, 233, 239, 240, 245, 256, 262, 272, 395

'TABLET,' the, 257
Talleyrand, 5, 25 *et seq.*, 72, 74, 76, 265*n*, 364
Tandy, Jas. Napper, 33, 56, 70, 71, 72, 73, 74, 75, 76, 77, 78, 79, 80, 81, 82, 83, 84, 88, 89, 90, 93, 98, 100, 218, 222, 223, 225, 226, 241*n*, 242, 243, 244, 294, 295, 341, 343, 344, 345, 346; 'Wearing of the Green,' 394
— James, 135, 181, 355 *et seq.*
Taylor, Wm. (Dublin Castle), 177
— W. C., author of 'Civil Wars,' 304
Teeling, 4, 5, 47, 51, 74, 86, 94, 292, 336, 337, 338, 339, 340
Temple, Lord, Viceroy, 119, 396
Tennent, Wm., 57
Thanet, Lord, 21
Thistlewood, Arthur, 306
Thomas, Jean (an *alias* for Samuel Turner), 20
Thurlow, Lord, 183
'Times,' the, 383
Toler, John, Lord Norbury, 125, 312, 314
Tone, T. Wolfe, 15, 45, 49, 53, 55, 58, 59, 74, 75, 106, 108, 109, 110, 111, 185, 231, 287, 294, 364, 389
Tooke, Horne, 114, 314, 328
Tracy, Miss Frances (legatee of the 'Sham Squire'), 124
Trafalgar, Incident at, 113
Traill, Mr., Dublin Castle, 386
Treason, High, two witnesses necessary to convict in, 320; one sufficient in Ireland, 374–8
Trimleston, Lord, 143
Trinity College, Dublin, 120, 126
Troy, Dr., R. C. Archbishop of Dublin, 150, 271, 274
'True Briton,' the, 53
Truguet, M., French Minister of Marine, 106, 113, 114
Tuite, the carpenter, 121
— Jacob, 55, 57
Turner, Samuel, LL.D., Barrister-at-Law, 8, 33, 38, 40, 41, 42, 43, 46, 47, 48, 49, 50, 52, 54, 55, 57, 59, 60, 61*n*, 63, 66, 67, 68, 69, 71, 72, 74, 75, 76*n*, 78, 79, 84, 91, 92, 93, 94, 96, 97, 98, 99, 100, 102*n*, 105, 125, 190, 196, 294, 295, 298, 308, 316, 335, 336, 339, 340, 347, 348, 383, 389, 394
Turner, Miss Anne, marries J. W. Armstrong, 333
— Bishop, *preface*
Tyburn Tree, 264
Tyrawley, Lord, 249*n*
Tythes (Father O'Leary in favour of), 250

ULM, Capitulation of, 294
Union, Legislative, 104, 178, 269, 286, 365
— 'Star,' the, 189, 300, 386, 387
United Irishmen—not treasonably disposed at first, 89
Urban, Sylvanus, 171, 186, 285

VALENCE, General, 3, 12, 78, 92
Vanbrugh, Sir T., 6
Venezuela, 207
Verdon, Dr., 390
Vereker, Colonel, 359
Vergennes, Count (French Premier), 215
Versailles, 5
Vicar-Apostolic, Military, 285
Vienna, 259
Villemarest, M. de, 25
Vincennes, murder of Duc d'Enghien at, 90
Vinegar Hill, 295
Volunteer Convention, 77, 232
Volunteers of 1782, Irish, 216, 232, 238, 245, 395

WAGRAM, Prince of, 290
Walcheren, Expedition to, 297
Wales, George, Prince of, 253, 270
Wall, Rev. Dr., 236
Wallace, Sir Richard, 260
Walstein, Miss, 204
Wardle, Major, 394
Warren, Thomas, 163
Warwick, Rev. Mr. (Presbyterian), hanged, 290
Watson, Dr., 306
'Wearing of the Green,' 78, 79, 391–4
Webb, R. D., 328
Weldon, Mr., 397
Wellington, Duke of, 93*n*, 96, 101, 102*n*, 137, 198*n*, 209, 345, 349, 351, 385, 386, 395, 399, 400

Wesley, Rev. John, 134
Westenra, W. W., Colonel (afterwards Lord Rossmore), 369–71
Westmoreland, Lord, 169, 219, 349*n*
Weymouth (Irish Secretary), 219
Wheatley, Hugh, 388, 389, 390
Whigs, the English, 9, 21, 183, 198, 249, 253, 257, 345
Whitbread, Mr., 21, 189
White, Esmonde, 208
— Luke, ancestor of Lord Annaly, 305
— Mr. T. Armstrong, 366, 369
— Miss, daughter of J. Sheares, 331
— R., created Lord Bantry, 363
Whiteboys, the, 217, 245, 249, 274
Whitechapel, Lord Edward Fitzgerald in, 91
Whiteside, Chief Justice, 377
Whitworth, Lord, 103*n*
Wickham, Rt. Hon. W., 21, 37, 39, 46, 48*n*, 49, 63, 65, 66, 68, 71, 72, 92, 94, 98, 110, 161, 162, 193, 280, 297, 298, 346, 347, 350, 364
Wilde, Lady, 313
Wills, Rev. James, 117*n*, 236*n*
Wolcot, John, 84
Wolfe, Stephen C. Baron, 1, 144, 189
Woodward, Bishop, 220, 251
Woolagan, Court-martial on, 332, 370
Wordsworth, Wm., 279
Worthington, Mr. Hall, 371
— Sir R., Police Magistrate, dismissed, 345
Wraxall, Sir N., 265, 271
Wright, Surgeon Thos., 168, 355
Wylde and Mahon sheltered by Lady Moira, 139
Wyse, Rt. Hon. Thos., 144, 231*n*, 237*n*

YARMOUTH, 30–50, 357
Yelverton, Baron, 211, 221, 235, 367
Yeomanry, the, 159, 333
York, Duke of, 81, 381, 391, 394
— Redhead, 309
Young, Charles (actor), 204
— Mr., 351

PRINTED BY
SPOTTISWOODE AND CO., NEW-STREET SQUARE
LONDON

1917669R0024

Printed in Great Britain
by Amazon.co.uk, Ltd.,
Marston Gate.